D1189927

Essays On and In the Chicago Tradition

Essays On and In the Chicago Tradition

Don Patinkin

The Hebrew University of Jerusalem

Duke University Press   Durham, N.C.   1981

Printed in the United States of
America by Kingsport Press

Library of Congress Cataloging in Publication Data

Patinkin, Don.
  Essays on and in the Chicago tradition.

  Includes bibliographies and index.
    1. Chicago school of economics—Addresses, essays,
lectures. I. Title.
HB98.2.P37   332.4′01   79-55770
ISBN 0-8223-0439-2

לנעמה, ארן, אילנה, ותמירה

For Naama, Aran, Ilana, and Tmira

Contents

viii   **Contents**

Photographs

Preface

The reader who hopes to find in this book a systematic disquisition on the perennial question of whether one can meaningfully talk about a "Chicago School"—and an accompanying analysis of its distinguishing characteristics—will be disappointed. That has not been my purpose. I have indeed provided such an analysis of a major aspect of the School's teachings during the 1930's and 1940's: namely, its monetary doctrines. But as for the rest, I have sufficed with a memoir on one of the School's leading members, with reminiscences of others, and with some reprinted articles of mine that provide a sample of the flavor of the Chicago tradition that I knew.

The precise nature of the "Chicago connection" of each of these articles (except two) has been indicated in the Introduction below. The two exceptions are Chapter 6 (which is actually a sequel to Chapter 5) and Chapter 9 (which deals with problems that are closely related to those of Chapter 8). As indicated, Chapter 9 was written jointly with my colleague, Nissan Liviatan, and my sincerest thanks to him for permitting its inclusion in this book.

For permission to reprint the previously published articles, I am indebted to the *American Economic Review, Canadian Journal of Economics, Econometrica, Economic Development and Cultural Change, Economic Journal, Jewish Social Studies, Journal of Law and Economics, Journal of Money, Credit and Banking, Quarterly Journal of Economics, Southern Economic Journal*, and the Stanford University Press. Unless otherwise indicated, these articles have been reproduced without change. In some cases, however, I have supplemented the original article with new material which appears in the form of a "Postscript." On occasion, I have also added new material in footnotes enclosed in braces. On the other hand, all material in square brackets appeared that way in the original publication as well.

For the sake of consistency and clarity, the line diagrams have all been redrawn, and I am grateful to Christopher Mueller-Wille of the Cartographic Services Unit of the Department of Geography at The University of Chicago for the excellent job he has done. An attempt has also been made to achieve consistency with respect to the citation practices and bibliographies of the reprinted articles; indeed, in many cases such bibliographies did not originally appear. In this connection I would like to explain that text references to works listed in these bibliographies as having been reprinted are to the date of original publication; for the convenience of the reader, however, the page references in the text follow the pagination of the reprinted form.

I would like to thank Lauchlin Currie, Mrs. Frank Knight, Mme. Felicja Lange, Lloyd Mints, John U. Nef, the late Jacob and Frances Viner, and Ellen Viner Seiler for kindly permitting me to reproduce correspondence and/or photographs. I am also very grateful to *Fortune Magazine* for its kind permission to reproduce its photograph

xii   **Preface**

of Henry C. Simons. Thanks too to Sonia and Lawrence Klein for supplying me with the group picture reproduced on p. 154 below. I am also indebted to the following institutions for their kind cooperation in providing me ready access to their respective collections of materials: The Joseph Regenstein Library of The University of Chicago for the Frank H. Knight Papers; the Franklin D. Roosevelt Library for the Henry Morgenthau Diaries; the Law School of The University of Chicago for the Henry C. Simons Papers; and the Princeton University Library for the Jacob Viner Papers. To George Stigler I am indebted for various materials. It is also a pleasure to express my thanks to Shlomo Maital, who at the time was visiting at Princeton from the Technion-Israel Institute of Technology, and whom I repeatedly burdened with requests for materials from the Jacob Viner Papers. And I have a special debt to David Laidler of the University of Western Ontario, whose good advice I have on several occasions sought.

In the course of preparing this volume for publication, I have benefited immeasurably from the assistance of Marc Levin, who with great care, initiative, and responsibility has checked texts and references and has pursued materials through various libraries and archives. He also carried out the difficult task of standardizing citation practices and bibliographies, and has most efficiently borne the main burden of checking galley proofs. My thanks too to Joshua Aizenman, who has helped to recheck the equations and diagrams. I am also grateful to Mrs. Marie Marchese and Ms. Mary Ellen Cross for so carefully and efficiently carrying out the task of typing. It has been a pleasure to have worked with all of them.

Fittingly enough, the manuscript of this volume was prepared—and both its beginning "Reminiscences" and concluding essay on "Keynes and Chicago" written—during a sabbatical year (1978–79) spent at the University of Chicago as Ford Foundation Visiting Research Professor in the Department of Economics and in the Graduate School of Business. The convenience that this afforded in access to archival materials—and, even more so, of discussions with people knowledgeable in the lore of Chicago—greatly facilitated my task. I am also indebted to the Department and the School for financial support that made the aforementioned technical assistance possible. But over and above all this I wish to express my appreciation to both the Department and the School for a stimulating and congenial atmosphere that made my visit a most pleasant and fruitful one.

The last stages of the publication of this volume were completed upon my return to Jerusalem. Here I have been helped greatly by Dale Knisely, particularly in connection with the preparation of the index. I am also greatly indebted to Yoseph Zeira for his invaluable aid in checking the page proofs of the mathematical portions, and to Bette Gorden for her most pleasant and efficient assistance in all that was connected with the final stages of the preparation of this book. My thanks too to the Ford Foundation for a research grant, administered by the Maurice Falk Institute for Economic Research in Israel, in support of this work.

Don Patinkin

Jerusalem
July 1980

Essays On and In the Chicago Tradition

Introduction: Reminiscences of Chicago, 1941–47*[1]

I came to The University of Chicago in the fall of 1941 as a third-year undergraduate student in the Department of Economics and (with one interruption) continued my studies there until receiving my Ph.D. degree in the summer of 1947.[2] These, as it turned out, were the final years of the traditional "Chicago School"—that School which, with due regard to the differences among them, can be identified with the teachings of Frank H. Knight, Jacob Viner, Henry C. Simons, and Lloyd W. Mints.[3] For by the academic year 1946–47—by which time my formal course work had been completed—Viner had moved to Princeton and Simons had died. And though in the same year Milton Friedman returned to Chicago (where he had taken his M.A. degree in 1933) to continue with the School's fundamental ideological advocacy of free-market economic liberalism, in other important respects Friedman's teachings dif-

---

*Though these reminiscences obviously constitute a personal document for which no one else can or does bear any responsibility, I have benefited greatly from comments on earlier drafts from colleagues at The University of Chicago (during a visit to which this was written), The University of Western Ontario, the Hebrew University of Jerusalem, as well as from various former Chicagoans. In particular, I am indebted to Gary Becker, Martin Bronfenbrenner, Marianne and Robert Ferber, Stanley Fischer, Jacob Frenkel, Peter Howitt, Ephraim Kleiman, Lawrence and Sonia Klein, J. Clark Leith, Gregg Lewis, Robert Lucas, Donald McCloskey, Yair Mundlak, Dvora Patinkin, Sherwin Rosen, T. W. Schultz, and George Stigler. I am especially grateful to David Laidler for his many thoughtful and fruitful criticisms and suggestions.

In writing these reminiscences I have drawn freely on my lecture notes from the period.

1. The reader should keep in mind that these are reminiscences of a department as seen through the eyes of a student; I hope that they will some day be complemented by the reminiscences of someone who saw the Department during this period as a member of its teaching staff.

2. A native Chicagoan, I also spent my first two years at a college in the city—namely, Central YMCA College, which subsequently evolved into Roosevelt University.

3. Some of these differences are indicated in the reminiscences that follow; others are described in chap. 1, p. 30, and pp. 44–45 below. See also p. 266 below for Viner's statement in a 1969 letter to me that he was not aware of the existence of such a "School" during the time he was at Chicago, and that in any event he did not consider himself, and was not fully considered, a member of it.

Despite all this, I am assuming that we can meaningfully talk about a "Chicago School" identified in this way. For additional views on this question, see the articles by Archibald, Friedman, Miller, and Stigler cited in the bibliography of chap. 1 below. See also Bronfenbrenner (1962), Friedman (1974), and Warren J. Samuels (ed.), *The Chicago School of Political Economy* (1976) and the references there cited. For the Chicago of yet an earlier period, see Coats (1963).

Insofar as the individual members of the Chicago School are concerned, see chap. 1 below on Knight (1885–1972), as well as the additional references to Buchanan and Dorfman there provided (p. 23, fn. 1). On Viner (1892–1970), see the tribute by Robbins (1970), as well as the articles by Machlup, Samuelson, and Baumol in the memorial issue of the *Journal of Political Economy* (1972); see also the article by Baumol and Ellen Viner Seiler (1979). On Simons (1899–1946), see John Davenport (1946), Herbert Stein (1968), and Stigler (1974); see also Friedman (1967), as well as chaps. 10–12 below. Aside from the listing in the A.E.A. *Handbook* for 1969, I have not been able to find any material on Mints (1888–   ); see, however, his letter to me reproduced in the Postscript to chap. 11 below.

fered significantly from those of the traditional Chicago School (see chapters 10–12 below).

Simons taught the undergraduate course in price theory, and Mints the one in money. Simons' course introduced us to partial-equilibrium analysis by means of Book 5 of Marshall's *Principles*, and to general-equilibrium analysis by means of chapter 4 of Gustav Cassel's *Theory of Social Economy* (1932). But our main text was Simons' own famous mimeographed *Syllabus*.[4] This began with a brief summary of Frank Knight's *Economic Organization* (1933, see chapter 1, p. 26, below)—to which we were also referred—which created the new and exciting vision of the market economy as an efficient system of allocating resources. (The term "invisible hand" was to appear only later, in Frank Knight's classes themselves). But the distinctive feature of the *Syllabus* was the challenging numerical problems in the theory of demand and supply under both perfect and imperfect competition which we had to solve, usually after intensive discussions amongst ourselves. (On one of the most challenging of these problems, chapter 4 below is based).[5] From this *Syllabus* I learned much more than the subject matter itself: I learned the hard way that just reading and listening was not enough; that full understanding of the principles of economic analysis could be achieved only after sweating through their application to specific problems, with pencil and paper in hand. I learned it then—and have applied it ever since in my own teaching.

Simons also gave an undergraduate course in public finance, in which context I read his famous pamphlet on *A Positive Program for Laissez Faire* (1934). I still remember my esthetic enjoyment of its clean and incisive style (Mozart, not Beethoven—he once told us—was the music for him), and my intellectual enjoyment of its trenchant argument. What was particularly exciting were the same qualities that made Marxism so appealing to many other young people at the time: simplicity together with apparent logical completeness; idealism combined with radicalism. For Simons carried out his approach to its logical extreme, with the unshaken and unshakable conviction of a world reformer that life would be better if only his policy recommendations were carried out. Market competition was to be assured by opposing with equal vigor all forms of monopoly, business as well as labor unions; a high degree of equality was to be achieved by a progressive income tax, applied to receipts of any kind—not only ordinary income, but capital gains, inheritances, and gifts as well; the instability of the banking system was to be solved by requiring 100 percent reserves; and, of course, mass unemployment—with the waste and sufferings that it represented—was to be prevented by a contracyclical policy of varying the quantity of money so as to stabilize the price level (see chapter 10 below).

---

4. The actual title of my copy of this *Syllabus* is *Economics 201: The Divisional Course in Economics*, with no indication of either author or date of publication. It was, however, common knowledge at the time that its author was Simons, and this is the name which I then wrote in on the title page of my copy. Simons also made use of this *Syllabus* in the more technical course for economics majors (Economics 209: "Intermediate Economic Theory"), which is the one described here. For further information on the *Syllabus*, see the bibliography below.

5. Another typical problem from Simons' *Syllabus* appears (with due acknowledgment) in George Stigler's text on *The Theory of Price* (3rd ed., 1966, pp. 191–93).

In contrast with these exciting ideas, so forcefully and systematically set out in his pamphlet, Simons' classroom presentations were somewhat haphazard. In my mental image of him he is slouched in one chair, with a knee drawn up over another, drawling on in a dry, laconic, half-cynical way. But despite his lethargic presentation, Simons' intellectual impact was such that we all left his classroom "simonized" to some extent or other.

Lloyd Mints' undergraduate course in money and banking was quite different: he lacked Simons' spark, nor did he aspire to it; [6] at the same time Mints' classroom presentations were clear, systematic, and very effective. We started with the quantity theory, and used Irving Fisher's equally clear and systematic *Purchasing Power of Money* (1913) as our textbook. And on the banking system we read another classic— C. A. Phillips' *Bank Credit* (1920). Led on by Mints, we shared that exciting moment of realizing that banks were not simply passive recipients of money deposits, but actually created these deposits.

Another one of my undergraduate teachers was Paul H. Douglas, who, though he more than shared the activist macroeconomic policy-view of the Chicago School, [7] did not share its free-market philosophy. By the time I took his course in labor economics (winter 1942), Douglas had already begun to shift his interests from the academic world to the political one. He had been elected city alderman in 1939, and ran for the democratic nomination for U.S. Senator in 1942. After failing in this bid, he volunteered (at the age of fifty!) for active duty in the Marine Corps. Indeed, the course I took was the last one Douglas gave before joining the Marines. [8]

For Douglas, more than for any of the other teachers in the department (with the possible exception of its chairman, Simeon E. Leland, with his red cheeks and booming voice) the classroom meeting was a dramatic encounter, and the classroom itself a stage on which to pace back and forth, declaiming more than lecturing, and pausing on occasion to fend off premature student questions by slowly intoning, with a wave of his hand, "Lead kindly light, one step at a time. . . ." Whenever we passed his open office door, we could see the three-dimensional representation (by means of small balls at the end of long, thin rods) of one of the famous production functions that Douglas had estimated empirically in his classic work on *The Theory of Wages* (1934, p. 216). But because of his impending departure from academic life, he was no longer very active in research. [9]

In a place by himself in the Department was John U. Nef, who gave the under-

---

6. See his letter to me of Sept. 1972, reproduced in the postscript to chap. 11 below.

7. See end of chapter 11 below; see also Davis (1971), pp. 47–60, and Tavlas (1977).

8. See Douglas' memoirs (1971), chaps. 9–13. T. W. Schultz has told me that there was much tension between Douglas and Knight, which in large part had originated in disagreements between them in the 1930s about the academic future of Simons (who had been a student of Knight's at the University of Iowa, and whom Knight had brought with him to Chicago in 1927 (see chap. 1, p. 44, fn. 24 below; see also Stigler 1974, pp. 1–2). I do not, however, recall that at the time we undergraduate students (who had practically no contacts with Knight) were aware of this tension. And when, as graduate students, we might have become aware of it, Douglas was no longer there.

As we all know, Douglas ran again for the Senate after the war, this time successfully; see below.

9. For a discussion of Douglas' contributions to economics, see the articles by Rees and Samuelson in the memorial issue of the *Journal of Political Economy* (1979). See also Cain (1979).

graduate course in European economic history.[10] Nef, the prototype of the soft-spoken, cultured European scholar-gentleman, opened a window for us on the life, language, and culture of France in particular. The subject of the course was the Industrial Revolution; but because of his own work on *Industry and Government in France and England: 1540–1640* (1940), Nef spent a disproportionate amount of time on this earlier period. Needless to say we read from the classics of modern European economic history: Tawney, Lipson, Clapham, Hammond, and Mantoux; but we also read Thorstein Veblen's *Imperial Germany and the Industrial Revolution* (1915) and learned from it about the advantages of the latecomer to industrialization. More than anything else, Nef was concerned with conveying a broad picture of historical development—a picture of the complex interrelationships of economics, politics, war, technology, and culture. It was the time of Toynbee's *Study of History*, and Nef had us read selected parts of its first volume and compare them with the introduction to Spengler's *Decline of the West* (1926). But what had even more of an impact on me was the "assignment" which consisted of the Epilogue to Tolstoy's *War and Peace*—and which in my case also served as the introduction to this book. Nef's course was the one *par excellence* which fulfilled that function of a university concerned with the transmission and development of broad cultural values.

I received the B.A. degree in early 1943, and after an interruption of almost a year returned to Chicago to begin with graduate studies in economics, supplemented by the study of mathematics. It was wartime, and there were few students: at most fifteen to twenty of us, in a closely knit group. Among my fellow-students were Marianne Abeles, later Ferber (now at the University of Illinois), Sonia Adelson, later Klein (now with The Wharton Econometric Forecasting Associates), Jacob Cohen (now at the University of Pittsburgh), Robert Ferber (University of Illinois), Bert Hoselitz (The University of Chicago), Ray Kosloff (Electrochemical Industries, Ltd., Haifa), Jack Letiche (University of California, Berkeley), and Rolf Weil (Roosevelt University).

On the other hand, the teaching staff of the Department at Chicago was barely touched by the exodus to Washington experienced by other economics departments in the United States. On the contrary, it was reinforced by two new groups of economists: a group of agricultural economists led by Theodore W. Schultz; and a group of mathematical economists and econometricians who formed the new nucleus for the Cowles Commission for Research in Economics, led by Jacob Marschak. The latter were to reestablish Chicago as a center of econometrics after its role in this field (and, indeed, in empirical economics in general) had almost come to an end as a result of Henry Schultz's untimely death in an automobile accident in 1938, as well as Paul Douglas' already noted shift in interest, both of which events took place against the background of Knight's continued antiquantitative bent and Simons' disinterest in

10. Nef has described some of his experiences at Chicago in an autobiography entitled *Search for Meaning* (1973); see especially pp. 106–13, 182–89.

There was also a course in U.S. economic history given by Chester Wright; but I took this only as a reading course.

such work. And though Viner's attitude to quantitative economics was basically positive, it was not enough of a counterweight.[11]

Most of my formal graduate instruction, however, was at the hands of the veteran teachers of the Department. Thus it was at this time that I had my first real contacts with Knight and Viner, both of whom gave courses in economic theory. On Knight I have written at length in the memoir reproduced in chapter 1; this also points out (pp. 24–25 below) that Viner was a more systematic and precise teacher than Knight, more sharply to the point in classroom discussion and in replies to student questions. Indeed, Viner's sharpness—as he sat, short and upright at the end of the large elliptical seminar table, holding in both hands on the table in front of him the index cards from which he lectured—sometimes deterred such questions. On the other hand, Viner was less dogmatic than Knight, less likely to see things in terms of black-and-white, much more a man of the world. Since their courses were so different (in both style and content) most of us took both of them, enjoying as a by-product the running debate between Knight and Viner on the relative merits of the opportunity-cost and cost-of-production theories of value (see chapter 1, p. 30, below). At the same time, their courses did have the common feature of using Marshall's *Principles* as the basic text and correspondingly devoting much attention to the nature of Marshall's demand curve and his related notion of consumer's surplus. This concern was the background of my later paper on "Demand Curves and Consumer's Surplus" reproduced in chapter 8 below.

Knight also gave his famous course in the history of economic thought. Here he had us read the classic works of Smith, Ricardo, and Mill and then write a term paper on the classical cost-of-production theory of value (see chapter 1, p. 34 below). Though Viner did not offer a formal course in the history of thought, he frequently dealt with questions of doctrinal history in his courses on international trade theory and policy, as well as in his theory course proper. Thus his international-trade course was based to a large extent on his classic *Studies in the Theory of International Trade* (1937), with their celebrated chapters on mercantilism and on the historical nineteenth-century English currency controversies.

Here again Knight's and Viner's approaches differed. For Knight tended to analyze doctrinal developments from the viewpoint of the current state of economic theory, against which he measured them; in contrast, Viner was more concerned with scholarship as such—with (as he was later to express himself) "the pursuit of broad and exact knowledge of the history of the working of the human mind as revealed in

---

11. On the attitudes of Knight and Simons, see below, chap. 1, p. 34 and chap. 11, pp. 282–83. Viner's attitude is implicit in his book (originally his thesis) on *Canada's Balance of International Indebtedness 1900–1913: An Inductive Study in the Theory of International Trade* (1924) and explicit in his subsequent cautiously encouraging comments on quantitative economics, as contrasted with alleged "statistical laws" (1928, pp. 45–46).

On Schultz's contributions to econometrics and economic theory, and on his classic *Theory and Measurement of Demand* (1938) in particular, see the memorial essays by Douglas (1939), Hotelling (1939), and Yntema (1939). See also Karl Fox (1968).

written records." [12] I will always remember with deep appreciation the patient help and interest with which he guided and encouraged my own first efforts in this direction. These took the form of a seminar paper on "Mercantilism and the Readmission of the Jews to England in the Seventeenth Century" for his course on "International Economic Policies." With Viner's further encouragement, I revised this paper for submission to one of the professional journals—and revised it again after it was initially rejected. The final published form of this paper is reproduced in chapter 3 below. Both because of its association with Viner, and because of its reflection of my joint interest in economics and Jewish studies, it has always been a source of gratification to me that this was my maiden scientific publication.

The main teacher of graduate economic theory was, however, Oskar Lange,[13] who had joined the Department in 1939 to continue, *inter alia*, with the work in mathematical economics that had been started by Henry Schultz.[14] In a sequence of systematic courses, Lange brought us to what were then the frontiers of knowledge in micro- and macroeconomic theory. These courses covered the imperfect-competition theories of Joan Robinson and Edward Chamberlin, against the background of the earlier duopoly theories of Cournot and Bertrand; Hicks' *Value and Capital* (1939) and the related Paretian welfare economics, together with Lange's (1936) and Lerner's (1944) confident application of the latter to the economics of a market-directed socialist economy; and business-cycle theory, beginning with a historical discussion of Say's law, continuing with an exposition of Marx, providing a detailed presentation of Keynes' *General Theory* (based on Lange's own "Rate of Interest and the Optimum Propensity to Consume" (1938)) and of the advantages of Keynesian macroeconomic policies, and concluding with the business-cycle theories of Kalecki and Kaldor. But Lange's most valuable course was the one on "Mathematical Economics" (i.e., on what was then called mathematical economics). Here he systematically took us through the Mathematical Appendix of Hicks' *Value and Capital* (1939), as well as Paul Samuelson's pathbreaking article on "The Stability of Equilibrium" (1941), subsequently reproduced as chapter 9 of his *Foundations of Economic Analysis* (1947). My lecture notes from this course served me as a "reference volume" for many years to come.

Lange was an excellent expositor—clear, systematic, and thorough, with the

12. Quoted from Viner's eloquent Brown University convocation address, entitled "A Modest Proposal for Some Stress on Scholarship in Graduate Training" (1950 (1958)), p. 369.

13. See the biographical articles on him by Tadeusz Kowalik in the Lange festschrift (1964) and by Stanislaw Wellisz in the *International Encyclopedia of the Social Sciences*; see also the obituary by Kalecki (1966).

During his Chicago period Lange spelled his first name with a "c." This spelling has been retained accordingly in the articles I wrote at the time (cf. chaps. 5–7 below).

14. Thus Schultz encouraged Theodore O. Yntema to write his thesis (which was subsequently published) on "A Mathematical Reformulation of the General Theory of International Trade" (1929). Later Schultz interested Martin Bronfenbrenner in writing his Ph.D. thesis on "Monetary Theory and General Equilibrium" (1939, p. iii) and served as the chairman of the thesis committee until his death. Schultz also inspired Jacob L. Mosak's interest in mathematical economics, which ultimately led Mosak to write his thesis on "General Equilibrium Theory in International Trade" (1941, p. ii), subsequently (1944) published as a Cowles Commission Monograph.

wonderful ability of getting to the essence of a problem and presenting it in as simple a way as possible. Indeed, too simply: for sometimes he left no intellectual challenge for the student, no need for the effort of understanding which is so akin to that of intellectual creation. Another characteristic of Lange's classroom performance was the slow and methodical way (so much in contrast with Viner's) with which he frequently answered student questions. Nor was Lange embarrassed if he had to think silently on his feet for several moments before offering an answer—sometimes concluding even such a pause with the simple statement that he had to give the question further thought and would defer the answer to the next class meeting. Then he would limp back to the blackboard and continue with his exposition.

During 1944 Lange became increasingly active in the affairs of the Polish government(s)-in-exile. These activities sometimes made it necessary for him to be out of town, at which times Leonid Hurwicz would meet his classes instead. There was that memorable occasion in 1944 when Lange was absent for an unusually long period—and when the mystery of his absence was suddenly solved by a front-page newspaper picture showing him meeting with Stalin in Moscow. After the summer quarter of 1945 Lange resigned from the University to become the first postwar Polish ambassador to the United States. According to the student gossip of that time, Lange decided to return to Poland in the hope of playing a leading role in a Socialist party which would function as a loyal opposition. If so, it was a hope that did not long endure. Ever since, I have thought of Lange as a tragic figure.

Together with these theory courses, I continued to take courses with Simons and Mints, as well as with Simeon Leland. The latter's course in public finance (with its frighteningly fat bibliography) was largely descriptive and institutional in nature. Simons' course on the "Economics of Fiscal Policy" emphasized the theoretical questions discussed in his closely reasoned monograph on *Personal Income Taxation* (1938), but dealt with other problems as well. Mints was less effective in his graduate courses than in his undergraduate one. He devoted about half of his graduate course on "Money" to the traditional quantity theory and the teachings of Hawtrey and Robertson, and the other half to Keynes' successive works—the *Tract*, *Treatise on Money*, and *General Theory*. In his course on "Banking Theory and Monetary Policy," Mints lectured from the manuscript he was then completing for his subsequent book on *A History of Banking Theory* (1945). By means of repeated arithmetical examples (*ibid.*, p. 34), he also gave us a life-time innoculation against the fallacies of the real-bills doctrine. Both Simons and Mints also devoted much attention to the question of proper monetary and fiscal contracyclical policy for an open economy (see chapter 10 below).

Mention has already been made of the two new groups of economists who joined the Department in 1943. The group of agricultural economists—Theodore W. Schultz, D. Gale Johnson, and William H. Nicholls—had been exiled from Iowa State for having dared to support research showing that margarine was as nutritious as the butter produced by that dairy state. Toward the end of my formal course work, I took a course with Nicholls on imperfect competition, an introductory course with Johnson on agricultural economics, and a graduate one in this field with Schultz (who by then had succeeded Leland as Department chairman, when the latter left Chicago to become dean of the College of Liberal Arts at Northwestern University). I must confess that what I remember best from these courses are not matters of agriculture but the painful struggle through the abstruse chapter on Alfred Marshall in Talcott Parsons' *Structure of Social Action* (1937), which Schultz had us read. Though this struggle was not completely successful, it did serve the important purpose of forcing us, at least momentarily, to consider the assumptions of economic analysis from a new viewpoint, the viewpoint of the forces at work in society as a whole. And it forced us in particular to ask ourselves why centers of economic power in a society would permit the development of the legal and institutional arrangements necessary for the functioning of a competitive economy that would curtail this power.

When I first came to Chicago, H. Gregg Lewis (who in addition to his teaching duties served as an invaluable adviser to all of us) was almost the sole active representative of econometrics, and indeed of quantitative economics in general. He had earlier assisted both Douglas and Schultz, and was then working on his doctoral thesis on "The Elasticity of Demand for Steel" (1947). Lewis' course on statistical correlation introduced us to the mysteries of multivariate regression analysis; and we were required to demonstrate our mastery of these mysteries by laboriously carrying out (on the mechanical desk-calculators of the time) a term-project consisting of the estimation of one such regression for four variables. That boring, time-consuming experience was enough to convince us of the desirability of devoting much thought to the economic meaning of an equation before undertaking the task of fitting it to the data—the kind of thought that is all too frequently missing in these days of instant estimation.

The temporarily lagging state of econometrics in Chicago was replaced by one in which Chicago once again became a leader in the field with the advent in 1943 of the second group of economists mentioned above—the group that constituted the Cowles Commission for Research in Economics, under the directorship of Jacob (or Jascha, as we rapidly learned to call him) Marschak.[15] Within a short time after Marschak's arrival in 1943, Ted Anderson, Trygve Haavelmo, Leo Hurwicz, Lawrence Klein, Tjalling Koopmans, Herman Rubin, and (somewhat later) Kenneth Arrow had joined the staff—some of them with joint appointments in the Department.[16] And it was my good fortune to receive a fellowship from the Social Science Research Council that enabled me to spend the academic year 1946–47 as a junior member of the Commission for the purpose of writing my doctoral thesis. After the completion of the thesis in 1947 I stayed on for another academic year as a research associate, with a joint appointment as assistant professor in the Department. So my memories of the Cowles Commission are from this two-year period.

After two false starts on subjects of an empirical nature I began to work intensively on a thesis which was ultimately entitled "On the Consistency of Economic Models:

15. On Marschak's contributions to economics, see Arrow (1979).
16. The connection between the Cowles Commission and The University of Chicago actually began before 1943; for details, see Carl Christ, "History of the Cowles Commission, 1932–1952" (1952), pp. 19–41.

A Theory of Involuntary Unemployment'' (1947). The chairman of my thesis committee was Marschak, and its other members were Gregg Lewis, Paul Douglas (who had returned to the University after being wounded in combat, but who was subsequently to leave for the United States Senate after his successful 1948 election campaign), and Theodore O. Yntema (who was actually no longer on campus[17]). Only with Marschak and Lewis, however, did I have some contacts. The thesis consisted of two parts: the first dealing with the mathematical consistency of a general-equilibrium system with money; and the second with unemployment interpreted as the manifestation of an inconsistent system. The main ideas developed in this second part were actually those with which I excitedly first came to Gregg Lewis, who in his characteristically quiet way was encouraging, while at the same time emphasizing that much work remained to be done. They are the ideas presented—in essentially the same form as in the original thesis—in my 1949 article on "Involuntary Unemployment and the Keynesian Supply Function," reprinted in chapter 7 below. At the time I considered these ideas to be the major contribution of the thesis. They were subsequently developed into chapter 13 of my *Money, Interest and Prices* (1956).

Practically all of the first part of my thesis appeared—almost verbatim—in two *Econometrica* articles: "Relative Prices, Say's Law, and the Demand for Money" (1948) [18] and "The Indeterminacy of Absolute Prices in Classical Monetary Theory" (1949), the latter of which is reprinted in chapter 5 below. However, the last ten paragraphs of this 1949 article—which presents what I then termed a "modified classical system" (pp. 144–47, below)—did not appear in the original thesis.

I hope I will be forgiven for digressing briefly on these ten paragraphs, for they have had a significance for me beyond their specific content. These paragraphs—which I have always considered to be the most important in the article—were added in galley proof. And I still have vivid memories of that "moment of truth" when everything suddenly fell into place: when after having long been troubled by the problem, I suddenly realized that the economically meaningful way for the commodity demand equations to depend on the absolute price level (and thus to avoid the invalid dichotomy) without violating the neutrality of money was to have them depend on the real value of money balances. In retrospect, it was clear that all the elements of this solution had been present in the original thesis discussion which these ten paragraphs replaced, but I had not realized it until that moment. Had I realized it, I would undoubtedly have written the earlier sections of the article with a different emphasis, and would accordingly also have entitled the article differently, in a

---

17. After completing his doctorate (see fn. 14 above), Yntema became a professor of statistics in the University's School of Business. At the time in question, he was on leave of absence from the School, at the Committee for Economic Development in Washington; shortly afterwards (1949) he resigned to become vice-president in charge of finance at the Ford Company.

18. Because of my failure at the time to realize that the economically meaningful way for money to enter the utility function is in the form of real balances (cf. the next paragraph), the emphasis of the concluding theorems of this article (namely, Theorems XII and XIV) is misguided. For that reason I have not considered it worthwhile reprinting here.

D. Gale Johnson, Herman Rubin, Tjalling Koopmans, Gershon Cooper

Trygve Haavelmo

Gershon Cooper's model of the U.S. agricultural sector

Herman Rubin, Gershon Cooper, Lawrence Klein, Jacob Marschak, Jack Hartog, unidentified participant, Tjalling Koopmans

Tjalling Koopmans, Jacob Marschak, Gershon Cooper

positive manner that would have highlighted this solution.[19] And it is this personal experience of knowing, but not knowing—knowing something, but not realizing its "obvious" implications until a later instant of time—that has strongly influenced my subsequent work on the history of doctrines, especially that dealing with the discovery of the "General Theory." For as presumptuous as it may be, we of necessity project from our own experiences in trying to understand how the minds of others work.[20]

Though Lange was no longer in Chicago at the time I wrote my thesis, his influence is apparent in it, particularly in that part reproduced in "The Indeterminacy of Absolute Prices in Classical Monetary Theory" (chapter 6 below). For though this article contains some criticism of Lange's work, its point of departure is clearly Lange's classic paper (in the Schultz memorial volume) on "Say's Law: A Restatement and Criticism" (1942).

The Cowles Commission provided the opportunity of personal discussions not only in connection with my thesis, but on general economic questions as well. Thus I remember in particular the long hours spent with Trygve Haavelmo as, pipe clenched between teeth, he discoursed quietly on a wide variety of subjects: the nature of the simultaneous-equation bias as analyzed in his pathbreaking "Probability Approach in Econometrics" (1944), through which he guided me; the meaning of a derivative in economic analysis; involuntary unemployment; Slutzky's analysis of the generation of cycles by random shocks; and the like. Indeed, I still have the notebook in which I would afterwards summarize the main points of these "private seminars." With Lawrence Klein there were stimulating discussions of the manuscript of his then forthcoming *Keynesian Revolution* (1947), and it was this excellent work which started me thinking about many of the problems discussed in the second part of my thesis. Equally stimulating were the discussions with Klein of the major work he was then beginning on providing empirical clothing for Keynes' theoretical model. (There were also our weekly squash games under the West Stands of Stagg Field, which came to an abrupt end when the courts were mysteriously closed off to the public; only after the war did Larry and I, together with the rest of the world, learn of the

19. A more concrete manifestation of my failure to recognize this solution at the time is the fact that what I then called the "Pigou effect" was represented in my thesis—and, correspondingly, in the aforementioned 1949 article on "Involuntary Unemployment"—by an expenditure function which depended, not explicitly on real money balances, but on the absolute price level (see p. 171 of chap. 8, below). The same was true of the savings function $S = \Gamma(r, Y, p)$ in the paper which I originally published on the Pigou effect, "Price Flexibility and Full Employment" (1948, p. 547), which is an extensive elaboration of the corresponding discussion in my thesis. Significantly enough, this function was rewritten as $S = \Gamma(r, Y, M/P)$ when I revised this article for republication in the American Economic Association's *Readings in Monetary Theory* (1951, p. 258). (In view of the fact that the revised form of this article has been reprinted several times, I have not done so again here).

20. See the discussion between Paul Samuelson and myself on the dating of Keynes' discovery of the "General Theory" in Patinkin and Leith (1977) pp. 80–87, 115–19, and 122–24. See also my paper in chap. 2 of that book and my forthcoming *Anticipations of the General Theory?* (1981)

In his contribution to the aforementioned discussion (pp. 115–16), Samuelson reminded us how ideas sometimes come suddenly, as in the case of Archimedes in his bathtub and Shackle while doing the dishes. I am glad to provide further support for this aquatic principle of discovery by noting that my idea came to me while standing next to our washing machine, watching the tumbler go around.

"alternative use" to which these squash courts had been put.) Similarly, there were many enlightening discussions with Kenneth Arrow and Herman Rubin of different aspects of statistical theory, as well as of certain mathematical problems that arose in the course of my work. Leo Hurwicz helped all of us in, among other things, clarifying the properties of homogenous functions. He also essentially tutored me through the multilithed edition of S. S. Wilks' *Mathematical Statistics* (1943).[21]

Besides contacts with Marschak at the Cowles Commission, I took a course with him (in which I was the sole student!) in mathematical economics devoted to the problems in the second half of R. G. D. Allen's *Mathematical Analysis for Economists* (1938). Marschak also gave a seminar in which we went through Tinbergen's pioneering econometric model of *Business Cycles in the U.S.A.: 1919–1932* (1939). On the other hand, I did not have too many contacts with Marschak in connection with the thesis. There was, however, one occasion on which he suggested that my frequent references in it to "classical economics" and "classical system" be supported by citations of the relevant literature. I remember my feeling at the time that this suggestion was needlessly nagging: for surely "everybody knew" what classical economics was. It was only after the unpleasant, though most salutary, experience of having my wrist publicly slapped in *Econometrica* (1951) by William Jaffé for having carelessly misinterpreted Walras' theory of money that I began to take a different view of Marschak's comment and to realize the importance of documenting allusions to, and *a fortiori* discussion of, the history of doctrine with references to the relevant texts.[22]

And then, of course, there were the valuable Cowles Commission seminars. Naturally enough, these were primarily devoted to reports on work-in-progress by staff members, like the one which Gershon Cooper (who subsequently left the academic world) presented in December 1946 on his proposed model of the United States agricultural sector (a seminar of which I happened to take some candid shots; see pp. 12–13 above). The presentation of these reports was followed (or rather, constantly interrupted) by critical comments, a recurrent theme of which was the necessity (emphasized especially by Marschak) for basing the analysis—and the resulting empirical equations—on the principle of profit or utility maximization.

Needless to say, there were also papers by visitors. Among these were Ragnar Frisch and Jan Tinbergen on the occasion of their respective first postwar visits to the United States. Once the famous atomic physicist Leo Szilard (who together with Enrico Fermi had played a leading role in generating the first sustained chain reaction during the wartime work of the Manhattan Project on campus, and who was also a friend of Marschak and Hurwicz) gave, at his (Szilard's) own request, a paper on a monetary scheme he had devised to solve the problem of underspending which he saw as the cause of depressions. The scheme involved the issuance of two kinds of

21. For more formal acknowledgments of these intellectual indebtednesses, see below (chap. 4, p. 116, fn.; chap. 5, p. 125, fn., and p. 132. fn. 4; and chap. 7, p. 155, fn.), as well as my "Relative Prices, Say's Law, and the Demand for Money" (1948, p. 135, fn.) and *Money, Interest and Prices* (1956, p. viii; p. 234, n. 4; and p. 275, fn. 3; 1965, p. xix; p. 336, n. 4; and p. 387, fn. 3).

22. For another instance of "sins of my youth" in connection with the interpretation of texts, see chap. 7. p. 170, fn., below.

money—one red, to be used for spending, and one green, to be used for saving and on whose holding a penalty was to be imposed. Though I do not remember, I suspect that it was (gently) pointed out to Szilard at the time that such schemes had long since been proposed by Silvio Gesell and other monetary cranks.[23]

The seminars were frequently attended also by people who were not members of the Cowles Commission. Among these were Herbert Simon, who was teaching at the Illinois Institute of Technology, elsewhere in the city (later he was to become more formally affiliated with the Commission). Milton Friedman, who had joined the Department of Economics in 1946, would occasionally participate too. Indeed, one of my sharpest memories is of a seminar by Lawrence Klein in which I first heard Friedman advance the simple but powerful suggestion that a minimum test for the predictive efficacy of an econometric model is that it do better than a "naive model" which stated that the future would be like the past. I have since often wondered whether or not Friedman thought that up on the spur of the moment, as well he might. In the year after receiving the Ph.D. degree—during which I was also a junior member of the Department—I benefited from additional contacts with Friedman. He was working on his "Monetary and Fiscal Framework for Economic Stability" (1948) and I on my "Price Flexibility and Full Employment" (1948), and I had stimulating discussions with him of both these papers. During this year I also had many fruitful contacts with Lloyd Metzler and Evsey Domar, both of whom had just joined the Department.[24]

Every research organization has its golden period when its members are unified with a sense of mission about a common goal. Since my own work was peripheral to it, I can safely express the opinion that those were the golden years of the Cowles Commission. Its mission was to base the estimation of structural equations from time series on firm probabilistic principles. And in accomplishing this mission it led to a revolution in econometric methodology by simultaneously demonstrating the inappropriateness of ordinary least-squares and developing alternative estimating procedures.[25] Thus was Error in the form of simultaneous-equation bias analyzed and exorcised, and Truth in the form of maximum-likelihood estimates identified and enthroned. Armed with this truth, Lawrence Klein developed his econometric models of the United States economy (1947, 1950), which were to become the prototype of much work in this field, and Tjalling Koopmans proclaimed the virtues of such models as compared with the "Measurement Without Theory" (1947) carried out by the National Bureau of Economic Research. But within a short time it became evident

23. I am indebted to Lawrence Klein for reminding me about the details of Szilard's scheme. To the best of Klein's memory, the title of Szilard's paper was "A Market Economy Without Trade Cycles."

24. Domar remained only for the year, and then moved on to Johns Hopkins. Metzler's career was tragically cut short by illness.

25. In addition to Haavelmo's seminal "Probability Approach in Econometrics" (1944), see the Cowles Commission's famous monographs 10 and 14: namely, *Statistical Inference in Dynamic Economic Models* (1950) and *Studies in Econometric Method* (1953), the former edited by Koopmans and the latter by Hood and Koopmans. The essential contributions of these monographs date from the period described here, namely, 1946–48. On the other hand, the contributions of the Cowles Commission to activity analysis as represented in its monograph 13 (*Activity Analysis of Production and Allocation* (1951), ed. Koopmans) date primarily from a slightly later period.

that despite the methodological superiority of the new estimating procedures, the predictions they yielded were no more accurate than the earlier ones. Since then, aided by the revolution in computer technology and by the great improvement in the quality and comprehensiveness of the data, econometric modeling has progressed[26] and has met the test of the market. Nevertheless, this experience at the Cowles Commission—reinforced by others[27] in the years which followed—left me with a good deal of skepticism about our ability to derive empirical macroeconomic structural relations which will stand up under the test of time.

That is the Chicago that I remember from my student days. It is undoubtedly an idealization of the past to think of it as a time when giants walked the earth. There are always giants. But it is not an idealization to say that of the giants in economics who did then exist, an unusually large number were walking the corridors of The University of Chicago. And the fact that they were giants of different views, varieties, and vintages only increased their impact on us lesser beings.

Bibliography

R. G. D. Allen. *Mathematical Analysis for Economists*. London, 1938.

K. Arrow. "Jacob Marschak." In *International Encyclopedia of the Social Sciences, Biographical Supplement*. New York, 1979. Pp. 500–507.

W. J. Baumol. "Jacob Viner at Princeton." *Journal of Political Economy*, Jan./Feb. 1972, *80*, 12–15.

_____ and Ellen Viner Seiler. "Jacob Viner." In *International Encyclopedia of the Social Sciences, Biographical Supplement*. New York, 1979. Pp. 783–87.

M. Bronfenbrenner. "Observations on the 'Chicago School(s).' " *Journal of Political Economy*, Feb. 1962, *70*, 72–75.

G. G. Cain. "Paul H. Douglas." In *International Encyclopedia of the Social Sciences, Biographical Supplement*. New York, 1979. Pp. 153–57.

G. Cassel. *The Theory of Social Economy*, trans., rev. ed., S. L. Barron. New York, 1932.

C. Christ. "History of the Cowles Commission, 1932–1952." In *Economic Theory and Measurement: A Twenty Year Research Report*, Cowles Commission for Research in Economics. Chicago, 1952. Pp. 3–66.

A. W. Coats. "The Origins of the 'Chicago School(s)'?" *Journal of Political Economy*, Oct. 1963, *71*, 487–93.

J. Davenport. "The Testament of Henry Simons." *Fortune*, Sept. 1946, *34*, 116–19.

J. R. Davis. *The New Economics and the Old Economists*. Ames, Iowa, 1971.

P. H. Douglas. *Theory of Wages*. New York, 1934.

_____. "Henry Schultz as Colleague." *Econometrica*, Apr. 1939, 7, 104–6.

_____. *In the Fullness of Time*. New York, 1971.

I. Fisher. *The Purchasing Power of Money*, rev. ed. New York, 1913.

K. A. Fox. "Henry Schultz." In *International Encyclopedia of Social Sciences*. New York, 1968. Vol. 14, pp. 65–66.

26. But so have the naive models, to which (by virtue of their ignoring structural relations) the present-day autoregressive integrated moving average (ARIMA) models correspond.

27. With the notable exception of the impressive developments with respect to the empirical consumption function.

M. Friedman. "A Monetary and Fiscal Framework for Economic Stability." *American Economic Review*, June 1948, *38*, 245–64. Reprinted in *Readings in Monetary Theory*, ed. F. A. Lutz and L. W. Mints. Philadelphia, 1951. Pp. 369–93.

_____. "The Monetary Theory and Policy of Henry Simons." *Journal of Law and Economics*, Oct. 1967, *10*, 1–13. Reprinted in *The Optimum Quantity of Money and Other Essays*. Chicago, 1969. Pp. 81–93.

_____. "Remarks." *The University of Chicago Record*, Feb. 21, 1974, *8*, 1–7.

T. Haavelmo. "The Probability Approach in Econometrics." *Econometrica*, July 1944, Supplement, *12*, 1–115.

J. R. Hicks. *Value and Capital*. Oxford, 1939.

H. Hotelling. "The Work of Henry Schultz." *Econometrica*, Apr. 1939, 7, 97–103.

W. Jaffé. "Walrasiana: The *Elements* and Its Critics." *Econometrica*, July 1951, *19*, 327–28.

M. Kalecki. "Oskar Lange 1904–1965." *Economic Journal*, Mar. 1966, *76*, 431–32.

J. M. Keynes. *A Tract on Monetary Reform*. London, 1923.

_____. *A Treatise on Money*, vols. 1 & 2. London, 1930.

_____. *The General Theory of Employment, Interest and Money*. London, 1936.

L. R. Klein. "The Use of Econometric Models as a Guide to Economic Policy." *Econometrica*, Apr. 1947, *15*, 111–51.

_____. *The Keynesian Revolution*. New York, 1947.

_____. *Economic Fluctuations in the United States, 1921–1941*. New York, 1950 (Cowles Commission Monograph No. 11)

F. H. Knight. *The Economic Organization*. Chicago, 1933 (multilith). Reprinted New York, 1951.

T. C. Koopmans. "Measurement without Theory." *Review of Economic Statistics*, Aug. 1947, *29*, 161–72.

_____, ed. *Statistical Inference in Dynamic Economic Models*. New York, 1950 (Cowles Commission Monograph No. 10).

_____, ed. *Activity Analysis of Production and Allocation*. New York, 1951 (Cowles Commission Monograph No. 13).

_____ and W. C. Hood, eds. *Studies in Econometric Method*. New York, 1953 (Cowles Commission Monograph No. 14).

T. Kowalik. "Biography of Oskar Lange." In *On Political Economy and Econometrics: Essays in Honour of Oskar Lange*. Warsaw, 1964. Pp. 1–13.

O. Lange. "On the Economic Theory of Socialism." Parts 1, 2, *Review of Economic Studies*, Oct. 1936, *4*, 53–71; Feb. 1937, *4*, 123–42. Reprinted in O. Lange and F. M. Taylor, *On the Economic Theory of Socialism*. Minneapolis, 1938. Pp. 55–143.

_____. "The Rate of Interest and the Optimum Propensity to Consume," *Economica*, Feb. 1938, *5*, 12–32; reprinted in *Readings in Business Cycle Theory*, ed. G. Haberler. Philadelphia, 1944. Pp. 169–92.

_____. "Say's Law: A Restatement and Criticism." In *Studies in Mathematical Economics and Econometrics*, ed. O. Lange, F. McIntyre, and T. O. Yntema. Chicago, 1942. Pp. 49–69.

A. P. Lerner. *The Economics of Control*. New York, 1944.

F. Machlup. "What the World Thought of Jacob Viner." *Journal of Political Economy*, Jan./Feb. 1972, *80*, 1–4.

A. Marshall. *Principles of Economics*, 8th ed. London, 1920.

L. W. Mints. *History of Banking Theory*. Chicago, 1945.

J. L. Mosak. *General Equilibrium Theory in International Trade*. Evanston, Ill., 1944 (Cowles Commission Monograph No. 7).

J. U. Nef. *Industry and Government in France and England: 1540–1640*. Philadelphia, 1940.
———. *Search for Meaning; The Autobiography of a Noncomformist*. Washington, D.C., 1973.
T. Parsons. *The Structure of Social Action*. New York, 1937.
D. Patinkin. "Relative Prices, Say's Law, and the Demand for Money." *Econometrica*, Apr. 1948, *16*, 135–54.
———. "Price Flexibility and Full Employment." *American Economic Review*, Sept. 1948, *38*, 543–64. Reprinted with revisions in *Readings in Monetary Theory*, ed. F. A. Lutz and L. W. Mints. Philadelphia, 1951. Pp. 252–83.
———. *Money, Interest, and Prices*. Evanston, Ill., 1956. 2nd ed., New York, 1965.
———. "The Process of Writing the *General Theory*: A Critical Survey." in Patinkin and Leith (1977), Pp. 3–24.
———. *Anticipations of the General Theory? And Other Essays on Keynes*. Chicago, 1981 forthcoming.
——— and J. C. Leith, eds. *Keynes, Cambridge and the General Theory: The Process of Criticism and Discussion Connected with the Development of the General Theory*. London, 1977.
C. A. Phillips. *Bank Credit*. New York, 1920.
A. Rees. "Douglas on Wages and the Supply of Labor." *Journal of Political Economy*, Sept./Oct. 1979, *87*, 915–22.
L. Robbins. *Jacob Viner: A Tribute*. Princeton, N. J., 1970.
W. J. Samuels, ed. *The Chicago School of Political Economy*. East Lansing, Mich., 1976.
P. A. Samuelson. "The Stability of Equilibrium: Comparative Statics and Dynamics." *Econometrica*, 1941, *9*, 97–120.
———. *Foundations of Economic Analysis*. Cambridge, 1947.
———. "Jacob Viner, 1892–1970." *Journal of Political Economy*, Jan./Feb. 1972, *80*, 5–16.
———. "Paul Douglas' Measurement of Production Functions and Marginal Productivities." *Journal of Political Economy*, Sept./Oct. 1979, *87*, 923–39.
H. Schultz. *Theory and Measurement of Demand*. Chicago, 1938.
*[H. C. Simons]. *Economics 201: The Divisional Course in Economics*. Chicago, n.d. (mimeographed).
———. *A Positive Program for Laissez Faire*. Chicago, 1934. Reprinted in *Economic Policy for a Free Society*. Chicago, 1948. Pp. 40–77.
———. *Personal Income Taxation*. Chicago, 1938.
———. *Economic Policy for a Free Society*. Chicago, 1948.
O. Spengler. *Decline of the West*. New York, 1932.
H. Stein. "Henry C. Simons." In *International Encyclopedia of the Social Sciences*. New York, 1968. Vol. 14, pp. 260–62.
G. J. Stigler. *The Theory of Price*, 3rd ed. New York, 1966.
———. "Henry Calvert Simons." *Journal of Law and Economics*, Apr. 1974, *17*, 1–5.
G. S. Tavlas. "The Chicago Tradition Revisited: Some Neglected Monetary Contributions:

---

*In the bibliography of Simons' writings which appears at the end of his posthumously published *Economic Policy for a Free Society* (1948, p. 313), this publication is listed as " 'Syllabus Materials for Economics 201.' Chicago: University of Chicago Bookstore, 1933 and rev. Pp. 62. (Mimeographed)." This was apparently an earlier edition, as is also attested by the fact that my copy (on whose title page I recorded the date of acquisition as "January 9, 1942") contains only 60 pages.

In a letter to me Gregg Lewis has confirmed that the *Syllabus* was revised at least once; indeed, he himself assisted in this revision.

Senator Paul Douglas (1892–1976)." *Journal of Money, Credit and Banking*, Nov. 1977, *4*, 529–35.

J. Tinbergen. *Business Cycles in the United States of America 1919–1932*. Geneva, 1939.

A. J. Toynbee. *Study of History*, vol. 1. London, 1934.

T. Veblen. *Imperial Germany and the Industrial Revolution*. New York, 1915.

J. Viner. *Canada's Balance of International Indebtedness 1900–1913: An Inductive Study in the Theory of International Trade*. Cambridge, Mass., 1924.

———. "The Present Status and Future Prospects of Quantitative Economics (Discussion)." *American Economic Review, Supplement*, March 1928, *18*, 30–36, as reprinted in Viner (1958), pp. 41–49.

———. *Studies in the Theory of International Trade*. New York, 1937.

———. "A Modest Proposal for Some Stress on Scholarship in Graduate Training." *Brown University Papers*, 1950, *24*, as reprinted in Viner (1958), 369–81.

———. *The Long View and the Short*. Glencoe, Ill., 1958.

S. Wellisz. "Oskar Lange." In *International Encyclopedia of the Social Sciences*. New York, 1968. Vol. 8, pp. 581–84.

S. S. Wilks. *Mathematical Statistics*. Princeton, N. J., 1943 (multilithed).

T. O. Yntema. *A Mathematical Reformulation of the General Theory of International Trade*. Chicago, 1932.

———. "Henry Schultz: His Contributions to Economics and Statistics." in *Studies in Mathematical Economics and Econometrics*, ed. O. Lange, F. McIntyre, and T. O. Yntema. Chicago, 1942. Pp. 11–17.

University of Chicago Ph.D. Dissertations

M. Bronfenbrenner. "Monetary Theory and General Equilibrium." 1939.

H. G. Lewis. "Studies in the Elasticity of Demand for Steel." 1947.

J. L. Mosak. "General Equilibrium Theory in International Trade." 1944.

D. Patinkin. "On the Consistency of Economic Models: A Theory of Involuntary Unemployment." 1947.

T. O. Yntema. "A Mathematical Reformulation of the General Theory of International Trade." 1929.

Unpublished Materials

Author's lecture notes from courses mentioned here.

Frank H. Knight (1955)

1. Frank Knight as Teacher*

I shall write of Frank Knight[1] as a teacher—and this is really the viewpoint from which I can best describe him. For I do not feel that I have the necessary expertise in the theory of uncertainty and in capital theory—and certainly not in social philosophy—to provide a critical evaluation of Knight's fundamental contribution to these fields. Nor do I have any basis to write of him as a colleague. On the other hand, my most vivid memories of Knight even today are from the days when he was one of my teachers at the University of Chicago (1941–47). Indeed, I saw him afterwards only a

Reprinted by permission from *American Economic Review*, Dec. 1973, *63*, 787–810.

*Appropriately enough, the first draft of this memoir was written while serving during the fall of 1972 as Ford Foundation Visiting Research Professor of Economics at The University of Chicago. And though the pages which follow are by their very nature a personal document, I have nevertheless greatly benefited from—and am grateful for—the opportunity afforded by this visit of discussing them with D. Gale Johnson, T. W. Schultz, George Stigler, Roger Weiss, and other people at Chicago who knew Frank Knight well. I am also indebted for helpful comments on earlier drafts to Yoram Ben-Porath, Martin Bronfenbrenner, Clarence Efroymson, Richard Freeman, William Ginzberg, Giora Hanoch, Ephraim Kleiman, Leonardo Leiderman, Akiva Offenbacher, David Marawetz, Jerome Stein, Lester Telser, Manuel Trajtenberg, and Menahem Yaari. In view of the personal nature of this memoir, it is really unnecessary to say that none of these individuals bear responsibility for the description that follows.

I would also like to express my appreciation to George Stigler for making Knight's unpublished papers (which are in his custody) available to me, and to Glen Gilchrist (who has catalogued these papers under Stigler's direction) for guiding me through them and xeroxing requested materials. {Since this article was published, the Knight papers have been placed in the Regenstein Library of The University of Chicago.} I wish finally to thank Mark Wang at the University of Chicago and Akiva Offenbacher at the Hebrew University of Jerusalem for their valuable technical assistance, and Kathryn Bates and, especially, Vera Jacobs for patiently and accurately typing this memoir through its various drafts. I am also grateful to the University of Chicago, the Central Research Fund of the Hebrew University, and the Israel Academy of Sciences and Humanities for research grants that made this and other assistance possible.

With regard to articles listed in the Bibliography, page numbers shown in the text refer to the reprinted version, and not to the original.

1. Frank Hyneman Knight: born, McLean County, Illinois, November 7, 1885; died, Chicago, Illinois, April 15, 1972.

The bare facts of Knight's academic career as given by the 1969 *Handbook of The American Economic Association* are as follows: Ph.B., Milligan College, Tennessee, 1911; B.S., M.A., University of Tennessee, 1913; Ph.D., Cornell University, 1916; instructor of economics, Cornell University, 1916–17, University of Chicago, 1917–19; associate professor and later professor of economics, State University of Iowa, 1919–27; professor of economics, University of Chicago, 1927–45; distinguished service professor of social sciences and philosophy, 1945–52; emeritus after 1952.

A bibliography of Knight's writings for the period 1915–35 appears at the beginning of his *Ethics of Competition* (1935, pp. 11–18). For other details of Knight's life, as well as a general description of his work, see James Buchanan (1968) and Joseph Dorfman (1959, pp. 467–79, 767–70, *et passim*). On Knight's days as a graduate student at Cornell—and his shift then from studying philosophy to economics—see the description of his renowned teacher there, Alvin Johnson (1960, pp. 227–28, 231). (I am indebted to Edward Shils for this reference.) See also the anonymous biographical sketch of Knight that appears in the December 1973 issue of the *American Economic Review*.

few times. Furthermore, my own work in economics has largely been in fields that were not his major concern, and so I read—or reread—little of his work after my student days.

Thus the picture of Knight that I shall draw here is primarily the one that I remember seeing as a student—through the window on the life of his teacher that is open to a student. It is thus a picture of only one aspect of Frank Knight's life—though obviously an important one. And I am fully aware that—like any picture based on personal impressions and memories—it is one that also reveals something about the viewer.

What is the mark of a great teacher? It is first and foremost the qualities he conveys by his very presence in the classroom: his personal integrity and his intellectual curiosity and stimulation; his humility and his breadth of interests.

And it is, secondly, the insights and understanding—the new ways of looking at things—that he transmits to his students. Frequently these insights are original to him; but even when they are not, they reflect his judgment as to what is important in the existing body of knowledge, and hence worthy of emphasis. And it is the mark of a great teacher that the insights he thus passes on to his students do indeed remain important: that they continue to guide their thinking many years later; and that these students in turn consider the insights so important as to wish to pass them on to their own students as well.

In all of these ways Frank Knight was a great teacher.

I am afraid that I did not think so in my first contact with him when I tried sitting in on his course on "Price and Distribution Theory" (Economics 301), the first course in economic theory required of all graduate students. I found myself then quite confused by the middle-aged (he was then in his late 50's), medium-height, plumpish and moustached man who stood at the side of the large elliptical wooden table in one of the seminar rooms on the first floor of the Social Sciences Research Building—leaning on the back of a chair, occasionally puffing on a corn-cob pipe—and rambling on in a high-pitched voice and in a disjointed manner on mysterious issues that certainly cast no light on the newly revealed truth which was then being enthusiastically explicated everywhere—in words, in graphs, as well as in mathematical formulas—of "marginal revenue = marginal cost." And after a few such bewildering experiences, I gave up in despair.

But not for long. The following year I registered for the course, and this time succeeded in taking fairly coherent classnotes. But I must admit that my greatest pleasure and benefit from the course came when, toward the end of my graduate studies, I sat through it once again.

Many factors lie behind this long road to understanding and appreciation. First of all, Knight gave little emphasis in his teaching to those things to which the beginning graduate student is normally attracted—namely the technical aspects of the discipline, and the newer the better. In part this was due to the fact that Knight was just not interested in these aspects—and in part because he took this knowledge for granted and wanted to get at the more fundamental issues that lay behind the assumptions and implications of the analysis. And this was not simply a reflection of the period and of the generation—for my classnotes of Jacob Viner's contemporaneous version of the

Economics 301 course show that Viner (in addition to being concerned with the broader issues of analysis and scholarship) gave considerably more emphasis to the technical aspects of the analysis than did Knight. Thus, for example—as might be expected from his famous article on "Cost Curves and Supply Curves" (1931)—Viner provided a fairly detailed presentation of the properties of these curves under the assumptions of imperfect as well as perfect competition, though (as I shall note later) Knight too discussed the theory of imperfect competition.

But this was not the only cause of the beginning graduate student's difficulties with Knight's course. For, quite frankly, Knight was not a good teacher in the sense of systematically introducing and developing a subject. Nor did he make a pedagogic effort to motivate the student to understand the subject in question by explicitly relating it to the general framework of economic analysis. All this, Knight took for granted as being known to the student— and devoted himself instead to forcing the student to rethink the basic issues of economic theory as he saw them.

Another difficulty with Knight's lectures was that at crucial points they frequently (and unawares to the student) turned into brief and cryptic summaries of views that Knight had developed at length in various of his writings—to which for the most part Knight did not explicitly refer. Thus a brief reference to the invalidity of "productivity ethics" or to "commutative justice *versus* distributive justice" could hardly convey the depth and meaning of Knight's famous essay on "The Ethics of Competition." Nor could passing references to "real-cost versus alternative-cost theories of value" mean much to a student who was not aware of Knight's many writings on this question.

For this reason I remember characterizing Knight's lectures at that time as being like a general-equilibrium system—which could not be solved until the student was familiar with the set of Knight's articles that specified the relationships between the various parts of the lectures, and thus converted their unknowns into knowns. And I still remember my feeling of satisfaction when I began to be able to see the system of equations as a whole—and things began to fall into place.

There is one further bit of background information that I feel is relevant to my picture of Knight. The teachers of economic theory during my student days at Chicago included not only Frank Knight and Jacob Viner, but also Oskar Lange—who was the antithesis of Knight, and not only on political grounds. Where Knight devoted much attention to probing (in his rambling and often obscure manner) into the meaning of the basic definitions and assumptions of the analysis ("perfect competition," "perfect foresight," "wants," "costs," "capital," "equality," and the like), Lange (in his contrastingly clear and systematic manner) was primarily concerned with drawing the logical implications of these assumptions. So where Knight taught economic theory in a loose, "literary," philosophical fashion—and was antipathetic to mathematical economics[2]—Lange was formal, rigorous, complete,

2. "The mathematical economists have commonly been mathematicians first and economists afterward, disposed to oversimplify the data and underestimate the divergence between their premises and the facts of life. In consequence they have not been successful in getting their presentation into such a form that it could be understood, and its relation to real problems recognized, by practical economists" (Knight 1923, p. 49).

and frequently made use of mathematical tools (not to mention his invaluable course in Mathematical Economics). And where Knight was basically not sympathetic to the new developments in economic theory (read: Keynes and Hicks)—and even, I would say, instinctively critical of them—Lange was an early convert as well as an efficient expositor and refiner.[3] Thus Knight and Lange complemented each other in a most wondrous way—thereby increasing the productivity of each of them in the teaching process. From the implicit dialogue that thus took place between these two teachers, we students were the direct beneficiaries.[4]

I. Knight the Theoretical Economist

What were the main features of this world of Knight's? First and foremost was ("If you don't learn anything else from me, then learn this . . .") the notion of social organization—and the economic system as a means of fulfilling certain basic functions of any such organization: the system whose exact structure varies from society to society, but which for every one of them must answer the basic questions about what goods and services to produce, how to produce them, how to distribute them among the members of the society, and how to provide for the future of the society. The fruitfulness of this view of economics is well attested by the fact that it has been adopted by such widely used elementary textbooks as those of Samuelson, Lipsey, and others, as to have become by now a commonplace.[5]

Another basic element of Knight's teaching was the view that the study of man—including economic man—could not proceed within the same deterministic framework as the study of nature. For the behavior of man must also express his freedom of will—to which there is no counterpart in the physical world. Hence "fully

3. See Lange's 1938 model of the *General Theory* in his "The Rate of Interest and the Optimum Propensity to Consume" and his use and elaboration of the analytical tools of *Value and Capital* in his *Price Flexibility and Employment* (1944).

4. Unfortunately, neither side to this dialogue—and even more unfortunately, practically nobody at Chicago at that time—represented the empirical approach to economics in the sense of the statistical analysis of quantitative data. From the death of Henry Schultz in 1938 and until the advent of the Cowles Commission in the mid-1940's (whose major concern at that time was not only the methodology of econometric models, but also the actual construction of such models for the U.S. economy), this component of a good education in economics was almost entirely absent from Chicago. It should, however, be noted that empirical economics had not achieved the recognized position it now has in the profession, and was accordingly absent from many (if not most) of the other leading academic centers as well.

5. Knight discussed these basic functions in his 1933 booklet on *The Economic Organization*. This reproduces the four chapters that Knight first published in 1932 in the book of readings that was prepared specially for the famous social science survey course developed during the 1930s at the College of the University of Chicago. In the bibliography of Knight's work that appears in the *Ethics of Competition* (1935c, p. 15) these chapters are described as "an abstract of material mimeographed for private circulation at the University of Iowa during the years 1922–25." (This is apparently the material that has been found among Knight's papers and catalogued in Boxes 8 and 9 under the title "*Economics, 1920's.*" In any event, this material does contain an approach to economic analysis in terms of the functions of an economy.) For further details on the dating of this material, see fn. 1 of the next chapter. An early version of the discussion of the functions of an economy is to be found in Knight's doctoral thesis, as revised and published in his classic *Risk, Uncertainty and Profit* (1921a, pp. 54 ff).

In connection with Samuelson's approach to economics in terms of these functions, see his reference to Knight in the second edition of *Economics: An Introductory Analysis* (1951, p. 14, fn. 1). See also fn. 8 below.

determined'' or ''perfectly rational'' human behavior is no behavior at all: for such behavior is entirely mechanistic, leaving no place for free choice on the part of the individual. (''Does the apple falling from the tree act rationally? The question is meaningless—since the apple is subject to mechanical forces.'') Indeed, the proper study of human behavior must take into account the possibility of error and the existence of exploratory and game-playing aspects of such behavior. Correspondingly, despite his occasional use of analogies from physics, Knight emphasized that we ''cannot transfer the laws of the physical sciences to where human beings are concerned'' (Classnotes: Econ. 305, 1945).

In the opening lecture of his theory course in 1942, Knight (according to my classnotes) set out his general approach to the analysis of the economic system:

> The main theme of traditional economics is that the investigation of theoretical problems can be settled by argument, without using inductive argument. Discuss things of common knowledge. Most questions solve themselves if correctly stated. No special technique necessary. The current tendency in the literature is a reaction against this view. Want to use inductive thinking—getting at facts. Also use mathematical techniques—statistics. Point of view of this course is not inductive or deductive in the sense of being beyond reach of any educated person. Simple principles of mathematics to be used. [Classnotes, Econ. 301, 1942]

Our basic readings for the course were from Marshall's *Principles* and Davenport's *Economics of Enterprise*.[6] In the opening lecture just mentioned, Knight referred in the following words to these writers and to what he planned to do in the course:

> Marshall was in many ways an eclectic combining supply and demand sides. He was a conservative and a defender of *laissez-faire*. Davenport was one of the most important and original thinkers.[7] He was a radical in the negative

6. The other reading materials to which we were referred (according to my 1942 classnotes from Knight's 301 course) were as follows: E. H. Chamberlin, *Monopolistic Competition* (1942) (mentioned, but not clear if assigned as reading); R. F. Harrod, ''Doctrines of Imperfect Competition'' (1934); J. R. Hicks, *Value and Capital*, ch. 1 (1939); F. H. Knight, *The Economic Organization* (1933a); A. P. Lerner, ''Statics and Dynamics in Socialist Economics'' (1937). In my 1945 classnotes, there is also a reference to Knight's ''The Business Cycle, Interest and Money: A Methodological Approach'' (1941).

Other of Knight's writings that we read in connection with this course included: *Ethics of Competition* (1935d), various essays; ''The Quantity of Capital and the Rate of Interest'' (1936); ''Diminishing Returns from Investment'' (1944a); and ''Realism and Relevance in the Theory of Demand'' (1944b). Interestingly enough, there is only one mention in my notes (in the context of a discussion of the nature of profits) of Knight's classic, *Risk, Uncertainty, and Profit*. Nor do I recall our reading this book as students. On the other hand, it is clear in retrospect that many of Knight's classroom discussions stemmed from it.

7. The deep impact—both intellectual and (I would conjecture) personal—that Davenport had on Knight is most evident from the biographical sketch of him that Knight wrote for the *Encyclopedia of the Social Sciences* (1931). Knight's first contact with Davenport (which—as the foregoing sketch makes clear—also included participation in the latter's classes) apparently took place at Cornell during 1916–17, which was the year that Davenport came to Cornell (Spiegel, 1968, p. 16), and also the year that Knight stayed on there as an instructor after receiving his Ph.D. (see fn. 1, above).

I might also note that the index to Knight's famous ''work of his youth,'' *Risk, Uncertainty, and Profit*, contains more references to Davenport than to any other writer besides J. B. Clark.

sense. . . . Davenport was a forerunner of Keynes. In certain paragraphs one can't tell whether reading Keynes or not.

Knight is for reading a couple of books and getting conclusions of subject rather than reading literature—what people have said (as Viner does). Knight interested in social applications of economic approach; not interested in associating points of view with writers, or in puzzle solving. The big job of economics is to divest people of prejudices—to have them see the questions as they are. Right now ordinary lay opinion should be forgotten as much as possible [by the students, presumably]. [Classnotes. Econ. 301, 1942]

The primary contrast that Knight drew in his lectures—and in much of his writings over the years—was that between two alternative systems for fulfilling the aforementioned functions: the competitive (capitalist) system and socialism. Most of his classroom analysis (as well as of his writings) was devoted to the competitive market system. Here Knight gave an overview of this system in terms of what he called "the familiar figure of the 'wheel of wealth' " (1933a, pp. 60–61, here reproduced in Figure 1), which has become even more familiar to a modern generation of economists through its use by Paul Samuelson in his introductory textbook.[8] Within the

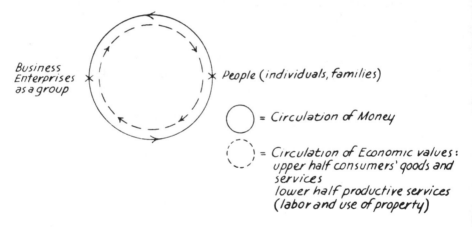

Figure 1 (Knight, 1933a, p. 61)

8. Knight's first use of such a diagram can be dated back to 1926 at the latest (see fn. 5 above). Insofar as Samuelson is concerned, see the circular-flow diagrams that appear in all editions of his *Economics: An Introductory Analysis* (e.g., 1948, p. 226; 1970, pp. 42, 170, and 607). I might note that Samuelson did his undergraduate work at the University of Chicago in the early 1930's—and that in reply to my query as to the possible origin of his circular-flow diagram in Knight's teachings, Samuelson has indeed confirmed that "I [Samuelson] was influenced by Knight's elementary (for him) explanation of how the economic system works. In the Social Science Survey Courses I or II, 1932–3 [see fn. 5 above], I am sure I was assigned it to read. And in early editions of my book, I cited Knight for How, What, and For Whom" (personal letter to author dated April 10, 1973, and cited with Samuelson's kind permission). (For his reminiscences of his days at Chicago, see Samuelson (1972a, pp. 158–61; 1972b, p. 5).)

The question of the origins of Knight's diagram itself is an intriguing one that I have discussed at length in the next chapter. This also describes the different uses that Samuelson has made of the circular-flow diagram in the various editions of his textbook.

framework of this diagram, Knight then proceeded to explain how the price system (and more specifically, the two sets of prices—those of final goods and services, and those of productive services) "control[s] the process of production and distribution under free enterprise" (1933a, p. 62).

The distinctive elements of Knight's exposition began with his criticism of the term "competition" as a description of the system. This term, emphasized Knight, had a connotation of *personal* competition: whereas the system of perfect competition was an impersonal one. With whom, asked Knight, was the farmer—producing his agricultural output in a perfect market—competing? Thus the use of the term was misleading in failing to bring out that the so-called system of *competition* was a system that actually brought about the *cooperation* (though again, in an impersonal manner) of economic units in carrying out the productive processes of the economy. The basic characteristic of this system—and once again Knight prefaced his discussion here (as in many other contexts!) with the injunction "If you don't learn anything else from me, then learn this . . . "—was that the exchanges which take place under this system are to the *mutual advantage* of both parties to the exchange. Indeed, this—according to Knight—was the major innovation of Adam Smith, though one that was frequently not understood even to this day. And he would frequently refer to the levying of tariffs as a flagrant example of the continued failure to understand this fundamental of economic analysis.

In analyzing the productive process, Knight emphasized that it was one in which (like in the usual production function of today) output was essentially simultaneous with input—and he thus criticized the classical model of (agricultural) production as well as the Austrian production-period model of capital theory, both of which presented output as following inputs with a time lag. Knight also emphasized that essentially what was produced (and, even more so, consumed) was not goods, but services—though (he admitted) the distinction tended to vanish in the case of perishable goods which were immediately destroyed in the process of consumption.

In his analysis of production, Knight devoted much attention to an explanation of the proper meaning of the law of diminishing returns. In this context he made the distinction—now to be found in many price-theory textbooks—among the three regions of the total output curve under the assumption of constant returns to scale (see Figure 2): region I, in which the average product of the variable factor, A, is rising; region II, in which both marginal and average product of A are declining; and region III, in which the marginal product of A is negative. Knight went on to emphasize the symmetry between regions I and III that expresses itself in the fact that just as the marginal product of the variable factor A is negative in region III, so must the marginal product of the fixed factor B be negative in region I. Hence, said Knight, in the real world we are always in region II (see 1921a, pp. 97–102).[9]

Within the foregoing framework Knight forcefully expounded an "alternative" or

9. For examples of textbook discussions of Knight's "three regions," see Stigler (1952, p. 115), Ferguson (1969, p. 130), and Grunfeld, Liviatan, and Patinkin (1963, pp. 15–19). Some price-theory textbooks today make use of the assumption of "free disposal" and thus draw the production curve as *Obce* instead of *Oabcd*, or else simply draw only the relevant segment of the curve, *bc*.

"opportunity cost" theory of value that he contrasted with the classical "real" or "subjective" or "pain cost" theory of value—to the clear disadvantage of the latter. I mentioned before that the beginning student frequently did not understand the issues that Knight was discussing in the classroom until he had found his way to those of Knight's writings that dealt with these issues (and in this case Knight's 1935 article on "The Ricardian Theory of Production and Distribution" was particularly relevant). I might now add that in this case the student's understanding was also advanced in the course of his studies as he became aware (through exposure to Viner's version of the Economics 301 course) that this was not a dead issue, but part of a running debate that Knight was carrying on with Viner. And I must admit that Knight's presentation of the issue in terms of absolute right and wrong (as he was wont to do) was less helpful than Viner's resolution of the debate in terms of including in the individual's calculation of alternatives his subjective tastes for the pains and pleasures he derived from the various labor services he could sell in the market.

In any event, I still find that it deepens one's understanding to follow Knight in emphasizing that Adam Smith's beaver was worth two deer not because of the fact per se that a unit of labor was involved in the catching of each, but because this fact implied that the cost of catching a beaver were the two deer that could alternatively have been caught. Hence (in Knight's terms) the market price for a beaver had to be two deer: for otherwise there would be a discrepancy between what the individual had to forego in order to obtain a (say) beaver "directly" (viz., by hunting it) and "indirectly" (viz., by hunting deer, and exchanging them for the beaver), so that market forces of excess supply (or demand) for beaver would automatically reestablish the price of two deer to one beaver, should it deviate from this level.

A basic part of Knight's theory course was devoted to the theory of demand, and to the Marshallian demand curve in particular. In this context Knight was less receptive than he might have been to indifference-curve analysis, and there may indeed be hints of a somewhat more positive attitude to this analysis in his Preface to the 1948 reissue of *Risk, Uncertainty, and Profit* (p. xlviii). After all, indifference-curve analysis did not challenge anything basic in Knight's general approach, so that I feel that his opposition to it was at least in part a reflection of his reluctance at that time to change traditional modes of thought.

Still, Knight's detailed critique of Hicks' exposition of indifference-curve analysis did provide the student with a deeper understanding of its assumptions. It also enabled Knight to draw a sharp and instructive distinction between the demand curve that Hicks generated by changing the price of the good in question while keeping all other prices and money income constant—so that real income changed along the demand curve; and the Marshallian demand curve, in the generation of which (according to Knight) other prices were changed so as to keep real income constant (1944b, 1946). This interpretation of the Marshallian demand curve was also stressed by Viner in his version of the Economics 301 course (Classnotes, 1944), and so can well be said to be part of a Chicago tradition.[10]

10. See the similar interpretations—based on texts from Marshall's *Principles*—in Friedman (1949) and Patinkin (1963, reproduced as ch. 8 below).

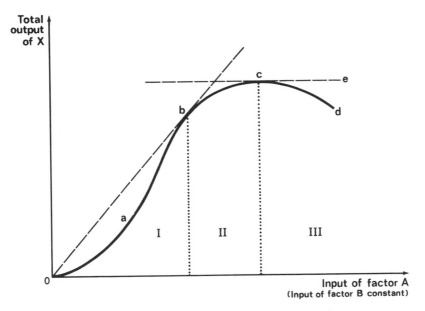

Figure 2

As already noted, Knight discussed (and referred us to the relevant readings on) the theory of monopolistic competition—indeed, to an extent greater than one might infer from some of the things that have been written on the attitude of the Chicago school to this theory.[11] It is, however, true that Knight was critical of Chamberlin's concepts of imperfect competition, and denied that the possibility that an ". . . enterprise can have a diminishing [i.e., negatively sloped] demand curve but still no monopoly profits . . . corresponded to fact" (Classnotes, Econ. 301, 1942).

The most distinctive part of Knight's theory course had to do with his theory of capital—and one cannot but be impressed by the modern flavor of what he taught here. First of all, Knight railed against the traditional classical "trinity of factors of production"—land, labor, and capital. There was little in the productive process that Knight was willing to identify with the "original and indestructible forces of nature" that the classical economists had defined as "land." Agricultural land, too—emphasized Knight—had to be developed and maintained just like any other capital good. Similarly, the productive process of labor reflected primarily not "native qualities," but the artificial qualities which constituted human culture. Thus there is no basic distinction between most of the income received by labor and that received by capital. In the terminology of the more recent "Chicago school" associated with the names of T. W. Schultz, Gary Becker, and others (and I suspect that Knight had some direct or indirect influence on their thinking, too), Knight viewed most of labor income as returns to "human capital" and stressed the role of the family (both genetically and

11. See Archibald (1961) and the references to Stigler and Friedman there cited, as well as the subsequent exchange (1963) between all three of these economists. See also Miller (1962, p. 67).

socially) in endowing its children with this capital. Thus Knight was not very far from classifying all of the factors of production under the one general title "capital."

In his more formal treatment of capital theory, Knight—like J. B. Clark before him (1899)—emphasized the basic distinction between specific capital goods in the concrete—which are periodically worn out and reproduced, and the stock of capital in the abstract—which is permanent, and which with the exception of a few historical periods (for example, periods of prolonged warfare) has been continuously growing over the course of human history. (See Knight, 1936, p. 434). And a capital good has value only by virtue of its being the source of the stream of services—and hence of income—that flows from it.

The economic explanation of the rate of interest is to be found in the productivity of capital. Time preference is not a cause of interest, but the result of it; because interest can be earned by deferring present consumption to the future and investing the savings in the meantime, the individual can not be in equilibrium unless a dollar's worth of present consumption exceeded the value to him of a dollar's worth of future consumption by precisely the interest that could alternatively be earned by abstaining now from consumption. I should also note that Knight's emphasis on the fact that capital in the abstract—or wealth—was continuously growing over time led him to reject the Fisherine notion that individuals save in the present only in order to finance increased consumption in the future.

And since the rate of interest is determined by the productivity of capital, it is (as Lerner (1953), Haavelmo (1960), and others were later to emphasize) the total *stock* of capital that is relevant to this analysis—and not the *flow* of current investment, which by its very nature is small relative to the total stock of existing capital, and hence can have little effect on its marginal productivity (see Knight 1932a, pp. 262–63; 1936, p. 622). (I might note that this concern with the time dimensions of the various economic variables was a constant characteristic of Knight's analysis— emphasized, for example, also in his treatment of the different "runs" of Marshallian cost and supply curves (Knight, 1921b, pp. 186–216).)

On the basis of this approach to capital theory, and with the aid of his historical perspective, Knight continued to insist—even in the face of the huge quantities of idle plant and equipment of the greatest depression in history, and the contrary contentions of the "secular stagnationists" who dominated economic thinking in the decade after the *General Theory*—that in the real world there is no tendency toward a diminishing return to capital, so that from the long-run viewpoint the demand for capital is infinitely elastic. Accordingly he rejected as unrealistic the classical notion of a long-run equilibrium quantity of capital that would characterize a stationary state to which the normal development of the economy would allegedly lead (Knight, 1936, 1944a).

These conclusions resulted from Knight's fundamental contention that the very process of increasing the stock of capital must of necessity change the "given conditions" which are supposed to generate diminishing returns. This contention was connected, first of all, with Knight's inclusive concept of capital as encompassing all factors of production, so that capital formation in the real world would lead to the augmentation of all productive agents, thus leaving no fixed factor which would be the source of diminishing returns.

Secondly, stressed Knight, ". . . it is practically impossible to imagine any investment activity in the real world which is not in some degree rationally experimental, in the sense of being reasonably expected to lead to new knowledge having some enduring economic significance. That is, all investment consists, in part, of investment in new knowledge." On the other hand, ". . . we can hardly think of new knowledge being applied without considerable accompanying expenditure on new instruments. This is even more unrealistic than the converse case, previously discussed" (1944a, pp. 40–42). In brief, Knight's "growth model" was one in which all investment generates "learning by doing," and all technological change is "capital-embodied."

Finally, another factor acting against diminishing returns was the fact that wants did not remain constant, but were changing. "Moreover, it is a familiar fact that in real life much investment actually takes the form of creating or changing consumers' wants and that the result appears in the capital and profit-and-loss accounts of an enterprise" (Knight, 1944a, p. 37).

As an aside, I might conjecture that we can find in Knight's capital theory one of the main sources of his objections (on theoretical, as distinct from political, grounds) to Keynes' *General Theory*. Knight could not accept the implications of this book that the rate of interest was related to the flow of current investment, and not (as Knight had emphasized) the existing stock of capital. Nor could Knight entertain the notion of a long-run stagnating economy in which the rate of interest was driven down to zero. Finally, Keynes' presentation of the rate of interest as a monetary, and not a real, phenomenon was anathema to Knight (1937, pp. 112–13; 1941, p. 221–23; see also 1960, pp. 81, 92).

In any event, Knight's continued emphasis on the dynamic and progressive aspects of the real world—and hence the inappropriateness of analyzing it in terms of a static model—was one of the most important messages that he conveyed to his students. As already noted, he conveyed this message not only with respect to the conditions of production, but also with respect to those of demand. Thus Knight never tired of emphasizing that wants did not remain constant, but constantly expanded over time; that the concept of "minimum" or "subsistence needs" was not a physiological one, but the value judgment of a society at a given point of time as to what the minimum standard of living of its members should be; and that, accordingly, this minimum increased over time with the society's general standard of living. Correspondingly, emphasized Knight, the theory that wages were exogenously determined by the subsistence needs of workers was nonsense.

In this context Knight also contrasted the view on the adjustment of wants to available resources in Western culture, as contrasted with ascetic cultures, such as the Buddhist one: the former attempts to make the adjustment by increasing resources; the latter, by denying wants. And I seem to recall Knight's commenting that from the long-run viewpoint, this denial of wants was the only way that a definitive adjustment of wants to resources could be achieved: for history had shown that

Western society created new wants just as fast as (if not faster than!) it expanded the means of satisfying them.

The social determination of wants was a theme that Knight also emphasized in his joint (with Charner M. Perry of the philosophy department) seminar on "Economics and Social Institutions" (Econ. 305). In this sense, then, Knight was an institutionalist. On the other hand, he was not an institutionalist in the sense of advocating the historical or statistical approaches to economics. On the contrary, as I indicated above, Knight's approach to economics was definitely non- (if not anti-) empirical. Indeed, I have a vague recollection of Knight (though it might have been Viner) referring to the excellent fits that have been achieved with the Cobb-Douglas function—and wryly adding that nobody really understood why such consistently good findings emerged from such variegated data! [12] In a broader sense of the term, however, Knight was much concerned with empirical facts: and I am referring once again to Knight's insistence on basing his analysis of investment and of the wants that lie behind demand on what he discerned as the salient dynamic features of the real world.

These were some of the distinctive features of Knight's teaching of economic theory. Actually, however, he also conveyed these messages in his teaching of the "History of Economic Thought" (Econ. 302), where his detailed critique of the Ricardian system (1935a) was the vehicle by which Knight made clear the main features of his own analytical framework. For this reason this history was live and current for us as students. Here too, however, I must admit that part of this liveliness stemmed from our realizing that the evaluation of Ricardo was also the subject of a running debate between Knight and Viner, where in contrast with the analytical genius whom Viner depicted, Knight depicted a Ricardo who represented a retrogression from the achievements of Smith: primarily I think, because of what Knight regarded as Ricardo's greater emphasis on—and formalization of—the labor theory of value. Indeed, Smith—according to Knight—did *not* believe in the labor theory of value (Classnotes, Econ. 302, 1945).

Knight devoted most of his "History of Thought" course to the classical school, and in this connection had us read the relevant texts from Smith, Ricardo, Senior, and Mill. He then set us the task of presenting what we had learned about this school in a term paper (which had become a standard feature of the course) on "The Classical Cost-of-Production Theory of Price." The remainder of the course was devoted to the Austrian "subjective-value revolution," with a few passing remarks added with reference to the institutionalists. As already indicated, there was much overlapping between this course and Knight's theory course proper—though the emphasis of the latter was on the Marshallian synthesis of the classical and Austrian approaches.

There is one aspect of Knight's treatment of the history of economic thought that continues to puzzle me: despite Knight's broad historical interests—and his 1926 translation of Max Weber's *General Economic History*—Knight made practically no

---

12. Still, one of the few instances in his writings in which Knight cited a statistical estimate of an economic magnitude was his citation of the Cobb-Douglas estimate of the elasticity of demand for capital! (1936, p. 623).

attempt to relate the development of economic thought to the contemporaneous historical developments. At one point in his "History of Economic Thought" course—after distinguishing several "epochs of economic thought" [13]—he went on to say that we "have to examine the historical contexts of the economic writings of these periods" (Classnotes, Econ. 302, 1945). But Knight himself did little further along these lines—except for some passing remarks in his discussion of Ricardo's work.[14] Instead, Knight's approach to the history of thought was that of providing a purely logical criticism of the nature of the assumptions made by the various schools of thought, and the validity of the conclusions that they drew from them; he was concerned almost solely with the logical consistency of the theories he was examining.

At the beginning of this memoir I referred to Knight's humility—and he was indeed humble with respect to the limits of knowledge in general, and of economics in particular. ("I once asked a historian of medicine when he thought doctors began curing more people than they killed. 'Well' he answered, 'I think that that will be in another generation or so.' ") But when it came to things that it was given to mortals to understand, Knight (as implied by my description here of his many disagreements with other economists) was a vigorous critic and polemicist—though more so in print and in formal lectures than in his classroom discussions. And even in those cases where it was Frank Knight against the field, we students were left in no doubt as to where the truth lay: "You can be with the majority—or you can be in the right."

II. Knight the Radical Economist—and the Conservative

The general image of Frank Knight in the profession is of a conservative economist whose outstanding students over the years (for example, Henry Simons in the 1920's, Milton Friedman and George Stigler in the 1930's, and James Buchanan in the 1940's) were and are among the leading representatives of this position. So it seems odd at first to think of Frank Knight as a radical economist—but that is one of the sharpest impressions that I have of him.

Knight was not, of course, a radical in the sense of being an advocate of Marxian economics: he had little patience with—and, indeed, had intellectual contempt for—the labor theory of value. His criticism of this theory was expressed in a general way in the course of his analysis of Ricardian economics, mentioned in the preceding section. But he also dealt in a direct—and pithy—manner with some of the basic

13. Namely: "I. Tribal Society and Ancient Empires—in which we do not know how much economic thought went on; II. Greece and Rome; III. Middle Ages; IV. Economic nationalism: Mercantilism (16th–18th centuries); and V. Individualism-liberalism" (Classnotes, Econ. 302, 1945).

14. "Ricardo in the main was not interested in equilibrium theory, but in the reasons for historical changes: especially in the pressure of increasing population on increasing wealth and constant natural resources. Ricardo was interested in what happens to wages. . . . If you project yourself to England of 1815 you can justify this somewhat in terms of what happened during Ricardo's life. About 1770 England began to export manufactured goods and import raw produce—whereas the converse was true before. There were great technological advances [in England]. Then the war cut off importation into England, and so had great increase in agricultural pressure on land. Ricardo was really thinking of revolutionary changes in relative value of agricultural and industrial products" (Classnotes, Econ. 302, 1945).

Marxist tenets. And here Knight revealed one of his major strengths: his ability to make telling points by resorting to obvious facts—whose implications, however, were not at all obvious until he drew them out.

Thus, said Knight, it was "nonsense" to say that labor created capital: "Capital was produced by *capital and* labor working together. Capital is as old as labor" (Classnotes, Econ. 302, 1945, emphasis in original).

Similarly fallacious was the subsistence theory of wages. First of all (as noted above) "subsistence" was itself a changing social concept affected by economic circumstances, and not a fixed physiological concept that could exogenously determine the level of wages. Second, if an employer were indeed free to determine wages at any level he chose, then ". . . an employer will not pay a free laborer a wage high enough to enable him to raise children, since there is no guarantee for the employer to gain by it" (Classnotes, Econ. 302, 1945).

But for the modern economist Knight was—or, more accurately, could have been—a far more effective radical than Marx: for in contrast to Marx, Knight understood the workings of the market system, but he went on by a deeper analysis of these workings to deny the ethical foundations of this system. Indeed, there is little in the writings of the modern day "radical economists" as described, for example, by Lindbeck, that was not more trenchantly said by Knight in his famous essay—published exactly fifty years ago—on "The Ethics of Competition" (1923, especially pp. 45–58). To my mind, these thirteen pages are among the most radical ever written in economics, and even now they remain sharply imprinted in my memory as among the most exciting things that I read during my student days.

Knight's major point in these pages was that ". . . in the conditions of real life no possible social order based upon a *laissez-faire* policy can justify the familiar ethical conclusions of apologetic economics" (1923, p. 49).

The reasons for this were, first of all, that

> . . . the freest individual, the unencumbered male in the prime of life, is in no real sense an ultimate unit or social datum. He is in large measure a product of the economic system, which is a fundamental part of the cultural environment that has formed his desires and needs, given him whatever marketable productive capacities he has, and which largely controls his opportunities. . . . It is plainly contrary to fact to treat the individual as a datum, and it must be conceded that the lines along which a competitive economic order tends to form character are often far from being ethically ideal. [1923, pp. 49–50]

Hence (said Knight) it cannot serve as a justification of the market system simply to say that it produces goods that satisfy the wants of individuals in the economy; for a far more fundamental test of any system is the nature of the wants themselves that it produces. " 'Giving the public what it wants' usually means corrupting popular taste" (1923, p. 57).

Or, again, the statement that the market system "works efficiently" is a normative statement, and not a descriptive one: for, said Knight (making use, as he was wont to do, of homely analogies from the world of physics) by the law of conservation of energy, total output is always exactly equal to total input; hence "efficiency" has meaning only as a measure of *useful* output to input, which means that a value judgment must be made as to the "usefulness" of the output to society. The market system "gets things done"; yes, said Knight, but what things?

So it should not surprise us that long before the recently renewed emphasis on the limitations of "consumer sovereignty" (see, for example, John Kenneth Galbraith, pp. 202–28), Knight was emphasizing that wants are not only the product of the system in general, but can also be specifically influenced by advertising:

> . . . skill in verbal utterance, or capacity in any form to "influence" other persons, is a form of economic power. Men have lived by their wits from time immemorial; it was no doubt one of the earliest uses of language. Persuasive power is, in the first place, a form of "productive capacity" in that skilful "puffing" makes a product more desirable to a purchaser and consumer, who in an individualistic system is the final judge of the merits of products. . . . Adam Smith and the classical economists, in advocating freedom of access to the market, do not seem to have thought about the possibilities of personal influence as a serious factor in economic relations; advertising and selling technique assumed importance after Smith's day [1935b, p. 292; see also 1923, p. 51, note]

Another deficiency of the market system is that it tends naturally towards monopoly:

> No error is more egregious than that of confounding freedom with free competition, as is not infrequently done. As elementary theory itself shows, the members of any economic group can always make more by combining than they can by competing. The workings of competition educate men progressively for monopoly, which is being achieved not merely by the "capitalist" producers of more and more commodities, but by labour in many fields, and in many branches of agriculture, while the producers of even the fundamental crops are already aspiring to the goal. [1923, p. 52]

I should note that in later years Knight came to consider labor unions—with their growing power—as the most harmful form of monopoly in the economy (see for example, 1960, pp. 168–70).

Knight's sharpest shafts were reserved for his critique of "productivity ethics"—the view (that Knight usually associated with the name of J. B. Clark) that one could attribute an ethical value to the income distribution generated by paying factors of production in accordance with their respective marginal products.

First of all, said Knight, because of market imperfections in the real world, "there is only a 'general tendency' to impute to each productive agent its true product" (1923, p. 55).

Second, the value of the marginal product depends on its price; and the

> money value of a product is a matter of the "demand," which in turn reflects the tastes and purchasing power of the buying public and the availability of substi-

tute commodities. All these factors are largely created and controlled by the workings of the economic system itself, as already pointed out. Hence their results can have in themselves no ethical significance as standards for judging the system. [1923, p. 55]

And to these two points, Knight added his most trenchant criticism of all:

The income does not go to "factors," but to their owners, and can in no case have more ethical justification than has the fact of ownership. The ownership of personal or material productive capacity is based upon a complex mixture of inheritance, luck, and effort, probably in that order of relative importance. What is the ideal distribution from the standpoint of absolute ethics may be disputed, but of the three considerations named certainly none but the effort can have ethical validity. [1923, p. 56]

Not only is there no ethical justification for the existing distribution of income (and, as can be seen from the preceding citation, Knight did not distinguish in this context between income from labor and income from property), but as a result of the cumulative processes at work in the market system, the distribution becomes increasingly worse:

. . . where the family is the social unit, the inheritance of wealth, culture, educational advantages, and economic opportunities tend toward the progressive increase of inequality, with bad results for personality at both ends of the scale. [1923, p. 50]

These words were written in one of Knight's first articles, when he was a relatively young man (around 35). And I am sure that there will be those who will say that they represent the "radicalism of youth" which Knight later "outgrew."

To this I can only say (on the basis of my own classroom experiences) that even twenty years later Knight continued to consider these criticisms sufficiently important to convey in his lectures to his students.[15] Furthermore, he had earlier repeated many of them in his major essay on "The Ethics of Liberalism" (1939a, pp. 45–74). I also find it significant that—at the age of 65—he returned to these points in what was essentially a statement of his credo in his presidential address to the American Economic Association (1951). Similarly, in one of the last articles he wrote (1966),[16] Knight made use of the foregoing points (and others) to present a sharp criticism of a would-be justification for the capitalist system by Henry Hazlitt.[17,18] Thus the

15. These discussions recurred in all of Knight's courses. They were, however, particularly emphasized in a joint seminar (again, with Charner M. Perry) on "Economic Theory and Social Policy" (Econ. 304).

16. I am indebted to Paul Samuelson for bringing this article to my attention.

17. Several readers of the first draft of this memoir have called my attention to a lecture before a student group which Knight gave during the presidential elections of 1932 and which was entitled "The Case for Communism from the Standpoint of an Ex-Liberal," a lecture of whose existence I was not hitherto aware. The main burden of this lecture, however, was not Knight's ethical critique of the economic functioning of the capitalist system that has just been described, but a scathing criticism of the inability of a democracy to govern itself rationally and efficiently by means of discussion—from which Knight concluded that government by a communist dictatorship might be preferable. This emphasis is also clear from the general title under which this lecture—as well as two others that Knight gave before student groups at roughly the

same time—were subsequently multilithed for private circulation: namely, *The Dilemma of Liberalism* (1933b). I might also note that Knight included the main substantive points of this criticism of the democratic process in his essay a few years later on "Economic Theory and Nationalism" (1935b), discussed below.

There is no copy of the *Dilemma of Liberalism* in The University of Chicago library, though there is a copy (to which I was directed by Maynard Kreuger) in the library of the London School of Economics. A copy (though without the title page) is also to be found among the papers that Knight left after him.

I might also note that the sections of the lecture on "The Case for Communism from the Standpoint of an Ex-Liberal" dealing with the genesis, character, and failures of the liberal regime (1933b, pp. 21–45) were reprinted in the eighth (1939) edition of the *Selected Readings* for the Social Science II survey course (Knight, 1939b). However, the title of the lecture from which these sections were taken (namely, "The Case for Communism . . .") is blackened out both in the Table of Contents of the *Selected Readings* and at the head of the reprinted sections, though it remains partly legible. A footnote attached to the blackened-out title indicates that the selection reprinted is an "excerpt from a privately printed pamphlet."

{After the publication of this memoir Mrs. Frank Knight gave me the following statement which she found among Knight's papers, and which is reproduced here with her permission:

STATEMENT

Frank H. Knight
  in account with   DILEMMA OF LIBERALISM
                           - - - - - - - - - - - - - - - - -

Outlay	Typing of MS, paid in cash		12.00
	(Besides work by Assistant paid by University of Chicago)		
	Manifolding 200 copies		91.45
		103.45	
	Own labor		000.00
			103.45

Return (To Apr. 7, 1933)

	56 copies at 50 cents		28.00
	1 copy at 52 cents (W. P. Brownlow)		.52
	1 copy at 51 cents (D. M. Slesinger)		.51
		29.03	
	1 dozen (more or less) polite (more or less) acknowledgements		???.??
	1 dozen (more or less) cynical pleasantries or pleasant (more or less) cynicisms, according to taste		???.??
	1 good letter (from a book peddler) really arguing the issues intelligently		???.???
	1 frank statement (from T. V. Smith) saying that it is the worst piece of writing he ever read, that he would be shot before he would put such stuff on paper		priceless

I understand from George Stigler and Warner Wick (Department of Philosophy, University of Chicago) that T. V. Smith was a popular philosopher who at the time was a colleague of Knight's at Chicago.}

18. I should, however, note the milder tone of some of these criticisms in Knight's 1960 book on *Intelligence and Democratic Action*, written as he approached the age of 75. Here Knight also wrote:

I may say that in the three decades or so since I laboriously worked up a lecture on "The Ethics of Competition" (given at Harvard University and later published as an article in the *Quarterly Journal of Economics*—and still later reprinted in a book) I have done quite a lot of thinking about ethics and economics, and have perpetrated some wordage in print as well as in several university classrooms. As a result, I have become even more hesitant about speaking very definitely and positively. [1960, p. 122]

evidence indicates that Knight's fundamental ethical critique of the actual operation of the market economy was an essential part of his thinking throughout his life.

And so at the Chicago of my student days it was, ironically enough, the socialist Oskar Lange who extolled the beauties of the Paretian optimum achieved by a perfectly competitive market—and Frank Knight who in effect taught us that the deeper welfare implications of this optimum were indeed quite limited.

All of which raises the question as to the sharp contrast between Knight's incisive criticism of the existing system, and his basically conservative opposition to various proposals made to reform it, and all the more so to change it radically. For this conservatism, too, was a fundamental element of Knight's teachings. Thus after summarizing his ethical critique of the market system in his 1939 "Ethics of Liberalism," Knight went on to conclude that

> . . . society has strong reasons for maintaining powerful brakes on departures from the "beaten path." Primitive society was wise in its conservatism, for it knew at least that the group had previously lived somehow, both as individuals and as a group. And liberal society, it now seems, has acted frivolously in switching over quite suddenly to an extreme opposite set of assumptions, that the new is better than the old, that the good consists in change, or at least in freedom of the individual to make changes, rather than in stability. This emphasis on the necessity of an *onus probandi* in favour of conservatism and against change, must stand as our last word at this point. [1939a, p. 74; see also 1935b, p. 286]

Similarly, in his 1950 presidential address he emphasized that ". . . the possible amount and speed of free and intelligent social change will always be quite narrowly limited" (1951, p. 276).

In some cases Knight's opposition to reform proposals stemmed from his belief that the proposals in question failed to reveal a proper understanding of market forces. Thus he opposed price and rent controls because he felt that these reflected a failure to understand the functioning of the price system in allocating scarce resources. He was particularly critical of reform proposals that in his eyes committed the original sin of offering "something for nothing," [19] and he continuously decried the age-old human failings that led to the belief in such a possibility. "A refrigerator generates cold," he would say in another one of his parables from physics, "only by conveying heat from the inside to some point on the outside. And people just never seem to be able to understand that simple fact."

But a far more basic source of Knight's conservatism was his view that as bad as the existing market system was, the alternatives were even worse! Indeed, this is the view to which he adverts in the concluding paragraph of his discussion in the aforementioned "thirteen pages" of his "Ethics of Competition":

> It is expressly excluded from the field of the present paper to pass any practical judgment upon the competitive system in comparison with any possible alterna-

---

19. From which view on life may have stemmed the more recent "Chicago tradition" that "there is no such thing as a free lunch."

tive. But in view of the negative tone of the discussion, it seems fair to remark that many of the evils and causes of trouble are inherent in all large-scale organization as such, irrespective of its form. It must be said also that radical critics of competition as a general basis of the economic order generally underestimate egregiously the danger of doing vastly worse. Finally, let us repeat that practically there is no question of the exclusive use or entire abolition of any of the fundamental methods of social organization, individualistic or socialistic. Economic and other activities will always be organized in all possible ways, and the problem is to find the right proportions between individualism and socialism and the various varieties of each, and to use each in its proper place. [1923, p. 58]

To the best of my knowledge, Knight never specified the criteria by which these "right proportions" were to be chosen—and I shall return to this point below. What I want now to explain is that the way in which Knight feared that the alternatives could ethically do "vastly worse" than the existing market system was primarily in their impact on individual freedom. For Knight, such freedom was an absolute value: even if people do not want freedom, they ought to want it. Furthermore (and here Knight's historical perspective reinforced his conservatism) liberalism and individual freedom were recent historical developments.[20] Indeed, they might even be said to have been the chance product of "a remarkable and temporary concourse of circumstances" that prevailed during the eighteenth and nineteenth centuries. Thus individual freedom was a fragile development—in constant danger of being destroyed (1935b, pp. 287–89, p. 305, note; see also 1960, pp. 38–39, 108).

"There has been, and must be, a question," said Knight in his critical review of Sumner Slichter's book in favor of economic planning,[21]

. . . how far it is *comparatively* better social policy (I am aware of the redundancy but wish to be clear) to have individuals make their own choices in economic life and how far better to have them dictated—by anybody else who can be thought of in the position of dictating them. . . . What I want from the preachers of control, and do not get in [Slichter's] *Modern Economic Society . . .* or anywhere else, is something I can understand on the subject of *who* is to make the economic choices for the individual who admittedly makes them quite "imperfectly," or *how* this choosing functionary is to be selected, and *how* the individual affected is to be brought to accept them; and, in general, what kind of (a) individuals and (b) social order the preachers are either assuming or working toward. [1932b, pp. 823–24, italics in original]

Looking back on all this now, I would conjecture that an important additional element of Knight's fundamental conservatism—and general opposition to "planning" or other government action whose declared aim was the improvement of the

20. The Greek city-states with their slaves were, in Knight's eyes, hardly in this tradition.
21. I am indebted to George Stigler for bringing this review article to my attention.

actual workings of the market economy—was his view of the "system of individual freedom" as representing a stage of unstable equilibrium in the course of human history. (I think it is significant that the instability of various aspects of the macro-world is a recurrent element of Knight's thought: it is reflected, as we have seen, in his discussion of the cumulative tendencies toward inequality and monopoly in a market economy; it is also reflected in his discussion (to which I shall now turn) of the cumulative tendency toward the concentration of power; finally, in a different context to be discussed below, it is reflected in his view of the business cycle—and particularly of the cumulative movement in it of the absolute price level.) In view of the existence of this knife-edge equilibrium, Knight feared that any encroachment by the state upon individual freedom in the attempt to "improve" the economy would generate cumulative departures from this freedom.

Be that as it may, the specific ways in which he feared that one of the possible alternatives to the market system—"democratic socialism" [22]—could "do worse" were spelled out by Knight in his lengthy 1935 essay on "Economic Theory and Nationalism." Knight's point of departure was that socialism was the extension of the political process to the business world. But if this extension were carried out within a democratic framework (as its advocates claimed to be interested in doing) then

> . . . the essential point is that, as it has worked out in practice in the modern world, *democracy is competitive politics,* somewhat as free enterprise is competitive economics (though inherently a competition for a monopolistic position), and shows the same weaknesses as the latter. [1935b, p. 295, italics in original]

In particular, competitive politics cannot be described as a system devoted to satisfying the given wants of the public; for this system—even more than competitive economics—tries by "advertising" (i.e., campaigning and political propaganda in general), to influence and form these wants themselves. Or, as Knight had succinctly expressed himself a few years earlier in sharp criticism of Sumner Slichter's defence of planning, ". . . between business and politics, it is as easy and as reasonable to assert that corruption goes one way as the other. . . . Both finally 'give the people what they want,' after doing their utmost to make them want what they want to give" (1932, p. 476). And, once again, the nature of the wants so generated by competitive politics are of questionable ethical value: ". . . in politics the appeal is almost exclusively to the crowd" (1935b, p. 299). Similarly questionable are the human qualities promoted by competitive politics as a means of succeeding in them.

---

22. By which Knight meant a representative democracy that continued to make use of the market, but in which

> . . . entrepreneurs and property owners . . . would be replaced by administrative officials, who, like their prototypes, would theoretically have no discretionary power over production, the details of organization being determined, just as under the theory of enterprise, by consumers' choices. [1935b, p. 307]

Presumably, Knight had in mind the kind of socialist system that Fred Taylor had described in his 1928 AEA presidential address, and which Lange (1936, 1937) and Lerner (1937) were later to explicate in greater detail.

Finally, the system of competitive politics that characterizes democracy and "democratic socialism" in particular will tend to generate more inequality in the real sense of the term than does the system of competitive economics. For ". . . the significance of consumption itself is largely symbolic; the inequality which really hurts is the unequal distribution of dignity, prestige, and power" (1935b, pp. 308–09; see also p. 298, note). And to this must be added the fact that the abilities which make for success in competitive politics ". . . are more unequally distributed among men by nature than is economic ability or power of any other kind, and also tend more strongly to cumulative increase through their own exercise" (1935b, pp. 296–97).

Thus not only does power corrupt, but it corrupts cumulatively. Nor can free elections be considered as a safeguard against this cumulative concentration of power in the hands of political leaders:

> In view of the way in which psychological principles work in politics, equal suffrage (even if it is respected in practice) provides little or no guarantee of equality in that field. The overwhelming majorities rolled up in plebiscites (more or less fairly conducted) on the question of dictatorship show where the realities lie. [1935b, p. 297; see also pp. 308–09]

(It should be recalled that Knight was writing these words a few years after Hitler had democratically reached power in Germany—as had Mussolini before him in Italy.)

The depth and intensity of Knight's feelings on the issues discussed in the preceding pages are well represented in the following paragraph from Knight's presidential address—or his "sermon," as he denoted it:

> The plea of communism, like that of Christianity, is justice, under absolute authority, ignoring freedom. (The former does extol progress, and progress through science, both of which Christianity despised; by the same argument, communism is overtly less devoted to law and tradition, more openly claims the right to ignore or break the law.) For liberalism, the primary value is freedom, self-limited by laws made by the community, ideally by general assent, in practice by representatives elected by a voting majority—one of its dangers. The laws of a liberal state will also be general, non-specific, but in a sense quite different from the Golden Rule or Law of Universal Love. The familiar figure is "rules of the road," in contrast with instructions where and when and how to travel, whether arbitrary or conformable to a traditional practice. But such freedom must be sweepingly limited by measures, not only of a "police" character in a broad sense, but also designed to equip the individual and family for social life by implanting wants and tastes in general conformity with the culture and endowing each with a minimum of productive capacity (or ultimately with final goods) without which freedom is a form empty of content. To take these units as "given" is flagrantly contrary to essential facts of life and means ignoring the major social problem. It is along this line that eighteenth- and nineteenth-century liberalism went to an extreme that has provoked a reaction which threatens to engulf all freedom, and justice too, in the modern conception

of it, if not to destroy civilization. Liberal states have been engaged, however, through their short life, in correcting this imbalance between freedom and justice; more intelligence and better judgment is our need, rather than any radical departure in method. [1951, pp. 277–78]

In concluding this discussion of Knight's political views, I would like to turn to a question that arises most naturally from it: what was the relationship between Knight and the "Chicago School"? From one viewpoint this is a rhetorical question: for in his emphasis on individual freedom as a basic value, Knight (together with Viner) can only be considered to be one of the "founding fathers" of this School. At the same time I think that Knight (as well as Viner) was less doctrinaire in his views than some of his younger colleagues and followers. And clearly Knight (and here he differed from Viner) did not have the policy-orientation that is one of the hallmarks of the Chicago School.[23]

Thus, as we have seen, Knight was sharply critical of the ethical deficiencies of the actual workings of the market system—and was particularly scornful of the "productivity ethics" by which this system was sometimes justified. Nor did he make an absolute distinction between "government by law" and "government by men"—for laws too are made by men. In particular, Knight emphasized that

. . . the primary difficulty with the notion of law as an ethical principle or norm is that the content of the law itself can never be taken as simply "given," or beyond dispute, even at a given moment . . . there was always and inevitably occasion for "interpreting" the law, in enforcing it, and also for making law outright, i.e., changing it, in consequence of changing conditions and standards. [1939a, pp. 62–63]

A similar picture holds with respect to the specific monetary policy with which the Chicago School of the 1930's and early 1940's is so strongly identified: namely, the contracyclical policy of adjusting the quantity of money so as to stabilize the price level. The rationale for this "monetary rule" had been developed most systematically during the 1930's by Henry Simons,[24] who continued to expound it in his courses and seminars with us on fiscal policy. And Lloyd Mints did the same thing in his courses on monetary theory and policy.

In contrast, as I have already shown in a paper on the monetary policy of the Chicago school,[25] though Knight recognized the importance of monetary disturbances in generating cycles of booms and depressions, he was skeptical about the

---

23. This should not be considered to be simply a reflection of the absence of an empirical orientation on the part of Knight. For Henry Simons and Lloyd Mints were not empirically oriented either.

24. Simons had been a student of Knight's at the University of Iowa, and had followed him to Chicago in 1927 as a lecturer.

25. See chap. 10 below, p. 245, fn. 8; pp. 258–59 and 264. In 1969, I sent a copy of this paper to Knight and asked him for his comments. But Knight replied that "to be quite frank, I'm very definitely 'retired' from economics"—and went on to write briefly about other matters, including his concern about the tensions in the Middle East. (Personal letter to author, dated March 19, 1969.)

extent to which these cycles could be controlled. As he expressed himself in one of his lectures:

In medieval times men didn't look for remedies since they thought everything was from God who was good—so everything was good. Now science is the God—and we think that there must be a remedy for every disease. Maybe there is no answer to the business cycle: maybe we have to let it take its course. [Classnotes, Econ. 301, 1945]

Correspondingly, I think it fair to say that Knight was less convinced than his younger colleagues, Simons and Mints, about the efficacy of the monetary rule of stabilizing the price level as a means of combatting the cycle. Indeed, in one of his lectures Knight said that he did "not know how to stabilize the price level—and at what height to stabilize it" (Classnotes, Econ. 301, 1945). I might also note that on at least one occasion in later years Knight expressed his preference for "administrative discretion" rather than "rules" in the carrying out of monetary policy (1960, pp. 105–6).[26]

But in all this—as well as in his failure noted above to specify the criteria by which to decide upon "the right proportions between individualism and socialism"—I think that we must see the manifestation of yet another basic element of Knight's character: that in what he regarded as the inherent contradiction between thought and action, Knight remained forever the man of thought: always critical, always probing, always asking questions—and always deeply aware of the complexities and inertias of the real world, and hence skeptical about the extent to which man could by deliberate policy-actions improve it.[27]

III. Knight the Social Philosopher and the Man

In my introductory reminiscences, I mentioned that I had heard Knight's "Price and Distribution Theory" course twice—and there is a distinct difference between my classnotes from these two exposures: for whereas the first is filled primarily with economic matters proper, the second contains less of these, and more of long digressions on the nature of man and society—and God.

But I do not think that this difference between the classnotes necessarily reflects a difference in the actual emphasis of these two courses. Instead, I suspect that it reflects the difference that had taken place in me, the listener. For by the second time I

26. It might be noted that Viner (1962), too, expressed his preference for discretionary action on the part of the monetary authorities. On the general relation of Viner to the Chicago school, see again below, p. 242, fn. 5; p. 245, fn. 8; p. 260 and pp. 265–71.

27. The following words from Knight's last book, written as he approached the age of 75, are revealing:

It has been said that fools ask questions and wise men answer them. . . . To that indictment I must plead guilty, and also that of being better at criticizing other people's asking and answering than at doing either myself, and more addicted to the former role. But I have a defense. . . . I think the role fits in with the concept of democracy, that the function of the intellectual leader, in the difficult field of social philosophy and policy, is to clarify issues, or at most suggest possible solutions and perhaps arguments, pro and con. Answering is rather the task of Adam Smith's insidious and wily animal, the statesman or politician, which in a democracy means the ordinary citizen. [1960, p. 121]

took the course I had already had several courses in economic theory proper, and I had also come to understand that the unique contribution that Knight as a teacher had to make to students—and not only to students!—was precisely in his rambling "digressions" on the nature of the world.

One of his major concerns in these digressions was religion—a concern that undoubtedly stemmed from Knight's growing up in the deeply religious atmosphere of rural Illinois at the turn of the century. After his youth, Knight was fighting religion all his life, and his strongest and most violent language were reserved for expressing his anticlerical views.

There were several dimensions to these views. First, the irrationality of religion—and even more specifically, its ban on intellectual curiosity and the asking of questions, its insistence on accepting its tenets without further thought. All this was anathema to Frank Knight—the eternal asker of questions ("Do parents in primitive societies correct their children's grammar?").

But I think that an even more important cause of Knight's anticlericalism was the discrepancy between the declarations of organized religions and their behavior. Again in the words of his presidential address:

> In Christianity, surely, we find the supreme "irony of history": that an original teaching centered ethically in humility, meekness, self-denial, and self-sacrifice became organized into corporations whose dignitaries have hardly been matched for arrogant grasping, using, and flaunting of power and wealth and for insistence on prerogative to the borderline of worship. One turns to Dostoevski's famous speech of the Grand Inquisitor for any adequate portrayal of this situation and its sinister indications of the nature of human nature. [1951, p. 277]

I believe that it was because of his confrontation with this discrepancy in his own cultural heritage that Knight's anticlericalism expressed itself in anti-Christianity, and anti-Catholicism in particular. I feel (though I may be prejudiced) that he expressed less opposition to Judaism: not because he thought any better of Judaism as a religion, but because the historical development of Judaism had been such as to leave it (in Knight's life experience) without the institutional framework and consequent power that so aroused his wrath in the case of Christianity.

In this context it is also significant that (to the best of my knowledge) Knight did not criticize Buddhism or Islam or any other of the great world religions in the same way that he did Christianity: and, I suspect, for the same reason just indicated—namely, that he had not directly experienced and been irritated by the workings of their institutional frameworks.

Here too we find the kind of contradiction in Knight's views that I noted above with respect to the question of social reform. He was highly critical of religion—and yet he recognized the vital function that it performed in maintaining the stability of any society: because the possibilities of social reform were limited—and could take place only slowly without endangering the existence of society—"men will always require, as a condition for maintaining any high civilization at all, some 'opiate' or some effective agent to prevent their demanding their rights" (1951, p. 276).

But if Knight was not a religious person in those things that concern man and God, in the things that concern man and man he exemplified the ethical qualities of moral rectitude and personal integrity that all religions teach us to aspire to. And he was an incessant and unswerving Seeker after the Truth.

I have mentioned Knight's opposition to the irrationality of religion. At the same time, however, he was the very opposite of those who turned rationality itself into a religion. Indeed, for Knight the very desire for rationality was one of the expressions of man's romantic nature. Knight never tired of quoting the saying—that he attributed to J. M. Clark (1918, p. 24)—about the "irrational passion for dispassionate rationality." And he always reminded us that it was not the people of low intelligence who spent their lives squaring the circle and inventing perpetual-motion machines.

Similarly, as already noted, he was deeply skeptical of the extent to which rational discussion could solve social problems: in part, because of the intrinsic difficulty of these problems themselves; but even more so because of the difficulty of reaching a consensus; and the more intelligent people were, the finer the distinctions they would insist on making, and hence the less likely they were to achieve such a consensus. And perhaps most important of all: free discussion in a democracy would not remain rational, but would degenerate into demagoguery: "Cheaper talk drives out of circulation that which is less cheap"—so "Frank Knight's First Law of Talk" (1933b, p. 8).

Indeed, here we find the deepest contradiction in Knight's view of human society: on the one hand, he regarded individual freedom as a basic value, and recognized that representative democracy was the only way in which a large society of free individuals could govern itself; on the other, he had basic misgivings about the actual workings of the democratic process—and was accordingly deeply pessimistic about its future. So much so that on some occasions he predicted the "natural" disintegration of democracy and its replacement by dictatorship.

Another of Knight's major themes (and an important component of his anti-religious position) was that it was not enough to want to do good: one had to have an understanding of the workings of social forces in order to be able actually to do good. The church might outlaw usury as unjust: but because of the workings of market forces all that this prohibition did was to change the form in which income from property was received—from the form of interest to that of rents or profits. The government might—in the face of "shortages" of critical goods—impose price controls: but this would not increase the quantities of these goods, and would indeed create artificial scarcities.

And "love thy neighbor as thyself" was not a prescription for social action. How do you know that your neighbor has the same tastes as you do? More important—to love everybody is to love nobody: for love by its very nature is a differential relationship.[28]

Knight was deeply concerned with the personal element of morality and the ethical problems created by an impersonal society. No one (Knight once said) would reinsert

---

28. See Knight (1935b, p. 312; 1939a, pp. 102–28; and 1945).

his coin into a public phone if it were accidentally returned to him after the completion of his call; indeed, if he were to do so, he would be considered a fool—not a saint. But was this not stealing?

Cynical? Perhaps. Though not the cynicism of an embittered man, but the cynicism of one who looked with understanding—and, though he would probably have denied it, even compassion—on the limitations of man and society. The cynicism of one who had resigned himself to the limitations of *la condition humaine*.

He was—as has been said of Ecclesiastes—a gentle cynic.

Bibliography

Anonymous. "In Memorium: Frank H. Knight." *American Economic Review*, Dec. 1973, *63*, 1047–48.

G. C. Archibald. "Chamberlin Versus Chicago." *Review of Economic Studies*, Oct. 1961, *29*, 1–28.

———. "Reply to Chicago." *Review of Economic Studies*, Feb. 1963, *30*, 68–71.

J. M. Buchanan. "Frank H. Knight." In *International Encyclopedia of the Social Sciences*. New York, 1968. Vol. 8, pp. 424–28.

E. H. Chamberlin. *The Theory of Monopolistic Competition*, 4th ed. Cambridge, Mass., 1942.

J. B. Clark. *The Distribution of Wealth*. New York, 1899.

J.M. Clark. "Economics and Modern Psychology." Parts 1, 2. *Journal of Political Economy*, Jan. 1918, *26*, 1–30; Feb. 1918, *26*, 136–66.

H. J. Davenport. *The Economics of Enterprise*. New York, 1913.

J. Dorfman. *The Economic Mind in American Civilization*, vol. 5. New York, 1959.

C. E. Ferguson. *Microeconomic Theory*, rev. ed. Homewood, Ill., 1969.

M. Friedman. "The Marshallian Demand Curve." *Journal of Political Economy*, Dec. 1949, *57*, 463–95. Reprinted in *Essays in Positive Economics*. Chicago, 1953. Pp. 47–99.

———. "More on Archibald Versus Chicago." *Review of Economic Studies*, Feb. 1963, *30*, 65–67.

J. K. Galbraith. *The New Industrial State*. Boston, 1967.

Y. Grunfeld, N. Liviatan, and D. Patinkin. *Lectures on Price Theory: Winter Term 1959/60*. Jerusalem, 1963 (Hebrew, mimeographed).

T. Haavelmo. *A Study in the Theory of Investment*. Chicago, 1960.

R. F. Harrod. "Doctrines of Imperfect Competition." *Quarterly Journal of Economics*, May 1934, *48*, 442–70.

H. Hazlitt. *The Foundations of Morality*. Princeton, N.J., 1964.

J. R. Hicks. *Value and Capital*. Oxford, 1939.

A. Johnson. *Pioneer's Progress*. Omaha, 1960.

J. M. Keynes. *The General Theory of Employment Interest and Money*. New York, 1936.

F. H. Knight (1921a). *Risk, Uncertainty, and Profit*. Boston, 1921. New York, 1957.

———. (1921b). "Cost of Production and Price Over Long and Short Periods." *Journal of Political Economy*, Apr. 1921, *29*, 304–35. Reprinted in *The Ethics of Competition and Other Essays*. New York, 1935. Pp. 186–216.

———. "The Ethics of Competition." *Quarterly Journal of Economics*, Aug. 1923, *37*, 579–624. Reprinted in *The Ethics of Competition and Other Essays*. New York, 1935. Pp. 41–75.

———. "Herbert Joseph Davenport (1861–1931)." In *The Encyclopedia of the Social Sciences*. New York, 1931. Vol. 5, pp. 8–9.

———. (1932a) "Interest." In *The Encyclopedia of the Social Sciences*. New York, 1932. Reprinted in *The Ethics of Competition and Other Essays*. New York, 1935. Pp. 251–76.

———. (1932b) "The Newer Economics and the Control of Economic Activity." Review of S. H. Slichter. *Modern Economic Society. Journal of Political Economy*, Aug. 1932, *40*, 433–76.

———. (1932c) "Modern Economic Society Further Considered." *Journal of Political Economy*, Dec. 1932, *40*, 820–25.

———. (1932d) "Social Economic Organization." "The Price System and the Economic Process." "Demand and Supply and Price." "Distribution: The Pricing of Productive Services Individually." In *Second Year Course in the Social Sciences (Social Sciences II): Syllabus and Selected Readings* (preliminary ed., multilith). Chicago, 1932.

———. (1933a) *The Economic Organization*. Chicago, 1933 (multilith). Reset and reprinted with different pagination, New York, 1951. (Reproduces the material of the preceding entry.)

———. (1933b) "The Case for Communism: From the Standpoint of an Ex-Liberal." In *The Dilemma of Liberalism*. Ann Arbor, Mich., 1933 (multilithed for private circulation).

———. (1935a) "The Ricardian Theory of Production and Distribution." Parts 1, 2. *Canadian Journal of Economics and Political Science*, Feb. 1935, *1*, 3–25; May 1935, *1*, 171–96. Reprinted in *On the History and Method of Economics*. Chicago, 1956. Pp. 37–88.

———. (1935b) "Economic Theory and Nationalism." In *The Ethics of Competition and Other Essays*. New York, 1935. Pp. 277–359.

———. (1935c) *The Ethics of Competition and Other Essays*. New York, 1935.

———. "The Quantity of Capital and the Rate of Interest." Parts 1, 2. *Journal of Political Economy*, Aug. 1936, *44*, 433–63; Oct. 1936, *44*, 612–42.

———. "Unemployment: And Mr. Keynes' Revolution in Economic Theory." *Canadian Journal of Economics and Political Science*, Feb. 1937, *3*, 100–123.

———. (1939a) "The Ethics of Liberalism." In "Ethics and Economic Reform." *Economica*, Feb. 1939, *6*, 1–29. Reprinted in *Freedom and Reform*. New York, 1947, 45–74.

———. (1939b) "The Genesis and Character of the Modern Liberal Regime," and "The Breakdown of the Liberal System: Its Weaknesses—Reasons for Failure." In *Selected Readings for the Second-Year Course in the Study of Contemporary Society (Social Science II)*, 8th ed. Chicago: Sept. 1939 (multilith, reproduces pp. 21–45 of 1933b).

———. "The Business Cycle, Interest, and Money: A Methodological Approach." *Review of Economic Statistics*, May 1941, *23*, 53–67. Reprinted in *On the History and Method of Economics*. Chicago, 1956. Pp. 202–26.

———. (1944a) "Diminishing Returns from Investment." *Journal of Political Economy*, Mar. 1944, *52*, 26–47.

———. (1944b) "Realism and Relevance in the Theory of Demand." *Journal of Political Economy*, Dec. 1944, *52*, 289–318.

———. "Liberalism and Christianity." In *The Economic Order and Religion*. New York, 1945. Pp. 13–126.

———. "Comment on Mr. Bishop's Article" [on the theory of demand]. *Journal of Political Economy*, Apr. 1946, *54*, 170–76.

———. *Freedom and Reform*. New York, 1947.

_____. "The Rôle of Principles in Economics and Politics." *American Economic Review*, Mar. 1951, *41*, 1–29. Reprinted in *On the History and Method of Economics*. Chicago, 1956. Pp. 251–81.

_____. *On the History and Method of Economics*. Chicago, 1956.

_____. *Intelligence and Democratic Action*. Cambridge, Mass., 1960.

_____. "Abstract Economics as Absolute Ethics." *Ethics*, Apr. 1966, *76*, 163–77.

_____ and T. W. Merriam. *The Economic Order and Religion*. New York, 1945.

O. Lange. "On the Economic Theory of Socialism." Parts 1, 2. *Review of Economic Studies*, Oct. 1936, *4*, 53–71; Feb. 1937, *4*, 123–42. Reprinted in O. Lange and F. M. Taylor, *On the Economic Theory of Socialism*. Minneapolis, 1938. Pp. 55–143.

_____. "The Rate of Interest and the Optimum Propensity to Consume." *Economica*, Feb. 1938, *5*, 12–32. Reprinted in *Readings in Business Cycle Theory*, ed. G. Haberler. Philadelphia, 1944. Pp. 169–92.

_____. *Price Flexibility and Employment*. Bloomington, Ind., 1944.

A. P. Lerner. "Statics and Dynamics in Socialist Economics." *Economic Journal*, June 1937, *47*, 253–70.

_____. *The Economics of Control*. New York, 1944.

_____. "On the Marginal Product of Capital and the Marginal Efficiency of Investment." *Journal of Political Economy*, Feb. 1953, *61*, 1–14.

A. Lindbeck. *The Political Economy of the New Left—An Outsider's View*. New York, 1971.

R. G. Lipsey. *An Introduction to Positive Economics*, 2d ed. London, 1966.

A. Marshall. *Principles of Economics*, 8th ed. London, 1920.

H. L. Miller, Jr. "On the 'Chicago School of Economics.' " *Journal of Political Economy*, Feb. 1962, *70*, 64–69.

D. Patinkin. "Demand Curves and Consumer Surplus." In *Measurement in Economics: Studies in Mathematical Economics and Econometrics in Memory of Yehuda Grunfeld*, ed. Carl Christ et al. Stanford, Calif., 1963. Pp. 83–112. [Reproduced as chap. 8 below.]

_____. "The Chicago Tradition, the Quantity Theory and Friedman." *Journal of Money, Credit, and Banking*, Feb. 1969, *1*, 46–70. Reprinted in *Studies in Monetary Economics*. New York, 1972. Pp. 92–117. [Reproduced as chap. 10 below.]

_____. "In Search of the 'Wheel of Wealth': On the Origins of Frank Knight's Circular-Flow Diagram." *American Economic Review*, Dec. 1973, *63*, 1037–46. [Reproduced as chap. 2 below.]

P. A. Samuelson. *Economics: An Introductory Analysis*. New York, 1948, 1951 (2d. ed.), 1958 (4th ed.), 1970 (8th ed.).

_____. (1972a) "Economics in a Golden Age: A Personal Memoir." In *The Twentieth Century Sciences: Studies in the Biography of Ideas*, ed. G. Holton. New York, 1972. Pp. 155–70.

_____. (1972b) "Jacob Viner, 1892–1970." *Journal of Political Economy*, Jan./Feb. 1972, *80*, 5–11.

S. H. Slichter. *Modern Economic Society*. New York, 1931.

H. W. Spiegel. "Herbert J. Davenport." In *International Encyclopedia of the Social Sciences*. New York, 1968. Vol. 4, pp. 16–17.

G. J. Stigler. *The Theory of Price*, rev. ed. New York, 1952.

_____. "Archibald Versus Chicago." *Review of Economic Studies*, Feb. 1963, *30*, 63–64.

F. M. Taylor. "The Guidance of Production in a Socialist State." *American Economic Review*, Mar. 1929, *19*, 1–8. Reprinted in *On the Economic Theory of Socialism*, by O. Lange and F. M. Taylor. Minneapolis, 1938.

J. Viner. "Cost Curves and Supply Curves." *Zeitschrift für Nationalökonomie*, Sept. 1931, *3*, 23–46. Reprinted in *The Long View and the Short*. Glencoe, Ill., 1958. Pp. 50–78.

————. "The Necessary and the Desirable Range of Discretion to be Allowed to a Monetary Authority." In *In Search of a Monetary Constitution*, ed. L. B. Yeager. Cambridge, Mass., 1962. Pp. 244–74.

M. Weber. *General Economic History*, trans. F. H. Knight. New York, 1927. Pp. 244–74.

Unpublished Materials

Frank H. Knight Papers. Joseph Regenstein Library, The University of Chicago.
Author's Lecture Notes of Following Courses:
    Frank H. Knight:
        Economics 301: "Price and Distribution Theory." Autumn 1942, Summer 1945.
        Economics 302: "History of Economic Thought." Winter 1945.
    Frank H. Knight and Charner M. Perry:
        Economics 304: "Economic Theory and Social Policy." Spring 1946.
        Economics 305: "Economics and Social Institutions." Spring 1945.
    Jacob Viner:
        Economics 301: "Price and Distribution Theory." Autumn 1944.

2. In Search of the "Wheel of Wealth": On the Origins of Frank Knight's Circular-Flow Diagram*

One of the memories that every former student of Frank Knight undoubtedly carries with him is that of the circular-flow diagram (reproduced on p. 28 above) which Knight used to illustrate "the exchange of productive power for consumption goods between individuals and business units, mediated by the circulation' of money" (1933, p. 60). To the best of my knowledge, the first appearance of this diagram in Knight's writings was in the mimeographed material that he prepared for teaching purposes at the University of Iowa in the early 1920's.[1] Knight first published the diagram, however, in the four chapters on the economic system that he wrote for the volume of *Readings* prepared for the famous undergraduate Social Science Survey

Reprinted by permission from *American Economic Review*, Dec. 1973, *63*, 1037–46. Appears here with significant revisions and additions.

*Without burdening him with any responsibility for the conclusions of this note, I would like to express my deepest appreciation and indebtedness to my colleague, Ephraim Kleiman, who encouraged me to write it, and who continued to be the source of many valuable suggestions and criticisms throughout its preparation—including the suggestion for its title! I am also indebted to Paul Samuelson for his stimulating comments on an earlier draft of this note; needless to say, he too does not bear responsibility for its conclusions. My thanks, too, to my colleague Nahum Gross who has checked the German references cited in this note.

I would also like to thank my assistants, Akiva Offenbacher and Reuven Nutkis, for their invaluable help with the detailed examination of the literature on which this note is based—a task which they carried out with gratifying care, accuracy, and responsibility. And my sincerest thanks to Vera Jacobs for her efficient and conscientious typing of this note through its various drafts; and to Margaret Eisenstaedt and David Raanan for so expertly preparing the diagrams for press.

Once again, I would like to thank George Stigler for making Knight's unpublished papers available to me, and Glen Gilchrist for providing xeroxes of requested materials from these papers. {Since this article was published, the Knight papers have been placed in the Joseph Regenstein Library of The University of Chicago.} I am also grateful to Stanley Fischer and Friedrich A. Lutz for providing me with xeroxes of material that was unavailable here in Jerusalem. I wish finally to thank the Central Research Fund of the Hebrew University and the Israel Academy of Sciences and Humanities for research grants that made this and other assistance possible.

1. This is the material that Glen Gilchrist has catalogued under the title *"Economics, 1920's"* and filed in Boxes 8–9 of Knight's papers. Gilchrist has informed me that " . . . most of the material in these boxes is undated, but I have found the date 1926 or 'revised 1926' on a couple of these items as well as a phrase indicating it was used as supplementary material for 'Economics IC' " (personal letter dated April 24, 1973). On the other hand, the bibliography of Knight's works which appears at the beginning of *The Ethics of Competition* (1935, p. 15, bottom) adds the following comment to its listing of Knight (1932): "These four items are an abstract of material mimeographed for private circulation at the University of Iowa during the years 1922–25." I presume that this is the mimeographed material in Boxes 8 and 9, and have accordingly dated this material 1922–26.

53

Course at the University of Chicago (Knight 1932). Subsequently, Knight reissued these chapters as a separate booklet entitled *The Economic Organization* (1933), in which form it became a standard feature of his graduate theory course at Chicago over the years, and from which the preceding passage has been quoted. So it was only natural for me to dwell upon this diagram in the preceding memoir.

I had always assumed that this diagram was original to Knight. Thus it came to me as a surprise to notice—in the process of writing this memoir—that Knight goes on in the passage just quoted to describe the diagram as one "suggesting the familiar figure of the 'wheel of wealth' " (1933, p. 60). My curiosity aroused, I began a search for the presumably earlier uses of this figure that rendered it so "familiar"—only to find myself being rapidly drawn into an ever-deepening mystery.

Let me first note that though this diagram is concerned with the circular flow of money, Knight used it not in the context of monetary theory, but in order to illustrate certain basic aspects of value theory: namely, the differentiated roles that families and businesses fulfill in the specialization and exchange that characterize a market economy; the ways in which the respective activities of these units are guided by the prices of productive services, on the one hand, and the prices of final goods and services, on the other; and the ways in which the interaction of these two sets of prices enables the economic system to fulfill its basic functions of determining what to produce, how to produce, and how to distribute the product.

As the first step in the search for the sources of this diagram,[2] I examined the standard American textbooks of the period in order to see if in addition to describing the process of specialization and exchange—and the role played by money in facilitating this process—they had also made use of the term "wheel of wealth" or of the diagram that Knight associated with it. Such an examination of the respective textbooks of Francis A. Walker (1887), Richard T. Ely (1893, 1937), Edwin R. A. Seligman (1905), Alvin S. Johnson (1909), Henry R. Seager (1909), Irving Fisher (1910, 1912), Frank W. Taussig (rev. ed., 1915), and Fred M. Taylor (1911, 1925) showed that they had not. The same is true of Herbert J. Davenport (1897, 1908, 1913)—to whom, as I have noted in my memoir, Knight had a special affinity. Nor does the term or diagram appear in the textbook by Leverett S. Lyon (1923), which was used at the University of Chicago Business School in the early 1920's. Similarly, no instances of such a term or diagram are to be found in such contemporary British standard works as Alfred Marshall's *Principles* (first ed., 1890; eighth ed., 1920), J. Shield Nicholson (1893–1901), Philip H. Wicksteed (1910; rev. 1933), Edwin Cannan (rev. ed., 1916), and Sydney Chapman (new ed., 1917). Similarly, there is no reference to the term or diagram "wheel of wealth" in Palgrave's *Dictionary of Political Economy* (new ed., 1925). And what lends added significance to the absence of such a diagram from all of these books is the fact that most of them did make use of analytical diagrams in other contexts.[3]

---

2. As an aside, I might note that the use of diagrams to describe the exchange of commodities goes back to Aristotle (Theocharis 1961, p. 4). Aristotle, however, used his diagram essentially to illustrate the labor theory of value, and not the circular flow of money and commodities. (I am indebted for this reference to my colleague Ephraim Kleiman.) See also Jaffé (1974), pp. 384–89.

3. Particular mention should be made here of the hydraulic diagrams—and even machines!—which

In view of the important influence of the Austrian school on Knight's thinking, I then turned to the Continental literature—only to find that there is no discussion or depiction of the wheel of wealth in the classic works of either Carl Menger (1871), Eugen v. Böhm-Bawerk (1888), or Friedrich v. Wieser (1889). The same is true of the earlier widely used textbook of that leading member of the old historical school, Wilhelm Roscher (13th ed., 1878). Nor does the "wheel" appear in the standard treatises of the turn of the century by Eugen von Philippovich (1897–99) and Adolph Wagner (1892–94, 1907–09) (see, however, fn. 17 below). Similarly, the wheel does not seem to have been referred to in the teaching of economics in Germany in the 1920's.[4] In any event, it does not appear in Gustav Cassel's book (1923, 1932), which was a standard text on the Continent at that time, though Cassel does provide a verbal description of the exchange by consumers of their productive services for goods produced by firms, in what is essentially a barter economy (Cassel 1932, pp. 43–44).[5] I must, however, admit that less significance can be attached to the absence of the wheel-of-wealth diagram from this literature as compared to the Anglo-American in view of the fact that this Continental literature generally did not make use of analytical diagrams in any context.

This consistent failure to find earlier instances of the wheel-of-wealth diagram then raised the possibility that perhaps the search was being conducted in the wrong direction: that perhaps the antecedents of the wheel were to be found not in the economic literature that was concerned primarily with value theory (as is largely the case with the foregoing works), but in that concerned with monetary theory and practice—and with the circular flow of money in particular.

Some students of the history of ideas claim that the idea of this circular flow appears already in Nicholas Oresme's fourteenth-century essay on *De Moneta* (ca. 1355), but I do not think that the passages they cite bear this interpretation.[6] Nor did Copernicus'

Irving Fisher constructed to illustrate the principle of equalizing the utility of expenditure at the margin (*Mathematical Investigations in the Theory of Value and Price* (1892), pp. 24–39; see also the photographs of the machines at the beginning of the 1925 reprint of this work). Fisher also made use of hydraulic diagrams to illustrate various points in his *Purchasing Power of Money* (1913), pp. 105–16.

4. I base this statement on information received from a sample of two: A. L. Gaathon (Gruenbaum) of the Bank of Israel Research Department, who completed his Ph.D. degree at the University of Berlin in 1934; and Freidrich A. Lutz of the Swiss Institute of International Studies in Zurich, who completed his at the University of Tubingen in 1925. Gaathon has also informed me that he has not found any references to the wheel of wealth in the textbooks by Adolph Weber, Wilhelm Lexis, and Othmar Spann, which were widely used in Germany during the first decades of this century.

5. Knight (1921–22) wrote a very favorable review article of the first edition of Cassel's book, though without any reference to the point now under discussion.

6. Thus Foley (1973, p. 126) supports this claim with a reference to p. 14 of Johnson's English translation (1956) of *De Moneta*; but all that Oresme seems to be discussing here is the "currency" of money, not in the sense of a flowing current, but in the sense of being in current use as a medium of exchange. (I am indebted to my late colleague and Professor of Classics at the Hebrew University, Chaim Wirszubski, for helpful discussions of this point). Similarly, Lowry (1974, pp. 435–36) cites a passage from Johnson's translation (pp. 43–44) which refers not to the circular flow of money, but to the harm done to an economy whose prince "draws to himself riches in excess as is done by altering the coinage." I should, however, note that Lowry himself presents this only as a "blurred premonition" of the idea of a circulatory flow. (Lowry's article is referred to in an unsigned note in the *History of Economic Thought Newsletter*, no. 17, Autumn 1976, p. 11. This also refers to an article by David M. Robinson on "The Wheel of Fortune" (1946) which, though interesting, does not bear directly on the present question).

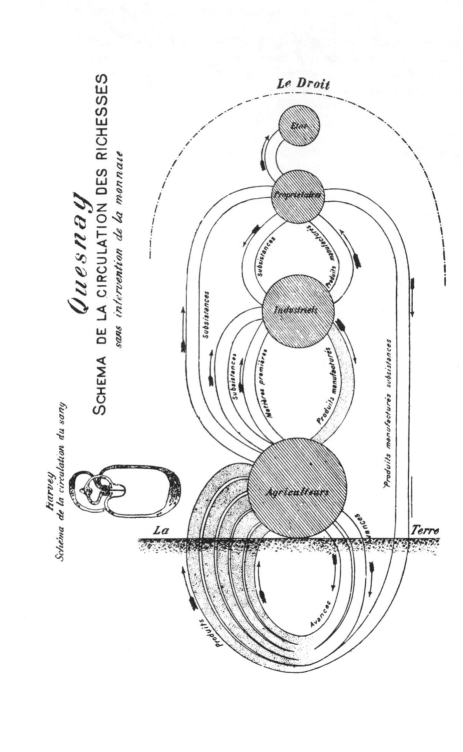

Harvey
Schéma de la circulation du sang

Quesnay
SCHEMA DE LA CIRCULATION DES RICHESSES
sans intervention de la monnaie

Le Droit

Etat

Propriétaires

Industriels

Subsistances

Subsistances

Produits manufacturés

Subsistances

Subsistances

Matières premières

Produits manufacturés

Produits manufacturés subsistances

Agriculteurs

La

Terre

Produits

Avances

Avances

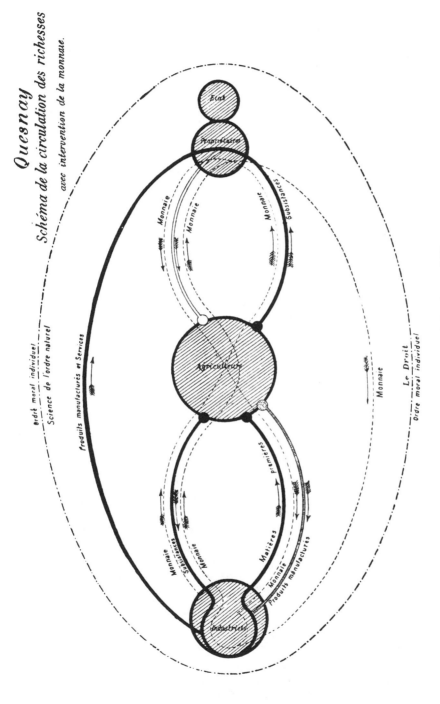

Figure 1 (Denis, 1904, vol. 1, following p. 353)

great discovery about the circulation of planets lead him, in his sixteenth-century tract on money (*Monete Cudende Ratio*, 1526), to a similar notion about money.[7,8] By the time of the seventeenth-century mercantilists, however, such notions do appear (cf., e.g., Monroe 1923, chs. 21–22; Holtrop 1929). Thus Petty (*Verbum Sapienti*, 1665) spoke of the "revolution" of money in "circles" (cited by Holtrop 1929, p. 503). Other mercantilists of this period (as Viner (1937, p. 37) has told us) often described the circulation of money as a medium of exchange by means of "analogies, especially with the circulation of blood, which William Harvey had discovered not long before." In the following century this analogy also influenced Quesnay (who was a doctor of medicine) [9] in the construction of his famed *Tableau Economique* (1758–59 (1972), pp. ii-iv),[10] in which the circulation of goods and money among different sectors (though not those designated by Knight) is analyzed and illustrated (though not by means of circles, and not for the purposes that concerned Knight).[11] And these same differences from Knight's diagram also hold for the circular-flow diagram by which, two and a half centuries later, Hector Denis (1904, v. 1, after p. 353) depicted Quesnay's system, vividly indicating its relation to Harvey's discovery (Figure 1).[12]

Quite naturally, the circular flow of money was also one of the topics frequently discussed in the quantity-theory literature. Thus in his pioneering work on the quantity-theory equation, Simon Newcomb emphasized that to the "monetary circulation" there corresponded a reverse "industrial circulation" of "wealth or services"—and used the term "societary circulation" to designate the combination of these two opposite circulations (1886, pp. 318–19, 326). Furthermore, Newcomb made use of diagrams (one of which is reproduced in Figure 2a) to illustrate this "societary circulation"—and explained that the "arrowheads" which showed the direction of the monetary circulation could "also be considered to represent the industrial circulation, the latter flowing in the opposite direction from that of the arrows, but along the same veins" (1886, pp. 318–19, 326). It is, however, clear

7. A corresponding statement holds for Newton's "Representations on the Subject of Money," written at the beginning of the eighteenth century, and reproduced by McCulloch (1856).

8. I have made use here of a French translation of Copernicus' work under the title *Traité de la Monnaie* (1864), and have benefited from a summary of it prepared by Gabrielle Brenner, who was my assistant at the time. Once again, I find myself in disagreement with Lowry, who cites an article by Taylor (1955, p. 540) in support of the statement that Copernicus "focused attention on the significance of the flow of funds within a country" (Lowry 1974, p. 436). I cannot find justification for such a statement in Taylor's article, which is largely devoted to providing an English summary of Copernicus' tract.

9. On the nature of this influence, see Foley (1973).

10. See also the passages on pp. 1–3 of the "Extract from the Royal Economic Maxims of M. de Sully," which appears as an appendix to the *Tableau*.

11. My colleague David Levhari has reminded me of Karl Marx's detailed discussions in *Capital* of his M-C-M (i.e., Money-Commodity-Money) circuit and variations thereof, which may stem in part from Quesnay. Once again, however, Marx's various circuits are quite different in both content and purpose from Knight's wheel of wealth. See *Capital*, vol. 1, part 1, ch. 3, especially p. 125; vol. 2, part I, especially p. 113. See also Sweezy (1942, pp. 56–59, 138–45). I might also mention Marx's graphical representation of his "process of reproduction" by means of a "*Tableau economique* which I [Marx] substitute for Quesnay's" (letter to Engels from 6 July 1863, translated and reproduced in Marx and Engels, *Selected Correspondence*, pp. 153–56; I am indebted to Arie Arnon of the Hebrew University for this reference).

12. I am indebted to William Jaffé, who, shortly after the original appearance of this paper, wrote me about Denis' diagrams, and subsequently published a brief note on them (1975).

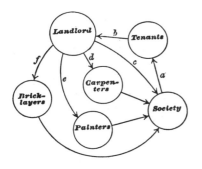

a. Newcomb (1886, p. 336)

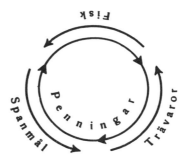

c. Wicksell (1901, vol. 1, p. 105)

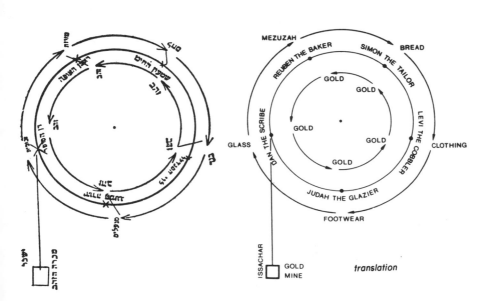

b. Hurewitz (1900, p. 112)

Figure 2

from Figure 2a that Newcomb was not concerned with the flows between the basic functional units (families and businesses) that concerned Knight; nor did Newcomb make use of his diagrams to illustrate the organization of production and distribution by the price system.

Much the same statements can be made for the many diagrams (for example, Figure 2b) illustrating the exchange of goods for money under different circumstances that appear in an early Hebrew textbook on money by Vienna- and Berlin-trained Chaim Dov Hurewitz (1900, pp. 105, 112, 119, 150, 153, and 156), which has recently been rediscovered by Ephraim Kleiman (1973). And the same can also be said for the diagram (Figure 2c) showing the opposite circular flows of goods and money that appears in Knut Wicksell's *Lectures on Political Economy* (1901, vol. 1, p. 105; vol. 1, p. 64 of the English translation)—whose purpose, however, is esentially to show how the use of money as a medium of exchange makes the "double coincidence" unnecessary. And in both cases one gets the clear impression that the authors present their diagrams not as original contributions on their part, but as something which they presume to be familiar to their readers from earlier sources— though they do not explicitly indicate what these sources were.[13,14]

13. In particular, as Kleiman (1973) has emphasized, "Hurewitz did not presume to present new theories, but rather wished to acquaint his readers with some part of what he considered to be the accepted corpus of economic theory." Still, as implausible as it may sound (and it *is* implausible—so that I would welcome counter-examples from the literature), Hurewitz's diagram is the first that I have been able to find that presents the opposite flows of goods and money in the by-now familiar "double-circle" form.

14. The literature on the circular flow of goods and money has been surveyed by Arthur W. Marget from a somewhat different—and much broader!—viewpoint in the course of his discussion of the history of "The Income Approach to the Theory of Prices" (1938, vol. 1, ch. 12; 1942, vol. 2, ch. 7). See also Joseph A. Schumpeter (1912; 1954, ch. 2).

Marget (1942, v. 2, pp. 356–57, fns. 18 and 19) also refers to circular-flow diagrams by Francesco Ferrara (1864; 1938, pp. 85, 86, 92) and Fleeming Jenkin (1887, p. 150). All of these diagrams, however, refer not to a money economy, but to the circular flow of goods in a barter economy as a result of barter exchanges of one good for another among the individuals of the economy. Corresponding-ly, these diagrams are not relevant to the present discussion. Nevertheless, I cannot re-sist reproducing here Jenkin's charming dia-gram illustrating the mutual benefits gener-ated by the trade that takes place " . . . among five little rudimentary people standing upright," where "the lines going out of the strokes to the right indicate produce, which each has to sell . . . [and the] line arriving at his left hand represents the goods which each man consumes" (1887, p. 150–51).

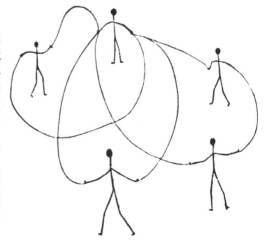

I might also note that unlike Ferrara, Jenkin (who was a professor of electrical engineering) also discussed (though *sans* diagram) the process of trade in a money economy and in this context referred to the "closed circuit (as we might say, borrowing a metaphor from electrical science) . . . round which the sixpence travelled from consumer to producer while the goods went the other way from producer to consumer." (1887, p. 143). The familiarity of such a concept at the time is well-attested by Francis Ysidro Edgeworth's statement in his biographical sketch of Jenkin in 1899 (1923, v. 2, p. 47) that this metaphor "enhances some elementary principles of economics." (*cont.*)

Perhaps Knight, too, considered his diagram to be such a "natural" description of the economic system that he took its familiarity for granted.[15] Still, I would conjecture that Knight's use of his diagram was directly inspired by certain earlier diagrams—though not those of Newcomb and Wicksell which (as already emphasized) only described the role of money as a medium of exchange, and did not depict any of the functional relations that were Knight's main concern. Instead, I think the relevant earlier diagrams were those that appeared in the literature of the first decades of this century that attempted to explain depressions in terms of inadequacies of demand generated by interferences (in the form of "excess" or "uninvested" savings) with the circular flow of money—and that, because of this denial of Say's law, grew up outside the mainstream of economic thought (though they ultimately led to the development of the money-flow analysis of Copeland [1952] and the flow-of-fund analysis of the Federal Reserve [1955]). Even more specifically, I would conjecture that the direct source of Knight's wheel of wealth was the diagram (Figure 3) showing what they called the "circuit flow of money" among different functional units that had been used in the foregoing context first by William Trufant Foster alone in an article in the *American Economic Review* (1922, p. 463), and then by Foster together with his colleague Waddill Catchings in their then widely discussed books on *Money* (1923, p. 305) and *Profits* (1925, p. 255), the latter of which Knight reviewed (1926).[16] I should also note Foster and Catchings' related contention that " . . . money spent in the consumption of commodities is the force that moves all the wheels of industry" (1923, p. 277; 1925, p. 234). Thus Foster and Catchings not only presented a diagram showing the opposite flows of money and commodities between the functional units, households and firms, but also connected this diagram with "wheels"—albeit not those of wealth!

Foster and Catchings (1923, p. 303) cite as their source of the diagram the almost identical one by M. C. Rorty (1922, p. 63)—one of the "two American amateur-

---

Though it, too, is not relevant for our purpose (since it refers to trade in a barter economy), I might finally mention the circular diagram used by Frédéric Bastiat to illustrate the benefits of economic progress ([1855] ch. 11, p. 331).

15. Thus see Schumpeter's clear verbal description of some of the basic features of Knight's wheel of wealth in his [Schumpeter's] influential article on "Money and the Social Product" (1917/18; 1956, pp. 152–53). I might at this point also cite John R. Commons' observation (1934, p. 294) that " . . . from Quesnay to the Twentieth Century economic theory was dominated, in large part, by his analogy of Circulation of commodities and money. In the latter part of the Nineteenth Century it began to take over the analogy of Turnover. The one is the analogy of a 'flow,' the other of a 'wheel.' " It is not clear from this passage whether Commons actually attributed the use of the term "wheel" to the nineteenth-century literature itself—or whether (as I suspect) this represents Commons' own (and hence post-Knightian) use of the term. Unfortunately, Commons does not provide the references to the nineteenth-century literature that would enable us to check this question. In any event, to the best of my knowledge, Commons himself did not use this term in his earlier writings; see, for example, Commons (1893).

16. The validity of specifically identifying the origin of Knight's wheel-of-wealth diagram with his review of Foster and Catchings' *Profits* depends, of course, on the assumption that the mimeographed material in which Knight first used this diagram was written in 1926—and I have above (see fn. 1) provided some evidence that this may indeed be the case. But even if Knight wrote this material earlier in the period 1922–26, it could still have been inspired by Foster and Catchings' earlier presentations of their circular-flow diagram—which, as indicated in the text, began in 1922. On the intensive discussions—both lay and professional—generated at the time by Foster and Catchings' work, see Dorfman (1959, pp. 339–50).

THE CIRCUIT FLOW OF MONEY

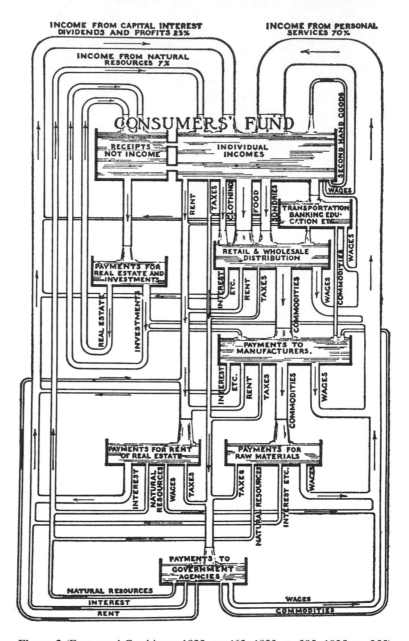

Figure 3 (Foster and Catchings, 1922, p. 463; 1923, p. 305; 1925, p. 255)

economists (cranks, some might say)'' to whose oversavings theory of the cycle Keynes was later to refer in his *Treatise* (1930, vol. 2, p. 100). Where did Colonel Rorty get it? He does not say. But I suspect that it can be traced back to the diagram (see Figure 4) which appears in the work of Keynes' other ''amateur,'' namely, Nicholas A. L. J. Johannsen, on *A Neglected Point in Connection with Crises* (1908, front matter). This diagram in turn, has its origin in an earlier one (to the best of my knowledge, the first of its kind in the literature) by the same author, writing this time as J. J. O. Lahn (a pseudonym formed from the initials of his name in reverse order) in a work entitled *Der Kreislauf des Geldes* (1903).[17] For though Johannsen was ignored by most of the profession, his contributions were appreciated by such economists as Wesley C. Mitchell,[18] who in 1920 became the first Director of the National Bureau of Economic Research, and to whom (among others) Rorty (who was among the founders of the Bureau, and its first President)[19] expresses his general indebtedness.

Let me conclude with two comments. First, even if the source of Knight's ''wheel of wealth'' was Foster and Catchings' diagram, it must be emphasized that Knight adapted this diagram to completely different purposes. In particular, as indicated at the beginning of this chapter, Knight's concern was with the allocative functions of the price system under the implicit assumption of full employment, not with the possible generation of unemployment as a result of inadequacies of aggregate demand. Thus no matter what the origins of Knight's wheel of wealth as a diagram, its use to illustrate basic aspects of price theory—as distinct from monetary theory— seems to have been original to him.[20]

17. I am indebted to Friedrich Lutz for bringing ''Lahn's'' diagram to my attention. Marget (1938, vol. 1, pp. 331–36) discusses the intellectual influences that Johannsen and Adolph Wagner exerted one on the other. Whatever the nature of these influences, it is clear that Johannsen did not derive his diagram from Wagner: for, as noted above, Wagner made no use of diagrams in his analysis in general—and this is true of his analysis of money-flows in particular (1909, pp. 158 ff.). Note also Johannsen's statement (1913, p. 5) that he first showed his circular-flow diagram to Wagner in 1898.

18. See the references to Johannsen in Mitchell's classic work on the business cycle (1913, pp. 18–19, 389, 580–81). In the revised edition of this work, however, these references are reduced to a single footnote (Mitchell 1927, p. 25, fn. 3); on the other hand, this edition contains several references to Rorty (consult index). See also Dorfman (1949, vol. 3, p. 413).

19. See Stone (1943) and Dorfman (1959, vol. 4, p. 195). See also title page of Rorty's book.

20. In this connection it is interesting to note the different uses that Samuelson has made of circular-flow diagrams in his *Economics: An Introductory Analysis*—the textbook by means of which Knight's wheel of wealth has become familiar to a modern generation of economists. (On the origins of Samuelson's diagram in Knight's teachings, see above p. 28, fn. 8.) All editions of Samuelson's textbook present a minor adaptation of Knight's description of the functions of the economic system in terms of ''what, how, and for whom'' to produce. But in the first three editions this discussion is not accompanied by Knight's wheel of wealth. Instead, Samuelson uses the circular-flow diagram in these editions only for the quite different purpose (to which Knight had also very briefly adverted (1933, p. 62)) of illustrating the equality between national income and national product (Samuelson 1948, p. 226; 1951, p. 231; and all subsequent editions up to the most recent—1970, p. 170). Only in the fourth (1958, p. 41) and later (e.g., 1970, p. 42) editions is Samuelson's discussion of the functions of the economic system illustrated by Knight's ''wheel of wealth,'' somewhat modified. In these editions Samuelson also makes use of the wheel in order to provide a detailed illustration of the simultaneous, mutual determination of prices in a general-equilibrium framework (1955, p. 597; 1958, p. 615; 1970, p. 607). Thus beginning with the fourth edition of *Economics*, Samuelson presents the wheel-of-wealth diagram at three different points in his textbook, each time in a somewhat different context.

Might I finally also mention here the use of Knight's diagram in the various editions of my own introductory text in Hebrew (e.g., 1949, p. 1; 1958, p. 21).

Figure 4 (Reprinted by permission of Augustus M. Kelley from Johannsen, 1908, front matter)

Second, after having in this way built conjecture upon conjecture in the search for the "familiar figure" with which Knight associated his circular-flow diagram, I must anticlimactically raise the possibility that this search has been a mistaken one: that Knight never made such an association to begin with. For in the mimeographed materials (1922–26) in which his circular-flow diagram first appeared (see above, p. 53), Knight began his analysis of the functions of the price system with the statement that ". . . the general character of an enterprise organization reduced to its very simplest terms can be indicated by a diagram which suggests the familiar figure *of speech*, the 'wheel of wealth' " (italics added). Thus what Knight referred to as "familiar" was not his diagram, but the figure of speech "wheel of wealth" which to his mind his diagram "suggested." In sum, though Knight was in all probability influenced by earlier diagrams (and that of Foster and Catchings in particular), he never did present his diagram as being similar to an earlier one. Correspondingly, there is nothing in Knight's presentation that controverts the original impression of my student days that his circular-flow diagram was largely his own construction (see above, p. 54).

But once again things are not so simple: for neither *Webster's New International Dictionary*, nor the *Oxford English Dictionary* nor any of the other standard reference works I have consulted list such a figure of speech. "Wheel of fortune," yes; "wheels of industry," yes; and, of course, "wheels within wheels." But not "wheel of wealth." Did Knight later delete the word "speech" from the 1932 version of his discussion because he became aware of this fact? Or was this deletion the result of a slip of the pen or typographical error? Or did a slip occur in the original mimeographed version in the very insertion of the word "speech"? I do not know.

Postscript*

Shortly after the appearance of this paper, E. F. Beach of McGill University called my attention to—and Shlomo Maital (now of the Technion in Haifa) and Tim Edwards sent me a draft of a note on—a 1906 book actually called *The Wheel of Wealth*, written by a Canadian doctor turned philosopher-economist-sociologist named John Beattie Crozier.[1] Maital and Edwards subsequently published their note (1975), and in a comment on it, Austin Robinson (1975) pointed out that Crozier's book was considered sufficiently important at the time to receive a four-page review by J. S. Nicholson in the *Economic Journal* of March 1907.

Despite this coincidence of names, Crozier's book has little, if anything, in common with Knight's diagram. Indeed, there is no diagram in the book. Furthermore, and more important, Crozier's concerns (which were somewhat on the crankish side) are different from Knight's. This is evident from the very title of the book, which is in full *The Wheel of Wealth: Being a Reconstruction of the Science and Art of Political Economy on the Lines of Modern Evolution*. It is even more evident from the passages in which Crozier explains what he means by the wheel of wealth:

> To begin with, then, we may say that the essential factors involved in the phenomena of wealth, and for the relationship between which some abstract symbol or formula must be found, may all be reduced to four, namely, Production, Consumption, the powers of Nature, and the powers of Man. And the first point we would notice is that the relationship between the first two factors is always the same, namely of production passing into consumption, consumption

---

*I am greatly indebted to Marc Levin for his invaluable assistance in connection with the preparation of this postscript.

1. Beach also informed me that the McGill library possesses a presentation copy of the book.

again into production, that in turn into consumption again, and so on continuously and without break or pause, like a revolving wheel [Crozier 1906, pp. 30–31].

The first point of identity then which we would note between a mechanical wheel and the wheel of wealth is that just as the two separate halves or aspects of a wheel are so rigidly bound together that the one side cannot be slowed or accelerated without slowing or accelerating the other, so too it is with the movement of wealth reproduction, where any brake put on the side of consumption is immediately transmitted to the side of production. For who will go on producing unless someone somewhere goes on consuming, and consuming precisely to the extent of the production? . . . On the other hand, again, when the consumption side of the wheel is stimulated for any reason, as from good harvests, easy credit, high wages, or business prosperity generally, the production side of the wheel is quickened to keep pace with it; so that everywhere production must keep time and pace with consumption, and consumption with production, as one side or aspect of a wheel keeps time and pace with the other . . . [ibid., pp. 32–33].

In brief, Crozier had in mind a single wheel representing the interdependence of production and consumption, and not (like Knight) two concentric and oppositely moving wheels representing the exchange of goods for money.[2] Furthermore, Crozier does not even advert to the exchange of the families' productive services for the firms' output of goods—which is a major element of Knight's diagram. Nor does Crozier develop Knight's basic notion of the price system as a means of organizing economic activity.

My conclusion from all this is that even if Knight got the term "wheel of wealth" from Crozier's book (and there is no evidence that he even knew of its existence[3]), this book did not provide the inspiration for the diagram itself.

But further reflection, together with evidence which I inexcusably overlooked in my original discussion, have now persuaded me that the word "speech" was indeed erroneously omitted from the passage in Knight's *Economic Organization* (1933, p. 60) which has served as the point of departure of this investigation, and that accordingly the term "wheel of wealth" which appears in this passage was actually intended to refer not to a "figure" but to a "figure of speech" (above, pp. 54 and 64–65). For one thing (to judge from my 1942 and 1945 lecture notes from Econ. 301), Knight himself did not designate his figure as the "wheel of wealth" in his classroom presentations; nor did Simons so designate it in his *Syllabus* (p. 10). And insofar as the failure of this figure of speech to be listed in the standard reference works is concerned, I now feel that this simply reflects the fact that Knight's language at this point was imprecise: that he was referring in a loose manner to the well-known

2. At a later point Crozier (1906, pp. 66–67) recognizes the role of money as a medium of exchange and says that money is "neither altogether on the wheel of wealth nor altogether off it," but serves to "accelerat[e] the speed of the revolutions of the wheel." Even though there is no reference in Crozier's book to Hume, this passage may well reflect the latter's influence; see below.

3. To the best of my knowledge, there is no reference to Crozier in any of Knight's writings. Nor have I been able to determine whether there was a copy of Crozier's book in Knight's library. There is, however, a copy (acquired in 1928) in The University of Chicago library.

metaphors employed by David Hume and Adam Smith in their writings on money. Thus the opening sentence of David Hume's celebrated essay "Of Money" (1752 (1970)) reads:

> Money is not, properly speaking, one of the subjects of commerce; but only the instrument which men have agreed upon to facilitate the exchange of one commodity for another. It is none of the wheels of trade: It is the oil which renders the motion of the wheels more smooth and easy.

In employing the metaphor "wheels of trade," Hume was presumably following the example set by John Locke some sixty years before in the following passage from his essay on "Some Considerations of the Consequences of the Lowering of Interest and Raising the Value of Money" (1691 (1823), vol. 5, pp. 21–22):

> The necessity of a certain proportion of money to trade (I conceive) lies in this, that money, in its circulation, driving the several wheels of trade, whilst it keeps in that channel (for some of it will unavoidably be drained into standing pools), is all shared between the landholder, whose land affords the materials; the labourer, who works them; the broker, i.e., the merchant and shopkeeper, who distributes them to those that want them; and the consumer, who spends them.

And Hume's passage in turn probably inspired Adam Smith some twenty-five years later to write in his *Wealth of Nations* (1776 (1937), book 2, ch. 2, p. 276; see also pp. 273–74):[4]

> Money, therefore, the great wheel of circulation, the great instrument of commerce, like all other instruments of trade, though it makes a part and a very valuable part of the capital, makes no part of the revenue of the society to which it belongs; and though the metal pieces of which it is composed, in the course of their annual circulation, distribute to every man the revenue which properly belongs to him, they make themselves no part of that revenue.

Now, Smith's *Wealth of Nations* was a work frequently discussed in Knight's writings and teachings (above, pp. 30, 34). Furthermore in his 1951 encyclopedia article on "Economics," Knight alluded to the preceding passage when he wrote, "Money, from the communal point of view, he [Adam Smith] held to be merely an instrument, a 'wheel of trade' " (Knight 1951, p. 8). And with due regard to the methodological danger in suggesting a connection between a man's writings separated by a twenty-five-year span, I feel that the very fact that Knight did not take care to distinguish here between Smith's "wheel of circulation" and Hume's "wheels of trade" only increases the likelihood that Knight's reference to the "familiar figure of speech, the 'wheel of wealth' " was simply a loose reference to these figures of speech, and possibly to the by-then more common "wheels of industry" as well (above, p. 61).[5]

The similarity of Hume's and Smith's figures of speech should not make us lose

---

4. Once again, I am indebted to E. F. Beach for bringing this passage, as well as Knight's reference to it (see below), to my attention.

5. Cf. also Commons' observation as cited on p. 61, fn. 15 above.

sight of the fact that there is actually a basic difference between them: for Smith money is a wheel, whereas for Hume it is not. This difference in metaphors implies a difference in their respective images. For Smith—and this is what made his discussion of particular interest to Knight[6]—the wheel represents circulatory motion, the motion of money in circulating goods. Hume's wheels, however, would seem to be the wheels of industrial machinery and accordingly represent the production of goods.[7,8] Indeed, as was clearly the case for Locke, the specific image Hume had in mind may well have been that of the water wheel, which was the major source of industrial power at the time.[9] In any event, by taking a few liberties, we can imagine Hume participating in a present-day discussion of micro-monetary theory and using his metaphor to claim that "money does not enter the production function, it merely raises the level of such a function."

Despite the difference in their metaphors, Hume's and Smith's message was the same: money is only a medium of exchange, to be sharply distinguished from the goods whose circulation it facilitates. For Knight, however, this was a relatively minor motif in the broad picture of the nature of economic organization that he was interested in drawing. And thus might Knight have transformed a familiar figure of speech into quite a different graphical figure, largely of his own construction, which, though not "familiar" when he first presented it, has certainly become so in the years since then.

6. Cf. Knight's description of his diagram as quoted at the beginning of this chapter.

7. This also seems to have been Marshall's interpretation of the metaphor: for in what is apparently an allusion to it, Marshall wrote:

> Money or "currency" is desired as a means to an end; but yet it does not conform to the general rule that, the larger the means toward a certain end, the better will that end be attained. It may indeed be compared to oil used to enable a machine to run smoothly. A machine will not run well unless oiled; and a novice may infer that the more oil he supplies, the better the machine will run; but in fact oil in excess will clog the machine. In like manner an excessive increase of currency, causes it to lose credit, and perhaps even to cease to be "current." (*Money Credit and Commerce*, p. 38).

I might also note Mill's likening of money to "a machine for doing quickly and commodiously, what would be done, though less quickly and commodiously, without it" (*Principles*, book 3, ch. 7, sec. 2; p. 488 of the Ashley edition).

8. This is obviously the case for today's more common metaphor "wheels of industry": witness the giant cog-wheel of modern industry that devours Charlie Chaplin. I would also conjecture that the reason this metaphor is more common today is precisely the fact that since the days of Hume the meaning of "trade" has narrowed from economic activity in general to activity related to the distribution of goods, as contrasted with their production.

9. I am indebted to my colleagues of the Department of English at the Hebrew University, Ruth Nevo and Adam Mendeloff, for first suggesting these interpretations of Hume's metaphor to me.

On the importance of the water wheel in seventeenth- and eighteenth-century England, see Mantoux (1928, pp. 252–53), Mathias (1969, pp. 123, 132–33), Stowers (1958), and Wilson (1954).

It is worth remembering in this connection that the major means of transporting goods at the time of Hume and Smith was not by wheels on the roadways, but by boats on the waterways (cf. Mathias 1969, pp. 106–18). Correspondingly, the likelihood then was much less than today that the word "wheels" would raise associations with vehicular motion. I should, however, note that (as my colleague Chaim Barkai has pointed out to me) in his discussion of paper money, Smith (1776 (1937), p. 305) did draw an analogy to "highways."

Bibliography

F. Bastiat. *Harmonies of Political Economy*, trans. from the 3rd ed. (1855) of the French by P. J. Stirling. Edinburgh, 1880.

E. v. Böhm-Bawerk. *The Positive Theory of Capital*. Innsbruck, 1888, trans. W. Smart. New York, 1891.

E. Cannan. *Wealth*, 2d ed. London, 1916.

G. Cassel. *The Theory of Social Economy*, trans. J. McCabe. London, 1923; trans. rev. ed. S. L. Barron. New York, 1932.

S. Chapman. *Outlines of Political Economy*, 2d ed. London, 1917.

J. R. Commons. *The Distribution of Wealth*. 1893, reprinted, New York, 1963.

——. *Institutional Economics*. New York, 1934.

M. A. Copeland. *A Study of Moneyflows in the United States*. New York, 1952.

N. Copernicus. *Traité de la Monnoie*, ed. M. L. Wolowski. Paris, 1864 (trans. of *Monete Cudende Ratio*, 1526).

J. B. Crozier. *The Wheel of Wealth: Being a Reconstruction of the Science and Art of Political Economy on the Lines of Modern Evolution*. London, 1906.

H. J. Davenport. *Outlines of Elementary Economics*. New York, 1897.

——. *Value and Distribution*. Chicago, 1908, reprinted, New York, 1964.

——, *The Economics of Enterprise*. New York, 1913.

H. Denis. *Histoire des systémes économiques et socialistes*, 2 vols. Paris, 1904–7.

J. Dorfman. *The Economic Mind in American Civilization*, vol. 3. New York, 1949, vol. 4. New York, 1959.

F. Y. Edgeworth. "Jenkin, Henry Charles Fleeming." In *Palgrave's Dictionary of Political Economy*, vol. 2, 1899; London, 1923, rev. ed. P. 473.

R. T. Ely. *Outlines of Economics*. New York, 1893; 6th ed., 1937.

F. Ferrara. "De l'équilibre dans l'échange des productions entre elles." In *Oeuvres Économiques Choisies*, 1864, trans. G. H. Bousquet and J. Crisafulli. Paris, 1938. Pp. 84–96.

I. Fisher. *Mathematical Investigations in the Theory of Value and Prices* (1892). Reprinted New Haven, Conn., 1925, and New York, 1965.

——. *Introduction to Economic Science* (Cover reads: *Elements of Economic Science*; actually 1st ed. of next entry). New York, 1910.

——. *Elementary Principles of Economics*. New York, 1912.

——. *The Purchasing Power of Money*. New York, rev. ed., 1913.

V. Foley. "An Origin of the Tableau Economique." *History of Political Economy*, Spring 1973, *5*, 121–50.

W. Foster. "The Circuit Flow of Money." *American Economic Review*, Sept. 1922, *12*, 460–73.

—— and W. Catchings. *Money*. Boston, 1923.

——. *Profits*. Boston, 1925.

M. W. Holtrop. "Theories of the Velocity of Circulation of Money in Earlier Economic Literature." *Economic History*, Jan. 1929, *1*, 503–24.

D. Hume. "Of Money," 1752. Reprinted in *David Hume: Writings in Economics*, ed. E. Rotwein. Madison, Wisc., 1970. Pp. 33–46.

C. D. Hurewitz. *Ha-Mammon: Perek ba-Kalkalah ha-Tzibburit (Money: A Chapter in Political Economy)*. (Hebrew.) Warsaw, 1900.

W. Jaffé. "Edgeworth's Contract Curve: Part 2. Two Figures in Its Protohistory: Aristotle and Gossen." *History of Political Economy*, Winter 1974, *6*, 381–404.

————. "A Wee Word on The Wheel of Wealth." *History of Economic Thought Newsletter*, Autumn 1975, *15*, 16–17.

F. Jenkin. *The Graphic Representation of the Laws of Supply and Demand, and other Essays on Political Economy*. London, 1887, reprinted London, 1931.

N. A. L. J. Johannsen. *A Neglected Point in Connection with Crises*. New York, 1908; reprinted, New York, 1971.

————. *Die Steuer der Zukunft*. Berlin, 1913.

————. See also listing under J. J. O. Lahn.

A. S. Johnson. *Introduction to Economics*. Boston, 1909.

E. Kleiman. "An Early Modern Hebrew Textbook of Economics." *History of Political Economy*, Summer, 1973, *5*, 339–58.

F. H. Knight. Review of *Theoretische Socialökonomie* by G. Cassel. *Quarterly Journal of Economics, 36*, 1921–22, 145–53.

————. Review of *Profits* by W. T. Foster and W. Catchings. *Political Science Quarterly*, Sept. 1926, *41*, 468–71.

————. "Social Economic Organization," "The Price System and the Economic Process," "Demand and Supply and Price," "Distribution: The Pricing of Productive Services Individually." In *Second Year Course in the Social Sciences (Social Sciences II): Syllabus and Selected Readings*, prelim. ed. Chicago, 1932.

————. *The Economic Organization*. Chicago, 1933, multilith. Reset and reprinted with different pagination, New York, 1951. (Reproduces the material of the preceding entry.)

————. *The Ethics of Competition and Other Essays*. New York, 1935.

————. "Economics." *Encyclopedia Britannica* (1951). Reprinted in *On the History and Method of Economics*. Chicago, 1956. Pp. 3–33.

J. J. O. Lahn (pseud. of N. A. L. J. Johannsen). *Der Kreislauf des Geldes und Mechanismus des Social-lebens*. Berlin, 1903.

J. Locke. "Some Considerations of the Consequences of Lowering the Interest and Raising the Value of Money," 1691. Reprinted in *The Collected Works of John Locke*, vol. 5. London, 1823. Pp. 1–117.

S. T. Lowry. "The Archaeology of the Circulation Concept in Economic Theory." *Journal of the History of Ideas*, July 1974, *35*, 429–44.

L. S. Lyon. *Education for Business*, 2d ed. Chicago, 1923.

S. Maital and T. Edwards. "On the Origins of Frank Knight's Circular-Flow Diagram: John Beattie Crozier's *The Wheel of Wealth* (1906)." *History of Economic Thought Newsletter*, Spring 1975, *14*, 9–13.

P. Mantoux. *The Industrial Revolution in The Eighteenth Century*, rev. ed. trans. M. Vernon. London, 1928.

A. W. Marget. *The Theory of Prices*, vol. 1, 1938; vol. 2, 1942, reprinted New York, 1966.

A. Marshall. *Principles of Economics*, 8th ed. London, 1920.

————. *Money Credit and Commerce*. London, 1923.

K. Marx. *Capital*, 3 vols., trans. from 3d German ed. by S. Moore and E. Aveling. Chicago, 1906.

———— and F. Engels. *Selected Correspondence of Marx and Engels*, trans. Dana Torr. London, 1934.

P. Mathias. *The First Industrial Nation: An Economic History of Britain 1700–1914*. London, 1969.

C. Menger. *Principles of Economics*, 1871, trans. and ed. J. Dingwall and B. F. Hoselitz, with an intro. by F. H. Knight. Glencoe, Ill., 1950.

J. S. Mill. *Principles of Political Economy* (1848), ed. W. J. Ashley. London, 1909.

W. C. Mitchell. *Business Cycles*. Berkeley, Calif., 1913.

_____. *Business Cycles: The Problem and Its Setting*. New York, 1927.

A. E. Monroe. *Monetary Theory Before Adam Smith*. Cambridge, Mass., 1923.

S. Newcomb. *Principles of Political Economy*. New York, 1886.

I. Newton. "Representations on the Subject of Money," 1712–1717. Reprinted in *A Select Collection of Scarce and Valuable Tracts of Money*, ed. J. R. McCulloch. London, 1856.

J. S. Nicholson. *Principles of Political Economy*. London, vol. 1, 1893; vol. 2, 1897; vol. 3, 1901.

_____. Review of *The Wheel of Wealth: Being a Reconstruction of the Science and Art of Political Economy on the Lines of Modern Evolution* by John Beattie Crozier. *Economic Journal*, Mar. 1907, *17*, 87–91.

N. Oresme. *De Moneta, c* 1355. Reprinted in *The De Moneta of Nicholas Oresme and English Mint Documents*, trans. C. Johnson. London, 1956. Pp. 1–48.

R. H. I. Palgrave. *Palgrave's Dictionary of Political Economy*, new ed., ed. Henry Higgs. London, 1925.

D. Patinkin. *Movoh le-Kalkalah: Sikkum Hartzaot* (*Introduction to Economics: Lecture Notes*), (Hebrew). Jerusalem, 1949 (1st ed., mimeographed); 1958 (4th ed., Students' Union of the Hebrew University of Jerusalem, multilithed).

_____. "Frank Knight as Teacher," *American Economic Review*, Dec. 1973, *63*, 787–810. [Reproduced as chap. 1 above.]

W. Petty. *Verbum Sapienti*, 1665. Reprinted in *Economic Writings of William Petty*, ed. C. H. Hull. Cambridge, Eng., 1899. Vol. 1, pp. 99–120.

E. v. Philippovich. *Grundriss der Politischen Ökonomie*. Freiburg, 1897–99.

F. Quesnay. *Tableau Economique, 1758–59*. In *Quesnay's Tableau Economique*, ed. M. Kuczynski and R. L. Meek. London, 1972.

A. Robinson. "Frank Knight's Circular-Flow Diagram and Crozier's *The Wheel of Wealth*." *History of Economic Thought Newsletter*, Autumn 1975, *15*, 17.

D. M. Robinson. "The Wheel of Fortune," *Classical Philology*, Oct. 1946, *41*, 207–16.

M. C. Rorty. *Some Current Problems in Economics*. Chicago, 1922.

W. Roscher. *Principles of Political Economy*. Stuttgart, 1854; (Eng. trans. of 13th German edition, Chicago, 1878).

P. A. Samuelson. *Economics: An Introductory Analysis*. New York, 1948, 1951 (2d ed.), 1955 (3rd ed.), 1958 (4th ed.), 1970 (8th ed.).

J. A. Schumpeter. *Economic Doctrine and Method*, 1912, trans. R. Aris. London, 1954.

_____. "Das Socialprodukt und die Rechpfennige." *Archiv für Socialwissenschaft und Socialpolitik*, 44, 1917/18. Trans. under the title "Money and the Social Product" in International Economic Association, *International Economic Papers* No. 6. London, 1956.

H. R. Seager. *Economics*. New York, 1909.

E. R. A. Seligman. *Principles of Economics*. London, 1905.

[H. C. Simons]. *Economics 201: The Divisional Course in Economics*. Chicago, n.d. (mimeographed).

A. Smith. *The Wealth of Nations*. 1776, New York, 1937 (Modern Library edition).

N. I. Stone. "The Beginnings of the National Bureau of Economic Research." In *The National Bureau of Economic Research Twenty-Fifth Annual Report*. New York, 1945.

A. Stowers. "Watermills, *c* 1500– *c* 1850." In L. Singer et. al., *A History of Technology: Volume IV: The Industrial Revolution*. Oxford, 1958. Pp. 199–213.

P. M. Sweezy. *The Theory of Capitalist Development*. New York, 1942.

F. W. Taussig. *Principles of Economics*. New York, 1911; rev. ed., 1915.

F. M. Taylor. *Principles of Economics*. 1st ed., New York, 1911; 9th ed., New York, 1925.

J. Taylor. "Copernicus on the Evils of Inflation and the Establishment of a Sound Currency." *Journal of the History of Ideas*, 1955, *16*, 540–47.

R. D. Theocharis. *Early Developments in Mathematical Economics*. London, 1961.

J. Viner. *Studies in the Theory of International Trade*. New York, 1937.

A. Wagner. *Grundlegung der Politischen Oekonomie*, 3 vols. Leipzig, Winter 1892–94.

_____. *Theoretische Socialökonomik*, 2 vols. Leipzig, Winter 1907–9.

_____. *Soziälökonomische Theorie des Geldes und Geldwesens*. Leipzig, Winter 1909. (Vol. 2, part 2 of preceding entry.)

F. A. Walker. *Political Economy*, 3d ed. New York, 1887.

K. Wicksell. *Föreläsningar I Nationalekonomi*, vol. 1, Lund 1901. Trans. as *Lectures on Political Economy*, vol. 1, E. Classen. London, 1934.

P. H. Wicksteed. *The Common Sense of Political Economy*. London, 1910; rev. ed., London, 1933.

F. von Wieser. *Natural Value*. 1889, trans. C. A. Malloch; reprinted New York, 1956.

P. N. Wilson. "Water Power and the Industrial Revolution." *Water Power*, Aug. 1954, *6*, 309–16.

Government Publications

U.S. Board of Governors of the Federal Reserve System. *Flow of Funds in the United States: 1939–1953*. Washington, D.C., 1955.

Unpublished Materials

Frank H. Knight Papers. Joseph Regenstein Library, The University of Chicago.

Jacob Viner (1956)

3. Mercantilism and the Readmission of the Jews to England*

The history of the Jews in modern England may be said to begin with the period of Oliver Cromwell, who came to power in the early 1650's. The proposal to readmit Jews as legal residents, thereby abrogating the measure for their expulsion in 1290, stirred up a heated controversy. In a re-examination of the sources bearing on the pros and cons of the Readmission,[1] with particular reference to the economic aspects of the polemic, the writer has come to the conclusion that the historians of English Jewry have not satisfactorily explained Cromwell's favorable attitude. Despite the fact that mercantilism dominated the contemporary English outlook and that the urge to expand foreign trade and accumulate gold within the country outweighed all other considerations, it can be demonstrated that this policy was not the decisive element in the minds of the writers who advocated the Readmission of the Jews. As for Cromwell himself, it will be seen that his personal motives in this matter had no particular relation to the mercantilist program.

It is well known that the only Jews living in England during the early seventeenth century were the handful of marranos in London, who never ventured to expose their secret faith. This situation continued for some decades and was not readily improved by the favorable attitude toward the Jewish people which developed among the Puritans in the course of their study of the Old Testament. Pamphlets urging the readmission of Jews began to appear in England, and in 1648 the Cartwright Petition was presented to the government. Thereafter the subject was debated widely and numerous pamphlets continued to be published. The controversy culminated in the Whitehall Conference (December 1655), at which the lawyers decided that there was no English statute barring the entry of the Jews; no decision was reached,

Reprinted by permission from *Jewish Social Studies*, July 1946, *8*, 161–78.

*I wish to express my appreciation to Professor Jacob Viner (University of Chicago) for his valuable suggestions. I am also greatly indebted to Professor Frederic C. Lane (Johns Hopkins University) for very helpful criticisms.

1. For a good account of the period, see Godfrey Davies, *The Early Stuarts* (1937); and G. N. Clark, *The Later Stuarts* (1940). See also Clark, *The Seventeenth Century* (1929). On mercantilism see the exhaustive study of Eli F. Heckscher, *Mercantilism* (1935). For a much shorter account, but nevertheless discussing most of the elements of mercantilism dealt with in this paper, see the first two chapters of Jacob Viner, *Studies in the Theory of International Trade* (1937). See also Samuel R. Gardiner, *History of the Commonwealth and Protectorate* (1894–1901); Charles H. Firth, *The Last Years of the Protectorate* (1909).

For the best study of the polemic literature on the resettlement (1648–56), see Mordecai Vilensky, *Shivat Ha-yehudim le-Anglia (The Return of the Jews to England)* (1943). For a very good shorter account, see Nathan Osterman, "The Controversy over the Proposed Readmission of the Jews to England (1665)" (1941) pp. 301–29. See also Montagu F. Modder, *The Jew in the Literature of England* (1939) pp. 31–46.

however, as to the conditions of the Readmission.[2] The question was ultimately settled by the typical English policy of "muddling through." In 1655 war broke out between England and Spain. The marranos were nominally Spanish subjects and pursuant to the proclamation of March 1656 their possessions were subject to seizure. When the property of one Antonio Rodrigues Robles was seized, the members of the community realized their danger and decided that the best course was to appeal to Cromwell. Accordingly they presented a petition to him openly declaring themselves to be Jews, and thus not Spanish. The petition was never acted upon but the case against Robles was quashed, and soon afterwards, in December 1656, a house was rented for use as a synagogue. Thus, by the use of a test case the legality of Jewish residence was recognized, and the long process, which culminated in the equalization of the Jews' status, began.[3]

Mercantilism in the Polemic Literature

While the economic motivation of the London marranos' petition, as well as of the steps taken by Menasseh ben Israel of Amsterdam and his group, is quite transparent, the motivation of Cromwell and of the others who advocated the Readmission forms an interesting and far from simple problem. The considerations which had once prompted European rulers to invite Jews into their territory were not relevant to the England of Cromwell. Credit facilities were fully adequate[4] and the advocates of Readmission on economic grounds based their argument on the economic activities of the existing Jewish community, which included neither moneylending[5] nor retail trade (the latter being restricted to those who had the freedom of the city). The state, moreover, had a relatively well-developed system of taxation and borrowing and required no assistance from the Jews in this field.[6]

We must, therefore, examine the possibility of the existence of economic motives of the contemporary type, namely, those dear to mercantilism. The main goal of mercantilism was to promote trade in order to increase the amount of bullion in the country, and it is from this perspective that we must analyze the sources. In considering the part played by mercantilist doctrine in the contemporary writings dealing with the Readmission, it must be noted at the outset that the writers divide themselves into two sharply defined classes: (1) the great majority who emphasized theological, political or other non-economic points of view;[7] (2) the "economic writers" who

2. Cecil Roth, *History of the Jews in England* (1941) pp. 132–49; H. S. Q. Henriques, *The Jews and English Law* (1908) pp. 62, 79–80; Roth, *A History of the Marranos* (1932) pp. 252–59; Lucien Wolf, "Crypto-Jews under the Commonwealth" (1893–94) pp. 55–89.

3. Roth (1941) pp. 164–66. The establishment of an open synagogue in London in 1656 implies the recognition of legal residence; Wolf, *Menasseh ben Israel's Mission to Oliver Cromwell* (1901) p. lvi f.; Wolf (1893–94) pp. 111–12. See also Wolf, "Status of the Jews after the Resettlement" (1899–1901) pp. 183–84; Roth (1941) pp. 211–12. On the Readmission in general, see ibid., pp. 149–73; Wolf (1901) pp. xi ff; W. K. Jordan, *The Development of Religious Toleration in England* (1938) vol. iii, pp. 208–18.

4. Cf. R. Tawney in the introduction to his edition of Thomas Wilson, *A Discourse on Usury* (1925).

5. Wolf, (1893–94) pp. 73–74; (1901) p. lxx.

6. Cf. Viner (1937) pp. 22–25; G. M. Trevelyan, *English Social History* (1942) p. 32.

7. See above, n. 2.

referred to the question only in passing as part of the general exposition of their economic policies. The writers who argued from a non-economic viewpoint, nevertheless, frequently emphasized the economic gain to be derived from the Jews. We see this, for instance, in the petition which David Abravanel Dormido (writing under the alias David Abravanel) of Amsterdam presented to Cromwell, emphasizing the increase in trade, the addition to the state coffers, the increased population and employment, and the growth of the sea-carrying trades—all matters of great concern for mercantilist policy.[8]

Menasseh ben Israel also came to realize the importance of the economic motives; his *Humble Addresses* (1655) contained practically nothing of his earlier religious arguments for Readmission (*Hope of Israel*, 1650), but dealt entirely with the alleged benefits the rulers of a nation could expect from the Jews. These benefits are the "Profit they [the rulers] may receive from them [the Jews]; Fidelity they hold toward their Princes; and the Nobleness and purity of their blood." The main emphasis is on profit: "Profit is a most powerfull motive, and which all the World preferres before all other things: and therefore we shall handle that point first" (p. 1).[9] Menasseh began his analysis by stating the general proposition: "It is a thing confirmed, that merchandising is, as it were, the proper profession of the Nation of the Jews." Princes have realized this fact and therefore have frequently invited Jews to settle in their lands, and have extended special privileges to them. And in each case the Prince has benefited by his action because the Jews enriched his realm (pp. 2–3). To substantiate this claim Menasseh proceeded to enumerate and describe the various Jewish communities in Europe and the Orient, laying special emphasis on their importance and power in the Turkish empire.[10] The Jews will by their trade provide commodities "not onely . . . requisite and necessary for the life of man; but also what may serve for ornament to his civill condition" (p. 3).[11]

In sum, Menasseh claimed, this trade offers five important benefits for the English nation:

1. The augmentation of the Publiq Tolls and Customes, at their coming and going out of the place.

2. The transporting and bringing in of marchandises from remote countries.

3. The affording of Materials in great plenty for all Mechaniqs; as Wooll, Leather, Wines; Jewels, as Diamants, Pearles, and such like Merchandize.

4. The venting and exportation of many kinds of Manifactures.

5. The Commerce and reciprocall Negotiation at Sea, which is the ground of

8. Text in Wolf, "American Elements in the Resettlement" (1896–98) pp. 88–90; cf. Viner (1937) pp. 51–57. On marranos trading under aliases, see Lionel D. Barnett, ed. and trans., *El Libro de los Acuerdos, Being the Records and Accompts of the Spanish and Portuguese Synagogues of London from 1663 to 1681* (1931), p. xi; Herbert I. Bloom, *The Economic Activities of the Jews of Amsterdam in the Seventeenth and Eighteenth Centuries* (1937) pp. 90 ff.

9. Menasseh did not discuss the last of these three benefits, on the ground that it had been sufficiently demonstrated by other writers (*ibid.*, p. 23). The references to the religious arguments occur only in the prefatory remarks.

10. Singled out because of the importance of the Levant trade.

11. Evidently a reference to the important part played by the Jews in the luxury trades.

Peace between neighbour Nations, and of great profit to their own Fellow-citizens.[12]

Jews will also increase the wealth of the realm, argued Menasseh, through their contacts with their marrano brethren in Spain. The latter are anxious to send out "their moneys and goods" to Jews in safe places in order to avoid total confiscation in case of apprehension by the Inquisition. [p. 3] [13] Further, there is no danger (as with other strangers admitted to trade) that the Jews will accumulate wealth and then return with it to their native land. For the Jews have no "proper place of their own" and wherever "the Jews are once kindly receaved, they make a firm resolution never to depart from thence." [p. 4]

Contemporary English writers also dealt with the economic aspects of the Readmission. Bishop Barlow, for example, mentioned in passing that when the Jews lived in England they had been an important source of revenue for the Crown.[14] One D. L. claimed that they could increase the wealth of the country;[15] to the contention that the Jews are dangerous he answered:

. . . why more here than in other Countreys? . . . in matter of trade they will be dangerous, they will quicken it, heighten, augment, advance it, and enrich it: but have they any Ships of transportation to Countreys to send wealth to; where can they lay it safe? . . . How does Turkie abound in all sorts of provisions notwithstanding all the Jews throughout the Emperor's Dominions? and therefore the danger is blown over, it is onely in conceit not in reality.[16]

As a further illustration, we find Major General Whalley writing to Secretary Thurloe in December, 1655:

. . . they bring in much wealth into this commonwealth; and where wee both pray for theyr conversion, and beleeve it shal be I know not why wee should deny the meanes.[17]

Outstanding among those who denied the validity of the economic arguments was William Prynne, whose book was published just before the Whitehall Conference.[18] Following an elaborate exposé of the legal and religious grounds to support his claim

12. The fifth point seems to be an expression of a current theological concept: by divine foresight, every nation is endowed with different kinds of resources. Consequently an international division of labor is created and international trade becomes necessary. In this way one nation is made dependent on the other, thus bringing about the divine purpose of encouraging peace and universal brotherhood among the nations; cf. Viner (1937) pp. 100–103. Menasseh refers to this argument again in his *Vindiciae Judaeorum* (1656) pp. 33–34.

13. The passage is obscure but this seems to be its meaning.

14. Thomas Barlow, *Several Miscellaneous & Weighty Cases of Conscience Learnedly & Judiciously Resolved* (1692) pp. 7, 74.

15. D. L., *Israel's Condition and Cause Pleaded; or Some Arguments for the Jews Admission into England* (1656) pp. 63–69.

16. *Ibid.*, pp. 72–73.

17. John Thurloe, *Collection of State Papers* (1742) vol. iv, p. 308.

18. William Prynne, *A Short Demurrer to the Jewes Long discontinued barred Remitter into England* (1656).

that the Jews had no right to be admitted, he turned to a refutation of those who believed in the possibility of converting the Jews and in the economic gain to be derived from their readmission. Prynne first entered a general denial of Menasseh's promise of economic gain. Though this is the argument Menasseh "most insists on," nevertheless, "he handles it so, that every eye may see he aims more at his own Nations profit, benefit, advance, than ours." Even if the truth of the claim is admitted, still "this argument, for their readmission, is but worldly, carnal, sensual." And if on the basis of it the Jews will be readmitted, then we will "betray and sell our Saviour Christ again to the Jews, like Judas, for thirty pieces of silver." Any possible gain to be derived from their readmission would be dishonest, and God would therefore destroy it.[19] Who will gain by the Readmission? From past experience, wrote Prynne, we know that it will not be the nation as a whole but only "the King and some of his bribed officers" who will gain by levying oppressive taxation on and by "plundering the poor Jews." [20] Furthermore, the Jews indulge in bad trade practices and take away the trade from English merchants. If the government is really desirous of improving the economic state of the nation, Prynne concluded, it would do much better to undertake more useful policies; for example, "the taking off all long continued, uncessant, new, illegal, Taxes, Excises, Imposts" and the like.[21]

One W. H., agreeing with Prynne, wrote a pamphlet specifically in answer to Menasseh's *Humble Addresses*. Rejecting the claim of material advantage, this author declared that even if it were true, there would still be no reason to admit the Jews:

> Profit is indeed the thing that all Kingdoms and States must look after, and with good reason, for money is the comfort of peace, and the sinews of war; but such profit is onely desirable, as is joyned with glory to God, honor to the Magistrate and Countrey, and the safety and prosperity of the subject.[22]

W. H. warned that the Jews would only displace the native merchants, thereby nullifying the contribution of the former in the form of increased customs and excises. "Might they not hereby ingross the Trade wholly to themselves, and serving one another, cheat the Natives in their Traffick?" Finally, he asked, if the Jews are a source of profit, as Menasseh claims, why are they always in search of new homes? [23]

The arguments bearing on the mercantilistic aspect of the question played an important role during the Whitehall Conference, especially at the last session held December 18, 1655. Whereas on previous days the Conference had discussed legal and religious questions, on that final day the argument concerned itself primarily with the commercial and economic aspects of the issue. The greatest opposition came, as would be expected, from the merchants of the City. A contemporary account tells us that they claimed that the result of the Readmission would be to "inrich foreigners,

19. *Ibid.*, pp. 119–20.
20. *Ibid.*, p. 121.
21. *Ibid.*, pp. 121–22.
22. W. H., *Anglo-Judaeus or the History of the Jews Whilst Here in England* (1656) p. 33.
23. *Ibid.*, p. 36 ff.

and impoverish English merchants.'' [24] The merchants were so vociferous that in his concluding remarks Cromwell is reported to have addressed a rebuke to them:

> You say that they [the Jews] are the meanest and most despised of all people. So be it. But in that case what become of your fears? Can you really be afraid that this contemptible and despised people should be able to prevail in trade and credit over the merchants of England, the noblest and most esteemed merchants of the whole world? [25]

The opposition of the merchants is further attested by the tentative report of the Council of State, drawn up as a result of the Whitehall Conference.[26] Considering the proposal that ''the Jewes deservinge it may be admitted into this nation to trade and trafficke and dwel amongst us as providence shall give occasion,'' the report listed several objections, among which we find the following:

> That great prejudice is like to arise to the natives of this Commonwealth in matter of trade, which besides other dangers here mentioned we find very commonly suggested by the inhabitants of the city of London.

There were, however, others at the Conference who did not consider the question solely in terms of the private interests of the merchant class. As Jessey tells us:

> Some judged, seeing the Jews deal chiefly in way of merchandise, and not in husbandry, not buying houses nor in manufactures, that the Jews coming, and so trading, might tend to the bringing lower the prices of all sorts of commodities imported: and to the furtherance of all that have commodities to be exported; and to the benefit of most of our manufactures, where they shall live, by their buying of them. And thus though the merchants gains were somewhat abated, it might tend to the benefit of very many in our nation, even in outward things, besides the hopes of their conversion; which time it is hoped, is now at hand, even at the door.[27]

A preacher named Newcomen also spoke very much along these lines.[28]

Thomas Collier undertook to refute Prynne's accusations.[29] To the claim that the Jews would ruin England's trade by flooding the market with goods, Collier offered several replies:

---

24. See the pamphlet on the Whitehall Conference attributed to Henry Jessey (1656), reprinted in *Harleian Miscellany* (1810), vol. 6, p. 450.

25. This speech has been reconstructed by Wolf from several contemporary reports (1901) p. liii. It is indeed very unfortunate that we have not been able to find any of Cromwell's speeches or letters on the question of the Readmission.

26. For the nature of this report, see Wolf (1901) pp. liv-lv; the text is reprinted on pp. lxxxiv f. This report was never acted upon.

27. [Jessey] (1656), p. 450.

28. Moses Margoliouth, *The History of the Jews in Great Britain* (1851) vol. ii, pp. 14–15.

29. *A Brief Answer to some of the Objections and Demurs made against the Coming in and Inhabiting of the Jews in this Commonwealth* (1656).

I suppose there might and are as well waise of exportation as of importation, the more is brought in, the more may be carryed out, &c.[30] . . . If it should be more loss to some rich Merchants, yet it would be advantage to the people in general, the more is brought in the plentier and cheaper it would be, what a few rich men might lose, a great many poor men might gain, and that would be indeed and in truth no loss at all. . . . Shall we prize a little merchants gain, before our duty to God, and good of soules; God forbid, sad will that gain be both the Merchants and others that is purchased at so dear a rate, it may cost them their own soules too for ought I know and what will it profit a man to get the world and lose his own soul? [31]

From the foregoing survey of the economic aspects of the polemic two very interesting questions arise: (1) what was the relative importance of these economic arguments in this literature, and (2) to what extent were they correct formulations of the prevalent mercantilist theory? The first question is the more easily answered: the literature on the Readmission was concerned primarily with the religious (conversionist and messianic) and legal rather than the economic aspects.[32] Prynne's *A Short Demurrer*, for example, is limited almost entirely to the legal and religious objections; Jessey's narrative of the proceedings at Whitehall consists almost entirely of scriptural exegesis; of the thirteen objections answered by Collier only two have economic implications, and this writer offered no economic counterarguments; John Dury likewise rejected all but the conversionist motive.[33]

As for the second question, there are indications that many of the writers on both sides did not have a thorough understanding of the mercantilist doctrines they were attempting to apply. For example, we know that the Jews of that period were prominent as bullion merchants, largely due to their importance in the Spanish trade.[34] For the mercantilist state, with its primary goal of increasing its stock of bullion, this would have been an argument of the utmost importance. Yet nowhere does Menasseh make mention of this point. Again, Menasseh repeatedly emphasizes in vivid detail the great increase of imports, especially of luxuries, that the Readmission will bring about, but makes only incidental references to the far more important question (for mercantilist policy) of the increase in exports that the Jews might

30. I do not believe that Collier had in mind here any necessity for equality between exports and imports. What he seems to say is that just as the superior abilities of the Jews enable them to import extensively, so will their superior abilities enable them to export large amounts.

31. *Ibid.*, p. 33. The "duty to God" here was the duty to admit the Jews in order to bring about their conversion. Thus Collier took Prynne's argument that economic gain should not predominate over religious principles (see above) and used it to demonstrate the opposite conclusion!

32. The preponderance of the religious emphasis in the polemics is evident from the publications listed in Roth, *Magna Bibliotheca Anglo-Judaica* (1937) section B 1. See also Vilensky (1943) preface; Osterman (1941).

33. See his *A Case of Conscience* . . . (1656); reprinted in *Harleian Miscellany*.

34. Cf. e.g. Wolf (1901) pp. xxix-xxx.

promote.[35] The only possible defense of Menasseh's emphasis on imports could be along the lines of the "policy of provision" (encouraging imports), which Heckscher has shown to exist as an undertone in many mercantilist writings. But from his discussion it appears quite unlikely that this policy applied to the import of luxuries; by the time of the Readmission, moreover, the "provision policy" had given way to the more typical mercantilist policy of protectionism.[36]

Further evidence of the existence in Menasseh's mind of views inconsistent with mercantilism is afforded in his list of benefits which the English might derive from the readmission of the Jews. Not only is the general tone of that section entirely out of keeping with mercantilist writings, but in his discussion of the fifth benefit Menasseh made use of a theological argument in favor of increasing international trade as much as possible. This very argument was, however, widely used in favor of free trade, for only by free trade could each nation make full use of its particular resources—a concept *diametrically opposed* to the traditional mercantilist policy of protectionism.[37] Menasseh's ineptitude in mercantilist theory is especially revealed in the sixth section of his *Vindiciae*, where he admitted that the "business of Merchandise" is "lesse pertaining to . . . [his] . . . faculty." Here his tone is quite different from that of his *Humble Addresses*; it is quite possible that this change resulted from adverse criticism of the earlier pamphlet with respect to its economic arguments.[38]

Most of the English writers were just as confused as Menasseh. Prynne contended, on the one hand, that the Jews will harm the English trade, but at the same time opposed their admission on religious grounds, to which he gave precedence over all other considerations. No "true" mercantilist would have invoked any spiritual factor in the formulation of policy; for mercantilism posited amoral, materialistic ends (increase of trade and bullion) to be pursued by amoral means. Similarly, the debate over the alleged usurious character of the Jews was irrelevant from the mercantilist viewpoint.[39] In general, few of the participants in the polemic failed to intersperse religious and superstitious diatribes among their economic arguments. Thus, all of them demonstrated their failure to understand the fundamentals of mercantilist policy.

Our problem accordingly is to explain why, in view of their unfamiliarity with mercantilist doctrine, these writers insisted on attempting to introduce economic considerations? Two explanations may be offered. First, we must consider the possibility that the study of mercantilist doctrine was in Cromwell's time limited to the theorists and had not achieved popularity. Consequently, the writers appealed to the masses in their own (non-mercantilist) terms. Inasmuch as writers like Prynne,

35. The criticism to which Collier replied (quoted above) may have been directed against Menasseh's overemphasis on imports; the latter's *Vindiciae Judaeorum* also seems to offer a rebuttal of such criticism. Thomas Violet likewise emphasized the danger of the great increase in imports that the Jews were expected to bring about; see below.

36. Cf. Heckscher (1935) vol. ii, pp. 80–111, 114–17, 289–93; cf. Viner (1937) pp. 90–91.

37. Cf. Viner (1937) pp. 100–103.

38. Menasseh (1656) p. 33; on p. 54, point 3, he also seems to confess lack of acquaintance with commercial practices. On the other hand, it should be noted that Menasseh was for some time the head of a publishing house.

39. Cf. Heckscher (1935) vol. ii, pp. 285–303.

however, were primarily interested in influencing the nation's policymakers (who definitely were followers of mercantilist thought) rather than the general public, this seems quite unlikely. Indeed, there did not exist a distinct body of professional theorists separated from the laity. Most mercantilists were ordinary businessmen, often using their writings to promote their personal interests.[40] Mercantilist opinion *was* popular opinion.

Secondly, the writers who engaged in this polemic were primarily propagandists who employed any argument that could be advanced to support their position. The predominance of mercantilist thought had created a conventionally accepted pattern of argumentation (or discussion) employing mercantilist terminology, concepts and symbols. Consequently, despite their primary interest in the religious aspects of the question, these writers presented some of their arguments in economic terms as a concession to the fashion of the time. Unfortunately they were not sufficiently versed in mercantilist doctrine to apply it correctly; they knew only its slogans but not their applications. The positions of these writers will appear more clearly when contrasted with that of the mercantilists to be discussed below.

The Economic Writers

The exponents of mercantilism were interested in expressing their opinions on the question of the Readmission only indirectly and only because in the general process of expounding their economic policies they were also called upon to discuss the relationship of trade to tolerance.[41] These writers undeviatingly and amorally directed their efforts toward the goal of increasing the trade of the country. In this they were greatly influenced by the example of Holland, the prototype of the successful mercantilist state.[42] Whatever Holland did was correct economic policy; Holland had adopted a system of complete tolerance, which included the Jews; *ergo*, complete tolerance was also the correct economic policy for England. Thus we find William Petty pointing out that one of the reasons for the economic success of the Dutch was their policy of "Liberty of Conscience." He then proceeded to give other examples of this principle, mentioning specifically the Jews in the Turkish empire.[43] Again, Roger Coke, in explaining how the "Dutch manage a Greater Domestick Trade than the English," gave as one of the reasons the fact that "The Dutch freely entertain men of all Nations in Trade, and give them equal freedom with the Natural born Dutch." [44]

40. Cf. Viner (1937) pp. 58–59; Erich Roll, *A History of Economic Thought* (1939) pp. 63–87.

41. A word of caution as to the limited validity of this method is appropriate here. It is important to remember that in the period under study one could argue for "toleration" with no intention of extending it to Jews. But in most of the references discussed here either the Jews are mentioned specifically or there are other reasons for assuming that the writer intended to include them.

42. Cf. Clark (1929) pp. 14–16; Maurice P. Ashley, *Oliver Cromwell* (1937) p. 269.

43. William Petty, *Political Arithmetick* (1690), vol. i, pp. 262–63.

44. Roger Coke, *Reasons of the Increase of the Dutch Trade*, Treatise II; published with and consecutively paged with Treatise I, *A Treatise Wherein is demonstrated that the Church and State of England are in Equal Danger with the Trade of it* (1671), pp. 109 ff; cf. also his *England's Improvements* (1675) pp. 77–88. Cf. Henry Robinson, *Certain Proposals In order to the Peoples Freedome and Accomodation in some Particulars. With the Advancement of Trade and Navigation of this Common-Wealth in generale* (1652) pp. 12–13. For another economic aspect of Robinson's program for toleration, cf. W. K. Jordan, *Men of Substance* (1942) pp. 223–24.

At a later date Sir Josiah Child justified the Readmission and argued for naturalization of the Jews on the ground that:

> The subtiller the Jews are, and the more Trades they pry into while they live here, the more they are likely to encrease Trade, and the more they do that, the better it is for the Kingdom in general, though the worse for the English Merchant, who comparatively to the rest of the People of England is not one of a thousand. . . . It is denied that they bring over nothing with them; for many have brought hither very good Estates and hundreds more would do the like, and settle here for their lives, and their Posterities after them, if they had the same Freedom and Security here as they have in Holland and Italy, where the grand Duke of Tuscany, and other Princes allow them not only perfect Liberty and Security, but give them the privilege of making Laws among themselves.[45]

Not all the commercial writers, however, took this position. On November 30, 1660 Thomas Violet presented a petition to the newly restored Charles II, purporting to demonstrate that historically the Jews had no legal right to remain in England.[46] In another petition presented to Charles in the following year Violet declared that the Jews

> . . . fill the Kingdom with unnecessary commodities, and make returns with our money, see their importation and exportation, this will be found true, they have cozened us of many score thousand pounds of our Gold and Silver.[47]

An antagonistic position was also taken by John Bland in his *Trade Revived* (1660). Bland claimed that historically, wherever Jews were admitted to a country, they exploited both rich and poor alike by their farming of the taxes. He also accused the Jews of counterfeiting coins. Even if England were in need of money, it should still not admit the Jews; for the Jews will lend only under the severest terms. He blamed the Jews as the cause of the doubling of the price English merchants had to pay for Canary Island wines, resulting in an outflow of bullion.[48] In general Bland denied that the admission of the Jews would bring about an increase in the volume of English trade, on the ground that "the Stock of England is too great for its own trade." [49] English merchants are already supplying their factors abroad with more than the latter can sell; and English merchants are already importing more "than the Nation can

45. Josiah Child, *A New Discourse of Trade* (1693) pp. 122–27.
46. The text of this petition is reprinted in Wolf, "Status of the Jews after the Resettlement" (1899–1901) pp. 188–92. It is very difficult to apply the classification adopted above to Violet. On the one hand he wrote from an economic point of view and so should be classified as an "economic writer." On the other, he had violent prejudices on the question of the Readmission and so could be considered as a "non-economic writer." Inasmuch as many of his other writings were of an economic nature, I have chosen the former category.
47. Thomas Violet, *A Petition Against the Jews Presented to the Kings Majestie & the Parliament etc.* (1661) p. 4.
48. Bland (1660), pp. 21–22.
49. *Ibid.*, p. 22.

spend.'' Consequently, Bland concluded, it is necessary ''that all Jews lately crept into this Nation, and its Dominions, be extirpated and banished. . . .'' [50]

Violet and Bland, however, remained the exceptions to the prevailing mercantilist position, and their importance is hardly comparable with that of men like Petty and Child. As Heckscher concludes, ''Toleration was the unanimous demand of all theoretical and practical economic politicians under mercantilism. . . . this much is clear, that the leaders of mercantilist policy wished to extend toleration even to Jews, and that this toleration was determined primarily by commercial considerations.'' [51]

The Historical Importance

We must now turn to the infinitely more involved question of the part played by mercantilist policy as a factor in the process which led to the Readmission. The historians of England have followed the Jewish historians in considering the primary causes to have been mercantilist in nature. Lucien Wolf has described the Readmission as ''one of Cromwell's own schemes—part and parcel of that dream of Imperial expansion.'' The Jews were to be used ''as very desirable instruments of his colonial and commercial policy.'' [52] In his recent history Cecil Roth has written: ''The whole question of the readmission of the Jews was, from one point of view, simply an episode in the Anglo-Dutch and Anglo-Spanish rivalry.'' [53]

The fundamental question is that of the *relative* importance of mercantilist policy. The England of our period had as its fundamental economic policy the increase of its trade. In order to achieve this end it adopted many measures. Since it appeared that the Jews residing in London could also do their bit to increase trade, among the measures adopted was one permitting them to remain in England. The decision to retain the Jews did not represent a special formulation of policy stimulated by the sudden recognition of the economic importance of the Jews. The England of Cromwell had

---

50. *Ibid.*, p. 20.

51. Heckscher (1935) vol. ii, pp. 303–35. Heckscher considers this attitude of mercantilism toward toleration as the reason for the improved position of the Jews in the seventeenth century ''in most western and central European countries.'' He cites the examples of Colbert in France (1673) and the Great Elector of Brandenburg (1671). Heckscher also recognizes that other factors besides ''commercial considerations'' were at work: specifically, ''the purely financial requirements of the state'' and ''sometimes even the religious interest in the mission among the Jews.''

52. Cf. [Jessey] (1656) and his report of the Conference: ''The protector shewed a favourable inclination towards our harbouring the afflicted Jews, professing he had no engagements, but upon Scripture grounds, in several speeches he made.'' (pp. 450–51) Even if Cromwell had had economic motivations, it is possible that he would have concealed them for fear of alienating the support of those advocating the Readmission on religious grounds; and for fear of further alarming the merchants of the City, to whom the prospect of Jewish competition was naturally distasteful; cf. Wolf (1901) pp. xl, xxix–xxx.

53. Roth (1941) pp. 157–58. But Roth recognizes the recent tendency to give less emphasis to Cromwell's economic and commercial interests, and suggests the possible need for a reinterpretation of Cromwell's attitude toward the Jews in view of this fact; cf. *ibid.*, p. 158, n. 1. For other writers on Cromwell's motives, cf., e.g., G. Burnet, *History of My Own Times* (1897) vol. i, p. 127; Ashley (1937) pp. 268–69.

already undergone great economic development during the Elizabethan period,[54] and the commercial activities of one or two hundred Jews could not have weighed much in the balance.[55] The decision to readmit the Jews was rather an incidental consequence of a general policy which had been formulated quite independently of the Jewish question.[56]

We must, accordingly, recognize the greater importance of the previously mentioned religious and messianic enthusiasts working for the Readmission. Again, the explanation of Cromwell's support of the Readmission may lie to a greater degree than has been realized in his personal character and in the particular circumstances confronting him. There is no doubt that Cromwell felt personally indebted to several Jews for services they had rendered to him. He was acquainted with several of the London marranos, and they had been of great assistance to him as intelligencers and army contractors. Lucien Wolf has especially emphasized the importance of these obligations and their influence on Cromwell's decision.[57] Even if it were granted that the Jews were of considerable economic importance, it would still be questionable whether we can attribute to Cromwell that degree of economic motivation which is assumed by the accepted hypothesis. In an essay on the general question of Cromwell's economic record, William Cunningham has shown that Cromwell neglected many matters relating to the economic welfare of England. He concerned himself little with the procuring of necessary imports, the obtaining of trade privileges and the like, and was not in favor of the Navigations Act of 1651. In general, Cromwell did little to remove the resentment against British traders which had been created by the beheading of Charles. Most of the commercial regulations of Cromwell's government were carry-overs from Charles, and "he was halfhearted or careless about matters that were essential to the growth of English maritime power . . . his ideas, so far from

54. Cf., e.g., E. Lipson, *The Economic History of England* (1931) vol. ii-iii; William R. Scott, *The Constitution and Finance of English, Scottish and Irish Joint-Stock Companies to 1720* (1912); J. U. Nef, *Industry and Government in France and England 1540–1640* (1940).

55. For estimates of the population of the London Jewish community about 1655, cf. Hyamson, *History of the Jews in England*, 2nd ed. (1928) p. 138 (200 persons); Wolf (1901) p. lxv (20 families); Wolf, "Jewry of the Restoration" (1902–05) p. 12 (150 persons). London's population was then around 350,000; Lipson, *op. cit.*, vol. ii, p. 249–50. On the other hand we should remember that Menasseh was arguing for the readmission of a large number of Jews, and most of the polemicists made this assumption. In many cases, nevertheless, the question of the retention or expulsion of the existing Jewish community was argued. This was especially true in later years, when it was apparent that there would be no large influx.

56. The extent to which the economic importance of the London Jewish community has been exaggerated can be demonstrated in yet another way. The Amsterdam Jewish community is usually considered as the richest and most powerful Jewish community during this period. Certainly its Jewish population was much larger (absolutely and relatively) than the London Jewish community. Furthermore, it was much older than the London community, probably dating back to the early part of the sixteenth century. Yet Bloom's detailed study of the economic activity of the Amsterdam community exploded the traditional picture of its economic importance; (1937), pp. 219–21. I feel, then, that an equally detailed study into the economic activities of the London Jewish community of this period would *a fortiori* yield the sobering conclusion that it was much less important than is usually thought. Consequently economic considerations could hardly have been as important a factor in the Readmission as claimed by Wolf and Roth.

57. Wolf, *Essays in Jewish History* (London 1934) pp. 102–11; Wolf (1901) pp. xxix-xxx; Roth (1941) pp. 150–60; Sombart, *The Jews and Modern Capitalism* (1913) p. 50; Wolf, "The First English Jew, Notes on Antonio Fernandez Carvajal" (1894–95) pp. 14–47; Ashley (1937) pp. 268–69.

being in advance of those of his contemporaries, were actually retrograde."[58] Furthermore, Cromwell's failure to reach an understanding with and thus obtain the full financial and commercial support of the City "indicates how little mercantile interests were primary considerations to him."[59]

There is, furthermore, one other factor which has not been sufficiently emphasized. We know that Cromwell was constantly in need of funds and that the City, which should have been the most likely source of these funds, had lost its early enthusiasm and was now quite unfriendly to Cromwell. There was as yet no Bank of England or other institution on which the government could depend. Consequently, it appears likely that a very important motive of Cromwell's action was simply his desire to assure himself and his government of dependable financial support in times of stress.[60] In this respect Cromwell was acting in much the same way as the medieval princes with reference to the Jews. But it cannot be overemphasized that this motive has little in common with the "economic motive" as stressed by Wolf and Roth. These writers speak of the supposed economic advantages to Great Britain *as a whole*, in terms of world power, commercial expansion, colonization, imperialism, and the like. The motive suggested here refers merely to certain financial aspects of the struggle for power conducted by Cromwell, the Royalists and other factions.

The importance of mercantilistic considerations in the Readmission has been greatly exaggerated; they played a minor role. The personal character of Cromwell and his need for trustworthy support, fiscal and otherwise, evidently were a more decisive factor in the decision to permit Jews to enter and settle in England than historians have hitherto recognized. Consequently, it is to be regretted that there has remained for us no original record of Cromwell's speeches and letters on the question of Readmission.

Bibliography

Primary Sources

T. Barlow. *Several Miscellaneous & Weighty Cases of Conscience Learnedly & Judiciously Resolved*. London, 1692.

J. Bland. *Trade Revived*. London, 1660.

---

58. William Cunningham, "The Imperialism of Cromwell" (1906) p. 115; Cunningham cites many historians who have emphasized the economic motivations of Cromwell. I am indebted to Professor Viner for this reference.
59. Maurice P. Ashley, *Financial and Commercial Policy Under the Cromwellian Protectorate* (1934) p. 4.
60. For the relationships of Cromwell to the City and the weakness of government credit there, cf. Ashley (1937) pp. 235–36; cf. also Ashley, *Financial and Commercial Policy* (1934) pp. 3–4. Substantially the same solution as is proposed here is offered by Cunningham; see above. Ashley (1934) p. 4, also suggests this solution as "within the bounds of legitimate speculation"; cf. *ibid.*, pp. 2–3.

G. Burnet. *History of My Own Time*, ed. by his son, Sir Thomas Burnet, London 1724–34; ed. by Osmund Airy, Oxford, 1897.

J. Child. *A New Discourse of Trade*. London, 1693.

R. Coke. *Reasons of the Increase of the Dutch Trade*, Treatise II; published with and consecutively paged with Treatise I, *A Treatise Wherein is demonstrated that the Church and State of England are in Equal Danger with the Trade of it*. London, 1675.

T. Collier. *A Brief Answer to Some of the Objections and Demurs made against the Coming in and Inhabiting of the Jews in this Commonwealth*. London, 1656.

J. Dury. *A Case of Conscience. . . .* London, 1656. Reprinted in *Harleian Miscellany*. London, 1810. Vol. 6, pp. 438–44.

W. H. *Anglo-Judaeus or the History of the Jews Whilst Here in England*. London, 1656.

[H. Jessey]. *A Narrative of the Late Proceedings at Whitehall*. London, 1656. Reprinted in *Harleian Miscellany*. London, 1810. Vol. 6, pp. 445–53.

D. L. *Israel's Condition and Cause Pleaded; or Some Arguments for the Jews Admission into England*. London, 1656.

Menasseh ben Israel. *Hope of Israel*. London, 1650.

――――. *Humble Addresses*. London, 1655.

――――. *Vindiciae Judaeorum*. London, 1656.

W. Petty. *Political Arithmetick*, 1676. Reprinted in *Economic Writings of William Petty*, ed. C. H. Hall. Cambridge, 1899. Vol. 1, pp. 233–313.

W. Prynne. *A Short Demurrer to the Jewes Long discontinued barred Remitter into England*, 2nd ed., enlarged. London, 1656.

H. Robinson. *Certain Proposals In order to the Peoples Freedome and Accomodation in some Particulars. With the Advancement of Trade and Navigation of this Common-Wealth in generale*. London, 1652.

J. Thurloe. *Collection of State Papers*, vol. 4. London, 1742.

T. Violet. *A Petition Against the Jews Presented to the Kings Majestie & the Parliament etc.* London, 1661.

Secondary Sources

M. P. Ashley. *Financial and Commercial Policy Under the Cromwellian Protectorate*. London, 1934.

――――. *Oliver Cromwell*. London, 1937.

L. D. Barnett, ed. and trans. *El Libro de los Acuerdos, Being the Records and Accompts of the Spanish and Portuguese Synagogues of London from 1663–1681*. London, 1931.

H. I. Bloom. *The Economic Activities of the Jews of Amsterdam in the Seventeenth and Eighteenth Centuries*. Williamsport, 1937.

G. N. Clark. *The Seventeenth Century*. Oxford, 1929.

――――. *The Later Stuarts, 1660–1714*. Oxford, 1934. Reprinted with corrections, Oxford, 1940.

W. Cunningham. "The Imperialism of Cromwell." In *The Wisdom of the Wise*. Cambridge, 1906.

G. Davies. *The Early Stuarts, 1603–1660*. Oxford, 1937.

C. H. Firth. *The Last Years of the Protectorate*. London, 1909.

S. R. Gardiner. *History of the Commonwealth and Protectorate*, 4 vols. London, 1894–1903.

E. F. Heckscher. *Mercantilism*, trans. M. Shapiro. London, 1935.

H. S. Q. Henriques. *The Jews and English Law*. London, 1908.

A. M. Hyamson. *History of the Jews in England*, 2nd ed. London, 1928.

W. K. Jordan. *The Development of Religious Toleration in England*, vol. 3. London, 1938.

_____. *Men of Substance*. Chicago, 1942.

E. Lipson. *The Economic History of England*, vols. 2 & 3. London, 1931.

M. Margoliouth. *The History of the Jews in Great Britain*, vol. 2. London, 1851.

M. F. Modder. *The Jew in the Literature of England*. Philadelphia, 1939.

J. U. Nef. *Industry and Government in France and England 1540–1640*. Philadelphia, 1940.

N. Osterman. "The Controversy over the Proposed Readmission of the Jews to England (1655)." *Jewish Social Studies*, 1941, 3, 301–29.

E. Roll. *A History of Economic Thought*. New York, 1939.

C. Roth. *A History of the Marranos*. Philadelphia, 1932.

_____. *Magna Bibliotheca Anglo-Judaica*. London, 1937.

_____. *History of the Jews in England*. Oxford, 1941.

W. R. Scott. *The Constitution and Finance of English, Scottish, and Irish Joint-Stock Companies to 1720*. Cambridge, 1912.

W. Sombart. *The Jews and Modern Capitalism*, trans. with notes by M. Epstein. London, 1913.

R. Tawney. "Introduction" to *A Discourse on Usury* by T. Wilson. New York, 1925.

G. M. Trevelyan. *English Social History*. London, 1942.

M. Vilensky. *Shivat Ha-yehudim le-Anglia (The Return of the Jews to England)*. Tel-Aviv, 1943 (Hebrew).

J. Viner. *Studies in the Theory of International Trade*. New York, 1937.

L. Wolf. "Crypto-Jews under the Commonwealth." *Transactions of the Jewish Historical Society of England*, 1893–94, *1*, 55–88.

_____. "The First English Jew, Notes on Antonio Fernandez Carvajal." *Transactions of the Jewish Historical Society of England*, 1894–1895, 2, 14–46.

_____. "American Elements in the Resettlement." *Transactions of the Jewish Historical Society of England*, 1896–1898, *3*, 76–100.

_____. "Status of the Jews after the Resettlement." *Transactions of the Jewish Historical Society of England*, 1899–1901, *4*, 177–93.

_____. *Menasseh ben Israel's Mission to Oliver Cromwell*. London, 1901.

_____. "Jewry of the Restoration." *Transactions of the Jewish Historical Society of England*, 1902–1905, *5*, 5–33.

_____. *Essays in Jewish History*. London, 1934.

Henry C. Simons (1944)

4. Multiple-Plant Firms, Cartels, and Imperfect Competition*

Although theories of imperfect competition have long since found a recognized place in textbooks, varying degrees of dissatisfaction with them have persisted due to their restrictive assumptions. To a very considerable extent this situation must continue until we have many more detailed studies of specific firms and industries and their methods of operation. The difficulty is, of course, the procuring of information. Even if many corporations overcame their reluctance to open their books to economists, those fundamental and intimate details of corporate policy formation which are not translatable into bookkeeping entries would still be lacking. To some extent, however, the empirical evidence already available to us provides a basis for significant improvement in the theory. Accordingly, I plan in this article (1) to extend the analysis to deal with multiple-plant firms[1] and (2) to present a generalized oligopoly solution which can be employed as a frame of reference in empirical studies.

I

To illustrate the problem of multiple-plant firms, I shall first consider a case of perfect monopoly. For simplicity assume a linear demand curve remaining constant throughout the discussion, completely unspecialized factors of production (precluding any monopsony power), and a single product. Assume that the monopoly firm consists of 100 individual (and identical) plants, each of the long-run optimum size and with cost curves indicated in Figure 1, where *ac, mc,* and *avc* represent average, marginal, and average variable costs, respectively. For convenience we have assumed that the plant marginal cost curve is composed of two linear sections.

Reprinted by permission from *Quarterly Journal of Economics*, Feb. 1947, *61*, 173–205, and Aug. 1947, *61*, 650–57, Copyright © 1947 by John Wiley & Sons, Inc.

* I cannot overemphasize my debt to Professor Henry C. Simons, on whose Economics 201 *Syllabus* (mimeographed, University of Chicago Bookstore) this article is so largely based. Although Professor Simons did not see the manuscript before his untimely death, I discussed with him several of the points involved. I am also indebted to Bert Hoselitz, H. Gregg Lewis, and William H. Nicholls (all of the University of Chicago), who read an earlier draft of this article and offered valuable criticisms and suggestions.

1. The usual one-firm-one-plant analysis is completely unrealistic. Thus, in 1937 the 50 largest manufacturing corporations owned 2869 plants, or an average of 57.4 per firm. No firm owned less than seven plants, while one owned 497. (TNEC, Monograph No. 27, The *Structure of Industry*, pp. 675–714.)

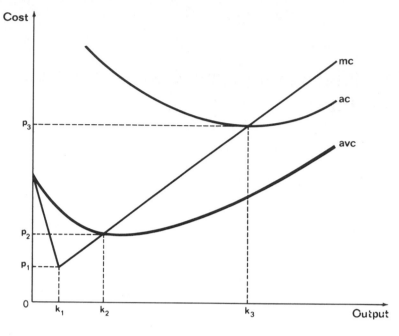

Figure 1

We turn now to the problem of constructing the monopolist's short-run marginal cost curve (Figure 2), noting that in the short-run (by definition) the monopolist cannot change the number of plants in existence. Consider a given output q_i.[2] The question is, how will the monopolist allocate this output among the different plants in order to minimize costs? The answer falls into two parts, according as q_i is greater or less than $q_2 = 100k_2$. In the former case the optimum allocation would be to have the output equally distributed among the plants. This readily follows from Figure 1. If one plant is producing more than another, its marginal cost will be higher; consequently, a reduction in total cost can be effected by shifting the output from the former to the latter.[3] This process will continue until all plants are producing the same amount. We thus get the right-hand part of the marginal cost curve in Figure 2. To construct the marginal cost curve for outputs less than q_2 we note that no plant *in operation* will produce less than k_2; any desired output $q_i < q_2$ will be produced by having x plants produce k_2 units apiece (where k_2 is the output corresponding to minimum average variable costs for the plant—cf. Figure 1), with the remaining $100 - x$ plants left idle. (x is obviously determined by the relationship $xk_2 = q_i$.) This may be proved as follows. In the short run the monopolist must bear the fixed expenses of the 100 plants. Therefore he will minimize total expenses for any given

---

2. The units of the abscissa of Figure 2 are related to those of Figure 1 by the equation $k_j = q_j / 100$ for any j.

3. This holds for the cost curves usually dealt with, but is not general. Cf. Section II below.

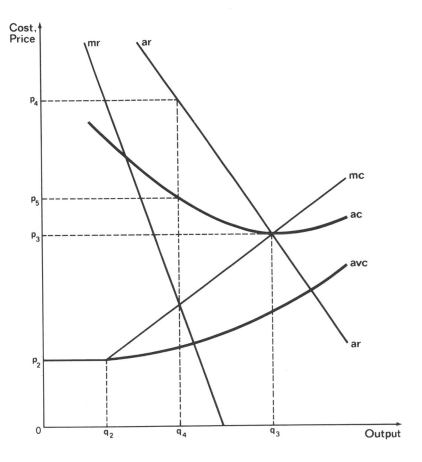

Figure 2

output by minimizing total variable expenses. Consider now the given output $q_i < q_2$. If this output were equally allocated among all plants, each plant would produce $k_i < k_2$ at an average variable cost of $p_i > p_2$. Then the total variable costs would be $100k_i\ p_i$. However, the total variable costs, if x plants were to produce k_2 apiece, would be $xk_2\ p_2$. But $100k_i\ p_i > xk_2\ p_2$, since $100k_i = xk_2 = q_i$ and $p_i > p_2$. This is perfectly general and holds for any $q_i < q_2$ and $k_i < k_2$. In this range the monopolist would operate keeping some plants idle. The average variable cost would be $xk_2\ p_2 / xk_2 = p_2$. Therefore, until q_2, the average variable cost curve is a horizontal line at a height p_2. By definition, the marginal cost curve, in this range, coincides with it.[4]

Strictly speaking the linear shape of the marginal cost curve is only an approximation which is approached as the number of plants increases. The actual shape is

---

4. The position of the marginal cost curve in this range can also be established by noting that it can never be less than p_2, for the total expenses can always be reduced by at least p_2 per unit simply by closing down a plant.

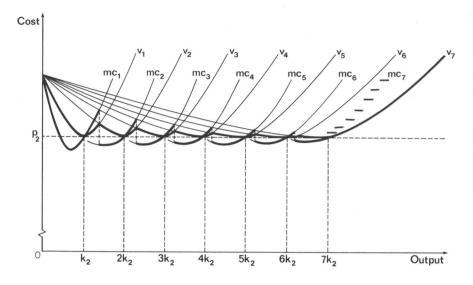

Figure 3

pictured in Figure 3; this may be considered as a "blowup" of Figure 2 (note the break in the vertical axis). For convenience, however, we have considered a firm consisting of only seven plants, each of the type described in Figure 1. v_i is the average variable cost of the firm, if i plants (neither more nor *less*) are used to produce a given output in the cheapest way possible. The v_i have a common origin, since one unit of output will always be produced by one plant producing one unit, regardless of the number of plants. As i increases, v_i tends to flatten out, since any given increase in output will increase the output per plant less the more plants there are. From our previous discussion we know that v_i will reach its minimum at an output of ik_2 and a height of p_2 ($i = 1, 2 \ldots 7$); that is, the minimum points are equidistant and at the same height.[5] The intersection of v_i and v_{i+1} indicates where it would be profitable to employ an additional plant. The heavy kinked [6] curve is thus the relevant average variable cost curve of the firm. It is tangent to the horizontal line (p_2 units high) at the outputs nk_2 ($n = 1, 2 \ldots 7$). Similarly, we construct a marginal cost curve mc_i for each v_i. For higher values of i, mc_i will approach closer to v_i since the latter tends to flatten out. It is possible that ranges may exist for which mc_i becomes a step function. This is especially true for the rising part, where the assumption that output will be equally allocated is more probable; mc_7 is drawn on this assumption. Then an output of $7k_2 + 1$ is produced, with six plants producing k_2 and one producing $k_2 + 1$; an output of $7k_2 + i$

5. These results are given more generally with the aid of some very neat mathematics in M. F. W. Joseph, "A Discontinuous Cost Curve and the Tendency to Increasing Returns" (1933), pp. 390–93. However, the exposition there is impaired by the unwarranted assumption that any output is equally allocated among plants. Cf. Section II of this article.

6. That is, a *continuous* curve with *discontinuous derivatives* at certain points. Curves of this type have been erroneously referred to in the literature as "discontinuous."

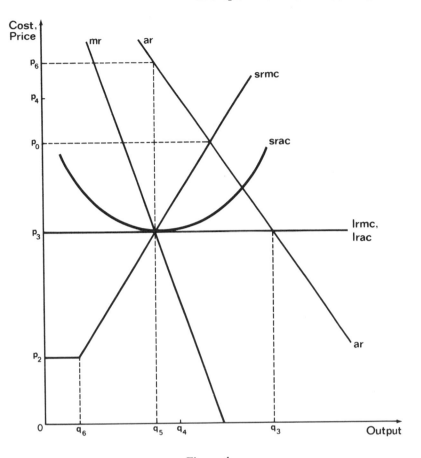

Figure 4

$(i=2, 3 . . . 7)$ is produced by having $7-i$ plants produce k_2 apiece, and i produce k_2+1—so that the marginal cost for all these outputs is the same. Thus, for outputs greater than $7k_2$, mc_7 is a rising step function, with steps seven units wide. On corresponding assumptions, in Figure 2 the marginal cost curve for outputs greater than q_2 is a step function with steps 100 units wide. As long as the width of the step is small relative to the scale of Figure 2, we can approximate the rising part of the curve by a straight line.

In fact, due to the decreasing portions of the v_i and mc_i curves, we cannot construct these curves by allocating the output equally among the i plants. There do not seem to be any short-cut rules to follow, and the curves can be constructed only by trial and error allocations of the given output in different ways among the i plants and noting which way minimizes total variable cost. Similarly, it is impossible to determine by any simple rule when v_i and v_{i+1} will intersect—that is, when a new plant will be brought into operation. There might even be multiple intersection of v_i and v_{i+1}. For differently shaped plant cost curves we get entirely different results. Thus, for example, in the case of two plants we can construct cost curves such that the total variable cost is minimized by having one plant produce on the *rising* part of its marginal cost curve, and the other on the *falling* part (see Section II of this article).

Since the allocation of any given output is now determined, we can construct the other cost curves in Figure 2, making use of the data in Figure 1. For the demand curve *ar* the optimum output is at q_4, and the per-unit monopoly profit is $p_4 - p_5$. The usual textbook analysis stops at this point, with the implication that the monopolist is not producing at the point of minimum average cost (q_3) and should make no attempt to do so if he is to maximize profits. This certainly holds for the short run, but in the long run the monopolist can change his position by adjusting the number of plants through investment and disinvestment.

The problem is then one of determining the long-run cost curves of the monopolist (cf. Figure 4). The fundamental fact which must be noted here is that even in the long run the monopoly will not proceed to build different sized plants; investment and disinvestment in the firm will take place only by changing the number of plants. This follows from our assumption that the existing plants are of the long-run optimum size.

The construction of the monopolist's long-run average cost curve is analogous to the construction of the short-run average variable cost curve for outputs less than q_2. The process is identical if we note that in the long run (by definition) all costs are variable costs. We need only to observe that in the argument p_2 is replaced by p_3 and q_2 becomes infinitely large. In the long run the monopolist will minimize the cost of producing any output q_j by arranging his investment and disinvestment policies so that he will have exactly y plants, each producing k_3 (cf. Figure 1), where y is determined by the relation $y = q_j / k_3$. In other words, the optimum method of producing any given output is to have each plant producing at its minimum average cost point, and adjusting the number of plants (by investment and disinvestment) so that the desired output can be produced. The total cost of *any* output q_j will then be $y k_3 p_3$ and the average cost p_3, so that the long-run average cost curve (*lrac*) will be a horizontal line at the height p_3; the long-run marginal cost curve (*lrmc*) will coincide with it.[7]

The long-run equilibrium price and output in Figure 4 (assuming *ar* to remain constant) are p_6 and q_5, respectively. The long-run price and monopoly profits are each greater than in the short run. Once the optimum long-run output q_5 is determined, the optimum number of plants in the long run—$m = q_5 / k_3$—is simultaneously determined. Thus, in the long run the monopolist will have m plants and the short-run average and marginal cost curves *srac* and *srmc* (Figure 4). *srac* will obviously have its minimum point at the output q_5, since for that output each of the m plants will be producing at its own minimum point k_3. Since $m < 100$, the marginal cost curve for the firm with m plants remains horizontal at p_2 over a shorter interval than when the firm consists of 100 plants. Specifically, for the case of m plants, *mc* remains constant only until $q_6 = m k_2 < q_2 = 100 k_2$. It is interesting to note that in the long run the monopolist will *of necessity* be producing at the minimum point of his short-run average cost

---

7. We must make reservations here analogous to those made above concerning the shape of the average variable cost curve for outputs less than q_2.

curve. We must now determine what particular assumption we have made that has led to this unusual result.

First let us distinguish between intraplant and interplant economies and diseconomies. Intraplant economies are what we usually have in mind when we speak of economies of large-scale production. These are derived from increases in the size of plant which enable use of more specialized and efficient machinery, develop skills in performing specialized tasks, eliminate movements of workers, and so on. Interplant economies are reductions in (social) cost following from the fact that two or more plants operate under a common management, instead of being separately owned. These take the form of economies in purchases and sales of materials, research, flexibility, "scientific management," riskbearing, financing, integration, etc. Diseconomies of both types are due to increasing difficulties of coördination, bureaucratic inefficiency, etc. That there are substantial and continuing intraplant economies has been shown to be true in many industries[8] but on the question of interplant economies very little empirical evidence is available. Similarly, we have little information about the diseconomies.

Let us now consider the long-run average cost curve (Figure 5).[9] The curve c_1 is the traditional Harrod-Viner envelope of the family of one-plant short-run cost curves s_1. The specific s_1 (say s_{11}) which is tangent to c_1 at the latter's minimum point is (by assumption) our curve of Figure 1. Consider now any specific curve of the s_2 family—say s_{21}. This curve is constructed by allocating a given output in the best way possible among two plants of *arbitrary size*. We construct an s_2 curve for every possible combination of different size plants. We then construct the c_2 curve by marking off for any given output an ordinate equal to that of the lowest point on any member of the family of curves s_2 for that given output. Strictly speaking, c_2 is not an envelope curve, since there can obviously be members of s_2 which do not touch it: for example, s_{22} in Figure 5. From our previous exposition we know that the s_2 curve tangent to c_2 at the latter's minimum point is that formed from two identical plants each of the size indicated in Figure 1. A similar interpretation holds for the other s_{jr} and c_i curves. The latter will tend to flatten out as i increases. We know from our preceding discussion that c_i will reach its minimum for an output of k_3i at a height of p_3 ($i=1, 2, \ldots \infty$); that is, the minimum points are equidistant and at the same height.[10] The intersection of c_j and c_{j+1} indicates where it would be profitable for the monopolist to build a $(j+1)$-st plant. The heavy kinked curve is therefore the long-run average cost curve. In the case of other indivisibilities, the c_i curves would also be kinked, resulting in the long-run average cost curve having still more kinks than pictured here. The long-run marginal cost curve is discontinuous and of the same general shape of that in Figure 3 (for outputs less than $7k_2$), except that it extends indefinitely out, approaching more and more to the horizontal line at p_3. In order not to make Figure 5 too cumbersome, this curve has not been included.

8. J. M. Blair, "The Relation between Size and Efficiency of Business" (1942), pp. 125–35; Joseph Steindl, *Small and Big Business* (1945).
9. Figure 5 may be considered as a blowup of Figure 4; note the break in the vertical axis.
10. Cf. note 5 above.

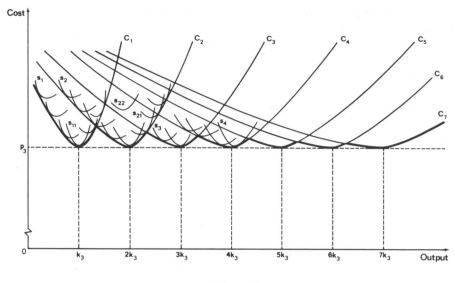

Figure 5

The declining portion of c_1 measures the extent of intraplant economies: the greater k_3 the greater their importance. The importance of interplant economies is measured by the relative positions of the successive minimum points of the long-run average cost curve. There are four major possibilities. (1) They may lie on a horizontal line; this is the situation depicted in Figure 5. It implies that there are no interplant economies or diseconomies, or that they offset each other identically for every output. (2) They may lie on a curve which remains a horizontal line for a significant distance and then begin to rise; here there are only interplant diseconomies. (3) The curve declines and then becomes horizontal; here there are only interplant economies. (4) The curve has the traditional U-shape pattern.

We see now that the previous unusual results for the monopoly case follow from our assuming situation (1) to hold; otherwise, there is no *necessity* for the monopolist to be operating at the minimum point of his short-run cost curve even in the long run. But it is essential to note that even in the traditional case (4), where from a purely probability viewpoint there is least likelihood that in the long run he will operate at the minimum point, the *probability* is greater than usually realized that his cost will be close to the minimum cost. This follows from the construction of the cost curves, which makes it impossible for the long-run *multiple*-plant cost curve (even if U-shaped) to be less flat-bottomed than the long-run *single*-plant cost curve.[11]

Formulation of the problem in this way focuses attention on the central policy problem of monopoly: optimum size of firm. Dissolution as the answer to monopoly

___

11. Though we have developed the theory of multiple-plant cost curves for monopoly only, it is clear that the construction of the cost curves is perfectly general and will hold in any of the cases of imperfect competition. These cases should be modified accordingly.

is subject to two fundamental criticisms. (a) If firms are to be of optimum size, there might not be enough independent firms resulting from the dissolution to make the operation of competition possible. In other words, we will replace monopoly with some oligopoly situation, and it is quite possible that we would be as badly off as under monopoly. We shall deal more fully with this in Section III. (b) Even if there are originally enough independent firms for competition to work, the situation might be unstable and develop into oligopoly.

Thus situation (1) is very favorable as far as (a) is concerned, depending only on the size of k_3 relative to market output. But the independent firms would then be in the familiar unstable situation of a long-run constant cost curve, and there would be no *economic* limit to their possible growth. The dissolution provisions would also have to define optimum firm and prevent firms from growing any larger.[12] Situation (2) is most favorable for a policy of dissolution, since it has the advantage over (1) that there is an economic limit to the growth of the independent firms. The case for dissolution is weakest under (3). Here again it depends on where the curve straightens out. Even if it is at a relatively small output (say $3k_3$, so that each competitive firm would consist of 3 plants), there would still be the problem of preventing indefinite growth. This problem would not be so bad under (4), but in either (3) or (4), if we insisted on making each plant a separate firm, we could do so only at the cost of efficiency in production. The cost would, of course, vary with the shape of the curve formed from the successive minimum points.

II

Our purpose in this section is to deal more mathematically with the short-run situation and show under what conditions equalization of marginal costs by equalizing outputs of the plants will not minimize costs to the firm.[13] We shall deal primarily with the case of a two-plant firm and offer (a) a geometric proof and then (b) a more general algebraic proof.

(a) Assume for convenience that each plant (A and B) has the same marginal cost curve reaching its minimum at b. For total outputs $x < 2b$ it is well known that equalization of marginal cost does not minimize cost (cf. (b) below). It is also obvious that in the case of a symmetric marginal cost curve an output of $2b$ can be produced either with each plant producing b or with one producing $b+d$ and the other $b-d$,

---

12. In the event that dissolution succeeded in placing each plant under separate ownership and making perfect competition work, in our preceding example we would have short-run equilibrium established at a price of p_0 (cf. Figure 4). This follows from our assumption that the ingredients are completely unspecialized, so that the supply curve for the competitive industry coincides with the marginal cost curve of the monopolist. This supply curve intersects the industry demand curve at the price p_0, thus establishing the short-run price for the competitive industry. Since this price exceeds minimum average cost (p_3) the industry is not in long-run equilibrium: firms will flow into the industry and the supply curve will shift over to the right until a price p_3 is established (again employing the assumption of a constant costs industry). This will be the case when there are 100 firms (with one plant each) in the industry (cf. Figure 2). Thus, in Cassels' terminology, for the monopoly we have no long-run excess capacity (in situation (1)), though there is under-investment if we accept perfect competition as a criterion. (J. M. Cassels, "Excess Capacity and Monopolistic Competition" (1936–37), pp. 440–43.)

13. This section may be omitted without disturbing the continuity between Sections I and III.

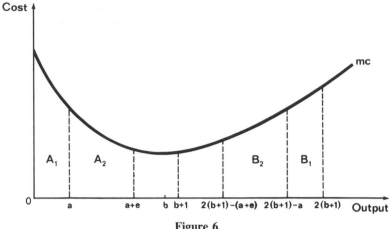

Figure 6

where d is any positive constant less than or equal to b. We shall ignore these more trivial cases and consider $x=2(b+1)$, which could be produced with each plant producing $b+1$. In order that it should be produced, instead, with A producing a and B producing $2(b+1)-a$, and *that this should be the only possible way of minimizing cost*, we have the following necessary and sufficient conditions (cf. Figure 6):

1. $A_1<B_1$—otherwise the entire output would be produced in B. This condition insures that *at least a* will be produced in A.

2. For any $0<e\leq b+1-a$ it is true that $A_2>B_2$. The most important value of $e=b+1-a$; for this insures that, even though we equalize the marginal costs by equalizing the outputs of the two operating plants, we are not minimizing costs. The statement must hold for the other values of e to insure that no other point on the falling part of the marginal cost curve is the minimizing one.

These two conditions are very general and impose no restrictions inconsistent with the generally accepted U-shaped marginal cost curve. In general the class of cost curves meeting these conditions will have the following characteristics: (*a*) sharply falling initial stages, (*b*) flattening out for a short interval, then (*c*) rising even more sharply. (*c*) brings about condition (1); (*a*) and (*b*) together tend to bring about condition (2). To prove the first statement in this paragraph, we offer the following actual example.

Let A and B each have the cost curves described in Table I. We must now construct the v_1 and v_2 curves (cf. Figure 3). The v_1 curve is, of course, represented by Table I. The v_2 curve is constructed in Table II. From a comparison of Tables I and II we see that v_2 intersects v_1 between outputs 11 and 12, so that the v_2 curve for an output of 12 is the relevant one. Yet this output, which could be produced by each plant producing at its minimum marginal cost output, is produced with one plant on the rising part of its marginal cost curve and the other on the falling.

(*b*) Consider again the case of a 2-plant firm.[14] Consider the plants as separate

---

14. I wish to express my appreciation to Trygve Haavelmo (University of Chicago) for his assistance in formulating the results of this paragraph.

factors of production, and let $c(x_1)$ and $c(x_2)$ be the total variable cost curves of A and B, respectively, where x_1 is the output of A and x_2 of B. Then for any fixed output k the monopolist will seek to minimize

$$C=c(x_1)+c(x_2)$$

subject to the side condition

$$x_1+x_2=k.$$

We employ the Lagrange multiplier and form

$$F=c(x_1)+c(x_2)-\lambda(x_1+x_2-k).$$

Minimizing F with respect to x_1 and then x_2 and eliminating λ we get as our first order conditions the familiar results

$$\partial c/\partial x_1=\partial c/\partial x_2.$$

In order that F should be a minimum, we need the second order conditions fulfilled[15]

$$D = \begin{vmatrix} 0 & \dfrac{\partial c}{\partial x_1} & \dfrac{\partial c}{\partial x_2} \\[2ex] \dfrac{\partial c}{\partial x_1} & \dfrac{\partial^2 c}{\partial x_1^2} & 0 \\[2ex] \dfrac{\partial c}{\partial x_2} & 0 & \dfrac{\partial^2 c}{\partial x_2^2} \end{vmatrix} = -\left(\frac{\partial c}{\partial x_1}\right)^2\left(\frac{\partial^2 c}{\partial x_2^2}\right) - \left(\frac{\partial c}{\partial x_2}\right)^2\left(\frac{\partial^2 c}{\partial x_1^2}\right) < 0.$$

Noting that $\left(\dfrac{\partial c}{\partial x_i}\right)^2$ is identically >0, and that $\dfrac{\partial^2 c}{\partial x_i^2} \lessgtr 0$ $(i=1, 2)$ according as marginal cost is falling, at a minimum, or rising, we can formulate the following results:

1. For outputs $x=x_1+x_2<b$ (where b is the output for plant minimum marginal cost), each plant will of necessity be producing on the falling part of the curve. Therefore $D>0$ and equalizing marginal cost will *maximize* total costs. Minimum costs are achieved by having one plant produce the entire output.

2. If $x_1=x_2=b$, then $D=0$ and this allocation may be neither a minimum nor a maximum.

3. If $x=x_1+x_2>2b$ and we equalize marginal costs by equalizing outputs then each plant is producing on the rising part of the marginal cost curve and $D<0$. This assures us that this allocation will minimize costs *relative to* all alternative allocations such that each plant is producing on the rising part of the marginal cost curve; that is, this allocation is the optimum one within a neighborhood such that every point is on the rising part of the curve. However, if we permit allocations such that one plant is producing on the falling part and one on its rising part, then for this allocation we may have $D>0$; thus the allocation achieved by equalizing marginal costs by equalizing outputs may be neither a minimum nor a maximum relative to the whole extent of the marginal cost curve.

15. Cf. J. R. Hicks, *Value and Capital* (1939), pp. 305ff.

Table I

Output	avc	tvc	mc
1	15.0	15	15
2	14.0	28	13
3	13.0	39	11
4	12.0	48	9
5	11.0	55	7
6	10.0	60	5
7	9.4	66	6
8	9.1	73	7
9	9.0	81	8
10	9.0	90	9
11	9.1	100	10
12	9.8	117	17
13	11.1	144	27
14	13.1	184	40
15	15.9	239	55

Table II

Output	Plant A		Plant B		TVC
	output	tvc(A)	output	tvc(B)	tvc(A)+tvc(B)
1	1	15	0	0	15
2	1	15	1	15	30
3	2	28	1	15	43
4	3	39	1	15	54
5	4	48	1	15	63
6	5	55	1	15	70
7	6	60	1	15	75
8	7	66	1	15	81
9	8	73	1	15	88
10	9	81	1	15	96
11	10	90	1	15	105
12	11	100	1	15	115
13	7	66	6	60	126
14	7	66	7	66	132
15	8	73	7	66	139

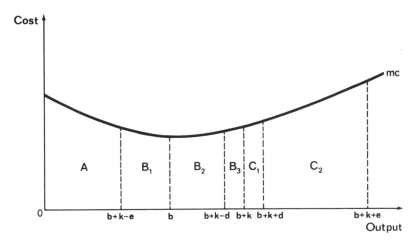

Figure 7

These results can be represented graphically with the aid of Figure 7. From the shape of the marginal cost curve (which reaches its minimum at the output b) we know, for an output of $2(b+k)$, $C_1>B_3$ as long as $d<k$. Therefore the total variable costs are less when the allocation is $b+k$ to each one than any other allocation $b+k+d$, $b+k-d$ (where $d<k$). Analogous results hold when total output is less than b: then from the shape of the curve we see that equalizing marginal cost will bring about a greater total variable cost than any other allocation. When, however, we permit the possibility of the allocation being $b+k-e$, $b+k+e$ (where $e>k$) we are no longer sure that $b+k$, $b+k$ will yield a smaller total variable cost than the former allocation. Specifically, the former allocation will be less when

$$2A+B+C<2(A+B)$$
$$\text{where } B=B_1+B_2+B_3; \ C=C_1+C_2.$$

This reduces to

$$C<B \text{ or } B_1>C-(B_2+B_3)>0.$$

Obviously by increasing the absolute value of the slope of the falling part of the marginal cost curve in the neighborhood of the minimum point, we can make B_1 as large as desired, while keeping the right side of this last inequality constant. Thus a marginal cost curve satisfying this inequality can easily be constructed.

These results can readily be generalized to the case of n plants, each with its own total variable cost curve $c_i(x_i)$, where the c_i are not necessarily the same. Our first and second order conditions are then:

$$\frac{\partial c_1}{\partial x_1} = \frac{\partial c_2}{\partial x_2} = \ldots = \frac{\partial c_n}{\partial x_n}$$

$$\begin{vmatrix} 0 & \dfrac{\partial c_1}{\partial x_1} & \dfrac{\partial c_2}{\partial x_2} \\[2ex] \dfrac{\partial c_1}{\partial x_1} & \dfrac{\partial^2 c_1}{\partial x_1^2} & 0 \\[2ex] \dfrac{\partial c_2}{\partial x_2} & 0 & \dfrac{\partial^2 c_2}{\partial x_2^2} \end{vmatrix} < 0 \quad \begin{vmatrix} 0 & \dfrac{\partial c_1}{\partial x_1} & \dfrac{\partial c_2}{\partial x_2} & \dfrac{\partial c_3}{\partial x_3} \\[2ex] \dfrac{\partial c_1}{\partial x_1} & \dfrac{\partial^2 c_1}{\partial x_1^2} & 0 & 0 \\[2ex] \dfrac{\partial c_2}{\partial x_2} & 0 & \dfrac{\partial^2 c_2}{\partial x_2^2} & 0 \\[2ex] \dfrac{\partial c_3}{\partial x_3} & 0 & 0 & \dfrac{\partial^2 c_3}{\partial x_3^2} \end{vmatrix} < 0$$

$$\ldots \quad \begin{vmatrix} 0 & \dfrac{\partial c_1}{\partial x_1} & \dfrac{\partial c_2}{\partial x_2} & \cdots & \dfrac{\partial c_n}{\partial x_n} \\[2ex] \dfrac{\partial c_1}{\partial x_1} & \dfrac{\partial^2 c_1}{\partial x_1^2} & 0 & \cdots & 0 \\[2ex] \dfrac{\partial c_2}{\partial x_2} & 0 & \dfrac{\partial^2 c_2}{\partial x_2^2} & \cdots & 0 \\[1ex] \cdot & \cdot & \cdot & & \\ \cdot & \cdot & \cdot & \cdots & \\[1ex] \dfrac{\partial c_n}{\partial x_n} & 0 & 0 & \cdot & \dfrac{\partial^2 c_n}{\partial x_n^2} \end{vmatrix} < 0.$$

These results leave us with the conclusion that it is impossible to formulate any general rules to determine how many plants (in the short run) will be used to produce a given output, except the one proved in the section above, namely, with k plants, each with minimum average variable cost at $x_i = g$, outputs of ng ($n = 1, 2, \ldots k$) will be produced by having n plants each produce g. Furthermore, it is theoretically possible that $x = x_1$ will be produced with j plants, $x = x_1 + d$ with $j + 1$ plants, and $x = x_1 + d + e$ with j plants again. Consequently our Figure 3 should allow for the possibility of multiple intersection of the v_i curves.

Finally, we should note that these problems do not arise under perfect competition, which may well explain why they have so long been neglected. In imperfect competition there is only a demand curve for the firm as a whole, and not for any individual plant. Therefore, before we can discuss equilibrium for the firm we must construct the aggregate cost curve for the firm as a whole. However, under perfect competition there exists a separate demand curve for each plant, namely, an infinitely elastic curve at the level of the market price. Consequently we can determine the equilibrium output of each plant independently of what takes place in other plants. In other words, the fact of the unlimited market which is present under perfect competition enables us to consider each plant separately.

Analytically this can be shown as follows. Consider a firm with n plants; the amount x_i is produced by the i-th plant, which has the total cost curve $g_i(x_i)$ $(i=1, 2, \ldots n)$. Let p=price of the product sold by the firm. By our assumption of perfect competition p is considered by the firm as given. Then the firm maximizes its profit

$$\pi = px - \sum_{i=1}^{n} g_i(x_i)$$

subject to

$$x = \sum_{i=1}^{n} x_i.$$

Substituting we have

$$\pi = p\sum_{i=1}^{n} x_i - \sum_{i=1}^{n} g_i(x_i)$$

from which follow our familiar maximizing conditions

$$\partial\pi/\partial x_i = p - \frac{\partial g_i(x_i)}{\partial x_i} = 0 \ (i=1, 2, \ldots n);$$

that is, the marginal cost of each plant must equal the market price, our usual condition for equilibrium under perfect competition.

III

In this section I shall assume that the monopoly has been dissolved and replaced by one hundred independent firms, and then consider the arrangements that might grow up between them in the absence of perfect competition. This failure of competition to develop may be due either to active desire to achieve monopoly gains, or to passive acceptance of noncompetitive arrangements due to interdependence and indeterminacy which make it impossible to adopt the rules of perfect competition.

We must recognize at the outset that in any realistic approach to the problem of monopoly and oligopoly we cannot deal in purely economic terms, but must introduce concepts and motivations which more closely approximate international power politics. On the one hand, corporation leaders have "corporationistic" feelings, together with a desire for power that is inherent in large size. On the other, corporations frequently undertake expansion programs for defensive purposes as well as for aggressive: vertical integration must be undertaken to assure strategic raw materials and market outlets—the corporation cannot allow itself to become dependent on other firms for these essentials. (The analogy to protectionism and war is complete.) In democratic societies the freedom of individuals becomes the ultimate limit to this integrative process; these societies prevent the corporation from achieving complete security by restricting its control over the factor of production labor, with its right to strike, and freedom of contract. Similarly, horizontal integration must be adopted, if the firm is to retain its position in the industry. The firm must accumulate large reserves, for in the event of a price war, victory is not to the most efficient but to the one with the largest reserves. In each case, it is the fear of imperfect competition which makes the corporation adopt methods of imperfect competition itself. This is what makes the oligopoly problem so difficult: it cannot be solved piecemeal. This vicious circle will continue until economists provide rules for the social control of oligopolies that will both protect the public and be workable: indeterminacy must be removed without leaving the door open to collusive exploitation. In brief, some criteria must be provided to distinguish "good" imperfect competition from "bad." It is quite likely that the controls devised will involve a much greater degree of direct government intervention than we have known heretofore.

Despite these qualifications, I now proceed to examine the workings of a market-sharing oligopoly arrangement among the newly independent firms. I shall attempt to show that this cartel arrangement (as we shall refer to it) should be used as a general model for practical studies of imperfect competition. This is not to say that as it stands it is realistic; in fact, its assumptions will prove to be quite arbitrary. However, it does provide a convenient "jumping-off" point from which modifications can be made to deal with actual cases.

Assume that the one hundred independent firms set up a central office which decides on a common price and output policy for the industry. The cartel allocates quotas among the different firms in such a way as to minimize the costs of any given output. We no longer continue with our unrealistic (monopoly) assumption that the cartel can control entry into the industry. In fact, and this is the distinguishing feature, we assume that, as a result of anti-monopoly laws or the pressure of public opinion, there is free entry. Specifically, we assume that the anti-monopoly laws prevent single ownership of the industry and restrictions on entry, but permit agreements (either tacit or explicit) among the supposedly competitive firms. The cartel must thus permit any firm which wishes to do so to enter the industry and become a member of the cartel. In order to determine the short-run and long-run equilibria of the cartel, we must first construct its cost curves.[16]

Let us first consider the short-run marginal cost curve. For outputs greater than q_2 (Figures 8 and 2) the cartel will minimize costs by equalizing marginal costs among all firms and having each produce an equal amount. For outputs less than q_2 the cartel will follow exactly the same procedure as the monopoly in allocating production: x firms will produce k_2 units apiece, where x is determined by the equation $xk_2=q_i$, where q_i is any output less than or equal to q_2. The short-run cartel situation is thus identical with short-run monopoly (Figure 2). Each firm will produce k_4 to give a total output for the industry of q_4 and a price of p_4. The firms will share according to their quotas (and therefore equally) the cartel profits, which are equal to the area of the rectangle $p_4r_1s_1p_{12}$.

In the long run the existence of these cartel profits will attract new firms into the industry.[17] Assume that these too become part of the cartel. We must now consider

16. The reader should make modifications to the shape and construction of these curves analogous to those pointed out for the curves in the preceding section. Since I have already dealt at length with this problem, it will be omitted here.

17. New investment might of course also come from the old firms' expanding in order to increase their quotas and relative standing in the industry. Or they might wait until a new firm establishes itself, and then buy it up along with its quota. This last was the pattern of the German potash cartel and is also characteristic of the American meat packing industry. Cf. George W. Stocking, *The Potash Industry* (1931); Wm. H. Nicholls, "Market-Sharing in the Packing Industry" (1940), pp. 225–40.

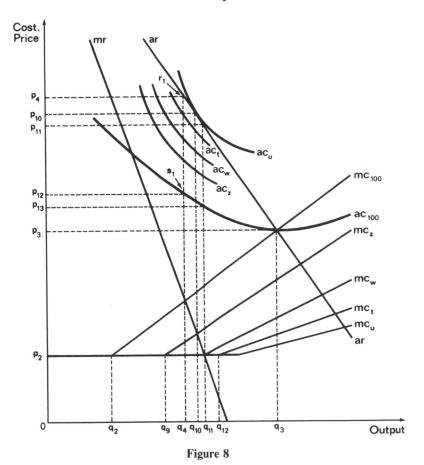

Figure 8

what happens to the short-run cost curves of the cartel as new firms enter. By assumption the existing plant is the optimum one; therefore, assuming no changes in technology or prices of factors, the new firms will build plants of exactly the same size. Assume also that one firm continues to operate only one plant.

As in the case of short-run monopoly, marginal cost can never fall below p_2. But in the long run, as new firms enter, the point corresponding to q_2 in Figure 2 moves over further to the right (cf. Figure 8). Specifically, for any number of plants $z > 100$, the marginal cost curve (mc_z) will be a horizontal line at the level p_2 until the point $q_9 = zk_2$. Outputs up to this point will be produced by keeping some plants idle and the remaining plants each producing k_2. For outputs greater than q_9 (with z firms), the cartel will allocate quotas equally among the firms and the marginal cost curve will rise. The marginal cost curve for z firms not only is horizontal for a longer stretch than that for 100 firms, but the slope of its rising part is smaller; therefore it will always lie below the marginal cost curve for 100 firms. This is true because for any given increase in output the increase in marginal cost for z firms is less than that for 100 firms, since the increased output can be shared among a greater number of firms. For example, for a given increase in the cartel output, with only 100 firms each one might have to increase output from k_1 to k_3; while for z firms, each one might only have to increase from k_1 to k_2, with a corresponding smaller increase in marginal costs (cf. Figure 1). Another way of looking at this is to note that the "steps" in the rising part of the curve become wider as more firms enter (cf. above, p. 95).

So much for the marginal cost curve. As more firms enter, the total fixed cost, and therefore the average fixed cost curve, will rise uniformly. But the average variable cost for the cartel with any number of plants $z>100$ will be less than, or equal to, the average variable costs with 100 firms. Until q_2 the curves will coincide as horizontal straight lines at the level p_2. For outputs from q_2 to q_9 the z curve will continue horizontally, while the other curve will begin to rise. For outputs greater than q_9 the average variable cost for z firms (avc_z) will also begin to rise, always remaining, of course, below its marginal cost curve. It will also lie below avc_{100}, since for any output $q_i>q_9$ each firm will produce a smaller output and will thus have lower average variable costs (cf. Figure 1). Consequently there is no definite relationship between the average cost curve for z firms and that for 100 firms: it might be higher in some intervals and lower in others. For example, if the cartel output were such that with 100 firms each firm were producing k_3 or less (Figure 1), an increasing number of firms would reduce (for the fixed cartel output) the output per firm and drive each firm to the left and higher on its average cost curve. Therefore, the cartel average cost for this output would be greater with z firms than with 100. If, on the other hand, cartel output were such that with 100 firms each one were producing immediately to the right of k_3, then for a slight increase in the number of firms the cartel average cost for that output would be decreased, as each plant was pushed down to its minimum point k_3; while for larger increases in the number of plants each one would be pushed up on the falling part of the average cost curve until the cartel average cost was higher than with 100 firms. If, finally, with 100 firms the output is such that each plant is far to the right on its average cost curve, then even for large increases in the number of firms, cartel average cost would be reduced. However, for the output q_3 with 100 firms, each firm is producing at its minimum average cost. We have thus the first situation described here, and therefore for any given output $q_j<q_3$ the cartel average cost with a greater number of firms will be greater than with a smaller number. For outputs greater than q_3 the other two situations will hold.

From our previous discussion we see that, as new firms enter, the marginal cost curve is pushed uniformly to the right. Since we have assumed that the average revenue (and therefore the marginal revenue) curve remains constant, this means that in the long run cartel price will fall and output increase. Thus, for z firms we have equilibrium with output $q_{10}>q_4$ and price $p_{10}<p_4$.

Let us suppose that even with z firms there are still cartel profits; then new firms will continue to enter. Assume that the number of firms increases to w where $w=q_{11}/k_2$. The same relationships hold between the cost curves of the cartel with w firms and the cartel with z firms as between z firms and 100 firms. The equilibrium output will be $q_{11}>q_{10}$ and the price $p_{11}<p_{10}$. Assume, now, that even with w firms

profits are still being made. Let the new number of firms be t, where $t=q_{12}/k_2$. Let us examine the effect of this new inflow of firms on the equilibrium situation.

The marginal cost curve (mc_t) is changed as indicated in Figure 8. The first significant point is that *the equilibrium output has not changed* and is still at q_{11}. Furthermore, the output q_{11} will be produced in exactly the same way as with w firms: w plants will produce k_2 each to yield a total output of $k_2w=q_{11}$. The remaining $t-w$ plants will remain idle and be paid their fixed costs and aliquot share of the cartel profits.[18] The other significant point is that average costs for an output q_{11} with t firms *will definitely be greater* than for w firms. This follows because average variable cost is the same in both cases ($=p_2$), while average fixed cost is greater in the former due to the additional fixed costs of the $t-w$ new firms. Thus per-unit profit is definitely smaller. If there are still profits, new firms will continue to enter, driving up the average cost curve for the output q_{11} until it is tangent to the demand curve at that output. At this point price will equal average expense and there will be no profits and no further inducements to enter. The industry will then be in long-run equilibrium.[19] It can be shown, however, that both in theory and in practice this equilibrium is a very unstable one.

The long-run equilibrium number of firms in the industry, u, can be determined as follows. Total profits P, when there are w firms, are

$$P=p_{11}q_{11}-(q_{11}p_2+wf)$$

where f is the total fixed cost per plant and p_2 the average variable cost. Then

$$u=w+\frac{P}{f}.$$

That is, the number of new firms above w is limited by the amount of cartel profits available to pay them their fixed expenses in order to keep them idle.[20]

The long-run equilibrium is thus one of both excess capacity (in the sense that the cartel is operating below its long-run minimum cost point) and overinvestment.[21] If we measure excess capacity in terms of the output that could be yielded if output were at a point where marginal cost equals price, the results are equally impressive. Although there are more plants in the cartel than under long-run competitive equilib-

18. Theoretically, at this point a new firm could obtain its share of cartel profits by merely *threatening* to build a new plant.

19. The classic case of a cartel in such a long-run equilibrium is the German potash cartel, which in 1928 operated only 60 of 229 plants. B. R. Wallace and L. R. Edminster, *International Control of Raw Materials* (1930), Chap. 4.

20. It is interesting to note that the graphic equilibrium obtained here is similar to that of the familiar Chamberlin product differentiation case. But here the curves refer to the *industry* as a whole, not to the individual firm. Also, here the equilibrium is obtained solely by shifts in the cost curves, while there the main shift takes place through the demand curve (for the individual firm).

21. Whereas under monopoly there was no excess capacity and underinvestment. This last pernicious and wasteful effect of the cartel is what makes many economists believe that a situation of out-and-out monopoly is preferable to a cartel. Cf. above, note 12.

rium, the industry output is less and the cost and price higher, with a very low (normal) rate of profit.[22]

Such long-run equilibria are highly unstable. This is clearly shown in our model by the discrepancy between the marginal revenue of the *firm* (which approximately equals price on the assumption of non-retaliation) and its own very low marginal cost. Each individual firm realizes the ease and profit with which it could sell additional units beyond its quota. Thus the temptation to "bootlegging," smuggling, and "chiseling" is strong. As cartel profits decrease with the influx of new firms, this pressure becomes irresistible, especially for the low-cost firms, and the eventual breakdown of cartel discipline is inevitable. The pernicious (for the cartel) fact remains that it is to the *maximum advantage* of each firm to stay out of the cartel and sell in unlimited quantities at the cartel price (or just below it), while all other firms remain members of the cartel and by their common restrictive policies hold up the price. This has been the pattern of breakdown of many cartels, with rubber (the Stevenson Plan) as the classic example.[23]

Another cause of instability lies in a fact from which our model abstracts by its assumption of uniform cost curves for all firms. There is a fundamental conflict of interest (within the cartel) between the low-cost and high-cost firms, with the latter insisting on high enough prices to cover their costs as the condition of their remaining in the cartel. There is also the very difficult problem of allocating quotas among the firms, which always creates much dissension and bickering. The forces described in this and the preceding paragraph go a long way in explaining the breakdown of many of our cartels. The cartel is in the unenviable position of having to satisfy everyone, for one dissatisfied producer can bring about the feared price competition and the disintegration of the cartel. Thus the successful cartel must follow a policy of continuous compromise.

In view of the difficulties of maintaining cartel discipline, it is not surprising that successful cartels have resorted to one or more of the following practices: (*a*) invoked government aid to compel membership and enforce cartel decisions (quotas and

22. Excess capacity is here presented as the outcome of cartel operations, and the cartel itself is depicted as beginning from a situation of perfect competition. As is well known, however, excess capacity frequently first arises through shifts in demand or technological changes, precipitates a disastrous period of "cutthroat competition," which is finally ended by setting up a cartel arrangment. This pattern has been especially important among products with low income elasticities of demand—the so-called primary products (e.g. the rubber, coffee, and wheat cartels). Thus excess capacity is itself a *cause* of the cartel. Cf. J. W. F. Rowe, *Markets and Men* (1936); Wallace and Edminster (1920), W. Y. Elliott et al., *International Control in the Non-Ferrous Metals* (1937).

23. Cf. Rowe (1936); K. E. Knorr, *World Rubber and Its Regulation* (1945); Rowe, "Studies in the Artificial Control of Raw Material Supplies: No. 2, Rubber" (1931); C. R. Whittlesey, *Governmental Control of Crude Rubber* (1931). The last two are excellent critical studies of the Stevenson Plan.

That the same pattern was at work in the U. S. copper export cartel after the first World War is evident from the following testimony of C. F. Kelley (president of Anaconda Copper Mining Co.) before the TNEC (Hearings, Vol. 25, pp. 13164–13165):

"The Copper Export Association finally broke up due to two causes. One was the withdrawal of certain members, led by the Miami Copper Co. . . . There was an increase in competition from nonmembers abroad. There was a constant undercutting of price, and certain members felt *that they were holding the umbrella,* and it was more desirable to have freedom, and so gradually by withdrawals it lost its importance" (italics mine).

prices)—especially true of Europe; (*b*) controlled entry into, and operation within, the industry through patents—a frequent practice in the chemical industries; (*c*) controlled entry into, and operation within, the industry by ownership over the scarce raw material cartelized, e.g. tin, potash, lead; (*d*) compelled membership or prevented insubordination by dumping at (temporarily) greatly reduced prices in the market area of the non-coöperating producer. The cartel is frequently prevented from following this last practice by force of law (especially anti-dumping tariffs) or public opinion.

IV

In the United States open cartel arrangements of the type analyzed here are not frequent, since they are strongly discouraged by antitrust law—even more so than outright merger. Nevertheless, I shall show that many of the (tacit) arrangements which do evolve in our economy have striking similarities to our cartel model. An unfortunate result of the classification of imperfect competition into several types is the failure to recognize that in actual life these types are inextricably mixed. Insofar as our economy can be characterized by a single pattern, I think it is one in which the given industry produces differentiated products and consists of a few (say three or four) very large firms doing the bulk of the business, plus many smaller "independents." The large firms act more or less as leaders for the industry in setting price policy, and so on. Some form of tacit or explicit market sharing arrangement (by percentages, market areas, recognized customers, etc.) exists to modify (if not remove) competition among the large firms. They might also proceed on the assumption that the other dominant firms will follow their prices both upwards and downwards. This gives results identical with our cartel model. The industry also has a trade association to help in maintaining discipline and implementing the price policies of the leading dominant firms.

The steel, petroleum, agricultural implements, anthracite coal, light bulb, cigarette, meat packing, and many other industries all fall within this general pattern.[24] In all these industries there has also been a decided tendency for the (original) dominant firms to decline in relative importance over the years. In some cases, this has been serious (steel, petroleum, meat packing); in others, relatively mild (anthracite coal, light bulb, cigarette). The decline has not taken place in absolute size; rather, the several industries have grown, but the dominant firms have grown at a slower rate. The dominant firms have apparently also attempted to pursue a policy of price stabilization, and have succeeded in varying degrees.

If we now interpret these facts in terms of our cartel model, we get very fruitful results. We must first consider the dominant firms as taking the place of the cartel "central office" and setting policies for the whole industry. They will discourage price-cutting by exhortation, "social" pressure, repeated stressing of the disaster which faces the industry as a result of price-cutting, and threats (explicit or implied) of underselling non-coöperating firms in their markets, if they persist. United States Steel and Standard Oil were, in their early years, notorious examples of this last

24. Cf. A. R. Burns, *The Decline of Competition* (1936), especially Chap. 3 and pp. 140–45.

practice. Through these methods the dominant firms are more or less able to maintain discipline within the industry and agreement on a common price. Even if the dominant firms are low-cost firms, they still may set a higher price than they themselves would prefer, in order to satisfy the other (high-cost) producers and prevent them from price cutting. As a rule, the dominant firms try to follow a policy of price stabilization. This may be due to the simplicity of the rule, or it may reflect the fear that arises every time the price is changed: whether the lead will be followed. In brief, the relationship between leaders and followers may be so delicate that the leaders take every care to prevent subjecting it to stress.

The decline in the relative position of the leader is readily explained as the familiar cartel phenomenon of the inflow of new firms and the expansion of old ones. The dominant firms themselves may not expand at the same rate as the industry, since they tend to be near their maximum size, and further expansion might involve them in many of the inefficiencies of large-scale operation. It is also possible that the dominant firms are high-cost producers and that the price set by them, though yielding relatively small profits in their case, would enable the other (low-cost) firms to earn much higher profits, thus increasing their incentive to enter the industry and expand. Finally, it should be noted that the decline in relative position may be due to weakness in the control exercised by the dominant firms. During periods of declining demand the "independents" will indulge in much more price cutting in order to increase their sales. It is quite possible (and seems to have been the case in steel and copper, for example) that the dominant firm will continue with its stabilized higher price and not retaliate for a time; that is, it expects it will still profit by this policy, although it is in the position of "holding the umbrella" for the other firms and restricting its own output relatively more than theirs.[25]

Finally, it is very instructive to examine those industries in which the dominant firms have declined relatively little. The results are what we might have expected from our cartel model (cf. above, pp. 110–11). General Electric has been able to maintain its position because it could control entry into the light bulb industry through ownership of vital patents. The dominant anthracite coal companies have control of most of the anthracite reserves. The "Big Four" in cigarettes have prevented entry by establishing monopoly through advertising. The depression, however, partly broke down this last monopoly by allowing the cheaper brands to establish themselves; and in recent years Philip Morris has established itself, in its turn, by a vigorous advertising campaign.[26]

The preceding paragraphs, though necessarily quite sketchy, provide a rough outline of the thesis I have tried to present in this section: that the cartel model is the most fruitful approach to economic analysis of our real world, focusing attention on the significant points of the problem. This general statement will now be amplified by applying the thesis to a specific industry and noting the particular ways in which the

25. Cf. Burns (1936), pp. 140ff.

26. Cf. A. A. Bright and W. R. Maclaurin, "Economic Factors Influencing the Development and Introduction of the Fluorescent Lamp" (1943), pp. 429–50; Burns (1936), p. 123.

cartel features appear. The example I have chosen is the milk distributing industry, whose striking resemblance to our cartel model makes it truly a "textbook case." [27]

Due to the perishability and high transportation costs of their product, milkshed coöperatives, made up of thousands of members, are able to operate more or less within a closed market. The coöperative bargains collectively with the distributors and sets a price on fluid (Class I) milk. It cannot, however, control the output of its members, and therefore all milk not used in fluid form is sold as surplus (Class II) milk at prices near competitive levels. This is used for butter, cream, condensed milk, and other processed dairy products. The individual producer is either allotted a quota on which he can receive the Class I price (receiving the Class II price on everything above this quota) or he receives the Class I price on a percentage of his sales equal to the percentage of the total coöperative sales which was used for Class I purposes. Over a period of time expansion takes place as (1) new producers are attracted into the dairy industry within the existing milkshed, (2) the individual members expand their production, and (3) the higher price set by the coöperative itself extends the geographical area of the milkshed.

As the size and output of the milkshed increase, the proportion of surplus milk increases still faster. This brings down the average price received by the producer. If there were completely free entry, the *average* price would tend to fall to the competitive level, with two possible results.

(1) At any time of the coöperative's existence, it is to the advantage of any individual producer to stay out of the coöperative and sell to non-participating dealers who sell primarily fluid milk. They will thus obtain a higher price than the average obtainable within the coöperative, but lower than the bargained Class I price. Note that this is also to the advantage of the nonparticipating distributor, since it (*a*) enables him to obtain Class I milk at a lower price than his competitor (participating) distributors and (*b*) throws a greater burden of surplus milk on them. Thus it is to the common interest of producers' and distributors' organizations to prevent free entry at both levels. When increasing amounts of surplus milk continuously lower the average price and increase the discrepancy between it and the Class I price, this unremitting pressure becomes overwhelming and, if not counteracted, causes the disintegration of the coöperative long before the "competitive" price is reached.

(2) But, of course, counter measures will be put into effect before this danger point is reached. Government assistance will be called in—health ordinances will be used to restrict the area of the milkshed and discipline recalcitrant producers. (The Rhode Island ordinance requiring milk from outside the state to be colored pink is classic.) Where this does not suffice, force can also be used (milk-dumping, for example). Action will also be directed at the non-participating distributors, for without these as an outlet the non-coöperating producer would be lost, unless he could do his own distributing. The producers' and distributors' organizations will thus try to eliminate

27. For the following account I have drawn heavily on John M. Cassels, *A Study of Fluid Milk Prices* (1937), Chaps. 5–6 and Appendix A; and Wm. H. Nicholls, *Imperfect Competition within Agricultural Industries* (1941), Chaps. 10–11.

them, either with government assistance (again via health ordinances) or pure coercion (their bottles broken or held back at the bottle-exchange, their workers beaten, and so on). Finally the Government itself is called in to fix and enforce the price, usually by arbitrating or participating in the bargaining between coöperatives and distributors and giving these results legal sanction.[28]

V

In conclusion it should be noted that to a large extent the general imperfect competition case described above can be dealt with by a market-sharing solution from the viewpoint of a single firm whose individual demand curve shifts to the left as new firms enter. For the following reasons, however, I believe that the cartel model is a more satisfactory analytical tool for revealing certain of the forces at work and should therefore be used in addition to the market-sharing analysis.

(1) There are some cases for which the cartel model is an exact, and not merely an approximate, description, in the sense that there is an actual body making and enforcing decisions from the viewpoint of the industry as a whole. The market-sharing analysis, with its emphasis on the individual firm, is obviously inapplicable here. In our own economy we have the examples of the milk industry, bituminous coal (Guffey Coal Act), oil (state proration laws and the Connally Act), and industries with strong trade associations. When we extend our view to the international scene, the examples become much more numerous: rubber, tin, wheat, sugar, coffee, etc. None of these can be satisfactorily analyzed from a market-sharing point of view.

(2) Even when the industry has not set up any official central office, our previous analysis has shown that through the interaction of dominant and independent firms we get approximate cartel results. Here, too, the dominant firms will make some decisions from the viewpoint of the industry. For example, they may not maximize short-run profits, in order not to attract new firms. But if we look at it from the viewpoint of each firm, the latter would not gain by foregoing its profit while the other firms retained theirs. The cartel model is necessary to bring out the nature of these industry decisions.

(3) The cartel model shows with graphic clarity the development of long-run excess capacity and overinvestment.

(4) Obviously, from a firm analysis we could not obtain the results of having new firms entering the industry and remaining idle.

(5) The cartel model reveals more precisely the inner mechanisms, forces, and conflicts leading to the disintegration of industry agreements and explains the resort to extra-economic methods of maintaining them.

---

28. Cf. TNEC Monograph No. 32, *Economic Standards of Government Price Control*, Part II, "Public Pricing of Milk" for government regulation of fluid milk marketing in Oregon, California, Indiana, Wisconsin, and New York. Federal price fixing is also discussed (pp. 57–229).

Multiple-Plant Firms: Comment by Wassily W. Leontief*

In his discussion of multiple-plant firms, Mr. Patinkin correctly states the well-known primary conditions of optimum capacity utilization at any given level of total output, which require that

(*a*) if two or more plants are operated simultaneously, the rates of output in all these plants must be such as to equate their marginal costs;

(*b*) no plant should be kept idle if its marginal costs at zero output are lower than the marginal costs of any other plant at its actual rate of operation.

He does not, however, state the important secondary conditions which also have to be satisfied if the given combined output of all plants is to be produced at lowest possible total costs, namely,

(*c*) not more than one plant should be operated at decreasing marginal costs;

(*d*) if one plant is actually operated at falling marginal costs, the reciprocal of their (negative) rate of decrease must not be smaller in its *absolute* magnitude than the reciprocals of the rates of increase of marginal costs of all other operating plants added together.

The equality of marginal costs of all operating plants (condition (*a*) above) as stated in mathematical terms—page 104 in his article—leads to radical simplification of the secondary conditions (inequalities) reproduced in their standard form on the same page below.

Subtracting from the first row of the smallest of his determinants, its second row multipled by c_1'/c_1'' and its third row multiplied by c_2'/c_2'' (I use c_i' for Mr. Patinkin's $\partial c_i/\partial x_i$ and c_i'' for his $\partial^2 c_i/\partial x^2_i$) one can reduce the first of his inequalities to the following simple expression: $(1/c_1'' + 1/c_2'') \cdot c_1'' \cdot c_2'' = c_1'' + c_2'' \geq 0$.

The equality sign can be added to the (now reversed) inequality sign used by Mr. Patinkin if one is interested in all distributions of any given combined output between different plants which will minimize its total costs. Since the numbers "1" and "2" can be attached to any two different operating plants, the last expression states our rule (*c*).

All other inequalities written out on page 104 can be reduced to similar simple expressions. The last one in particular can be written as:

$$(1/c_1'' + 1/c_2'' + \ldots + 1/c_n'')\, c_1'' \cdot c_2'' \ldots c_n'' > 0.$$

If none of the second derivatives is negative, the condition will obviously be satisfied; if only one of them is negative, it will be satisfied, provided the expression in parenthesis is not positive. This situation is covered by rule (*d*) stated above. Rule (*c*) excludes all cases with more than one non-positive second derivative.

Mr. Patinkin's second and all other intermediate inequalities do not represent independent conditions, since they are necessarily fulfilled if conditions (*c*) and (*d*) are satisfied.

* {I am indebted to Professor Leontief for permission to reproduce his comment.}

Note on the Allocation of Output*

Professor Leontief's comment provides two very interesting theorems on the allocation of output in the case of multiple-plant firms. His theorems hold for any output. Usually, however, we are concerned only with the output for which the firm maximizes profits; for this "optimum output" it is possible to derive stronger theorems than those developed by Professor Leontief.

Assume, for the sake of simplicity, that all plants are in operation. Let x_i be the output of the ith plant and $c_i = c_i(x_i)$ ($i=1 \ldots n$) be its total cost curve. Let the total revenue curve of the firm be

$R = R\left(\sum_{i=1}^{n} x_i\right)$. The firm then maximizes its profits

(1)
$$R\left(\sum_{i=1}^{n} x_i\right) - \sum_{i=1}^{n} c_i(x_i)$$

with respect to the x_i to yield the first order necessary conditions for a maximum

(2)
$$R' - c_i' = 0 \qquad (i=1 \ldots n).$$

These are the familiar conditions for the equality of marginal revenue and the marginal cost of each (operating) plant.

In general, the allocation of output among the plants derived from (2) will not be unique. Furthermore, some of these allocations may correspond to minimum profits. These are excluded by imposing the second order necessary conditions for a maximum:

(3)
$$(-1)^k \begin{vmatrix} R'' - c_1'' & R'' & R'' & \cdots & R'' \\ R'' & R'' - c_2'' & R'' & \cdots & R'' \\ R'' & R'' & R'' - c_3'' & \cdots & R'' \\ \cdot & \cdot & \cdot & \cdots & \cdot \\ \cdot & \cdot & \cdot & \cdots & \cdot \\ R'' & R'' & R'' & \cdots & R'' - c_k'' \end{vmatrix} \geqq 0$$
$$(k=1 \ldots n)$$

where R'' (c'') is the slope of the marginal revenue (cost) curve. For $k=1$ and $k=2$ this reduces to

(4)
$$R'' \leqq c_1''$$

and

(5)
$$c_1'' c_2'' \geqq R''(c_1'' + c_2'')$$

respectively. Now assume that both c_1'' and c_2'' are negative. Multiplying (4) by $(c_1'' + c_2'')$ we obtain

(6)
$$R''(c_1'' + c_2'') \geqq c_1''(c_1'' + c_2'') = (c_1'')^2 + c_1'' c_2''.$$

*I am indebted to Kenneth J. Arrow (Cowles Commission, University of Chicago) for very helpful suggestions. {Today the following problem would be dealt with by means of the Kuhn-Tucker theorem.}

Comparing (5) with (6) we see that (assuming $c_1'' \neq 0$) there is a contradiction. Since any two plants can be considered as the "first and second," this proves that at the "optimum output" not more than one plant will be operating on the falling part of its marginal cost curve. This is Professor Leontief's statement (c) applied to a specific output: the optimum market output.

By this result we can eliminate some of the allocations determined by (2). The remaining admissible ones will all be of one of the following types: (a) all plants operating at the same marginal cost on rising parts of their respective marginal cost curves; and (b) all plants operating at the same marginal cost, but one operating on the falling part of its curve, and the rest on the rising part of theirs. However, we have used only the first two conditions of (3). By using the n-th, even some of these remaining allocations can be rejected as not satisfying the second order necessary conditions for a maximum.

Consider now (3) for $k=n$. Subtract the last row from each of the other rows. This reduces (3) to

$$(7) \quad (-1)^n \begin{vmatrix} -c_1'' & 0 & \cdots & 0 & c_n'' \\ 0 & -c_2'' & \cdots & 0 & c_n'' \\ \cdot & \cdot & \cdots & \cdot & \cdot \\ 0 & 0 & \cdots & -c_{n-1}'' & c_n'' \\ R'' & R'' & \cdots & R'' & R'' - c_n'' \end{vmatrix} \geqq 0.$$

Now multiply the j-th row ($j=1 \ldots n-1$) by $\dfrac{R''}{c_j''}$ and add to the last one, so that (7) reduces to

$$(8) \quad (-1)^n \begin{vmatrix} -c_1'' & 0 & \cdots & 0 & c_n'' \\ 0 & -c_2'' & \cdots & 0 & c_n'' \\ \cdot & \cdot & \cdots & \cdot & \cdot \\ \cdot & \cdot & \cdots & \cdot & \cdot \\ 0 & 0 & \cdots & 0 & R'' - c_n'' + R'' c_n'' \left(\sum_{j=1}^{n-1} \dfrac{1}{c_j''} \right) \end{vmatrix}$$

$$= (-1)^n (-1)^{n-1} \left[\prod_{j=1}^{n-1} c_j'' \left\{ R'' - c_n'' + R'' c_n'' \left(\sum_{j=1}^{n-1} \dfrac{1}{c_j''} \right) \right\} \right]$$

$$\geqq 0.$$

Multiplying and dividing by c_n'' we have

$$(9) \qquad \prod_{i=1}^{n} c_i'' \left(R'' \sum_{i=1}^{n} \dfrac{1}{c_i''} - 1 \right) \leqq 0.$$

There are several cases to consider: (α) allocation (a) with $R'' < 0$; (β) allocation (a) with $R'' > 0$; (γ) allocations (b) with $R'' < 0$; and (δ) allocation (a) with $R'' = 0$. Note that by (4) (since the plant operating on the declining part of its marginal cost curve can be considered as the "first") there are no cases of allocation (b) and $R'' \geq 0$.

(α) Since $\Pi c_i'' > 0$ and $R'' < 0$, (9) reduces to

(10)
$$\sum_{i=1}^{n} \frac{1}{c_i''} \geq \frac{1}{R''}$$

By assumption, the left side of this inequality is positive, and the right negative; therefore it is always satisfied. Consequently, it is impossible to reject (on the basis of (9)) an allocation (a) when $R'' < 0$.

(β) Since $\Pi c_i'' > 0$ and $R'' > 0$, (9) reduces to

(11)
$$\sum_{i=1}^{n} \frac{1}{c_i''} \leq \frac{1}{R''}$$

where, by assumption, both sides of the inequality are positive. In this case it is possible to reject allocation (a) if the c_i'' are not sufficiently large.

(γ) Since $\Pi c_i'' < 0$ and $R'' < 0$, this reduces to

(12)
$$\sum_{i=1}^{n} \frac{1}{c_i''} \leq \frac{1}{R''}.$$

This will not be satisfied if the absolute value of the reciprocal of the negative c_i'', does not exceed the sum of the reciprocals of the marginal costs of the other plants by an amount $\geq \left| \frac{1}{R''} \right|$. Thus some of the allocations (b) can be rejected on the basis of (12).

(δ) Since $R'' = 0$, (9) reduces to
(13)
$$- \Pi c_i'' \leq 0.$$
This is always satisfied for any allocation (a).

These results can be summarized in the following:

Theorem: All the allocations that will maximize profits are included under types (a) *or* (b). *Allocation* (a) *can be rejected in the case where $R'' > 0$ and* (11) *is not satisfied. Allocation* (b) *can be rejected for $R'' < 0$, if* (12) *is not satisfied; and for $R'' \geq 0$, in all circumstances.*

As was to be expected, the conditions of rejection formulated in this theorem are broader than those proposed by Professor Leontief. This is due to the fact that he discusses all outputs, while I am concerned only with the optimum output. Thus, Professor Leontief does not reject any allocation (a) (cf. first sentence of next to last paragraph of his note), while our theorem does reject some of these in the case $R'' > 0$ (cf. (β)). Similarly, for allocations (b), Professor Leontief rejects if "the reciprocal of the (negative) rate of decrease is greater in its *absolute* magnitude than the reciprocals of the rates of increase of marginal costs of all other plants added together." In our theorem, we reject (in the case of $R'' < 0$) if the absolute magnitude does not exceed this sum by an amount $\geq \left| \frac{1}{R''} \right|$

The reader can establish for himself the fact that there are only three independent restrictions in (3): $k=1, 2, n$. If these are satisfied, those for $k=3 \ldots n-1$ are also satisfied.

The fundamental point here is that even on the basis of our theorem, there may still remain several unrejected allocations. Furthermore, it is possible that they will satisfy the sufficient conditions for a relative maximum, viz., (3) with the equality sign removed. Under these assumptions, each of the remaining allocations will then maximize profits relative to all allocations within a neighborhood. But we are interested in the *absolute* maximum—i.e. the highest of all these relative maxima. (This is analogous to the discussion in my article under point 3, on page 101 above.) For this purpose, conditions (3) can give us no additional information. It may be necessary actually to compute the profit at these different allocations in order to discover the one which gives the highest profit.

There is an interesting special case of the preceding analysis. This is the case of perfect competition. By this assumption $R''=0$ so (9) reduces to

$$(14) \qquad\qquad -\prod_{i=1}^{n} c_i'' \leqq 0.$$

This establishes the following:

Corollary: Under perfect competition, it is impossible to have any plant of a multiple-plant firm operating on the declining part of its marginal cost curve.

So far, we have abstracted from the possibility of non-operating plants. Introducing this possibility complicates the problem considerably. Let us consider a fixed output x, and determine the conditions under which a plant will not be operated. These have been stated by Professor Leontief under his propositions (a) and (b); but it is interesting to consider the rigorous analytic proof of these propositions.

The firm minimizes its costs $\sum_{i=1}^{n} c_i (x_i)$ subject to the constraint that

$$(15) \qquad\qquad \sum_{i=1}^{n} x_i = x > 0.$$

For our purposes we must specifically introduce the additional restrictions, always tactitly assumed,

$$(16) \qquad\qquad x_i \geqq 0 \qquad i=1 \ldots n$$

i.e. no plant can produce a negative output. It can be shown that the problem of minimizing total costs subject to (15) and (16), is equivalent to minimizing

$$(17) \qquad\qquad \sum_{i=1}^{n} c_i(x_i) - \lambda\left(\sum_{i=1}^{n} x_i - x \right) - \sum_{i=1}^{n} \mu_i x_i$$

with respect to the x_i to yield the n equations

$$(18) \qquad\qquad c_i' - \lambda - \mu_i = 0 \qquad (i=1 \ldots n)$$

(where λ and μ_i are Lagrange multipliers), and imposing the $n+1$ restrictions

$$(19) \qquad\qquad \mu_i x_i = 0 \qquad (i=1 \ldots n)$$

and (15). By (15), at least one of the x_i is greater than zero. Let this be x_1. Then by (19), $\mu_1 = 0$. Substituting in (18) we obtain

$$(20) \qquad\qquad c_1' = c_j' - \mu_j \qquad j=2 \ldots n$$

There are two possibilities (a) $x_j > 0$; (b) $x_j = 0$. If $x_j > 0$, then by (19) $\mu_j = 0$. Substituting into (20), we see that the marginal cost of all operating plants must be equal. Now assume $x_j = 0$. Then there are two possibilities to consider: $\mu_j < 0$ and $\mu_j \geqq 0$. Assume $\mu_j < 0$; then by (20)

(21) $$c_1'(x_1) > c_j'(0)$$

i.e. the marginal cost of the operating plant is greater than that of the idle one. Consider the expression

(22) $$c_1(x_1 - t) + c_j(t)$$

as a function of t, where t is restricted to positive values. Differentiating this function at $t=0$, and employing (21) we obtain, as the expression for the derivatives

(23) $$-c_1'(x_1) + c_j'(0) < 0.$$

Hence, by the continuity of $c_1(x_1)$ and $c_j(x_j)$, it follows from (23) that for sufficiently small (positive) t

(24) $$c_1(x_1 - t) + c_j(t) < c_1(x_1) + c_j(0).$$

The left member of (24) represents total cost when the first plant produces $x_1 - t$, and the j-th, t. The right member represents total cost for the allocation x_1, 0. Hence assuming $\mu_j < 0$ leads to a contradiction of the assumption that the allocation x_1, 0 minimizes costs. Thus if $x_j = 0$, we must have $\mu_j \geqq 0$. Consulting (20), we see that this proves that every non-operating plant will have marginal costs (at zero output) greater than the marginal costs of any operating plant (at its actual rate of output). It can be readily proved that this same rule holds (without further restriction) for the profit-maximizing output too.

There are many additional (and very interesting) problems with respect to the allocation of output in multiple-plant firms. First of all, it may be possible to set an upper bound to the number of admissible allocations corresponding to relative profit-maximizing outputs. Second, I conjecture that it is possible to have situations where outputs of $x = x_0$ are produced with j-plants, $x = x_0 + d$ with $j+1$ plants, and $x = x_0 + d + e$ with j plants again. I have not yet been able to develop the conditions under which this would be true. Finally, there is the very general problem of choosing among relative maximum or minimum positions. I hope to treat some of these problems in the future.

Postscript[1]

The initial horizontal segment of the short-run marginal cost curve of the cartel with (say) 100 firms in Figure 8 (p. 107 above) corresponds to the initial (dashed) straight-line segment Ob in the production function depicted in Figure 2 on p. 31 above (see also p. 29, fn. 9). That is, it reflects the assumption that the fixed factor (in this case, the number of plants) is divisible, and that until output q_2, the actual input of this factor (i.e., the number of plants actually operated) is adjusted so as to maintain a constant proportion between it and the input of the variable factor. Correspondingly, the marginal and average products of the variable factor over this

---

1. Based on Yehuda Grunfeld, Nissan Liviatan, and Don Patinkin, *Lectures on Price Theory: 1959/1960* (Hebrew) Jerusalem, 1960 (mimeographed), pp. 239–53.

interval—and hence the marginal and average costs of the cartel—are constant and equal.

One can, however, readily think of a situation in which no firm will agree to be closed down, for fear (say) of eventually losing its rights to cartel profits; and in which accordingly the cartel divides output (say) equally among all its firms, no matter what the level of cartel output. In such a case, the short-term cartel marginal cost curve will be a blowup of the mc curve in Figure 1 (p. 92, above). Clearly, cartel output, price, and profits in this case (to be designated for simplicity as cartel Type II) will differ from those in the preceding one (cartel Type I) only if the mr curve should intersect the mc curve in Figure I (now interpreted as referring to the cartel as a whole, and with the k_i accordingly replaced respectively by the $q_i = 100k_i$) at an output less than q_2. In such a case the output of cartel Type II will be less or greater than the output of cartel Type I according as the point of intersection between the mr curve and the blown-up mc curve is above or below p_2. In any event, the fact that at outputs less than q_2, cartel Type II is operating under an additional restriction (viz., equal allocation of output among firms), means that its profits at such outputs must be less than or equal to the corresponding profits of a Type I cartel.

We might finally consider a cartel (to be designated as Type III) which operates only as a marketing organization: in particular, it fixes the price at which it will purchase any quantity an individual member-firm decides to produce, and also fixes the price at which it will sell the total cartel output so obtained. Cartel profits are then divided among the member-firms in accordance with their respective outputs. This arrangement avoids the administrative problem of fixing production quotas for the individual member-firms, a problem which increases in difficulty with differences in the size and efficiency of these firms.

For simplicity, however, let us continue with the assumption that our 100 cartel-firms are identical. For outputs greater than or equal to q_2 in Figure 8 (p. 107, above), the mc curve of the Type III cartel coincides with the mc_{100} curve there depicted, which now also represents the buying-price the cartel must fix in order to obtain the designated output. There is, however, no buying price that the cartel can fix that will cause its members to produce a greater-than-zero output below q_2: for the buying-price p_2 will cause q_2 to be produced, while any price below that will cause output to become zero—for such a price will not cover the minimum average variable costs of the member-firms (Figure 1, p. 92 above). Thus if the optimum sales of the cartel should be of a quantity less than q_2, it will fix the buying-price at p_2, and destroy the surplus quantity produced. In other words, for any output less than q_2, the cartel has no variable costs: it has only fixed costs, consisting of the ordinary fixed costs *plus* the total variable costs of producing q_2 units of output. Correspondingly, the marginal cost to the cartel of selling any quantity less than q_2 is zero.

It follows that if the mr curve should intersect the mc_{100} curve to the right of q_2, then there is no difference between the three types of cartel. Thus in the case of Figure 8, cartel Type III will fix its buying-price at the height where mr intersects mc_{100}, and will fix its selling price of the q_4 units so obtained at p_4. If, however, at the height p_2, the mr curve should be to the left of q_2, then the behavior of cartel Type III will differ from that of Type I both in the quantity produced (which in the case of Type III will in any event be q_2) and in the quantity sold (which in the case of cartel Type III will be determined by the intersection of *mr* with the *x*-axis or with the vertical dotted line at q_2, whichever should occur first, and which will therefore be greater than in the case of cartel Type I).[2] Once again, however, the fact that cartel Type III operates under more restrictions than cartel Type I (namely, the inability of the former to produce an output less than q_2) means that its total profits must be less than or equal to those of a Type I cartel.

These possible differences between cartels of different types should not make us lose sight of the fact that they all share two basic characteristics that have been emphasized in connection with the original model: first, on the assumption of free entry, the existence of cartel profits will continue to attract firms into the industry until profits are eliminated; second, though the cartel's marginal revenue and costs are equal, the marginal revenue (= cartel price) of the individual member-firm exceeds its marginal costs, and thus creates disruptive internal pressures which may ultimately lead to the breakdown of the cartel organization.

Bibliography

J. M. Blair. "The Relation between Size and Efficiency of Business." *Review of Economic Statistics*, Aug. 1942, *24*, 125–35.

A. A. Bright and W. R. Maclaurin. "Economic Factors Influencing the Development and Introduction of the Fluorescent Lamp." *Journal of Political Economy*, Oct. 1943, *51*, 429–50.

A. R. Burns. *The Decline of Competition*. New York, 1936.

J. M. Cassels. "Excess Capacity and Monopolistic Competition." *Quarterly Journal of Economics*, May 1937, *51*, 426–43.

———. *A Study of Fluid Milk Prices*. Cambridge, Mass., 1937.

W. Y. Elliott et al. *International Control in the Non-Ferrous Metals*. New York, 1937.

J. R. Hicks. *Value and Capital*. Oxford, 1939.

M. F. W. Joseph. "A Discontinuous Cost Curve and the Tendency to Increasing Returns." *Economic Journal*, Sept. 1933, *43*, 390–98.

K. E. Knorr. *World Rubber and Its Regulation*. Stanford, Calif., 1945.

W. H. Nicholls. "Market-Sharing in the Packing Industry." *Journal of Farm Economics*, Feb. 1940, *22*, 225–40.

———. *A Theoretical Analysis of Imperfect Competition with Special Application to the Agricultural Industries*. Ames, Iowa, 1941.

J. W. F. Rowe. "Studies in the Artificial Control of Raw Material Supplies: No. 2, Rubber." *London and Cambridge Economic Service*, Memorandum No. 34, 1931.

———. *Markets and Men*. New York, 1936.

J. Steindl. *Small and Big Business*. Oxford, 1945.

G. W. Stocking. *The Potash Industry*. New York, 1931.

2. I am assuming here that the total revenue is greater than or equal to the total variable costs of producing q_2 units; if it is not, the cartel will maximize profits—or rather, minimize losses—by not producing at all.

B. B. Wallace and L. R. Edminster. *International Control of Raw Materials*, Washington, D.C., 1930.

C. R. Whittlesey. *Government Control of Crude Rubber*. Princeton, N.J., 1931.

Government Publications

U. S., Temporary National Economic Committee. *Hearings*, vol. 25, Jan. 17, 1940, 13164–13165. Washington, D.C., 1940.

U. S., Temporary National Economic Committee. *The Structure of Industry* by W. L. Thorp. Monograph No. 27. Washington, D.C., 1941.

U. S., Temporary National Economic Committee. *Economic Standards of Government Price Control* by D. H. Wallace. Monograph No. 32, 1941.

Oskar Lange (ca. 1960)

5. The Indeterminacy of Absolute Prices in Classical Economic Theory*

Summary

Classical economic theory postulates two parallel dichotomies: the real and monetary sectors of the economy on the one hand, and relative and absolute prices on the other. In the real sector all economic behavior depends solely on relative prices; conversely, once the behavior of the real sector is specified (in the form of demand and supply functions), relative prices are uniquely determined. Similarly, absolute prices play a role in and are determined by the monetary sector alone.

Something is wrong with this neat picture. It lies in the fact that in a monetary economy a bridge is inevitably created between the real and monetary sectors: individuals cannot make decisions in the real sector independently of their decisions in the monetary sector. In particular, the only way people can obtain money is by selling goods; hence the demand for money is identical with the supply of all goods. That is, when people determine how much to supply of every good, they simultaneously determine how much money to demand. Classical economists recognized this dependence, and in fact made use of it. But they overlooked one of its simple implications: If the supply of all goods depends only on relative prices, then, of necessity, the demand for money can depend only on relative prices. Thus absolute prices appear nowhere in the system, and hence obviously cannot be "determined" by it.

In brief, the only way to have behavior in the monetary sector depend on absolute prices is to have these prices appear in the real sector. Conversely, if the real sector depends only on relative prices, then so must the monetary sector. The classical dichotomy is self-contradictory (section 10).

Once this point is recognized it is immediately seen that the only way to have the system determine absolute prices is to have them appear in the real sector of the economy too. Nor will any patchwork attempt to retain the "main sense" of the

Reprinted by permission from *Econometrica*, Jan. 1949, *17*, 1–27. {As indicated in the Introduction (above, p. 11), except for its last ten paragraphs, this article is an almost verbatim reproduction of parts of my Ph.D. thesis. In the works by Lange cited in this and the following two chapters, his first name is given as Oscar and not Oskar; this spelling has accordingly been retained in these chapters. See above, p. 8, fn. 13.}

*This article has been reprinted as Cowles Commission Papers, New Series, No. 28. It represents the results of studies undertaken during the tenure of a Social Science Research Council Fellowship.

I am indebted to Trygve Haavelmo (formerly of the Cowles Commission; now of the Oslo Institute of Economics) who first stimulated and encouraged my interest in the problems discussed in this paper. I am also grateful to my colleagues of the University of Chicago Department of Economics and of the Cowles Commission for Research in Economics for many valuable suggestions and criticisms.

dichotomy by introducing just "a few" absolute prices work. For it will be shown that the only way in which all absolute prices can be determined is to have each and every one play a role in the real sector of the economy. The purge of relative prices from the real sector must be complete. *A money economy without a "money illusion" is an impossibility* (sections 11 and 14).

The classical school frequently introduced the assumption of Say's law. This law served to remove other contradictions from the classical system; but it did so at the expense of making it impossible to determine all prices. The reason for this can be seen intuitively in the following way: the meaning of Say's law is that people spend all they receive, regardless of prices. Another way of saying the same thing is that people maintain their money stocks constant regardless of prices. Thus prices play no role in the monetary sector; consequently the monetary sector can have no influence on the determination of prices. This throws the whole burden of determining prices on the real sector alone. But the real sector does not provide enough information to complete this task; at most it can determine all but one of the prices as functions of the remaining one. Hence the assumption of Say's law renders the system incomplete. This difficulty remains even if the real sector depends also on absolute prices (section 13).

From the above it is clear that if absolute prices are to be determinate, the classical system must be modified. However, modifications that do not completely break away from the classical dichotomy are doomed to failure. In particular, it will be shown that Lange's system runs into exactly the same type of difficulties as the classical one and hence is inconsistent (section 12). The only way out of this difficulty is to discard completely the classical dichotomy between the real and monetary sectors, and to recognize that prices are determined in a truly general-equilibrium fashion, by both sectors simultaneously (section 14). Nevertheless, it is possible to reconstitute the classical theory in such a way that the following familiar proposition still holds: An increase in the amount of money will merely cause a proportionate increase in the prices of all commodities, without in any way affecting the demand and supply for these commodities or the rate of interest (section 14).

I. Introduction

1. When Walras and Pareto began the task of formalizing economic theory in a rigorous, mathematical structure, they were concerned with assuring an equality between the numbers of variables and equations. They sought this equality in order to be sure that their systems should be both *complete* (in the sense of determining a specific value for each of the variables) and *consistent* (in the sense that there should exist a set of values for the variables which would satisfy simultaneously all the stipulated equations). To insure the completeness, they specified at least as many equations as unknowns (i.e., the system should not be underdetermined); to insure the consistency, they were careful not to impose more restrictions (in the form of equations) than could be satisfied by the variables (i.e., the system should not be overdetermined). A simple example will help clarify these concepts.

Consider the market for sugar, and assume that our theory states that the amount of sugar demanded (x) is a function of its price (p), i.e.,

(1.1) $$x=D(p).$$

If this were the extent of our theory, we should have an underdetermined system. That is, the price and quantity could correspond to any one of the infinite number of points lying on the curve $D(p)$ in Figure 1. If we went on to postulate a supply function

(1.2) $$x=S(p),$$

then the price and quantity would definitely be established at (p_0, x_0), since this is the only point satisfying both (1.1) and (1.2). If in addition we should state that the government fixes the price at

(1.3) $$p = p_1,$$

we should have an inconsistent (overdetermined) system. For by postulating (1.1)–(1.3), we are in effect saying that there exists at least one set of values for p and x that will simultaneously satisfy (1.1)–(1.3); but from Figure 1, it is clear that such a set cannot exist; hence the inconsistency.

2. Unfortunately, Walras and Pareto failed to realize that, within the domain of real numbers, equality in number of variables and equations is neither a necessary nor a sufficient condition for a complete and consistent system. The nonnecessity is proved by the following example of a single equation in two variables:

(2.1) $$x^2 + y^2 = 0.$$

For the domain of real numbers, equation (2.1) uniquely determines $x = 0$ and

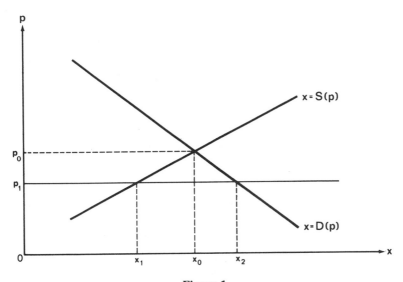

Figure 1

$y = 0$. Similarly, even if there are more equations than unknowns, the system may still possess a consistent solution. Consider, for example, the following system:

$$x^2 - 6x + 9 = 0,$$

(2.2)

$$x^3 - 3x - 18 = 0.$$

Even though the system consists of two equations in only one variable, it nevertheless possesses the consistent solution $x = 3$. Similarly, the insufficiency is proved by the following system

$$x^2 + y^2 = 1,$$

(2.3)

$$x + y = 20,$$

which cannot be satisfied for any pair of real values (x, y).

3. There are no simple criteria for determining when a system of equations is consistent. (Suffice it to say that except in the linear case such criteria are not provided by the Jacobians of the system.) In this paper we shall not deal with this general problem. Instead we shall assume throughout that for the systems under study equality in numbers of equations and variables is a necessary, but not sufficient, condition for the existence of a unique solution. In particular, we shall assume that any system considered here with more independent equations than unknowns is inconsistent; and that any system with fewer equations than unknowns cannot yield a unique solution for all its variables.

4. The primary purpose of this essay is to examine critically the "classical system." As in the examination of any school of thought, the problem of textual interpretation immediately arises. To minimize this problem, I shall confine myself to the mathematical economists of this school. These can be classified as follows: (a) those who start from the theory of individual behavior and build up to market relations on this basis (e.g., Walras, Pareto); (b) those who start from the market relations themselves (e.g., Cassel).

This essay will deal primarily with the classical system as formulated by Cassel;[1] this is the form in which it is most familiar to us now. In addition some criticisms will also be made of modifications that have been proposed for this system.

II. Some Preliminary Theorems

5. In this chapter I shall construct a general model with respect to which models considered in the following chapter can be considered as special cases. The purpose of constructing this model here is to develop several preliminary theorems that are fundamental to the subsequent argument. Specifically, I shall first discuss the re-

---

1. The examination of the Walras-Pareto system is presented in an earlier article. "Relative Prices, Say's Law, and the Demand of Money" (1948a) {see Introduction, p. 11 above}. This will be referred to henceforth as "The Demand for Money." The present paper is referred to in the earlier one by the title "The Indeterminacy of Absolute Prices in the Casselian System." This original title has since been changed to the one now appearing at the head of this article.

lationship between the static models discussed in this essay, and dynamic economic models. This will be followed by an analysis of the relationship between two alternative ways of looking at the demand for money: the demand for money considered as a flow, and the demand for money considered as a stock. It is shown that these two alternatives are really equivalent and consequently can be substituted for one another without affecting the theory. Finally the class of functions known as homogeneous functions is studied, and several fundamental theorems deduced.

6. Consider an isolated economy with n commodities, the nth commodity being paper money. Let p_i = the number of units of money necessary to purchase one unit of the ith commodity, i.e., the price of the ith commodity. Then $p_n = 1$. Assets are assumed to be nonmarketable, with only their services saleable. (I follow Keynes in ignoring the effect of the production of new assets—net investment—on current supply functions.) Let D_i (S_i) represent the demand for (supply of) the ith commodity or service per unit of time. Express D_i and S_i as functions of the prices p_i.

$$(6.1) \qquad D_i = f_i(p_1, p_2, \ldots, p_{n-1}) \qquad (i = 1, \ldots, n),$$

$$(6.2) \qquad S_i = g_i(p_1, p_2, \ldots, p_{n-1}) \qquad (i = 1, \ldots, n),$$

$$(6.3) \qquad D_i = S_i \qquad (i = 1, \ldots, n).$$

These are the demand functions, supply functions, and equilibrium conditions, respectively. (6.1), (6.2), (6.3) each consist of n equations. Thus there is a total of $3n$ equations in the $3n - 1$ variables: p_i $(i = 1, \ldots, n - 1)$, D_i $(i = 1, \ldots, n)$, S_i $(i = 1, \ldots, n)$. However, not all the equations are independent. Following Lange[2] we note that within this system the only way people can acquire money is by supplying commodities; and the only way to dispose of money is by demanding commodities. Thus the demand for money per unit of time is identically equal to the aggregate money value of all goods supplied during the period: when people determine how much to supply of every good at different prices and incomes, they simultaneously determine how much money to acquire at different prices. A corresponding statement holds for the supply of money. Thus we have for the demand and supply of money, respectively,

$$(6.4) \qquad D_n \equiv f_n(p_1, p_2, \ldots, p_{n-1}) \equiv \sum_{i=1}^{n-1} p_i g_i(p_1, p_2, \ldots, p_{n-1})$$

identically in the p_i, and

$$(6.5) \qquad S_n \equiv g_n(p_1, p_2, \ldots, p_{n-1}) \equiv \sum_{i=1}^{n-1} p_i f_i(p_1, p_2, \ldots, p_{n-1})$$

identically in the p_i. Subtracting (6.5) from (6.4) we have what Lange has called "Walras' law":

$$(6.6) \qquad D_n - S_n \equiv \sum_{i=1}^{n-1} p_i(S_i - D_i).$$

2. Oscar Lange, "Say's Law: A Restatement and Criticism" (1942).

Thus in (6.3), if $D_i = S_i$ is satisfied for $i = 1, 2, \ldots, n - 1$, then it follows from (6.6) that the equation $D_n = S_n$ is simultaneously satisfied and is not an additional restriction. Assume that the remaining equations are independent, so that there are $(n - 1)$ independent equations in (6.3). For the moment I shall assume that as a result of this dependence any one equation of (6.3) can be dropped. (I shall return to this assumption below in section 12.) We have then $3n - 1$ independent equations in $3n - 1$ variables. The system (6.1)–(6.3) thus enables us to solve for the quantities D_i and S_i, and the absolute prices p_i. Insofar as the "counting" criterion applies, our general model is thus exactly determinate.

7. Before continuing with the analysis of (6.1)–(6.4), it will be necessary to deal (in this and the two following sections) with several preliminary points.

First I must make clear in what sense the system (6.1)–(6.3) [and especially (6.3)] is supposed to hold. The system (6.1)–(6.3) is a static model; but it is directly related to a dynamic one. Assume that individuals' plans (decisions) are made not continuously, but at discrete points of time, with the intention of carrying out the plan during an ensuing finite time interval. Call this time interval a "period." Then at the beginning of the period, individuals plan their demand and supply flows (D_i and S_i) for the entire period. The system (6.1)–(6.3) can then be considered as the limiting position of that dynamic model which has become familiar through the work of Samuelson and Lange.[3] This dynamic model is identical with (6.1)–(6.3) except that it replaces the $n - 1$ independent equations of (6.3) by the dynamic market-adjusting equations

$$(7.1) \qquad \frac{dp_i}{dt} = H_i(D_i - S_i),$$

where

$$(7.2) \qquad \text{sign } \frac{dp_i}{dt} = \text{sign } (D_i - S_i),$$

i.e., price rises with excess demand and falls with excess supply. As long as (6.3) is not satisfied for all commodities, we see from (7.2) that the system will not be in stationary equilibrium but will continue to fluctuate. Thus the existence of a solution to the static system (6.1)–(6.3) is a necessary condition for the existence of a stationary solution for the dynamic system (6.1)–(6.2), (7.1). Throughout this paper, all models in which the equality of demand and supply for different commodities is postulated must be understood in this same sense: viz, that the existence of a solution to the postulated static model is a necessary condition for the existence of a stationary solution for the dynamic system underlying the static model.

8. As can be seen from the beginning of the previous section, the demand and supply for money, D_n and S_n, are considered in the sense of *flows* per planning period. D_n is the planned flow of money in exchange for commodities supplied (i.e., planned receipts), and S_n the planned flow in exchange for commodities demanded (i.e.,

---

3. P. A. Samuelson, "The Stability of Equilibrium: Comparative Statics and Dynamics" (1941), pp. 97–120. Oscar Lange, *Price Flexibility and Employment* (1944), pp. 91 ff.

planned expenditures). It is more usual in economic theory to discuss the demand for and supply of money as a *stock*. From this viewpoint, instead of assuming the individual to plan, at the beginning of the period, the *flows* of money during the ensuing period, assume that he plans at the beginning of the period the stock of money (cash balances) he will hold at the end of the period. Denote this by M_D. Similarly, those economic units (e.g., government and banks) which control the stock of money in existence are also assumed to plan at the beginning of the period the stock they will supply (M_s) at the end—i.e., the amount of money they will permit in circulation. Assume M_D and M_S to be functions of prices. We have then

$$(8.1) \qquad M_D = F_n(p_1, p_2, \ldots, p_{n-1}),$$

$$(8.2) \qquad M_S = G_n(p_1, p_2, \ldots, p_{n-1}).$$

Divide the economy into two sectors: the private P sector; and the bank-government B sector. Denote the planned demand of the P sector for cash balances by M_D^P, the demand flow planned by the B sector by D_n^B, etc. Assume that the B sector has no demand for cash balances; therefore

$$(8.3) \qquad M_D \equiv M_D^P + M_D^B = M_D^P.$$

Let M_S^0 be the supply of cash balances at the beginning of the period and M_S the supply planned for the end of the period. Then we have the following relationships:

$$(8.4) \qquad M_D \equiv M_S^0 + D_n^P - S_n^P \text{ identically in the } p_i,$$

$$(8.5) \qquad M_S - M_S^0 \equiv S_n^B - D_n^B \text{ identically in the } p_i.$$

The first equation states that the planned excess of inflow over outflow of the private sector ($D_N^P - S_N^P$) is identically equal to the planned increase in cash balances of the P sector ($M_D - M_S^0$). The second states that the B sector plans to increase (decrease) the amount of money in circulation (cash balances) by planning a greater injection (withdrawal) of money into the economy than a withdrawal (injection). Subtracting (8.5) from (8.4) we have

$$(8.6) \qquad M_D - M_S \equiv D_n - S_n \quad \text{identically in the } p_i,$$

where

$$(8.7) \qquad D_n = D_n^P + D_n^B$$

and

$$(8.8) \qquad S_n = S_n^P + S_n^B.$$

Denote the left-hand member of (8.6) by M_x and the right-hand by X_n. Then we can write

$$(8.9) \qquad M_x \equiv X_n \quad \text{identically in the } p_i.$$

Equation (8.9) relates the demand for and supply of money considered as a stock and the demand for and supply of money considered as a flow. By virtue of (8.9) we can replace, in (6.3), the equation

$$(8.10) \qquad\qquad\qquad X_n = 0$$

by the equivalent restriction

$$(8.11) \qquad\qquad\qquad M_x = 0.$$

In the subsequent exposition we shall make frequent use of this substitution.

9. In economic theory frequent use is made of a class of functions known as "homogeneous functions." In this section I shall develop certain properties of these functions which will subsequently prove useful.[4]

A function

$$(9.1) \qquad w = f(x_1 , x_2 , \ldots , x_m , y_1 , \ldots , y_n)$$

is homogeneous of degree t in $x_1 , x_2 , \ldots , x_m$ if

$$(9.2) \qquad \begin{aligned} &f(\lambda x_1 , \lambda x_2 , \ldots , \lambda x_m , y_1 , \ldots , y_n) \\ &\equiv \lambda^t f(x_1 , \ldots , x_m , y_1 , \ldots , y_n) \end{aligned}$$

identically in the x_i, y_j, and λ, where λ may be any number. Putting in particular $\lambda = 1/x_m$ and substituting in (9.2) we get

$$(9.3) \qquad \begin{aligned} f\left(\frac{x_1}{x_m}, \ldots , \frac{x_{m-1}}{x_m}, 1, y_1, \ldots , y_n\right) \\ = \frac{1}{x_m^t} f(x_1, \ldots , x_m, y_1, \ldots , y_n). \end{aligned}$$

Consider now the system of $n + m$ independent equations in $n + m$ variables

$$(9.4) \qquad \begin{aligned} f_i(x_1 , \ldots , x_m , y_1 , \ldots , y_n) = 0 \\ (i = 1, \ldots , m, m + 1 , \ldots , m + n), \end{aligned}$$

where f_i is homogeneous of degree t_i in the variables $x_1 , \ldots , x_m$. By (9.3) we can then write

$$(9.5) \qquad \begin{aligned} f_i\left(\frac{x_1}{x_m}, \ldots , \frac{x_{m-1}}{x_m}, 1, y_1, \ldots , y_n\right) \\ \equiv g_i(z_1, \ldots , z_{m-1}, y_1, \ldots , y_n) = 0 \qquad (i = 1, \ldots , m + n), \end{aligned}$$

where

$$(9.6) \qquad\qquad\qquad z_j = \frac{x_j}{x_m} \qquad\qquad (j = 1, \ldots , m - 1).$$

4. The development in this section follows more or less that of an unpublished note on homogeneous functions, prepared by Leonid Hurwicz and circulated among members of the Cowles Commission in June, 1945. [The specialization consists in assuming t *constant*. If t is considered as any function of the variables involved, no special "class" of functions is segregated. EDITOR] {This bracketed comment was inserted by Ragnar Frisch, then editor of *Econometrica*}.

Thus the system of equations $g_i = 0$ consists of $m + n$ equations in $m + n - 1$ variables and is therefore inconsistent (cf. above, section 2). We have proved the following:

THEOREM: *If every equation of a system of K independent equations in K variables is homogeneous of some degree t in the same set of variables, then the system possesses no solution (i.e., it is inconsistent), with the possible exception of the one which sets each of the variables equal to zero.*[5]

The theorem obviously holds when every equation is homogeneous in all the variables. However, if every equation is homogeneous, but not in the same set of variables, the theorem does not hold. Thus, for example, the system of independent equations

$$(9.7) \qquad h_i(x, y, z) = 0 \qquad (i = 1, 2, 3)$$

(where h_1 and h_2 are homogeneous of degree t_1 and t_2 (respectively) in x and y, and h_3 is homogeneous of degree t_3 in x, y, and z) is not overdetermined. For by (9.3) the system (9.7) can be rewritten as

$$q_1\left(\frac{x}{y}, z\right) = 0,$$

$$(9.8) \qquad q_2\left(\frac{x}{y}, z\right) = 0,$$

$$q_3\left(\frac{x}{y}, \frac{z}{y}\right) = 0.$$

The first two equations determine x/y and z; the last determines z/y. From these we can then derive the values for x and y separately.

As a corollary of this theorem note that if we have $n + m - 1$ independent equations

$$(9.9) \qquad \phi_j(x_1, \ldots, x_m, y_1, \ldots, y_n) = 0$$
$$(j = 1, \ldots, m, m + 1, \ldots, m + n - 1),$$

where ϕ_j is homogeneous in $x_1, \ldots, x_m$ of degree t_j, then (9.9) can be solved for $z_r = x_r/x_m$ ($r = 1, \ldots, m - 1$) and the y_i ($i = 1, \ldots, n$).

Finally, we should note that a linear combination of any finite number of functions, each homogeneous of the tth degree in the same variables, is homogeneous of the tth degree in the same variables. That is, if

$$(9.10) \qquad w_j = w_j(x_1, \ldots, x_m, y_1, \ldots, y_n) \quad (j = 1, \ldots, k)$$

---

5. The zero solution will definitely hold in the case $t > 0$, and might possibly hold in the case $t = 0$. Since the zero solution is economically unimportant, we shall disregard it in the future discussion.

I am indebted to Professor Ragnar Frisch for pointing out the necessity of adding the qualifying phrase at the end of this theorem.

is homogeneous of degree t *in* $x_1, \ldots, x_m$, then $W = \sum\limits_{j=1}^{k} \alpha_j w_j$ (where the α_j are some designated constants) is also homogeneous of degree t in the same variables; for

$$W(\lambda x_1, \ldots, \lambda x_m, y_1, \ldots, y_n)$$

(9.11)
$$= \sum_{j=1}^{k} \alpha_j w_j(\lambda x_1, \ldots, \lambda x_m, y_1, \ldots, y_n).$$

$$= \lambda^t \sum_{j=1}^{k} \alpha_j w_j(x_1, \ldots, x_m, y_1, \ldots, y_n) \equiv \lambda^t \ W.$$

III. Analysis of the Classical System

10. This chapter begins with an examination of the classical system as presented by Cassel and demonstrates its inconsistency. This inconsistency is shown to be due to the traditional assumption that the demand for goods depends only on relative prices. The demonstration is then generalized to prove that even when some absolute prices enter the demand functions, the system may still be inconsistent. A modified classical system proposed by Lange is then considered and its inconsistency shown. Finally, the role of Say's law is examined, and its effect on the consistency of the system described.

In contrast with Walras and Pareto, Cassel does not concern himself with microeconomic analysis. Instead his system consists of equations of the form (6.1)–(6.3). (For simplicity, I consider only his analysis of an exchange economy.) The "classical" element is introduced into this system by his particular assumptions about the properties of the functions (6.1)–(6.2). These stipulated properties (supposedly holding for a paper-money economy) are that the actual values of D_i and S_i ($i = 1, \ldots, n - 1$) depend only on relative prices, and are independent of the absolute price level.[6] Whether the latter is 100 or 200 should not affect the working of

---

6. Gustav Cassel, *The Theory of Social Economy* (1932), pp. 154–55: "It is clear that the functions [D_i and S_i] . . . will remain unchanged if all the [p_i] expressed in the money unit are multiplied by any multiplier whatever. . . . The demand can only be determined by the relative prices."

Other mathematical economists make similar statements. Thus F. Divisia, *Economique rationelle* (1928), pp. 413–16, makes this assumption most explicitly. Walras is less clear. He concludes that the D_i and S_i are functions of the absolute price level. But he maintains that this dependence is very weak ("Ils n'en dépendent que très indirectement et très faiblement") and may be disregarded, so that the general price level is determined apart from the demand and supply equations for commodities. ("En ce sens il s'en faut de peu que l'équation de la circulation monétaire [which determines the general price level], dans le cas d'une monnaie non marchande, ne soit en réalité extérieure au système des équations de l'équilibre économique.") [L. Walras, *Elements d'économie politique pure* (1926), p. 311.] (Walras's logic is really incorrect, as was pointed out in "The Demand for Money" (Section 3).)

Cf. also K. Wicksell, *Lectures on Political Economy* (1934), I, pp. 65–68: ". . . all the quantities involved can . . . be expressed in terms of the $n - 1$ relative prices of the commodities." By these prices are meant "the $n - 1$ ratios between the money prices of the n commodities." [Wicksell is dealing with a case where there are a total of $n + 1$ commodities. The $(n + 1)$th being money.]

I must emphasize that what these classical economists mean by relative prices are the $n - 2$ ratios p_j/p_{n-1} ($j = 1, \ldots, n - 2$), and *not* the $n - 1$ "ratios" p_i/p_n ($i = 1, \ldots, n - 1$). Since p_n is by definition equal to unity, these latter are *absolute* prices. The last quotation from Wicksell (recalling that he is concerned with a system of $n + 1$ commodities) should make this clear.

the economy. In other words, the functions $(6.1)-(6.2)$ (for $i = 1, \ldots, n - 1$) are homogeneous of degree 0: instead of depending on the absolute values of the $(n - 1)$ variables $p_1, p_2, \ldots, p_{n-1}$, they depend only on the $(n - 2)$ ratios $p_1/p_{n-1}, \ldots, p_{n-2}/p_{n-1}$. Thus when each of the $n - 1$ variables is changed in the same proportion μ, so that the general price level is also changed in the proportion μ, the relative prices (and therefore D_i and S_i for $i = 1, \ldots, n - 1$) remain the same. This follows directly from (9.2) by setting $t = 0$.

The classical analysis assumed that the equation dropped in (6.3) [by virtue of the interdependence shown by (6.6)] was one of those referring to commodities (as distinct from money), say the equations for $i = 1$. This left $3n - 4$ commodity equations determining the $3n - 4$ variables D_i, $S_i (i = 1, \ldots, n - 1)$, and p_j/p_{n-1} $(j = 1, \ldots, n - 2)$.[7] Thus the quantities of goods bought and sold were determined in the "real" part of the model, independently of what happened in the money market. The equations referring to the money market were used only to determine the absolute level of prices. In reality, the theory discussed the demand and supply for money in terms of stocks, and assumed (using the notation of section 8)

$$(10.1) \qquad M_s = M = \text{const},$$

$$(10.2) \qquad M_D = K \sum_{i=1}^{n-1} p_i S_i = p_{n-1} K \sum_{i=1}^{n-1} \frac{p_i}{p_{n-1}} S_i,$$

$$(10.3) \qquad M_s = M_d .$$

Therefore

$$(10.4) \qquad M - p_{n-1} K \sum_{i=1}^{n-1} \frac{p_i}{p_{n-1}} S_i = 0.$$

This is essentially the familiar "Cambridge equation" for the demand for cash balances, where K is an institutionally determined constant. The p_i/p_{n-1} and S_i being given by the "real" part of the system, (10.4) determined p_{n-1} and thereby all the absolute prices.[8]

Despite its apparent elegance, the preceding theory involves logical contradictions on several scores. We will discuss two of these here. In the following section we will discuss a third.

(a) In (6.4) and (6.5) make the classical assumption that the f_i and $g_i (i = 1, \ldots, n - 1)$ are homogeneous of degree 0 in all the variables. Then

---

7. Cf., for example, F. Modigliani, "Liquidity Preference and the Theory of Interest and Money" (1944), pp. 45–88, esp. p. 69.

8. Cassel (1932), pp. 454–59. Cf. also F. Divisia (1928), ch. 19; Walras (1926), pp. 302–12. The interpretation of Walras as supporting a cash-balance equation follows A. W. Marget, "Leon Walras and the 'Cash Balance Approach' to the Problem of the Value of Money" (1931), 569–600. Note again that in order to fit Walras' analysis into the mold of the classical analysis as presented here, we must apply rigorously his assumption that the dependence of the S_i on absolute prices can be ignored. Cf. above footnote 6.

$$f_n(\lambda p_1, \ldots, \lambda p_{n-1}) \equiv \sum_{i=1}^{n-1} \lambda p_i g_i(\lambda p_1, \ldots, \lambda p_{n-1})$$

(10.5)
$$\equiv \lambda \sum_{i=1}^{n-1} p_i g_i(p_1, \ldots, p_{n-1})$$

$$\equiv \lambda f_n(p_1, \ldots, p_{n-1})$$

identically in λ and the p_i. A similar statement holds for g_n. We have thus proved the following:

LEMMA: *If the g_i (f_i) ($i = 1, \ldots, n-1$) are homogeneous of degree 0 in all the variables, then f_n (g_n) is homogeneous of degree 1 in the same variables. More generally, if the g_i (f_i) ($i = 1, \ldots, n-1$) are homogeneous of degree t in all the variables, then f_n (g_n) is homogeneous of degree $t + 1$ in the same variables.*

Note, however, that if each of the functions is homogeneous of the tth degree in the same *subset* of variables, then f_n (g_n) is not necessarily homogeneous of any degree in any of the variables. For example assume the g_i ($i = 1, \ldots, n-1$) to be homogeneous of degree 0 in $p_1, \ldots, p_{n-2}$. Then, if $\lambda \neq 1$,

$$f_n(\lambda p_1, \ldots, \lambda p_{n-2}, p_{n-1}) \equiv \sum_{j=1}^{n-2} \lambda p_j g_j(\lambda p_1, \ldots, \lambda p_{n-2}, p_{n-1})$$

(10.6)
$$+ p_{n-1} g_{n-1}(\lambda p_1, \ldots, \lambda p_{n-2}, p_{n-1}) \equiv \sum_{j=1}^{n-2} \lambda p_j g_j(p_1, \ldots, p_{n-1})$$

$$+ p_{n-1} g_{n-1}(p_1, \ldots, p_{n-1}) \neq \lambda f_n(p_1, \ldots, p_{n-1}).$$

A similar statement holds for $g_n(p_1, \ldots, p_{n-1})$.

For convenience form the excess-demand functions

(10.7) $X_i(p_1, \ldots, p_{n-1}) \equiv f_i(p_1, \ldots, p_{n-1}) - g_i(p_1, \ldots, p_{n-1})$

and rewrite (6.1)–(6.3) as

(10.8) $X_i(p_1, \ldots, p_{n-1}) = 0$ ($i = 1, \ldots, n$).

Employing the classical homogeneity assumption, the preceding lemma, and the last paragraph of section 9, the first $n - 1$ of these equations are homogeneous of degree 0 in all the variables, and the last equation homogeneous of degree 1 in all the variables. Thus no matter what equation of (10.8) we drop (by virtue of their interdependence) we are left with ($n - 1$) independent equations in ($n - 1$) variables, where each of the equations is homogeneous in all the variables. By virtue of the theorem proved in section 9 and the preceding lemma we can then state the following:

THEOREM: *If the f_i and g_i ($i = 1, \ldots, n-1$) in (6.1) and (6.2) are independent and homogeneous of degree t' in all the variables, then the system (6.1)–(6.3) is overdetermined. In particular, the Casselian system (6.1)–(6.3) is inconsistent.*

An additional word of explanation is in place with reference to this last theorem. There is a belief that Wald has proved the consistency of the Casselian system under certain specified assumptions as to the properties of the demand functions.[9] Undoubtedly Wald does prove the consistency of the system he considers; *but this system is not the Casselian system*. Specifically, in the system considered by Wald, *the assumption is tacitly made that the demand functions are not homogeneous of degree 0 in $p_1, \ldots, p_{n-1}$*. Wald's system is stated in terms of the inverse functions of f_i (i.e., price as a function of quantities); and a necessary condition for the existence of these inverse functions is that the functions f_i ($i = 1, \ldots, n - 1$) not be homogeneous of degree 0 in $p_1, \ldots, p_{n-1}$. This can easily be proved as follows:

A necessary condition for the existence of the inverses of f_i ($i = 1, \ldots, n - 1$) is that the Jacobian

(10.9)
$$\begin{vmatrix} f_{1,1} & f_{1,2} & \ldots f_{1,n-1} \\ f_{2,1} & f_{2,2} & \ldots f_{2,n-1} \\ \cdot\; \cdot & & \cdots \qquad \cdot\; \cdot \\ f_{n-1,1} & f_{n-1,2} & \ldots f_{n-1,n-1} \end{vmatrix}$$

(where $f_{i,j}$ is the partial derivative of f_i with respect to its jth argument) should not vanish identically. Now assume the f_i to be homogeneous of degree 0 in $p_1, \ldots, p_{n-1}$. Multiply the ith column of (10.9) by p_i ($i = 1, \ldots, n - 1$) and add it to the last column. The determinant (10.9) then becomes

(10.10)
$$\begin{vmatrix} f_{1,1} & f_{1,2} & \ldots f_{1,n-2} & \sum_{r=1}^{n-1} p_r f_{1,r} \\ f_{2,1} & f_{2,2} & \ldots f_{2,n-2} & \sum_{r=1}^{n-1} p_r f_{2,r} \\ \cdot\; \cdot & & \cdots \qquad\qquad \cdot\; \cdot \\ f_{n-1,1} & f_{n-1,2} & \ldots f_{n-1,n-2} & \sum_{r=1}^{n-1} p_r f_{n-1,r} \end{vmatrix}$$

But by Euler's theorem on homogeneous functions we have

(10.11) $$\sum_{r=1}^{n-1} p_r f_{i,r} \equiv 0 \qquad\qquad (i = 1, \ldots, n - 1)$$

identically in the p_r. Consequently the last column of (10.10) becomes zero, and the Jacobian (10.9) vanishes identically. This proves that a necessary condition for the existence of the inverse function of f_i ($i = 1, \ldots, n - 1$), is that the f_i not be homogeneous of degree 0 in $p_1, \ldots, p_{n-1}$.

(b) From (a) we have seen that under the classical homogeneity assumptions, the equation

(10.12) $$X_n(p_1, \ldots, p_{n-1}) = 0$$

is homogeneous of degree 1. But by (8.9)

9. A. Wald, "Über die eindeutige positive Lösbarkeit der neuen Produktionsgleichungen" (1933–34), pp. 12–20; "Über die Produktionsgleichungen der ökonomischen Wertlehre" (1934–35), pp. 1–6; "Über eines Gleichungssysteme der mathematischen Oekonomie" 7, (1936), pp. 637–70.

(10.13) $$M_x \equiv X_n .$$

Thus the classical homogeneity assumptions imply that M_x is homogeneous of degree 1. That is, (10.4) must be homogeneous of degree 1. But this is impossible if K and M are constants. Thus we have shown that *the classical homogeneity assumption is logically inconsistent with the classical monetary equation.*

11. The discussion in the last section has shown that the overdeterminacy of (10.8) [and consequently of (6.1)–(6.3)] is due to the fact that the homogeneity of the first $n - 1$ equations implies the homogeneity of the nth. Let us now consider a situation in which this will not be true. Specifically, assume that the $X_i (i = 1, \ldots, n - 1)$ are homogeneous of degree 0 in all the prices but one, say p_1. Then by (10.6) we see that X_n is not homogeneous. Therefore the theorem of section 9 does not apply. Nevertheless I shall show that even under these assumptions the system (10.8) will not in general possess a solution.

For convenience rewrite (10.8) as

(11.1) $$X_j(p_1, \ldots, p_{n-1}) = 0 \quad (j = 1, \ldots, n - 2),$$

(11.2) $$X_{n-1}(p_1, \ldots, p_{n-1}) = 0,$$

(11.3) $$X_n(p_1, \ldots, p_{n-1}) = 0,$$

where the X_j and X_{n-1} are homogeneous of degree 0 in $p_2, \ldots, p_{n-1}$. The approach of, for example, Modigliani [10] is to deal with the system (11.1)–(11.3) as follows: "The excess demand function to be eliminated, by virtue of the interdependence, is arbitrary; we may, if we choose, eliminate one of the $n - 1$ referring to commodities, say $X_{n-1} = 0$; we are then left with $n - 2$ commodity equations (11.1) to determine the $n - 3$ price ratios $p_i/p_{n-1}, i = 2, \ldots, n - 2$, and p_1. To determine the absolute prices we use (11.3) as was done with (10.4)."

The procedure seems straightforward. But an obvious hint of an inconsistency somewhere in the argument follows from the fact that if the dropping of the extra equation is as symmetrical a process as Modigliani implies, we should get the same results no matter which equation we choose. But if we drop (11.3) instead of (11.2) we are left with $n - 1$ homogeneous equations in $n - 1$ variables, which (by section 9) are overdetermined and thus in general do not possess a consistent solution!

Let us analyze in detail what is involved in the process of dropping (11.2). Consider first (6.6), which we rewrite [using (10.7)] as

(11.4) $$- X_n(p_1, \ldots, p_{n-1}) \equiv \sum_{i=1}^{n-1} p_i X_i(p_1, \ldots, p_{n-1})$$

---

10. Modigliani (1944), pp. 68–70. In the next sentence of the text I have paraphrased Modigliani's words to fit in with the models set forth here. Otherwise there is no change from his original statement. In reality, Modigliani's analysis is incorrect even without the analysis of this section; for he assumes that the first $n - 1$ equations are homogeneous of degree 0 in *all* the variables (*ibid.*, p. 68, especially footnote 24).

identically in the p_i. From the system (11.1), (11.3) (which is the system Modigliani considers) we obtain solutions for the p_i $(i = 1, \ldots, n - 1)$ which when substituted in (11.4) yield

(11.5) $\qquad\qquad p_{n-1}X_{n-1}(p_1, \ldots, p_{n-1}) = 0.$

From this Modigliani concludes that (11.2) is satisfied with the same set of values p_i $(i = 1, \ldots, n - 1)$ obtained by solving (11.1), (11.3). But (11.5) implies (11.2) *only if* $p_{n-1} \neq 0$. It will, of course, be answered that since this is an economics problem, we can assume that all the $p_i \neq 0$. Thus implicit in Modigliani's procedure is the assumption that *in general the system (11.1), (11.3) has a solution with* $p_{n-1} \neq 0$. I shall show that *in general this assumption is not true.*

Consider the systems (11.1), (11.2) and (11.1), (11.3). If the system (11.1), (11.3) has a solution with $p_{n-1} \neq 0$, then from (11.5) we see that (11.2) is also satisfied so that the system (11.1), (11.2) has a solution. Thus we have proved:

THEOREM: *A necessary condition for (11.1), (11.3) to have a solution with* $p_{n-1} \neq 0$, *is that (11.1), (11.2) have a solution.*

Now since (11.1), (11.2) is a system of $n - 1$ homogeneous equations in $n - 1$ variables it will in general (by section 9) be inconsistent and not possess a solution. Therefore *in general* (11.1), (11.3) does not possess a solution with $p_{n-1} \neq 0$. That is, in general, the solution (if any) of (11.1), (11.3) will yield $p_{n-1} = 0$, and therefore [cf. (11.5)] the solution of (11.1), (11.3) will *not* in general satisfy (11.2).[11]

The reader can immediately generalize these results to the following:

THEOREM: *If in (11.1)–(11.3), each of the X_i $(i = 1, \ldots, n - 1)$ is independent and homogeneous of degree t in the same subset of $2 \leq m \leq n - 1$ price variables, then the system (11.1)–(11.3) will in general be overdetermined.*

These results are also useful as a guide to general procedure. For note that any solution of (11.1)–(11.2) will always (regardless of the values of the p_i) satisfy (11.3). This is true because X_n enters (11.4) without a price coefficient. Thus, as a general rule, in dropping the equation due to the interdependence shown by (11.4), we should always first drop the excess-demand equation for money. Then we should examine the remaining equations. If, in general, they have a solution, then (and only then) we can reinstate the money equation and drop any other equation we might desire without affecting the results.

12. I shall now consider another set of assumptions about the system (10.8) and examine it for consistency. These assumptions (and the resulting system) are the ones set forth by Oscar Lange in his recent book.[12]

In the beginning of section 6, I assumed that no assets could be bought or sold. Assume now that there does exist one (and only one) asset that is marketable. Let this asset be bonds that are perpetuities paying one dollar per period. Represent these bonds by the $(n - 1)$th commodity. Thus bonds and money are assumed to be the

---

11. I am indebted to D. Zelinsky (Institute for Advanced Studies, Princeton) for his advice on formulating the preceding theorem rigorously.

12. Lange (1944).

only nonphysical assets. Abstracting from uncertainty, and assuming all bonds to be identical we have .

(12.1)
$$p_{n-1} = \sum_{t=1}^{\infty} \frac{1}{(1 + r)^t} = \frac{1}{r} ,$$

where r is the rate of interest. Thus the price of bonds, p_{n-1}, is the reciprocal of the rate of interest. Our commodities are then divided into three types: goods, bonds, and money. Assume with Lange [13] that the excess demand functions for goods are homogeneous of degree 0 only in the first $n - 2$ prices—i.e., in all prices except the rate of interest. Consider now the demand for bonds. Assume that a given individual possesses q bonds, each paying \$1 per period. The real value of this payment measured in terms of the ith good is $\$q/p_i$. If all prices increase by the proportion ϵ, then the real value of $\$q$ in terms of the ith good decreases to $1/(1 + \epsilon)$ of its former value. Since prices of all goods are assumed to increase in the same proportion ϵ, the real value of $\$q$ in terms of any good decreases to the same extent. Assume again with Lange [14] that the individual will then increase the number of bonds he holds in the proportion ϵ so that the real value of the bond yield after the price rise will be the same as it was originally, i.e., $\$q(1 + \epsilon)/p_i$ $(1 + \epsilon) = \$q/p_i$. This implies that the excess demand for bonds is homogeneous of degree 1 in the prices $p_1, \ldots , p_{n-2}$.

For convenience, we can again consider the system (11.1)–(11.3) where now the X_j are homogeneous of degree 0 in $p_1, \ldots , p_{n-2}$, and X_{n-1} is homogeneous of degree 1 in the same variables. How do these assumptions affect X_n? From (11.4) we have

$$- X_n(p_1, \ldots , p_{n-1})$$

(12.2)
$$\equiv \sum_{i=1}^{n-1} p_i X_i(p_1, \ldots , p_{n-1})$$

$$\equiv \sum_{j=1}^{n-2} p_j X_j(p_1, \ldots , p_{n-1}) + p_{n-1} X_{n-1}(p_1, \ldots , p_{n-1})$$

identically in the p_i. Consequently

$$- X_n(\lambda p_1, \ldots , \lambda p_{n-2}, p_{n-1})$$

(12.3)
$$\equiv \sum_{j=1}^{n-2} \lambda p_j X_j(\lambda p_1, \ldots , \lambda p_{n-2}, p_{n-1})$$

$$+ p_{n-1} X_{n-1}(\lambda p_1, \ldots , \lambda p_{n-2}, p_{n-1}).$$

Since the X_j are homogeneous of degree 0 in $p_1, \ldots , p_{n-2}$, and X_{n-1} is homogeneous of degree 1 in these same variables, this reduces to

---

13. *Ibid.*, ch. 3.

14. *Ibid.*, pp. 15–16, especially footnote 6, p. **16**. **Lange's mathematical argument in this footnote is really inconsistent with the assumptions of the rest of his book.** Cf. ''The Demand for Money,'' footnote 22.

$$(12.4) \quad \lambda \left[\sum_{j=1}^{n-2} p_j X_j(p_1, \ldots, p_{n-2}, p_{n-1}) + p_{n-1} X_{n-1}(p_1, \ldots, p_{n-2}, p_{n-1}) \right]$$

$$\equiv \lambda[- X_n(p_1, \ldots, p_{n-2}, p_{n-1})]$$

identically in λ and the p_i. Therefore X_n is homogeneous of degree 1 in the variables $p_1, \ldots, p_{n-2}$. This is a generalization of the lemma proved in part (a) of section 10.[15]

Thus Lange's assumptions imply that the X_j are homogeneous of degree 0 in $p_1, \ldots, p_{n-2}$, and X_{n-1} and X_n are homogeneous of degree 1 in the same variables. Then we can immediately apply the overdeterminacy theorem of section 9; for no matter which equation in (11.1)–(11.3) is eliminated by virtue of the interdependence between them, we are still left with $(n - 1)$ equations homogeneous of some degree in the same subset of variables. Consequently Lange's system is overdetermined.[16]

Lange, in fact, generalizes the results of (12.3)–(12.4) to the following: [17] If the X_r $(r = 1, \ldots, m)$ are homogeneous of degree 0 in $p_1, \ldots, p_t$; and the X_s $(s = m + 1, \ldots, n - 1)$ are homogeneous of degree 1 in the same variables, then X_n is homogeneous of degree 1 in $p_1, \ldots, p_t$. Using this and the theorem of section 9, we can generalize the theorem of section 10(a) as follows:

THEOREM: *If in (10.8) the X_r $(r = 1, \ldots, m)$ are homogeneous of degree 0 in $p_1 \ldots, p_t$ and the X_s $(s = m + 1, \ldots, n - 1)$ are homogeneous of degree 1 in the same variables and if all these equations are independent, then the system (10.8) is overdetermined.*

Similarly, it is readily seen that the objections of section 10(b) are still valid: for with a constant K, (10.4) cannot be homogeneous of degree 1 in $p_1, \ldots, p_{n-2}$. Lange's system thus involves exactly the same contradictions as were discussed in section 10.

13. In the classical theory another special assumption (in addition to the homogeneity assumptions) was sometimes made with reference to the system (6.1)–(6.3). This was the assumption of Say's law.[18] According to this law the only reason people supply commodities is in order to use the receipts to purchase other commodities. The decision to supply simultaneously involves a decision to spend the receipts. People do not sell to obtain and hold money; money is only a "veil" concealing the true barter nature of the economy. Thus aggregate demand for all commodities must always equal aggregate supply—regardless of prices. That is,

$$(13.1) \quad \sum_{i=1}^{n-1} p_i f_i(p_1, \ldots, p_{n-1}) \equiv \sum_{i=1}^{n-1} p_i g_i(p_1, \ldots, p_{n-1})$$

identically in the p_i, or, using the notation of (10.7),

---

15. Cf. Lange (1944), pp. 99–100. The difference between this result and that of the preceding section is due to the fact that there X_{n-1} was assumed to be homogeneous of degree 0.

16. Lange's system is presented mathematically in his *Price Flexibility and Employment*, Appendix, section 4. L. Hurwicz was the first one to point out its overdeterminacy (cf. above, footnote 4).

17. Lange (1944), pp. 99–100.

18. Cf. Divisia (1928), pp. 411–12.

$$(13.2) \qquad \sum_{i=1}^{n-1} p_i X_i (p_1, \ldots, p_{n-1}) \equiv 0$$

identically in the p_i. This is the mathematical formulation of Say's law.[19]

What is the effect of Say's law on our system? It can be shown that it reduces the number of independent equations in (10.8) to $(n - 2)$. For from (11.4) we see that when (13.2) is satisfied, $X_n = 0$ is simultaneously satisfied. Therefore this equation is not independent. Consider now the first $(n - 2)$ equations of (10.8), homogeneous of degree 0 in the $n - 1$ variables $p_1, \ldots, p_{n-1}$. By the corollary to the theorem of section 9, these equations can be solved for the price ratios p_j/p_{n-1} $(j = 1, \ldots, n - 2)$. [Or if the functions are homogeneous in only $p_1, \ldots, p_{n-2}$, then they can be solved for $p_r/p_{n-2}(r = 1, \ldots, n - 3)$ and p_{n-1}.] In either case, by substituting this solution in (13.2) we obtain

$$(13.3) \qquad p_{n-1}X_{n-1}(p_1, \ldots, p_{n-1}) = 0.$$

Since in general we can assume that none of the prices (or price ratios) determined by the first $(n - 2)$ equations are 0 or infinity, we can divide both sides of (13.3) by p_{n-1} to yield

$$(13.4) \qquad X_{n-1}(p_1, \ldots, p_{n-1}) = 0.$$

Consequently the solution derived from the first $n - 2$ equations will also satisfy the $(n - 1)$th. So this equation is not independent either.

Thus the assumption of Say's law removes the overdeterminacy from the system; for it reduces (10.8) to $n - 2$ independent homogeneous equations in the $n - 1$ variables $p_1, \ldots, p_{n-1}$. By the corollary to the theorem of section 9, (10.8) can then be solved for the p_i/p_{n-1} $(i \equiv 1, \ldots, n - 2)$. *But Say's law removes the overdeterminacy only at the expense of leaving the system definitely underdetermined.* For as a result of Say's law we are left with $n - 2$ independent equations in $n - 1$ variables $p_1, \ldots, p_{n-1}$; therefore at the most we can solve only for the price ratios. The absolute prices must remain indeterminate.

IV. Conclusions

14. From the preceding analysis it is clear that it has not been possible to construct a system satisfying the classical dichotomy of determining relative prices in the real part of the model, and absolute prices through the money equation. It must be emphasized that *there is no monetary equation that we can use to remove this indeterminacy of the absolute prices.* For any monetary equation will either be (a) homogeneous or (b) not homogeneous. It is impossible for (b) to be true, since as has repeatedly been shown, this contradicts the homogeneity assumptions made with reference to the nonmonetary equations. Therefore (a) must hold. But if (a) holds, we

---

19. Cf. Lange, "Say's Law" (1942), pp. 49–53.

see from the second paragraph of section 10 [or (9.4)] that the monetary equation itself is a function of relative prices only, and therefore cannot determine absolute prices. We are caught on the horns of a dilemma: if the monetary equation is useful (in determining absolute prices) then it is inconsistent with the rest of the system; on the other hand, if it is consistent with the rest of the system, it is useless. Furthermore, although the assumption of Say's law removes the overdeterminacy of the system, it simultaneously renders absolute prices indeterminate.

What are the implications of these conclusions? They are, in brief, that the classical theory never really dealt with the monetary aspects of our economy. Classical analysis was restricted to examining those aspects of an economy which are similar to a barter economy; or, at most, to an economy in which transactions take place with goods against goods, with money acting only as a counting unit. But it did not explain why people held actual cash balances.[20]

It is equally clear that for a real monetary theory, at least one of the $n - 1$ equations of (11.1)–(11.2) cannot be homogeneous.[21] From the viewpoint of the determination of absolute prices, it makes no difference which one this is. However, in accordance with the results of section 11, we must be sure that the introduction of the nonhomogeneous equation effectively eliminates all relative prices from the real sector.

By proper selection of the nonhomogeneous equation it is, in fact, possible to achieve results very close to those desired by the classical school. For example, assume again (cf. section 12) that the $(n - 1)$th commodity is bonds. Let X_j $(j = 1, \ldots, n - 2)$ each be homogeneous of degree 0 in $p_1, \ldots, p_{n-2}$, with p_{n-1} again representing the reciprocal of the interest rate. However, assume that, for some unspecified reason, the excess-demand equation for the bond market, X_{n-1}, is not homogeneous of degree 1 in $p_1, \ldots, p_{n-2}$. Then the development (12.3)–(12.4) is no longer valid, so that X_n is not homogeneous of degree 1 in $p_1, \ldots, p_{n-2}$, and the overdeterminacy theorem of section 9 cannot be applied.

Owing to the interdependence following from Walras' law (6.6) drop (11.3). Then (11.1) consists of $n - 2$ homogeneous equations in $n - 1$ variables. By (9.9) they can in general be solved for the relative prices. Then the absolute prices can be determined from the nonhomogeneous equation (11.2). Since (11.1)–(11.2) is thus in general consistent, we can, according to the procedure justified in section 11, reinstate the money equation (11.3) and eliminate the bond equation (11.2). Then the classical dichotomy would hold—with relative prices determined in the "real" part (11.1), and absolute prices through the monetary equation (11.3).

Keynesian theory usually assumes nonhomogeneity for another equation: the supply of labor, which is assumed to be a function of money, and not real, wages.[22] The results are completely analogous to those just discussed and need not be repeated.

---

20. The rigorous proof of this last statement requires microeconomic analysis. Cf. "The Demand for Money," section 2.
21. Once again, the full implications of this nonhomogeneity can be developed only through microeconomic analysis. Cf. "The Demand for Money," section 5, especially theorem XVI.
22. J. M. Keynes, *The General Theory of Employment, Interest and Money* (1936), pp. 7–14. Cf. also W. Leontief, "The Fundamental Assumption of Mr. Keynes' Monetary Theory of Unemployment" (1936–37), pp. 192–97.

But neither of these approaches is really acceptable: they both resort to tricks. What justification is there for singling out one particular equation and assuming it to be nonhomogeneous? A satisfactory solution to our problem cannot be achieved by such *ad hoc* and arbitrary assumptions.*

There is, however, a straightforward solution that can be readily formulated. The key to the problem lies in distinguishing between two assumptions of classical monetary theory which have hitherto been indiscriminately lumped together. The first postulates a twofold dichotomy between relative and absolute prices on the one hand, and the real and monetary sectors on the other. The second asserts that the quantity of money makes no difference for the determination of the equilibrium flows of goods and services. This last assumption is as basic and intuitively obvious today as it was in "classical" times. It is equivalent to the proposition that no difference will be made for the functioning of the economy if the dollar is replaced throughout by the peso. But the first assumption is neither obvious nor helpful. In fact, the inconsistencies and inadequacies of the classical system that have been repeatedly demonstrated in this paper are due entirely to this assumption.

The usual confusion of these two assumptions arises from the fact that in the classical system the first is made as a means of implying the second. Hence, the classical theory did not distinguish between them. But if we are to solve our difficulties we must find a way in which we can have the logically necessary results of the second assumption, without involving the treacherous implications of the first.

Fortunately, this can be done. First, the absolute price level is introduced into every equation of the system; this immediately eliminates the dichotomies. In particular, we argue that the excess demand for each commodity is affected by the value of all assets (monetary as well as nonmonetary) in the economy.[23] In other words, every excess-demand function depends on the money value of these assets divided by the absolute price level. The modified classical system can now be written down with the aid of the following symbols: r = rate of interest, p = absolute price level, Y = real national income,[24] M = amount of money, and A = *money* value of all other assets. We now write our system

(14.1) $X_i(p_1/p, \ldots, p_{n-2}/p, r, A/p, M/p) = 0 \ (i = 1, \ldots, n - 2)$,

(14.2) $\quad X_{n-1}(p_1, \ldots, p_{n-2}, r, p, A, M) = 0$,

(14.3) $\quad\quad X_n(p_1, \ldots, p_{n-2}, r, p, A, M) = 0$,

(14.4) $$p = \sum_{i=1}^{n-2} w_i p_i.$$

Equation (14.4) defines the absolute price level p as a weighted average of all the prices, where the w_i represent the given weights. Following section 12, we assume the

---

* {The material from this point to the end of the chapter was added at the time in galley proof; see Introduction, p. 11 above.}

23. The rationale of this hypothesis is provided by A. C. Pigou, "The Classical Stationary State" (1943), pp. 343–52. Cf. also D. Patinkin, "Price Flexibility and Full Employment" (1948b), pp. 543–64.

24. In what follows it should be kept in mind that $Y = \sum_{j=1}^{m} p_j S_j/p$—where $S_j (j = 1, \ldots, m)$ are the amounts supplied of the *finished* goods of the economy.

first $n - 2$ equation to be homogeneous of degree 0 in $p_1, \ldots, p_{n-2}$, and p, A, and M. This assumption has already been effected by writing the arguments of equations (14.1) in ratio form; from these forms it is clear that, say, a 10 per cent change in all prices *and the amount of money and the monetary value of all other assets* will leave the excess demands unchanged. Equation (14.2) represents the excess demands for bonds. Here it is assumed that this is homogeneous of degree 1 in $p_1, \ldots, p_{n-2}$, *and* p, A, M. That is, a 10 per cent change in *all* these variables will cause a corresponding 10 per cent change in the amount of bonds purchased. By a simple extension of the theorems developed in section 12 it can be shown that under these assumptions the excess-demand equation for money—(14.3)—must be homogeneous of degree one in $p_1, \ldots, p_{n-2}$, and p, A, M. In particular, the excess-demand equation

$$(14.5) \qquad pL(r, Y) - M = 0,$$

where $L(r, Y)$ is any function of r and Y, meets these conditions; for a 10 per cent change in p and M [and, of course, $p_1, \ldots, p_{n-2}$, and A, which do not appear in (14.5),[25] and hence can be ignored] will cause a corresponding 10 per cent change in the excess demand for money. As a particular case of (14.5) we can assume $L(r, Y)$ to have the form

$$(14.6) \qquad L(r, Y) = KY,$$

in which case (14.5) reduces to the familiar Cambridge equation (above, section 10).

The reader might ask whether these assumptions have not again brought us within the scope of the inconsistency theorems of sections 9 and 10. The answer is no. True that we have a system of n independent equations, each of which is homogeneous; but the equations are not homogeneous in the dependent (or endogenous) variables of the system; the homogeneity holds only with respect to the independent (exogenous) and dependent variables taken together. Under these conditions the reader can establish for himself that there is no analogue to the basic inconsistency theorem of section 9.

The distinction can be seen intuitively as follows: A and M are the independent variables of the system: they are stipulated *numbers* determined by factors outside the economic system. Once these numbers are given, our system of n independent equations, (14.1)–(14.4), will then determine the values of the n dependent variables, $p_i (i = 1, \ldots, n - 2)$, r, and p. If the reader will again consult section 9, he will see that the crucial step in the proof of the inconsistency there is justified by our ability to rewrite equations (9.4) in the form (9.5). In other words, the inconsistency derives from the fact that the homogeneity assumptions enable us to reduce the number of dependent variables by one: instead of depending on the individual value of each of these variables, the functions depend on their ratios. For example, instead of depending on $y_1, \ldots, y_m$, the function will depend on the $m - 1$ ratios $y_1/y_m, \ldots, y_{m-1}/y_m$. But in the case of the system (14.1)–(14.4) it is impossible to do this. For assume that the values of the independent variables are specified as $M = 100$ and

---

25. Except indirectly through Y, as in the preceding footnote. Clearly, a constant percentage change in all prices will leave Y, as defined in the preceding footnote, unchanged. Hence, we need not consider it here.

$A = 1,000$—or any other numbers, for that matter. Then the last two ratios of (14.1) become $100/p$ and $1,000/p$. Clearly, then, it is no longer possible to consider the functions of (14.1) as depending only on the *ratios* of p and the p_i.

Let us now summarize the properties of the system (14.1)–(14.4). First of all, the absolute price level appears everywhere in the system. It is, in general, impossible to break down the system into two distinct parts: one to determine relative prices, and one absolute. Both these sets of prices are determined in a truly general-equilibrium manner—by the system as a whole. In particular, it is impossible to say, as Cassel and others did, that a proportionate change in all prices, including the price of assets, will leave the real part of the system completely unaffected; for inspection of equations (14.1) shows that there will be a change in M/p, the real value of cash balances, which in turn will change the excess demands. In this way we have completely freed ourselves of the troublesome classical dichotomies.

Nevertheless, the effects of an increase in the amount of money are completely classical in nature. Assume that this increase (say, a doubling) results in a proportionate change in all prices, including that of assets. (Throughout this discussion it is assumed that the *real* value of nonmonetary assets remains fixed.) We shall show that in this case no other change (except for a doubling in the number of bonds) will occur in the economy. Examine first equations (14.1). Here it is clear that the flows of real goods and services are not affected at all: the doubling of money, value of assets, and all prices cancels out everywhere. Furthermore, this increase has absolutely no effect on the rate of interest. Equation (14.2) shows that there will be a doubling in the number of bonds. Equation (14.5)—which, for simplicity, we take as the form of (14.3)—is completely consistent with our assumptions: r and Y are constant, as was shown in the discussion of (14.1), and the sole effect of the doubling of M is to double p. Equation (14.4) is also obviously satisfied: the doubling of all prices corresponds to the doubling of the general price level.

One more point must be noted in connection with the rate of interest. As we have seen, despite the fact that it appears in the excess-demand equation for money, the rate of interest remains constant after a change in the money supply. Thus, we can simultaneously accept both the Keynesian proposition, that the rate of interest influences the amount of money people want to hold, and the classical proposition, that changing the amount of money will not affect the rate of interest. This seeming paradox is explained by the assumption of equation (14.5), on the one hand, that variations in the rate of interest will affect only the amount of *real* balances people want to hold; and by the proof, on the other, that changes in the amount of money will cause a proportionate change in all prices, thus leaving *real* balances constant. Finally, it should be emphasized that, in contrast to both the classical and (radical) Keynesian position, the rate of interest is not determined by any one particular equation, but, just like any other variable, by the system as a whole.

In this way, I believe it is possible to reconstitute the classical theory. As frequently in such cases, once the reformulation is completed, it is possible to go back to the texts and show that it is really closer to what the original propounders had in mind. What we have in essence done is to solve the problems arising from the classical homogeneity assumptions by assuming still more homogeneity. That is, we argued that the excess-demand functions were homogeneous of degree zero in the monetary value of assets as well as in prices. This is really closer to the classical position, which, when arguing for the lack of any effect of an increase in the amount of money, assumed that the prices of all things—including assets as well as currently produced goods—changed proportionately. Until assets are explicitly introduced into the demand functions of (14.1), this classical proviso with regard to the price of assets has no counterpart in the mathematical analysis.

System (14.1)–(14.4) is closer to the original classical formulation in yet another way. A re-examination of the utility-maximization theory developed by Walras and Pareto will make it obvious that the excess-demand equations derived from this theory must depend also on the amounts of assets in the economy.[26] However, since it was usually assumed that these assets were held constant, there was no point including them in the excess-demand equations. Now that we are interested in the effects of an increase in these assets (i.e., an increase in the amount of money), it is necessary to re-introduce them into our equations.

Bibliography

G. Cassel. *The Theory of Social Economy*, trans. rev. ed. S. L. Barron. New York, 1932.

F. Divisia. *Economique rationelle*. Paris, 1928.

J. M. Keynes. *The General Theory of Employment, Interest, and Money*. New York, 1936.

O. Lange. "Say's Law: A Restatement and Criticism," in *Studies in Mathematical Economics and Econometrics*, ed. O. Lange, F. McIntyre, and T. O. Yntema. Chicago, 1942. Pp. 49–69.

———. *Price Flexibility and Employment*. Bloomington, Ind., 1944.

W. Leontief. "The Fundamental Assumption of Mr. Keynes' Monetary Theory of Unemployment." *Quarterly Journal of Economics*, Nov. 1936, *5*, 192–97.

A. W. Marget. "Leon Walras and the 'Cash Balance Approach' to the Problem of the Value of Money." *Journal of Political Economy*, Oct. 1931, *39*, 569–600.

F. Modigliani. "Liquidity Preference and the Theory of Interest and Money," *Econometrica*, Jan. 1944, *12*, 45–88.

D. Patinkin. "Relative Prices, Say's Law, and the Demand for Money," *Econometrica*, Apr. 1948, *16*, 135–54. (a)

———. "Price Flexibility and Full Employment," *American Economic Review*, Sept. 1948, *38*, 543–64. (b)

A. C. Pigou. "The Classical Stationary State." *Economic Journal*, Dec. 1943, *53*, 343–51.

P. A. Samuelson. "The Stability of Equilibrium: Comparative Statics and Dynamics," *Econometrica*, Apr. 1941, *9*, 97–120.

A. Wald. "Über die eindentige positive Lösbarkeit der neuen Produktionsgleichungen." *Ergebnisse eines mathematischen Kolloquiums*, 1933–34, *6*, 12–20.

———, "Über die Produktionsgleichungen der ökonomischen Wertlehre," *Ergebnisse eines mathematischen Kolloquiums*, 1934–35, *7*, 1–6.

26. Cf. "The Demand for Money," section 1, especially the parenthetical remark at the bottom of p. 137.

_____. ''Über eines Gleichungssysteme der mathematischen Oekonomie,'' *Zeitschrift fur Nationalökonomie*, 1936, 7, 637–70.

L. Walras. *Elements d'économie politique pure*, definitive ed. Paris, 1926.

K. Wicksell. *Lectures on Political Economy*, trans. E. Classen and ed. with an introduction by L. Robbins. London, 1934.

6. Reflections on the Neoclassical Dichotomy*

And Samuel answered Saul, and said: I am the seer . . .
And as for thine asses that were lost three days ago,
set not thy mind on them, for they are found.
(I Samuel 9:19–20).

I have hesitated until now to comment on Paul Samuelson's treatment of the neoclassical dichotomy in his recent interpretation of "What Classical and Neoclassical Theory Really Was" (1968) both because this treatment expresses substantial agreement with the one presented in my *Money, Interest, and Prices* (1956, pp. 105–15; 1965, 171–86) and earlier writings—and because discussions of the dichotomy in the literature have long since passed the point of diminishing returns. Nevertheless, there are differences in emphasis between Samuelson's treatment and my own. Hence—in view of the continued attention which Samuelson's paper has drawn—I would like to make a few observations.

Samuelson's description of the dichotomy is based on his personal recollections. As he writes (1968, p. 15):

> From 2 January 1932 until an indeterminate date in 1937, I was a classical monetary theorist. I do not have to look for the tracks of the jackass embalmed in old journals and monographs. I merely have to lie down on the couch and recall in tranquility, upon that inward eye which is the bliss of solitude, what it was that I believed between the ages of 17 and 22.

Let me start with some of my own recollections on the subject. For convenience of comparison, I shall present them in terms of the notation used by Samuelson.

Over twenty years ago, I published an article (1949, reproduced as the preceding chapter) which demonstrated the invalidity of the traditional dichotomy. According to this dichotomy, the excess-demand equations of a model with n commodities (with their respective prices $p_1, \ldots, p_n$) and money are divided into the "real subset"

$$X_1(p_2/p_1, \ldots, p_n/p_1) = 0,$$
$$\ldots\ldots\ldots\ldots\ldots\ldots\ldots\ldots\ldots ,$$
$$A': \quad \ldots\ldots\ldots\ldots\ldots\ldots\ldots\ldots\ldots ,$$
$$\ldots\ldots\ldots\ldots\ldots\ldots\ldots\ldots\ldots ,$$
$$X_n(p_2/p_1, \ldots, p_n/p_1) = 0,$$

Reprinted by permission from *Canadian Journal of Economics*, May 1972, 5, 279–83. Published originally under the title "Samuelson on the Neoclassical Dichotomy: A Comment."
*I am indebted to my colleagues Yoram Ben-Porath and Giora Hanoch for very helpful criticisms of an earlier draft of this paper.

where $X_i(. . .)$ is the excess-demand equation for the i-th commodity; and the "monetary subset," consisting of the quantity-theory equation

$$B': p_1[Q_1^* + (p_2/p_1)^*Q_2^* + . . . + (p_n/p_1)^*Q_n^*] = \bar{M}V,$$

where the $(p_i/p_1)^*$ are the equilibrium relative prices which emerge as the solution of A'; the Q_i^* are the corresponding equilibrium quantities (as determined by the respective commodity demand functions, which could also be added to A'); $\bar{M}$ is the given quantity of money; and V is Fisher's constant velocity of circulation. Thus relative prices are determined in the "real sector," A', and the absolute price level in the "monetary sector," B'. This is what Samuelson calls "the (A', B') split."

In technical terms, my criticism of this dichotomy was that, because of Walras' law, the excess-demand function for money—say $\phi (. . .)$—has the form

$$\phi(. . .) \equiv - \sum_{i=1}^{n} p_iX_i(p_2/p_1, . . . , p_n/p_1),$$

which—by virtue of its being homogeneous of degree 1 in the p_i—is inconsistent with the form of this function as presented in B'.[1] The economic meaning of this criticism (which, I must admit, became fully clear to me only subsequently)[2] is simple and straightforward: by the budget restraint, the excess demand for money is identical with the excess supply of commodities; hence the inconsistency of the (A', B') dichotomy reflects itself in, for example, the fact that whereas the commodity sector A' does not contain money balances as a variable, and thus implies that a change in these balances has no effect on the system—money sector B' contains such balances, and thus implies the opposite. More generally, even though (for the reason just noted) A' and B' must be mirror images of one another, A' implies that money has no role to play in the economy, whereas B' implies the opposite.

My 1949 article did not stop with criticism, but went on (in its concluding section) to present a remedy in terms of what I described as the "modified classical system"

$$
\begin{aligned}
& G_1(p_2/p_1, . . . , p_n/p_1, M/p_1) &&= 0, \\
& \cdots\cdots\cdots\cdots\cdots\cdots\cdots\cdots\cdots\cdots\cdots\cdots && ., \\
A: \quad & \cdots\cdots\cdots\cdots\cdots\cdots\cdots\cdots\cdots\cdots\cdots\cdots && ., \\
& \cdots\cdots\cdots\cdots\cdots\cdots\cdots\cdots\cdots\cdots\cdots\cdots && ., \\
& G_n(p_2/p_1, . . . , p_n/p_1, M/p_1) &&= 0, \\
& G_{n+1}(p_2/p_1, . . . , p_n/p_1, M/p_1) &&= 0,
\end{aligned}
$$

where $G_i(. . .)$ $(i = 1, . . . , n)$ and $G_{n+1}(. . .)$ represent the excess-demand equa-

---

1. Though it does not bear on the present discussion, it is clear from this that Samuelson's statement (1968, p. 15) that "no version of Walras' Law relates B' to A' " is incorrect.
2. See my "Invalidity of Classical Monetary Theory" (1951), pp. 147–51; *Money, Interest, and Prices* (1965), pp. 174–83, especially pp. 178–79.

tions for commodities and real money balances, respectively (above, p. 144). A few years later,[3] I supplemented this subset of equations with the subset

$B: \quad M = \bar{M},$

and noted that the resulting system (A, B) is dichotomized in the sense that the equilibrium values of all real quantities (including relative prices and real money balances) are determined in A, after taking due account of the equational dependence implied by Walras' law; and that nominal prices are then determined by the specification of B. Accordingly, I called this "the first, valid dichotomy," to be distinguished from the "invalid dichotomy" described above. This is what Samuelson terms "the (A, B) split."[4]

But let me return to recollections of my 1949 paper. After presenting the "modified classical system" A, I went on to emphasize that though the commodity excess-demand functions did not satisfy the then-accepted "homogeneity postulate" (viz., the dependence of these functions solely on relative prices), the system nevertheless possessed the classical quantity-theory property that a change in M causes an equi-proportionate change in the p_i. Correspondingly, I suggested that the advocacy of the "invalid dichotomy" was the consequence of the mistaken notion that the "homogeneity postulate" was a necessary condition for the validity of the quantity theory. I also explained that—by virtue of its specifying the real-balance mechanism by which an increase in the quantity of money increased the demand for commodities—the "modified classical system" was "really closer to what the original propounders [of the classical theory] had in mind" (above, p. 146).

Having presented the matter in this light, I thought at the time that my paper would be accepted as a simple correction of a technical point in the classical model which did not affect any of its substantive conclusions—and that this would be the end of the matter. If this has not turned out to be the case—and, unfortunately, it certainly has not!—it is because my criticism has continued to attract counter-critics from two opposite extremes: those who have continued to assert the validity of the (A', B') dichotomy (and more about them below)—and those who have denied that anyone ever really believed in this dichotomy (of whom Paul Samuelson is the latest example).

Samuelson agrees "that the principal neoclassical writers (other than Walras) had failed to *publish* a clear and unambiguous account of the (A, B) equations" (1968, p. 6; italics in original).[5] Along the same lines, he contends that "few economists in those days tried to write down formal equations for what they were thinking" and that "classical writers, when they did full justice to their own views, did not believe that

3. In my *Money, Interest, and Prices* (1956), pp. 103–4 and p. 333.

4. From this it is clear that there is no cause for Samuelson's fears (1968, p. 6) that I might "prefer not to call the (A, B) split a dichotomy".

The (A, B) model which Samuelson actually presents (*ibid.*, pp. 7–11) is considerably more compli-cated; but its essential properties—for the issue at hand—are validly represented by the foregoing one.

5. I must, however, emphasize once again that though "I have not succeeded in finding an example spelled out in detail of the valid $[(A, B)]$ dichotomy between money and relative prices . . . it is implicit in any of the frequent statements in the literature that a change in the quantity of money causes a proportionate change in prices" (*Money, Interest, and Prices*, supplementary note I:1).

[the (A', B')] formulation was more than a provisional simplification'' (1968, pp. 2 and 4).[6]

Unfortunately, in making these statements Samuelson ignores the existing contrary evidence which shows that: (1) many economists *did* ''write down formal equations for what they were thinking''—and *whenever* they did so it was in the form of the (A', B') dichotomy;[7] (2) Walras did *not* publish an account of the (A, B) dichotomy— and indeed, there are some indications that he might have been the source of the invalid (A', B') dichotomy itself.[8]

This brings us to Samuelson's provocative question: ''In what sense can one say that a man believes one thing when he says something else? In this nonoperational sense: if one could subpoena Cassel, show him two systems and the defects in one, and then ask him which fits in best with his over-all intuitions, I believe he would pick (A, B) and not his own (A', B')'' (1968, p. 14).

Actually, however, such experiments are not only operational, but have been carried out—indeed, in Samuelson's own presence—only to yield results opposite to those predicted by him!

In particular, Samuelson tells us that he ''did discuss the present issue at the Econometric Society meetings of 1940, of which only an incomplete abstract appeared, and also at its 1949 meetings, where W. B. Hickman, Leontief, and others spoke'' (1968, p. 4). But what Samuelson forgets are the papers which Hickman and Leontief presented at the session of the 1949 meetings over which he (Samuelson) presided as chairman—and which they subsequently published.[9]

These papers were criticism of my 1949 article described above. Despite the explanation in this article that all of the good, classical features of the (A', B') dichotomy were in the (A, B) dichotomy, and none of its bad ones—and that system (A, B) was actually closer to the classical spirit than system (A', B')—Hickman and Leontief nevertheless proceeded to choose (A', B') over (A, B).[10] And the same

6. Actually, Samuelson does not deal with my basic criticism of neoclassical monetary theory—which is that it did not fully integrate the real-balance effect into its analysis. The invalid dichotomy is one piece of evidence which I adduce in support of this criticism; but the first and main piece of evidence presented in chap. VIII:1 of my book is the absence of stability analysis (with reference to the absolute price level) in the monetary theory of Walras and the Cambridge economists. By this I mean (in the case of the Cambridge economists) nothing more complicated than the fact that in the diagrams in which they presented a demand curve for money (as a function of $1/p$) intersecting with a fixed supply, they did not carry out the simple graphical exercise (that they always carried out with their demand-and-supply curves of value theory) by which they showed the automatic market forces (in this case, the real-balance effects) that would be generated to bring the equilibrium price back to this intersection point—should there be any deviation from it. (For detailed documentation of this criticism see the references to Marshall, Pigou, Robertson, and others in supplementary note G:2 of my *Money, Interest, and Prices*.)

This broader question (of the role of the real-balance effect in neoclassical monetary theory) has not been dealt with in the subsequent discussion in the literature—which has, unfortunately, concentrated instead on the dichotomy issue.

7. See detailed discussion of François Divisia, Oscar Lange, Franco Modigliani, Eric Schneider, and other writers in supplementary note I:3 of my *Money, Interest, and Prices*.

8. *Ibid.*, 2nd ed., p. 183 and pp. 560–63.

9. W. B. Hickman, ''The Determinacy of Absolute Prices in Classical Economic Theory'' (1950), pp. 9–20; W. W. Leontief, ''The Consistency of the Classical Theory of Money and Prices'' (1950), pp. 21–24.

10. Note in particular Leontief's statement (1950, p. 21) that my criticism of the (A', B') dichotomy ''is aimed at the logical foundations of the non-Keynesian theory of general equilibrium.''

choice was made several years later by Archibald and Lipsey.[11] Surely Paul Samuelson should have drawn the proper conclusion from this revealed preference of recognized scholars.

I cannot explain this preference. Nor can I explain the persistence with which writers even today make strained attempts to present conditions under which the (A', B') dichotomy is (allegedly) valid. And this makes it all the more difficult for me to understand Samuelson's implication that nobody (or hardly anybody) ever "really" believed in this dichotomy.

The pleasures and fascination of *dogmengeschichte* are many. But surely it is only fair to ask anyone who wants to enjoy them to pay an admission fee in the form of supporting citations of chapter and verse for any interpretation that he wishes to advance. Postulated stylized facts are not a substitute.

Bibliography

G. C. Archibald and R. G. Lipsey. "Monetary and Value Theory: A Critique of Lange and Patinkin." *Review of Economic Studies*, Oct. 1958, *26*, 1–22.

W. B. Hickman. "The Determinacy of Absolute Prices in Classical Economic Theory." *Econometrica*, Jan. 1950, *18*, 9–20.

W. Leontief. "The Consistency of the Classical Theory of Money and Prices." *Econometrica*, Jan. 1950, *18*, 21–24.

D. Patinkin. "The Indeterminacy of Absolute Prices in Classical Economic Theory." *Econometrica*, Jan. 1949, *17*, 1–27. [Reproduced as chap. 5 above.]

――――. "The Invalidity of Classical Monetary Theory." *Econometrica*, Apr. 1951, *19*, 134–51.

――――. *Money, Interest, and Prices*. Evanston, Ill., 1956; 2nd ed., New York 1965.

P. A. Samuelson. "What Classical and Neoclassical Theory Really Was." *Canadian Journal of Economics*, Feb. 1968, *1*, 1–15.

11. G. C. Archibald and R. G. Lipsey, "Monetary and Value Theory: A Critique of Lange and Patinkin" (1958), pp. 9–17. Again, note Archibald and Lipsey's claim that "nearly all modern value theory presupposes the validity of the classical $[(A', B')]$ dichotomy"—and that if my criticism of this dichotomy is correct, "then most existing real static theory, e.g., of international trade, must be radically at fault" (*ibid.*, pp. 1 and 10).

Trygve Haavelmo and author (December 1946)

In front of the Social Science Building (ca. 1945). Top row: Jacob Cohen, author, Ray Kosloff. Bottom row: Lawrence Klein, Robert Ferber, Leo Hurwicz.

7. Involuntary Unemployment and the Keynesian Supply Function*

I. Introduction

1. Within the framework of traditional Keynesian economics there are at least two basic issues which have not yet been settled. The first one centers in the frequently heard complaint that Keynesian models neglect the supply side of the market. The second is concerned with the very question which brought forth the *General Theory*: involuntary unemployment. Examination of the Keynesian theory shows that (even granted its argument) it explains primarily the level of employment; it is inadequate in providing either a criterion for the measurement of *un*employment, or a justification for calling it "involuntary."

The only serious attempt to deal with this last question proceeds by assuming a special shape for the supply curve of labor,[1] as in Figure 1. Here N represents employment; w, the money wage; and $w = f(N)$, the supply curve of labor. By

Reprinted by permission from *The Economic Journal*, published by Cambridge University Press, Sept. 1949, *59*; 360–83.

{This article errs both in its substantive analysis of the aggregate supply function and in its statement that there is no such function in the *General Theory*. I have nevertheless reprinted it here for the reasons indicated on p. 11 above.

I might also note that in the years since the publication of this article, I have attempted to amend both of the foregoing errors. Thus a correct analysis of the aggregate supply function was presented in ch. 9, sec. 3, and ch. 13, sec. 2 of my *Money, Interest, and Prices* (1956 and 1965); and a detailed examination of Keynes' treatment of it in the *General Theory* was more recently provided in my "Study of Keynes' Theory of Effective Demand," *Economic Inquiry*, April 1979, *17*, 155–76. Here it is shown that though Keynes did indeed present an aggregate supply function in the *General Theory*, his analysis of it is deficient in several respects.}

* Research in connection with this paper was undertaken under a Social Science Research Council fellowship. The paper has been reprinted as Cowles Commission Paper No. 38.

I should like to express my general indebtedness to two of my former colleagues at the Cowles Commission for Research in Economics: to Lawrence R. Klein (now of the National Bureau of Economic Research), whose excellent book, *The Keynesian Revolution* (New York: Macmillan and Co., 1947), read in manuscript form, started me thinking about many of the problems discussed in this paper; and to Trygve Haavelmo (now of the Oslo Institute of Economics), who was a constant source of stimulation and encouragement.

I am also particularly indebted to the following individuals, who read earlier drafts of this paper and offered many valuable criticisms and suggestions: James Buchanan (University of Tennessee); Robert and Marianne Ferber (University of Illinois); Malcolm Hogg (University of Illinois); Everett E. Hagen (University of Illinois); and D. Gale Johnson, H. Gregg Lewis and Jacob Marschak (University of Chicago). I am also grateful to many former colleagues of the University of Chicago Department of Economics and of the Cowles Commission with whom I have discussed the ideas presented in this essay.

1. Cf., e.g., Oscar Lange, *Price Flexibility and Employment* (1944), p. 6.

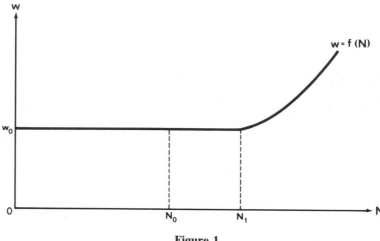

Figure 1

assumption, this supply curve is horizontal at the "customary money wage," w_0, until the amount of employment N_1. In other words, it is assumed that until a certain point money wages are completely rigid. If the amount of labor employed is N_0, then involuntary unemployment to the extent $N_1 - N_0$ is said to exist—since this many additional workers would be willing to work at the prevailing market wage. The artificiality of this definition is sufficiently demonstrated if one considers the case in which the supply curve, instead of being horizontal until the point N_1, rises at an extremely slow rate.

In the following sections it will be shown that the two seemingly independent issues raised above are, in fact, vitally interrelated. In particular, it will be argued that the key to our difficulties lies in explicitly introducing supply functions into the standard Keynesian models: once this is done, the problem of defining and measuring involuntary unemployment is simultaneously solved.

II.   The Supply Function

2.   The traditional tools of Keynesian analysis are the consumption and invest-ment functions. In the very simple Keynesian models these are assumed to depend only on the level of real national income; this is the situation in Figure 2. Here C, I and E are "desired" real-consumption expenditures, investment expenditures and total expenditures, respectively. Y is real national income, and E^* is actual, as distinct from "desired," total real expenditures. $G(Y)$ and $H(Y)$ are the "desired"-consumption and "desired"-investment functions, respectively. The total-expenditures function, $F(Y)$, is obtained by the vertical addition of $G(Y)$ and $H(Y)$.

First of all, we must make clear the sense in which the term "desired" is being used. It refers to nothing more than the schedule of alternative actions (as represented by the demand and supply curves) of traditional economic theory. Consider, for example, the "desired"-consumption function. This can be considered as the end-

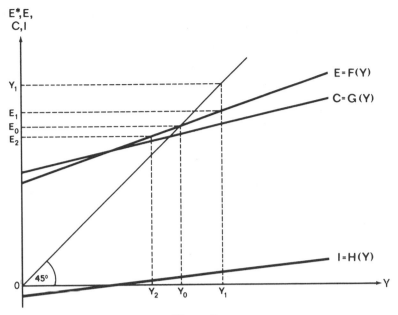

Figure 2

product of the following experiment: Every individual in the economy is approached, told that he must stay within his income and asked how much of each particular good he will buy at different sets of prices and personal income. This gives us the usual individual demand curves of Walrasian general-equilibrium economics. If we sum up these demand curves for all individuals and for all goods, we obtain the aggregate "desired"-consumption function. Under certain assumptions[2] this desired-consumption function will be of such a form that aggregate real desired-consumption will depend only on aggregate real income. These assumptions have been implicitly made in the preceding paragraph; consequently, our desired-consumption function there is written as $C = G(Y)$. It tells us the aggregate amounts the economy desires to consume at different income levels.

Thus the desired behavior of consumers is defined as their behavior under certain specified conditions—a behavior that is described by their Walrasian demand curves. In a similar way we can specify certain conditions under which the firm must operate (*e.g.*, the transformation function) and derive the desired-investment function. The conceptual experiment here is the following one: We ask each firm how much it will invest at different sets of prices and national income, subject to the restriction that the firm's inputs and outputs are related in a specified way (*i.e.*, subject to the firm's transformation function). The results of these experiments will, after aggregation, give us the desired-investment function, $I = H(Y)$. (Admittedly, there are many more

2. Namely, (*a*) that the individual demand curves depend only on relative prices and real income; and (*b*) that in deflating money consumption expenditures and money national income we use a certain price index which emerges from the aggregating process itself. For an example of the derivation of the consumption function in this way see L. R. Klein, "A Post-Mortem on Transition Predictions" (1946), pp. 300–301.

conceptual difficulties in doing this than in constructing the desired-consumption function; but these need not detain us now.) The total expenditures function, $F(Y)$, being the vertical sum of the consumption and investment function, thus represents the total expenditure people desire to make at any given level of real income.

3.   Once the total desired-expenditures function $F(Y)$ is given, the equilibrium level of real national income is determined as follows: First, a 45° line through the origin is drawn. This line (whose equation is $E^* = Y$) represents the fact that, by definition, real national income is equal to actual real expenditures: no one can receive income except as a result of expenditures by someone else.[3] Now consider the income level Y_1. At this level people desire to spend only the amount E_1, which is less than Y_1. In other words, if the income Y_1 is to be maintained, people must continue spending more than they desire to the extent $Y_1 - E_1$. For example, inventories will be accumulated above the amount indicated by the desired-investment function. This undesired spending cannot continue indefinitely. To use again the example of inventories, people will attempt to reduce their undesired accumulations, and, as a result of this attempt, the level of real income prevailing in the system will change. Hence Y_1 cannot be an equilibrium position.

Similarly, the equilibrium level cannot be Y_2; for at that level people would try to correct the resulting undesired disinvestment that would be occurring. To use again the example of inventories, people will try to replenish inventories that have been drawn down below their desired levels, and by this action will change the level of income. By reasoning along these lines we see that the equilibrium level must be at Y_0. At this point—which is given by the intersection of the 45° line and the total desired-expenditure function—desired and actual aggregate expenditures are equal. Hence, within the framework of the given conditions, there exists no force acting to change the income level from Y_0.[4]

4. So much for the standard Keynesian analysis. However, a little reflection will make it obvious that there are some missing links in the argument. Consider again Figure 2. The careful reader will have noted that all that was said about the income level Y_1 or Y_2 was that they were not equilibrium levels; nothing was said about the direction in which the forces set up by the resulting disequilibria would cause the income level to move. In other words, no attempt was made to show that if the economy were, say, at the income level Y_2, automatic forces would be set up to push the income in the direction of the equilibrium level, Y_0. If we were to try to follow through such a dynamic analysis, the omission of certain factors from the Keynesian analysis represented by Figure 2 would immediately become evident. For the standard dynamic analysis runs along the following lines (cf. Figure 2): if the income level were Y_1, the resulting accumulation of undesired inventories would drive prices down and therefore discourage production. As an immediate result, income payments, and

---

3. Many complications are hidden in this simple statement—such as the practice of considering inventory accumulation as purchases of the firm from itself. But these complications need not concern us here.
    4. I abstract here from the difficulty that this equilibrium is only aggregative, and may be disturbed by the disequilibrium of individual firms. Cf. Arthur F. Burns, *Economic Research and the Keynesian Thinking of our Times* (1946), p. 9.

hence national income, would decline. This process would continue until the income level Y_0 is reached. Similarly, if the income level were Y_2, prices would be driven up, and production increased.

The significant point about the preceding dynamic analysis is that it calls into play factors completely outside the analytical framework of Figure 2. It presupposes some type of behavior (*e.g.*, responses to changes in inventories) from the supply side of the market which is never explicitly introduced into the analysis. This procedure is a sharp contrast with that employed in, say, the dynamic analysis of partial equilibrium in one particular market. There both sides of the market are represented by the traditional demand and supply curves. If the price is higher than the equilibrium one, the analysis itself indicates the force (viz., the excess supply) which drives prices down. There is no need to appeal to outside forces to explain the movement toward equilibrium.

From all this there follows but one conclusion: something must be done to complete the Keynesian picture; and that "something" must clearly be the explicit introduction of the supply side into the analysis. It is to this task that we turn in the section which follows.

5. To start from fundamentals, it is clear that a complete explanation of the economic system can be presented only through a Walrasian general-equilibrium system. Unfortunately, for practical analytical purposes such a system is entirely too large and cumbersome. Aggregation is necessary to reduce it to manageable terms. Thus, we have seen that in the preceding Keynesian models all the Walrasian demand curves for finished goods are aggregated into two functions: the consumption and investment functions. But these represent only one side of the market—the demand side. The system presented in Figure 2 provides no aggregate counterpart to the supply functions of the general-equilibrium system. But clearly such an aggregate function can be built up from the Walrasian supply functions in exactly the same way that the consumption and investment functions were built up from the Walrasian demand functions. Furthermore, the interpretation of such an aggregate function will be completely analogous to that of, say, the aggregate desired-consumption function. The Walrasian supply functions from which the aggregate supply function is constructed represent the behavior of suppliers within a specified framework (profit maximization, given transformation curves, etc.); these supply functions, by definition, represent the desires of suppliers. Hence, the function we get by aggregating them also represents the desires of suppliers. We call this function "the aggregate desired-supply function." It shows the aggregate amount of finished goods and services suppliers desire to provide at different levels of income.

In other words, the equilibrium position of the Walrasian system is determined by the joint influence of the demand and supply functions. In the process of aggregation we do lose a lot of detailed information. This we are willing to sacrifice for the sake of manageability. But one characteristic of the general-equilibrium system which we should carry over to the aggregate (or macro-) system is that supply factors, as well as demand factors, influence the equilibrium position. No such influence is provided for in our Keynesian model of Figure 2. In order to bring it in, our macro-system must

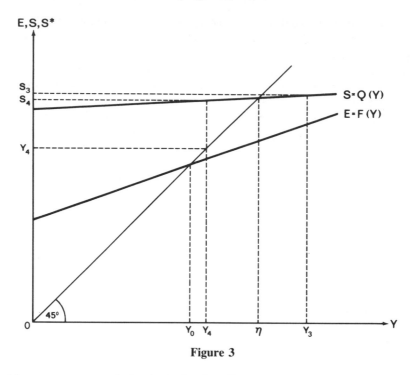

Figure 3

provide an aggregate desired-supply function (corresponding to the aggregate desired-consumption and -investment functions) which should play a co-equal role in the determination of the equilibrium position.

What might the form of this aggregate desired-supply function be? By making assumptions similar to those made for the consumption function we can have aggregate real desired supply, S, depending only on real income, Y. In Figure 3 this function is drawn as $S = Q(Y)$.

What is the form of $Q(Y)$? It can be shown that the assumptions made in aggregating the supply function imply that the real return to productive services is constant; that is, the price of finished goods is always proportionate to the price of productive services.[5] This should lead us to suspect that the function $Q(Y)$ might have a special

---

5. Limitations of space prevented the publication of the mathematical appendix to this article in which this was proved. The general argument is related to footnote 2 on p. 157, above. The price index that comes out of the aggregation there is for finished goods only; but the price index resulting from the aggregation here is for productive services as well. If the supply function is to depend on the same measure of real income, Y, that the expenditure function does, then the two price indexes must be the same, which means that the prices of finished goods and productive services must be proportionate.

{The assumption that these prices always change proportionately actually contradicts the law of diminishing returns, which implies that the increased input of productive services necessary for an increase in the output of finished goods, Y, will cause a decrease in the marginal productivity of the services and hence in their price relative to that of finished goods. This is the major analytical error alluded to in the footnote added at the beginning of this article.

The mathematical appendix mentioned here has now been reproduced at the end of this chapter.}

form. In particular, since the real return is constant, suppliers might desire to provide the same amount of goods regardless of the level of income. In that case the aggregate supply function would be a horizontal line at, say, the level η. This extreme position was not taken in Figure 3; but some allowance for it was made by giving $Q(Y)$ a small slope with respect to Y. In other words, it was assumed that the desired supply does not vary much with the level of income.

Lest there be any misunderstanding on this point, it should be made clear that the assumption of a constant real wage is regarded as completely unrealistic. We shall, in fact, remove this assumption later (§ 14). However, the main point here is that for the purposes of this article it is only the *existence*, and not the *form*, of the aggregate supply function which is of importance. We shall return to this point again (§ 14).

6. Let us for the moment ignore the expenditure function in Figure 3 and concentrate on the relationship between the 45° line and the desired-supply function. Introduce the variable $S*$ which equals actual, as distinct from desired, aggregate real supply of finished goods and services. Previously we used the fact that national income is equal to aggregate expenditures. Now we note that, by definition, real national income is also equal to the actual real value of finished output, $S*$. So the 45° line also represents this equality, *i.e.*, $S* = Y$.

In a manner completely analogous to that of the discussion of the expenditure function, it can now be showed that the level of income η (Figure 3) is the equilibrium level determined by supply conditions. For consider the income level Y_4. At this level firms desire to supply the amount S_4, which is greater than Y_4. In other words, if the income level Y_4 is to be maintained, firms must continue supplying less than they actually desire, to the extent $S_4 - Y_4$. Consequently, an effort will be made (via price reductions) to correct this disappointment of desires, and in the process the level of income will change. Similarly, Y_3 cannot be an equilibrium value; for to maintain that level firms must supply more than they actually desire. The only possible equilibrium from the supply side is $Y = \eta$. At this level, since desired and actual supply are equal, there is no stimulus for any change in the system.

If we now consider Figure 3 as a whole, it is immediately evident that the macro-system we have built up from our Walrasian system is one which can never be at equilibrium. For the income level Y_0, which equilibrates the demand side of the economy, leaves the supply side in disequilibrium. Conversely, the income level η, which equilibrates the supply side, leaves the demand side in disequilibrium. There is no level of income which will simultaneously equilibrate both of these sets of forces in the economy. What is the economic interpretation of this inability to reach a consistent equilibrium position? This is the problem discussed in Part III. There it is argued that the inconsistency created by the explicit introduction of the aggregate supply function into Keynesian systems provides the key to the theory of involuntary unemployment implicit in Keynesian economics.

7. One more point must be made, an important one for our later analysis. In the discussion of Figure 3 it was tacitly implied that there is no way of resolving the inconsistency of having two "equilibrium" positions. There are, however, *a priori* grounds (formulated by Pigou) for claiming that the initial duo-equilibrium itself

brings into play automatic market forces which tend to remove the inconsistency.[6] Specifically, suppliers at, say, the income level Y_0 in Figure 3, will find themselves supplying less than they desire. Hence they will reduce the general price level in an effort to increase their sales. The fall in the price level will in turn increase the real value of the cash holding of individuals. As a result, their willingness to spend out of income will increase so that the whole expenditure function in Figure 3 will shift upwards. (In other words, the expenditure function is now assumed to depend on the absolute price level, p, as well as the level of real income, Y.) Under certain assumptions, if the price decline continues long enough, the expenditure function can be shifted so far up that it intersects the 45° line at the same income level, η, at which the supply function intersects. (This is the situation pictured in Figure 5 below.) Thus, a unique equilibrium position is determined and the inconsistency removed.

In addition to these forces there is the more traditional Keynesian effect on the expenditure function through variations in the interest rate. An excess supply will drive interest rates down and thereby raise the expenditure function. If it has sufficient interest elasticity, the expenditure function might eventually be driven up to its position in Figure 5. It is clear that for the purpose of this paper the interest rate and the price level play completely equivalent roles. Hence, whenever in the subsequent argument the reader will find the phrase "price level," he can add "and interest rate."

As we shall see later, this argument makes no fundamental change in our analysis. At most, it requires that we shift from a static to a dynamic viewpoint. The full implications of these remarks will become clearer in the exposition which follows.

III. The Concept of Involuntary Unemployment

8. Involuntary unemployment involves what might be called "relative coercion": people cannot fulfil their desires as freely as under some other situation which serves as a norm of reference; hence in order to give concreteness to the concept of coercion we must first define this norm of reference. Thus, it is theoretically meaningless to speak of involuntary unemployment without introducing a comparison between two alternative models: the actually existing one and some designated norm. The extent of involuntary unemployment is then measured by the difference between the existing amount of employment, and the amount that would have existed under the norm.

I must emphasize that coercion and freedom are defined in a relative sense only. People acting with the "normal" freedom (*i.e.*, under the restrictions to be found in the norm of reference) will (for the sake of brevity) be defined as fulfilling their desires freely. People acting under more than the "normal" restrictions will be said to be coerced and prevented from fulfilling their desires. In what follows our norm of reference is defined as a model in which perfect competition reigns and the economic unit is restricted only by the budget restraint and technological relationships (*e.g.*, the

---

6. The argument of this paragraph is presented in its barest details, since it has already been discussed at length in my article "Price Flexibility and Full Employment" (1948), pp. 543–65. This will be referred to henceforth as "Price Flexibility."

production function). Thus, by definition, our norm is a system of equations. Within this norm of reference the individual will be defined as fulfilling his desires—though he may be poor and unhappy. In other words, an individual will be said to be acting freely as long as he is on his Walrasian demand and/or supply curves.

Partial equilibrium analysis provides an illustration. Consider the classical demand (D) and supply (S) curves for labor (N) in terms of the real wage w/p (Figure 4). By definition, the demand curve, D, represents the desires of employers under normal restrictions, and the supply curve, S, represents the desires of workers under normal restrictions. Now, if the real wage, w/p, is always at the intersection of D and S, then within this model there can be no involuntary unemployment. No matter how far D shifts over to the left and employment drops, workers will be working as much as they desire: Workers and employers will be fulfilling their desires as long as the equilibrium wage and employment are always at the intersection of the curves. Only if some force entered which established the equilibrium value at, say, the wage $(w/p)_2$ and the employment N_2, a point off the supply curve of labor, could coercion, and therefore involuntary unemployment (to the extent $N_1 - N_2$), be said to exist in the system.

One fundamental qualification must be introduced into the discussion of Figure 4. If the wage $(w/p)_2$ has been set and maintained by monopolistic tactics of a trade union, it is clearly a distortion to say that "involuntary" unemployment exists in the economy. (Of course, those workers unable to find jobs because of the union wage policy might be said to be "involuntarily" unemployed; but this involves a completely different usage from the customary one, which implies that the workers are

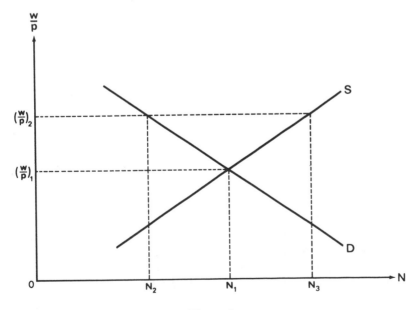

Figure 4

unemployed neither through their fault, nor through that of their brethren.) This paper does not deal with any of these difficulties; it is concerned solely with the definition of involuntary unemployment within an actual competitive framework. Within this framework we can think of the wage $(w/p)_2$ being maintained despite wage flexibility if, for example, the price level were to fall proportionately with the wage level and so keep the real wage constant. In such a case, workers would truly be involuntarily unemployed—despite all their efforts to correct the situation by money-wage reduction.[7]

More generally, in a dynamic framework, we can think of the price decline as being less than proportionate to the money-wage decline, so that the real wage falls only slowly. During the time it takes for it to fall, workers are involuntarily unemployed; but the amount of involuntary unemployment is continuously decreasing. Eventually, if the real wage falls to $(w/p)_1$ (cf. Figure 4) a full-employment condition may be re-established.

9. Let us apply the concepts of § 8 to the analysis of Figure 3. Clearly a full-employment level of income in this model must mean a level of income at which suppliers are able to supply exactly what they desire—in the sense of § 8. In other words, suppliers must be employed to the full extent they desire. From the analysis of Figure 3 it immediately follows that η is the full-employment level of income; for at any other level there would exist a discrepancy between the amount sellers desire to supply, and the amount they actually do. Hence we choose as our norm of reference a model in which this level of income could be maintained indefinitely; $i.e.$, a model whose equilibrium level of national income (for both the demand and supply sectors) is η. This norm of reference is drawn in Figure 5.

Assume now that, in contrast with this norm, the actual desires of individuals are represented by the expenditure and supply curves in Figure 3. This figure reveals an initial incompatibility of interests—with demanders desiring the income level Y_0, and suppliers the level η. Several possibilities now present themselves. First consider the case in which the prevailing level of national income is always Y_0. In other words, only the desires of demanders influence the determination of the national income, while the desires of suppliers are completely ignored. We would then have as a measure of the extent of involuntary unemployment (U) in the system

$$U = \eta - Y_0.$$

That is, involuntary unemployment is measured by the difference between the level of national income in the norm of reference, η, and the level actually prevailing, Y_0 (cf. § 8).

What are the implications of assuming that the income level will remain at Y_0? It is with respect to this question that the remarks of § 7 are pertinent. It will be recalled that at the income Y_0 suppliers will reduce their prices in an attempt to eliminate the discrepancy between the quantity they are selling and the quantity they desire to sell. Now, if these price reductions have no effect on spenders—that is, if the expenditure

7. This is clearly the argument of Keynes in his *General Theory* (1936), pp. 11–13.

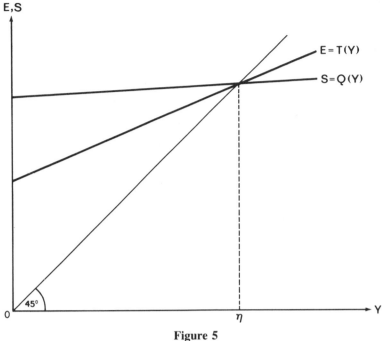

Figure 5

function does not shift upwards at all, despite all price reductions, no matter how far down they go or how long they are maintained—then the income level will remain indefinitely at Y_0. In the case of such insensitivity of spenders to general price declines we can say that suppliers are in a "weak strategic position." At the other extreme is the case where the slightest price decline instantaneously shifts the expenditure function to the position it has in Figure 5, so that full employment is established. In this case we can say that suppliers are in a "strong strategic position." Midway between these extremes is the case illustrated in Figure 6. Here it is assumed that by price reductions we can shift the expenditure function upwards; but that (to repeat the phrase of the preceding paragraph) despite all price reductions, no matter how far down they go or how long they are maintained, it is impossible to shift the expenditure function up to its position in Figure 5. That is, say, the expenditure function cannot be pushed above its position in Figure 6. Under these circumstances the income level Y_6 will be maintained; correspondingly, the amount of involuntary unemployment is measured by $\eta - Y_6$. In this case we can say that suppliers have an "intermediate strategic position."

Thus, the strategic position of suppliers is essentially a measure of the sensitivity of spenders to changes in the absolute price level (*i.e.*, to changes in their real cash balances) and interest rate. The strategic position is stronger the smaller the price (interest) decline required to shift the expenditure function a given amount within a given period. Similarly, it is stronger the shorter the time required to shift the expenditure function to a given position by a given price (interest) decline. And, of

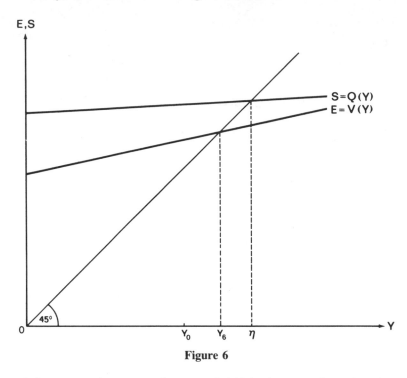

Figure 6

course, it is stronger the greater the upward shift in the expenditure function corresponding to a given price (interest) decline maintained for a given period. Finally, there is the case where the initial price (interest) decline creates expectations of further price (interest) declines and causes the expenditure function to drop even further downwards.[8] In this case suppliers are clearly in an extremely weak strategic position: all their attempts to extricate themselves from the unemployment situation will perversely plunge them ever deeper into it. Corresponding to each of the above cases, the unemployment will be defined as permanent, temporary or prolonged, according to the strategic position of the suppliers.[9]

There is one further (and, perhaps, even more fundamental) sense in which we can speak of suppliers as being in a weak strategic position. Assume that we start out with the incompatibility of Figure 3, but that by a series of price declines we are finally able to reach the situation of Figure 5. We can conceive of two opposite ways in which this dynamic adjustment might take place. The first is the one that has been assumed up to now in this section. The income level starts out at Y_0 (cf. Figure 3); as the price level falls, the desired-expenditure function rises, and for each period of time the actually prevailing income is determined by the intersection of this function with the 45° line, until finally the income level η is reached. At the other extreme we might consider the income starting out at η and remaining there all the time the expenditure function is

8. Cf. "Price Flexibility," 811
9. *Ibid.*, p. 564.

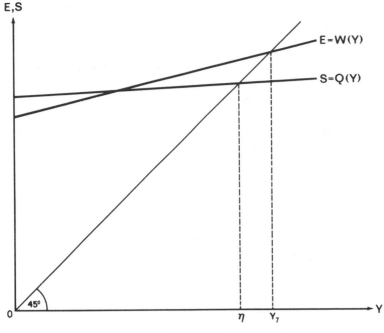

Figure 7

moving upwards. In other words, under the first method the prevailing income is always at a level desired by demanders, throughout the adjustment process; while under the second method it is always at the level desired by suppliers.

In our economy it is easy to think of suppliers selling less than they desire; but it is difficult to conceive of demanders buying more than they desire. Hence, when we start off from a situation such as that of Figure 3, it is the first type of adjustment that takes place. Thus, throughout the period of adjustment, even if income finally succeeds in reaching η, demanders are obtaining an income level they desire, while suppliers are not. This is another very real sense in which suppliers are in a weak strategic position relative to demanders.

10. Until now we have dealt with involuntary unemployment; but using exactly the same concepts of § 8 we can also define involuntary over-employment. Consider the case where the desired expenditure function is $E = W(Y)$ as in Figure 7. This situation implies that despite price increases suppliers are unable to bring the expenditure function down to the point where it intersects the 45° line at η. In brief, the level of national income desired by spenders (Y_7) is greater than that desired by suppliers. If the level of national income is actually Y_7, then a measure of the extent to which suppliers are over-employed is the negative quantity

$$U = \eta - Y_7.$$

That is, involuntary over-employment is measured by the difference between the level of national income in the norm of reference, and the level actually prevailing. Clearly, the same concept applies when suppliers do succeed in bringing the expenditure function down somewhat, so that an intermediate level of national income— between η and Y_7 —prevails.

A situation of over-employment may well have existed during the War. Here the Government provided almost an unlimited demand for goods, which was not diminished by higher prices. Then it resorted to patriotic appeals to persuade the supplier to produce more than they really desired. It might be argued that this patriotic appeal caused an upward shift in the supply function itself, so that suppliers were "really not" involuntarily over-employed. The danger in this type of argument is that eventually it will define away the whole concept of involuntary action. It leads to such nonsense statements as: a man held up at the point of a gun "voluntarily" gives up his wallet because he "desires" to save his life! This example simply points up the necessity of stating a norm of reference (arbitrary as it may be) whenever we wish to speak of involuntary actions. In our economic norm suppliers are presumed to be acting like "economic men," completely devoid of any nationalistic motivations. Hence, when they are influenced by patriotic appeals, they can properly be said to be acting involuntarily.

Another way in which suppliers can meet a situation of over-employment is by rationing. That is, if price increases prove ineffectual in reducing the expenditure function sufficiently, suppliers may decide that nevertheless they will produce only the output they desire, and allocate it among consumers on some arbitrary rationing basis (first come first served, fixed percentage of purchases in previous years, etc.). In this case it is the spenders who are forced into involuntary actions: they must buy less than they actually desire.

The elimination of peace-time involuntary over-employment seems to be a simpler task than the corresponding elimination of involuntary unemployment. (Once again the reader is reminded that we are abstracting here from all monopolistic forces in the economy.) This follows from the supposition that price rises are a much more effective means of shifting the expenditure function down, than price declines of shifting it up. There is no inconsistency here; as in many other places in economic theory, there is no reason to expect symmetry of reactions. Thus, under conditions of over-employment the strategic position of suppliers, in the first sense of § 9, is stronger than that under unemployment. The suppliers' strategic position is also stronger in the second sense; for the income level may remain at η during the whole period of adjustment in which the expenditure function is being forced down. For example, suppliers may resort to rationing during this whole period.

IV. Keynes and the Classics

11. From the perspective of the preceding analysis it is now possible to examine, and contrast, the assumptions of the Keynesian and classical positions. Consider first the conventional Keynesian analysis of §§ 2–3. Explicitly, the supply function is not introduced at all. Implicitly, it is assumed that under unemployment conditions suppliers are in a weak strategic position, in both of the senses of § 9. First of all, spenders respond little, if at all, to price-level and interest-rate reductions.[10] Secondly, the actually prevailing level of income is always determined by the intersection of the expenditure function and the 45° line. Hence, there is no need to introduce the supply function, since the prevailing level of income is determined by demand factors alone. This level of income is then compared with an arbitrarily selected level, designated as the full-employment income, and the difference used as a measure of unemployment. The advantage of the preceding argument is that it makes this element of arbitrariness unnecessary: the full employment level of income is defined by the same analytical apparatus which determines the actually prevailing level of income. In addition, we differ from the usual Keynesian analysis in saying that the income level need not remain at the original intersection of the expenditure function with the 45° line. True, for each period of time the level of income is determined by the intersection of the expenditure function with the 45° line. But this level increases over time as the expenditure function is pushed upwards.

It is important to understand the dynamic theory implicit in this interpretation of the Keynesian theory.[11] Essentially we divide the economy into two markets: one for finished goods and services, and the other for productive services. From the preceding paragraph it is clear that we assume that equilibrium is rapidly restored in the first market. In other words, if a disturbance should suddenly shift the expenditure function downwards, the level of income would quickly fall to the new intersection point with the 45° line. All this means is that undesired inventories are rapidly eliminated from the system (cf. § 3). Thus no stimulus for any further movement in prices comes from the finished-goods market. Nevertheless, the system continues with its dynamic adjustment due to the fact that the market for productive services is not in equilibrium. By analogy, one might say that the involuntary unemployment in this market represents "undesired inventories of productive services." In any event, the presence of unemployed productive services drives the price level down as long as equilibrium is not re-established in this market too.

12. In the classical position, involuntary unemployment could not arise in this way. For a basic assumption of that position was Say's law; and under this assumption full employment was always assured.

The meaning of Say's law is that regardless of the level of income, people desire to spend their entire incomes; or, what is the same thing, people will not use their money incomes to add to their cash holdings. In the words of J. S. Mill, in his chapter on Say's law:[12]

> Could we suddenly double the productive powers of the country, we should double the supply of commodities in every market; but we should, by the same

---

10. Actually, Keynes never considered the effect of the price level on the expenditure function; but, as I have argued elsewhere ("Price Flexibility," pp. 563–64) it does not seem too difficult to extrapolate his position on this matter.

11. In the formulation of this paragraph I have benefited from discussions with Kenneth J. Arrow of the Cowles Commission for Research in Economics.

12. J. S. Mill, *Principles of Political Economy*, book 3, ch. 14, § 2; p. 558 of the Ashley edition.

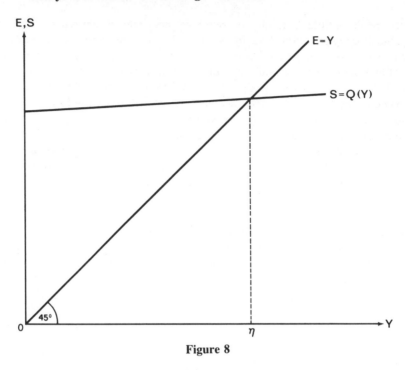

Figure 8

stroke, double the purchasing power. Everybody would bring a double demand as well as a supply: everybody would be able to [and, presumably, would]* buy twice as much, because everyone would have twice as much to offer in exchange.

What does this mean as far as the shape of the aggregate expenditure function is concerned? Under Say's law the expenditure function must always coincide with the 45° line, as in Figure 8. This coinciding is the graphical counterpart of the statement that at every level of income people want to spend their entire income. Analytically this means that the expenditure function has the form $E = Y$. Under this assumption it is clear that there exists only one equilibrium level of the national income, a level jointly desired by both spenders and suppliers. Therefore, in the classical system full employment is always established; the income of the community is limited only by supply factors. Thus, Say's law, far from precipitating the economy into a state of unstable equilibrium (as is sometimes assumed), instead removes a possible inconsistency from the system, and insures the rapid achievement of a unique, stable, full-employment equilibrium.

* {The insertion of these words actually distorts Mill's meaning in this passage, which—in present-day terms—simply states that national income *equals* national product. This distortion (of which Keynes on p. 18 of the *General Theory* was also guilty) was subsequently noted in my *Money, Interest, and Prices* (1956), pp. 473–74; (1965), pp. 646–57.}

13. Keynes, of course, violently disagreed with the assumption of Say's law. This is the sum and substance of his liquidity-preference theory: out of any given income, people may have a net desire to add to their cash balances. Hence, the expenditure function need not coincide with the 45° line; and hence, the level of income established by the intersection of the 45° line and the expenditure function need not be the full-employment level. Thus Keynes denied the basic proposition of classical economics: namely, that the economic system would automatically generate full employment.

It should, however, be emphasised that *the classical position as revised by Pigou no longer needs Say's law*. In this system automatic full employment is brought about by interest, wage and price flexibility regardless of the form of the expenditure function.[13] Correspondingly, as I have argued elsewhere,[14] the Keynesian attack shifts its concentration from Say's law to the dynamic instability of our economic system—its inability to restore full employment within a reasonable time after being subjected to a shock of one type or another.

Actually it can be said that everyone simultaneously accepts and rejects Say's law: rejects it, in the sense that no one believes the short-run-expenditure function must have the form it has in Figure 8; accepts it, in the sense that everyone recognizes that in the long run people want goods, and not money.

V. The Argument Generalized

14. There have been many occasions in this paper where the analysis has pressed hard against the confines of our oversimplified model. Essentially, the trouble is that the model explicitly provides for only one price level (finished goods), while implicit in the analysis is that of yet another (productive services). This is one reason why the aggregate supply function appears like such a monstrosity. Actually, it should depend on both of these prices; however, our oversimplified assumption that these prices are proportionate (cf. § 5, above) forces us to write it as dependent on neither. Nevertheless, it was claimed in § 5 that the general analysis developed on the basis of this oversimplified model could be readily extended to more realistic ones. This and the following sections attempt to make good this claim.

First, we shall briefly sketch the way in which the concepts of this article appear in a somewhat more extended model. Let Y = national income, r = rate of interest, p = absolute price level, E = aggregate demand for finished goods, N^D = demand for labor, N^S = supply of labor, M^D = demand for cash balances and M^S = supply of cash balances. It must be emphasised that these last five variables represent *desired* quantities demanded or supplied—in the sense used in § 2 and throughout this paper. Consider now the following system:—

(1) $$E = \psi\,(Y,\, r,\, p)$$
(2) $$Y = \phi\,(N^D)$$
(3) $$E = Y$$

13. Cf. "Price Flexibility," §§ 1–8.
14. *Ibid.*, § 14.

$$(4) \qquad N^D = f(w/p)$$
$$(5) \qquad N^S = g(w, p)$$
$$(6) \qquad N^D = N^S$$
$$(7) \qquad M^D = L(Y, r, p)$$
$$(8) \qquad M^S = \text{const.}$$
$$(9) \qquad M^D = M^S.$$

This model divides up the economy into three markets: finished goods, labor and money.[15] For each market there are two behavior equations and one equilibrium condition. Starting from the last triplet of equations, we have in (7) the desired-demand for cash balances (*i.e.*, the liquidity preference equation); in (8), the desired-supply of cash balances (assumed for simplicity to be a constant); and, in (9), the condition that the money market is not in equilibrium unless desired supply and demand for money are equal. The next triplet furnishes corresponding information for the labor market. Here we have followed Keynes in assuming that the supply of labor depends on money, and not real, wages; but this is not a necessary part of the argument which follows. The demand for labor is assumed to depend on real wages; this is not essential to the argument either.

In the first triplet, the first and third equations are quite familiar. The only difference between equation (1) and the expenditure function used throughout this paper is that (1) provides explicitly for the possible influence of the rate of interest. Equation (3) is the equilibrium condition for the finished-goods market, as explained in § 3. Equation (2) is the only new-comer: this is the production function.[16] In this model the production function is completely interchangeable with the aggregate supply function. This follows from the relationship between equations (2) and (4). If suppliers of finished goods are faced with a given real wage rate, the amount of labor they will purchase is determined by (4). If we insert the resulting labor input in (2), we get the output of finished goods that suppliers will provide for this labor input, *i.e.*, at the designated real wage. In other words, by substituting (4) into (2) we come out with the familiar aggregate supply function. It differs from the one used in this paper in that it depends on the real wage rate, now no longer (cf. § 5) assumed to be constant.

The use of the production function in (2) instead of the equivalent aggregate supply function was deliberate. There is no doubt that the former function is a much more familiar and accepted tool of economic analysis. In fact, one can find in the literature several examples of models very similar to the one above.[17] Consequently, these models have implicit in them the aggregate supply function developed in this paper. My only objection to these other presentations is that they make no satisfactory interpretation of the supply function; in particular, they fail to see the relationship

15. Implicit in the model is yet a fourth market: that for bonds. This can be ignored since, by "Walras' law," it is considered here as residual. Cf. ch. 5 above, §§ 6 and 14.

16. For simplicity we are assuming the amount of capital to be held constant. Hence the production function depends only on the rate of labor input, N^D.

17. As a case in point cf. Franco Modigliani, "Liquidity Preference and the Theory of Interest and Money" (1944), pp. 47–48.

between it and involuntary unemployment. This is the problem we shall now examine.

Assume, for simplicity, that our model is consistent:[18] that is, it has a solution. Let the solution values for income and employment be $Y = \eta$ and $N^D = N^S = \sigma$, respectively. Then, by definition of the functions of our model, these are the full-employment values of the respective variables. Assume now that a sudden disturbance in the economy causes a downward shift in the expenditure function. This sets up a whole chain of dynamic events. During this process there is no reason why any of the equilibrium conditions—(3), (6) and (9)—should be satisfied. We assume, however, that equilibrium in the finished goods and money markets is quickly re-established. The only pressure for continued movements of the variables comes from the failure to satisfy (6) (cf. above, § 11). Correspondingly, as long as this equilibrium condition is unsatisfied, the level of employment is less than σ. Hence, by definition, there is involuntary unemployment within the system (cf. above, § 8). The level of this unemployment will continue to fluctuate as the system tries to correct the disequilibrium in the labor market. In some cases it is possible that the system will finally succeed in restoring a full-employment equilibrium.

15. The preceding section extended the analysis by applying it to a model with more equations. Another method of extension is to go back to the maximizing behavior from which the equations themselves are derived. In this way it is possible to make the concept of involuntary action even more vivid.

Consider, for example, the demand function of an individual for a certain commodity. Assume that the norm is given by the condition that he must stay within his budget. Then inability to be on his demand curve (for example, the commodity may be rationed by the government) means, in mathematical terms, that besides being subject to the (normal) budget restraint when maximizing utility, the individual is also subject to at least one additional restraint or side condition (viz., that arising from the rationing). This additional restraint is an indication of the extent to which he must act involuntarily. On the other hand, an individual who maximizes his utility subject only to the (normal) budget restraint (say, an individual exempt from the rationing regulations), is said to be acting freely and fully satisfying his desires. This interpretation can readily be generalized to any type of maximizing activity.

16. So far we have dealt with particular extensions. Let us now see how the basic concepts presented in this article can be extended to a perfectly general system.

Consider a model with n equations. For the moment, assume that the model is a static one. Its n equations will be of various types: some will be behavior equations for various sectors of the economy, some equilibrium conditions and some definitions. Assume that the behavior equations represent behavior under the restrictions of the norm; in other words, assume that they represent the desires of the respective sectors, in the sense used in this paper. Mathematically, there are two possibilities: the static system may be consistent, or it may be inconsistent. To say that the system is mathematically inconsistent is equivalent to saying that the desires of people, as

---

18. The implications of an inconsistent model are discussed below, § 16. On this whole paragraph see in particular § 11, above.

reflected by this system, are incompatible: they cannot all be satisfied simultaneously. Let us examine in detail the implications of this proposition.

If the system is inconsistent, then there exists no point (*i.e.*, no set of prices, quantities, incomes, etc.) which will simultaneously satisfy all the equations of the system. In other words, no matter at what point the economy may be, some of its behavior equations cannot be satisfied; that means, no matter what happens some people must be off their (desired) behavior curves, and hence must be acting involuntarily. From this it follows that the system can never be in equilibrium; for no matter at what point it is, it cannot remain there; the members of the economy left dissatisfied at that point will try to achieve their desired behavior, and thereby move the system away from whatever point it happens to be at.

An example of such an inconsistent static system is provided by Figure 3—under the assumption that nothing can be done to move any of the curves presented in it. As pointed out in the discussion of this figure (§ 6), no matter at what point the system happens to be—that is, no matter what the income and the price level (for by the preceding sentence we are assuming that the expenditure function is completely insensitive to the price level)—it is impossible for both demanders and suppliers simultaneously to fulfil their desires; at least one of them must be forced into involuntary action. Correspondingly, the system can never be at equilibrium.[19]

Now assume that the static system is consistent. Does that mean that everyone in the society will always fulfil his desires? In order to answer this question we must turn to dynamic analysis. The general proposition that can be made is: The existence of a consistent equilibrium position for the static system is a necessary, but not a sufficient condition for the elimination of involuntary action within the economy.[20] In other words, the argument of the preceding paragraph has shown that the system cannot be free of involuntary action unless it is consistent; but that does not mean that once it is consistent we can be sure of the elimination of involuntary action. For example, assume that the system does have the consistent solution represented in Figure 5. Assume further that due to a certain disturbance in the system the expenditure function falls to its position in Figure 3. This sets up price-level and interest-rate declines, and we now assume that these declines shift the expenditure function upwards. But in certain cases it may be that, due to dynamic expectation factors, no matter how far the price level and interest rate falls, it is impossible to shift the expenditure function back to its position in Figure 5.[21] Under these assumptions we may continue to have involuntary action within the system for an indefinitely long period.

But we need not go to such an extreme case—again, a mathematical, not necessarily a realistic, extreme. Assume now that by price-level and interest-rate declines the expenditure function is eventually brought back to its position in Figure 5. But all this takes time; and during this period of movement and adjustment some individuals must

---

19. Another example of an inconsistent static system is provided by Figure 3 and § 3 in "Price Flexibility."

20. Cf. "Price Flexibility," p. 560, footnote 30.

21. This particular argument is developed in much greater detail in "Price Flexibility," § 12.

be off their behavior curves; that is, they must be forced into involuntary action.[22] Here, too, we can define our concept of strategic position. The strategic position of any behavior group is defined in terms of how much it must give up its desires, for what period of time. The one that can stay "closest" to its desired behavior curve during the period of adjustment is the "strongest."

From the framework just described, we can appreciate the major significance of the classical position. It is, in brief, that the behavior equations are so sensitive to price and interest changes that the market will automatically and quickly establish a position in which everyone's desires are satisfied. That is, the market will make the desires of people consistent. Correspondingly, we can appreciate the nature of the Keynesian argument: its denial of the efficacy, and even existence, of these delicate balancing operations; and its insistence that the end result of leaving the market to its automatic functioning must inevitably be the frustration of desires somewhere in the system.

Mathematical Appendix*

The nature of the Keynesian model which figures so prominently in §§ 2–7 can best be appreciated if it is actually aggregated from the demand and supply functions of traditional economic theory. This we shall now proceed to do.

Consider an economy consisting of n goods: the first $n - 1$ being finished goods; and the n-th, paper money. Let D_i, S_i, and p_i ($i = 1, \ldots, n$) equal the amount demanded, the amount supplied, and the price of the i-th good, respectively. By definition $p_n = 1$. Let $\mathcal{Y}$ = money national income. Then we can write the following (modified) Casselian system:

(1) $\quad D_i = f_i(p_1, \ldots, p_{n-1}, \mathcal{Y})$

(2) $\quad S_i = g_i(p_1, \ldots, p_{n-1}, \mathcal{Y}) \qquad (i = 1, \cdots, n)$

(3) $\quad D_i = S_i$

(4) $\quad \mathcal{Y} = \sum_{i=1}^{n-1} p_i S_i.$

Equations (1) and (2) are the demand and supply equations, respectively. These are assumed to depend on national income as well as the prices of all goods. They tell us how much of each good the individuals of the economy desire to buy at different sets of prices and income. Equations (3) are the equilibrium conditions of the system. The last equation defines the money national income as the value of the total output of finished goods.

---

22. Cf. above, § 9; "Price Flexibility," § 14.

* Originally unpublished.

We now define aggregate money expenditure $\mathcal{E}$ as the sum of expenditures on all goods, so that the aggregate money expenditure function becomes

$$(5) \qquad \mathcal{E} = \sum_{i=1,}^{n-1} p_i f_i \, (p_1, \, \cdots, \, p_{n-1}, \, \mathcal{Y}).$$

The function (5) gives the desired aggregate money expenditure on goods and services corresponding to given levels of prices and money income. It must be emphasized that $\mathcal{E}$ includes investment as well as consumer expenditures. Assume that the functions f_i are of such a form that aggregate expenditure, $\mathcal{E}$, is a function of only money income, $\mathcal{Y}$, and a suitable general price index, p, derived from the aggregation process (5). That is, assume the f_i are of such a form that the following relationship holds:

$$(6) \qquad \mathcal{E} = \sum_{i=1}^{n-1} p_i f_i \, (p_1, \, \cdots, \, p_{n-1}, \, \mathcal{Y}) = H(p, \, \mathcal{Y}).$$

Assume further that the function $H(p, \, \mathcal{Y})$ is of such a form that a given percentage change in the general price level and in money incomes results in the same percentage change (in the same direction) in aggregate money expenditures. (That is, H is assumed to be homogeneous of degree 1 in p and $\mathcal{Y}$.) Under this assumption we can then rewrite the aggregate expenditure function as

$$(7) \qquad \frac{\mathcal{E}}{p} = H\left(1, \, \frac{\mathcal{Y}}{p}\right) = F\left(\frac{\mathcal{Y}}{p}\right).$$

Let real expenditures $\mathcal{E}$ be represented by E; similarly let real income $\mathcal{Y}$ be represented by Y. Then we can rewrite (7) as

$$(8) \qquad E = F(Y).$$

This is the aggregate real expenditure function of Figure 2.

As an example of the preceding development, consider the case where the f_i are of the form

$$(9) \qquad D_i = \sum_{j=1}^{n-1} \gamma_{ij} \frac{p_j}{p_i} + \delta_i \frac{\mathcal{Y}}{p_i} \qquad (i = 1, \, \cdots, \, n-1)$$

where the γ_{ij} and δ_i are known constants. Then, by (6), the aggregate expenditure function has the form

$$(10) \qquad \mathcal{E} = \sum_{i=1}^{n-1} p_i \left[\sum_{j=1}^{n-1} \gamma_{ij} \frac{p_j}{p_i} + \delta_i \frac{\mathcal{Y}}{p_i} \right]$$

$$(11) \qquad = \sum_{j=1}^{n-1} \left[p_j \sum_{i=1}^{n-1} \gamma_{ij} \right] + \sum_{i=1}^{n-1} \delta_i \mathcal{Y}$$

Let p be a general price index of the form

(12)
$$p = \sum_{j=1}^{n-1} \omega_j p_j$$

where the weights, ω_j, are determined by the equations

(13)
$$\omega_j = \sum_{i=1}^{n-1} \gamma_{ij} / \nu \qquad (j = 1, \ldots, n-1)$$

where ν is a known constant. Also define a new constant

(14)
$$\delta = \sum_{i=1}^{n-1} \delta_i.$$

Substituting from (12), (13), and (14) into (11) we obtain

(15)
$$\mathcal{E} = \nu p + \delta \, \mathcal{Y}.$$

Dividing through both sides by p we obtain

(16)
$$E = \nu + \delta Y$$

which is clearly of the form (8).

Until now we have discussed only the demand side of the macrosystem. There is also a supply side, built up from equations (2). By a curious asymmetry this side of the macrosystem was rarely considered by Keynesian analysis. But it is clear that (completely analogous to aggregate money demand) we can define aggregate money supply, $\mathcal{S}$, and the aggregate money supply function

(17)
$$\mathcal{S} = \sum_{i=1}^{n-1} p_i g_i (p_1, \ldots, p_{n-1}, \mathcal{Y}).$$

This function gives us the amount people desire to supply (in dollars) at any given set of prices and national income. Making similar assumptions to those made in (6) above, rewrite (17) as

(18)
$$\mathcal{S} = J(p', \mathcal{Y})$$

where p' is again a general price index arising out of the aggregating process. If we again assume homogeneity of degree 1 for the function J, (18) can be rewritten as

(19)
$$\frac{\mathcal{S}}{p'} = J\left(1, \frac{\mathcal{Y}}{p'}\right) = Q\left(\frac{\mathcal{Y}}{p'}\right).$$

If we assume that p and p' are the same,[1] then (19) can be rewritten as

(20) $S = Q(Y)$.

This is the aggregate real supply function of Figure 3.

The assumption that p and p' are the same is heroic, to say the least. But as emphasized in the text, our main concern is to demonstrate the existence of an aggregate supply function; its particular form need not concern us here.

In Figure 3, however, one assumption is made about the shape of the supply function. Specifically, it is assumed that its slope with respect to Y is smaller than that of the expenditure function. The reason for this distinction lies back in equations (1) and (2). The dependence of the demand function on income is a familiar result of the theory lying behind equation (1)—a theory which considers individuals maximizing their utilities subject to the restraint of a fixed income. Due to this restraint, income enters the demand functions. But no such theory exists on the supply side; nor is it clear that these equations depend on national income. In the extreme case where $\mathcal{Y}$ does not appear in any of the supply equations, (2), the aggregate real supply function in (20) is independent of Y; in other words, aggregate real supply is equal to a constant, say,

(21) $S = \eta$.

In this extreme case, the supply curve in Figure 3 would be a horizontal line at the height η.

So far we have made use of only equations (1) and (2) of the Casselian system. We have yet to form the macroeconomic counterparts of equations (3) and (4). This is readily done. Multiply each side of (3) by p_i and sum up over all $n-1$ finished goods in the economy; then divide through by the general price level. This provides our macroeconomic equilibrium condition

(22) $E = S$.

In a similar way divide both sides of (4) by p to obtain

(23) $Y = S$.

Here, too, we have used the assumption that p and p' are the same.

Thus our Keynesian macrosystem consists of the four equations, (8), (20), (22), and (23), in the three variables E, S, and Y: the system is overdetermined. The meaning of this overdeterminacy has been presented in the analysis of Figure 3 where it was shown that there existed no level of income which would simultaneously equilibrate both the demand and supply sides of the market. In other words, the system is inconsistent.

1. p is essentially a price index of finished goods and services; while p' is an index of the prices of productive services as well. The assumption that they are the same implies that these two sets of prices always move proportionately. In other words, the real rate of return to productive services is constant. These reflections would seem to strengthen the speculations below that the aggregate supply function (under these assumptions) has the form (21).

{See the paragraph added to footnote 5 on p. 160 above.}

The entire preceding development has been concerned with building up a Keynesian macrosystem dealing only with the real variables of the system. If in addition we would want to have a system explaining the absolute price level, it would be necessary to include those equations of (1)–(3) which were ignored in the construction of (8), (20), and (22). Specifically, we would have to include the excess demand equation for money derived from (1) and (2) for $i = n$.

Under the Pigou assumption the expenditure function (8) depends also on the absolute price level, p.[2] That is,

(24) $E = G(Y, p)$.

Our Keynesian macrosystem (24), (20), (22), and (23) would then have an equal number of variables and equations. However, this does not insure its consistency.[3] Even if it is consistent, the concept of involuntary unemployment enters in a dynamic sense as in § 16 above.

Bibliography

A. F. Burns. *Economic Research and the Keynesian Thinking of our Times* (Twenty-sixth Annual Report of the National Bureau of Economic Research, 1946). New York, 1946.

J. M. Keynes. *The General Theory of Employment, Interest, and Money.* New York, 1936.

L. R. Klein. "A Post-Mortem on Transition Predictions of National Product." *Journal of Political Economy*, Aug. 1946, *54*, 289–308.

———. *The Keynesian Revolution.* New York, 1947.

O. Lange. *Price Flexibility and Employment.* Bloomington, Ind., 1944.

J. S. Mill. *Principles of Political Economy* (1848), ed. W. J. Ashley. London, 1909.

F. Modigliani. "Liquidity Preference and the Theory of Interest and Money." *Econometrica*, Jan. 1944, *12*, 45–88.

D. Patinkin. "Price Flexibility and Full Employment." *American Economic Review*, Sept. 1948, *38*, 543–65.

———. "The Indeterminacy of Absolute Prices in Classical Economic Theory." *Econometrica*, Jan. 1949, *17*, 1–27. [Reproduced as chap. 5 above.]

2. On this whole paragraph, cf. "Price Flexibility," §§ 1–8, especially § 8.
3. Cf. above, ch. 5, § 2.

8. Demand Curves and Consumer's Surplus*

The assumptions underlying the construction of a demand curve—and their implications for the problem of measuring consumer's surplus—have been much discussed in recent years. Similarly, there has been a renewed interest in the nature of Marshall's demand curve. The present paper adds little in a technical way to these discussions; nevertheless, it is hoped that the graphical device of Section 1 will clarify the nature of the interrelationships among the various demand curves that have been employed in the literature. Similarly, it is hoped that the approach to consumer's surplus in Section 2 will place it in a somewhat broader context than heretofore, as well as bring out its common-sense meaning. Particular attention will also be devoted to an analysis of consumer's surplus within a general-equilibrium framework. These two sections will then serve as the basis for an interpretation of the Marshallian demand curve, offering a simple solution to the prolonged debate that has taken place on this question in recent years.

1. Three Types of Demand Curves

1.1 Consider an individual who comes to market with an initial endowment of the (composite) good Y and exchanges part of it for the (composite) good X. Let A in

Reprinted by permission from *Measurement in Economics: Studies in Mathematical Economics and Econometrics in Memory of Yehuda Grunfeld*, by Carl Christ and others, Stanford, 1963, pp. 83–112. Copyright © 1963 by Stanford University Press. A few minor changes have been made.
{As indicated above (p. 7 and p. 30, fn. 10), my interest in the nature of the Marshallian demand curve stemmed from the attention which Knight and Viner devoted to this subject in their lectures. For some reason, however (perhaps because I took it for granted), I failed to indicate this relationship when this article was first published. I might, however, note that my interpretation of Marshall's demand curve in Section 3 below actually differs—though, as explained there, not operationally—from the one which Knight presented in these writings; cf. again p. 30 above.}
*This paper was completed while I held a Ford Foundation Visiting Research Professorship at the University of California, Berkeley. I have benefited greatly, on questions of exposition as well as substance, from the searching and patient criticism of E. J. Mishan. There are, however, still some points on which we remain in disagreement. I am also indebted to William J. Baumol, Nissan Liviatan, and Jerome Rothenberg for their helpful comments.
The subject of this paper is one that was close to the heart of Yehuda Grunfeld. In keeping with his Chicago training, he was continuously concerned with the assumptions that underlie the demand curve, and I remember many absorbing hours spent with him discussing this subject. One of Grunfeld's planned projects was a critical examination of the literature on empirical demand functions, the purpose being to bring out the implicit definitions of "real income" used in these studies, and to show that the failure to understand the economic significance of these definitions had frequently led to an incorrect interpretation (in terms of substitution and income effects) of the estimated parameters.
This paper was written after Grunfeld's death. But I did discuss with him the material of Section 1, and particularly the interrelationships of Figure 2. As always, his comments were quick, to the point, and provocative.

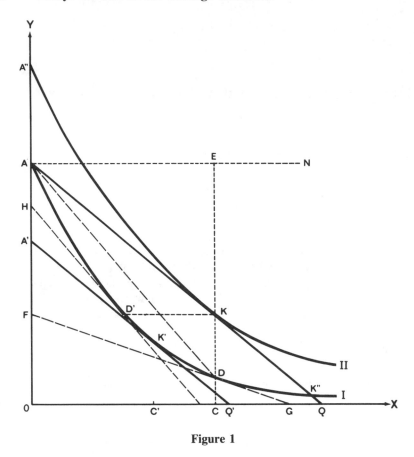

Figure 1

Figure 1 represent the individual's initial position. Assume now that we confront the individual with a price of X represented by the slope of the budget line AQ and ask him to tell us the respective amounts he will buy of X under the following three alternative conditions:

(a) The individual is to buy the maximum amount of X that he can buy without making himself worse off than he was in his initial position A. This will bring him to point K'' on the original indifference curve, I. For reasons that will become apparent below, let us denote the demand curve generated by varying the price in this sort of experiment an "all-or-none demand curve." It is represented by MP in Figure 2. The assumed convexity and negative slope of the indifference curve imply that the slope of this demand curve must always be negative.[1]

(b) The individual is to buy the amount of X that will maximize his utility. This will bring him to point K on the higher indifference curve II. Clearly, K cannot lie

---

1. If the indifference curve through A should intersect the X-axis, then this curve is not defined for prices corresponding to budget lines which intersect this axis rightward of this point of intersection.

I am indebted to Eytan Sheshinski for this observation.

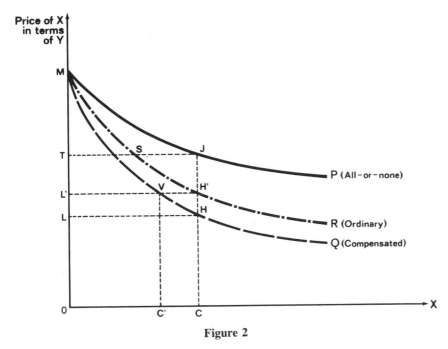

Figure 2

rightward of K'' on AQ, for under no circumstances will anyone freely choose to carry out a market transaction that will make him worse off. Indeed, we can see from the graph that K must actually lie leftward of K''. This is the obverse side of the fact that the individual in experiment (a) is forced to go beyond his optimum. The demand curve generated in this way will be called an "ordinary demand curve" and is represented in Figure 2 by MR. As just explained, it must lie leftward of the all-or-none curve.

(c) As in (b), the individual chooses the utility-maximizing amount of X; but in contrast to (b), compensating variations are made in his initial endowment of Y ("income") to keep him on indifference curve I. In the case at hand, this means that we deduct AA' units of Y from his initial endowment so that the individual chooses the optimum point K' on the budget line, $A'Q'$ (parallel to AQ in Figure 1). If X is a normal good (i.e., income elasticity greater than zero), K' must lie leftward of K. Hence the "compensated demand curve," MQ, in Figure 2 must lie leftward of MR. The convexity of the indifference curve once again implies that MQ must be negatively sloped—whether X is normal or inferior. This is simply an expression of the familiar fact that under the convexity assumption the Hicksian substitution effect—which is what our experiment actually isolates—is always negative. (Note that in the present case we cannot generate MQ by compensating variations in prices instead of income. For as long as income is unchanged, the budget line must go through the initial point A, and hence can be tangent to indifference curve I only at that point.)

The above experiments derive the demand curves in Walrasian fashion by confronting the individual with a given price and asking him to specify the quantity demanded. A more precise relationship among these curves can be derived by conducting the experiments in the alternative Marshallian way: by asking the individual to tell us the maximum he is willing to pay for X under different circumstances, on the assumption that he is consuming a given quantity of it (say, OC). Thus the all-or-none demand curve (and this, of course, is the reason for the name) is derived by determining the maximum per-unit price the individual is willing to pay for OC of X rather than go entirely without it. In Figure 1, the maximum *total* amount the individual is willing to forego for this quantity is ED. Hence the maximum *per-unit* price is $ED/OC = ED/AE$, which is the slope of the radius vector AD with respect to AN. From this viewpoint we also see that the convexity and negative slope of the indifference curve imply that the all-or-none demand curve is not only negatively sloped, but also of greater-than-unity elasticity. Note too that since the decision here is *not* a marginal one, the individual is at a point on his indifference curve where the marginal rate of substitution is *not* equal to the price.

In contrast, the ordinary demand curve is derived by asking the individual to tell us the maximum price he is willing to pay for X at the margin—when he is consuming OC units of it, and when he obtains all units at the price he designates. Alternatively, and equivalently, the individual is asked to specify the maximum per-unit price he is willing to pay for X when he is free to buy *any* amount of it up to and including OC units. This is Marshall's "marginal demand price." [2] The fact that in this case the individual is making a marginal decision means that he must be at a point on an indifference curve whose marginal rate of substitution equals the price he designates; and the fact that all units are purchased at the same price means that he must be on a straight budget line originating in point A in Figure 1. Hence the "marginal demand price" must equal the slope of that budget line originating in A and tangent to an indifference curve at the given quantity of X. On the assumption that the demand curve is single-valued, any other budget line originating in A will intersect an indifference curve at this quantity; hence its slope will represent a price different from the one the individual "is just willing to pay." In Figure 1 the marginal demand price for OC of X is thus equal to the slope of AQ with respect to AN, which is necessarily less than that of AD.

Finally, the compensated demand curve is derived in the same way as the ordinary one—with the difference that compensating changes are made in income to keep the individual on indifference curve I. For OC of X, this compensating reduction in income is AF. The corresponding maximum price is given by the slope of FG with

2. "Suppose, for instance, that tea of a certain quality is to be had at 2s. per lb. . . . he buys perhaps 10 lbs. in the year; that is to say, the difference between the satisfaction which he gets from buying 9 lbs. and 10 lbs. is enough for him to be willing to pay 2s. for it: while the fact that he does not buy an eleventh pound, shows that he does not think that it would be worth an extra 2s. to him. That is, 2s. a pound measures the utility to him of the tea which lies at the margin or terminus or end of his purchases; it measures the marginal utility to him. If the price which he is just willing to pay for any pound be called his *demand price*, then 2s. is his *marginal demand price*" (Marshall, 1920, pp. 94–95; italics in original).

I believe the conceptual experiment described here is also the one Marshall had in mind in Note II of his "Mathematical Appendix" (ibid., pp. 838–39). Correspondingly, the phrase "price which he is just willing to pay for an amount x" that appears there should be understood as "total amount" that he is just willing to spend—when he can buy all units at the "marginal demand price" of the amount x.

respect to *AN*—represented by *OL* in Figure 2. Alternatively, we can conceive the compensated demand curve as representing the maximum price the individual will pay for an additional unit of *X*—on the assumption that we have exacted from him the respective maximum prices that he is willing to pay for each preceding unit. For this too is measured by the marginal rate of substitution of indifference curve I at the quantity of *X* in question.

From this last description it is clear that the compensated demand curve is related to the all-or-none as the marginal is to the average (Hicks, 1956, pp. 84–88). This can be seen most simply by turning Figure 1 upside down and comparing the slopes of *FG* and *AD* with respect to *AD*. Hence we can make use of the familiar relationship between average and marginal to state that the fact that *MP* in Figure 2 is always declining (see above) implies that *MQ* must lie below it.

At first there seems to be something paradoxical about the fact that the all-or-none and compensated experiments—both of which keep the individual on the same indifference curve I—should nevertheless yield different demand curves. But as has just been seen, this simply reflects the difference between the curves that are, respectively, average and marginal to the same indifference curve. A less technical way of resolving the paradox is to note that in the case of curve *MQ* the individual surrenders *Y* both in payment for *X* and in payment of compensation; in the case of the curve *MP*, however, he surrenders *Y* only in payment for *X*. Since for any given quantity of *X* the total amount of *Y* surrendered must be the same in both cases (in order to remain on the same indifference curve), this implies that the per-unit market price in the all-or-none case must be higher.

Indeed, this line of reasoning brings us to the familiar fact that we can measure in Figure 2 the size of the compensating variation *AF* in Figure 1. For the total amount of *Y* surrendered in the all-or-none case is represented in Figure 2 by the area *OCJT*. In the compensated case, however, only area *OCHL* is surrendered via the market place. This means that an amount of *Y* equal to area *LHJT* (= *OCJT* − *OCHL*) must have been surrendered via the compensating mechanism. Alternatively, by the marginal-average relationship existing between curves *MQ* and *MP*, area *OCJT* = area *OCHM*; hence the compensating variation is represented by the area of the triangle-like figure *LHM* (= *OCHM* − *OCHL*).

Consider now the special and much discussed case in which the good *X* has zero-income elasticity throughout. This implies that parallel shifts in the budget line in Figure 1 will generate points of tangency corresponding to the same quantity of *X*. In other words, the indifference curves must be parallel for every value of *X*. This in turn implies that, for example, points *K'* and *D* must coincide. Hence the ordinary demand curve *MR* in Figure 2 must coincide with the compensated curve *MQ*. The fact that in this way the same demand curve describes the individual's behavior both when his utility is constant and when it is changing (as he moves along the curve) should not disturb us, for the essence of the zero-income-elasticity assumption is precisely that changes in the level of utility (''real income'') do not affect the demand for *X*.

1.2. Before leaving this discussion, three further—and unrelated—points might be noted. First, only the second of the six experiments described above can be conducted solely on the basis of observation of the individual's behavior.[3] Hence only this experiment, with its resulting demand curve, is properly part of "positive economics." All the others—and particularly all of the Marshallian ones—are not, for they can be conducted only if the individual provides us with true information about the positions or slopes of his (to us) unobservable indifference curves. An individual intent on bluffing (designating prices really below his maximum) could not be detected.

Second, the negative slope of the all-or-none curve has some simple implications for the case of the perfectly discriminating monopolist. Consider in particular the familiar problem of a monopolist whose costs are too high to permit him to operate if all units must be sold at the same price. This implies that the total costs of producing the first unit are greater than the demand price for that unit. Hence the negative slope of the all-or-none curve implies that even perfect discrimination will not enable the monopolist to operate unless he enjoys decreasing average costs over a certain region. This is clearly a necessary and not sufficient condition, for in order to reach a profit situation, the monopolist's average costs must fall more sharply than the all-or-none price over the relevant region.

Third, if we conceive the foregoing demand curves as being aggregated over all individuals, then the compensated demand curve would represent a "constant real income" curve in the sense of describing movements along a given (community) indifference curve. It would *not* represent a constant "real income" curve in the sense of describing the demand that would prevail under the assumption of constant productive capacity and techniques.[4] Hence even an exogenous change that shifts the economy to another point on the same production-possibility curve will generally involve a shift in the compensated "constant-real-income" demand curve no less than in the ordinary one.

On the grounds of invariance under such a change, then, there is little to choose between the compensated and ordinary demand curves as analytical tools. But even if this were not so, I can see little point to a *methodenstreit* on this question.[5] We need exactly the same amount of information to carry out an analysis with one type of curve as with another. And if account is taken of all the interrelationships, the results obtained by using the alternative demand curves must be the same. In technical terms, the way in which we choose to take two-dimensional cross sections of a demand function dependent on relative prices and "real income" can obviously not affect the

3. There is, however, a variant of the third experiment that also comes within this category; in this variant, the compensation is of the Slutzky type (that is, enabling the individual to buy his initial basket). As Mosak (1942, pp. 69–74) has shown, for infinitesimal changes the Hicks and Slutzky substitution effects are equal. But this equality obviously does not hold for finite changes.

4. The way in which such a "constant-productive-capacity" demand curve can be derived is neatly shown by Bailey (1954).

5. The recrudescence of this *methodenstreit* is, of course, due to Friedman (1949). Friedman's methodological criticism of the ordinary demand curve has been restated in an even more extreme way by Buchanan (1958). See footnote 7.

For a detailed discussion of the issues involved, see Yeager (1960).

outcome of the general-equilibrium analysis of a problem.[6] Thus it would seem to me that the only valid—if not very edifying—methodological prescription that can be given here is that we should adopt a general-equilibrium approach to our problems that will take account of these interrelationships. There would, nevertheless, be a point to insisting on the advantages of using the compensated demand curve if it were to be shown that the failure to use this curve has tended to lead to a neglect of these interrelationships and to consequent error. This is a meaningful hypothesis that can be tested empirically by adducing relevant evidence from the literature, but no such valid evidence has as yet been adduced.[7]

2. The Common Sense of Consumer's Surplus[8]

2.1. A given individual with a given "money" income achieves different levels of welfare under different trade situations; this is the essence of consumer's surplus. It follows that the magnitude of this surplus is a function of the situations being compared. If utility were a cardinal quantity, we would be able to measure this surplus in terms of "utils." But if utility is only ordinal, we must resort to other—and necessarily arbitrary—measures.

The ordinary way in which we measure a difference in welfare is by means of a quantity index. In its "true" form this measures the magnitude of a shift from one level of utility to another by the ratio of the respective minimum money costs of acquiring these levels under competitive conditions (Samuelson, 1947, pp. 160–61; cf. next chapter, pp. 214–15). Clearly, this ratio depends on the prices used to compute these costs. Consider then the individual in Figure 3 whose income is OA and who is initially permitted to trade in a competitive market at price p_1, so that he is at B on indifference curve I_1. Let the individual now be permitted to trade at the lower price p_2, so that he moves to point C on the higher indifference curve I_2. If we measure this increase in welfare by a quantity index using the original prices (i.e., evaluating the respective indifference curves at the price p_1), we obtain OA_1/OA. On the other hand, if we use the final prices, we obtain OA/OA_2. In principle, however, there is no

6. It is worth noting that Friedman himself shows just this in the example he considers (1949, pp. 59–62).

7. It is noteworthy that Friedman concedes that the type of error he is interested in averting by use of the compensated demand curve had already been corrected by other economists, who did not make use of such a construct (1952, pp. 101–2, fn. 3). See also his reply to Bailey (1954).

Ironically enough, Buchanan's treatment of the hypothesis just mentioned actually reduces it to a tautology. For he attempts to prove that failure to use the compensated demand curve has led to error by dividing his examples from the literature into two categories: those in which this failure has been accompanied by error, and those in which this failure has not so been accompanied, but in which (it is asserted) error is absent despite the failure to use the compensated-demand curve, and not because of it! (1950, pp. 262–69). Thus Buchanan's procedure makes it impossible ever to refute the hypothesis he wishes to test.

It might also be noted that Buchanan's emphasis on the desirability of points on demand curves being potentially observable (1950, p. 264) is much more fruitfully discussed as part of the general problem of identification, so familiar from the econometric literature.

8. For a critical survey of the "new" development of this subject by Hicks, Henderson, Little, and others, see Mishan (1960), pp. 238–45; fig. 3 is reproduced from p. 240 of this article.

On the arbitrariness of the measure of consumer's surplus, see Samuelson (1947), pp. 195–202.

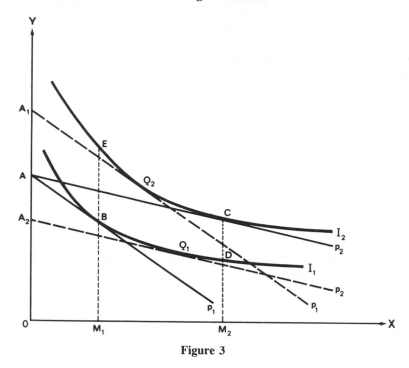

Figure 3

reason to restrict ourselves to these two alternatives, and we can measure the shift from I_1 to I_2 in terms of a true quantity index using any set of prices that we choose.

In actual practice, of course, the indifference map is unknown, and so resort is had instead to the Laspeyres and Paasche approximations. Unfortunately, however, these approximations fail us in just that case which plays such a crucial role in the theory of consumer's surplus: the one depicted in Figure 1, in which the two situations being compared are those of no-trade (point A) and competitive trade at a given price (point K), respectively. For the impossibility of trading at A is represented by an infinite price for X, which renders the Laspeyres quantity index meaningless, while the fact that A and K are by assumption on the same budget line implies that the Paasche index must always be unity. This indicates, as it must, an increase in welfare, but it obviously fails to reflect the elementary fact that the lower the price at which trade is opened up, the greater this increase.

Whether or not for this reason, the traditional discussion of consumer's surplus has never been in terms of the relative movement measured by index numbers but in absolute, money terms. This obviously does not diminish—and might even be said to increase—the arbitrariness already noted in connection with measures of changes in utility. Thus, corresponding to the true quantity index OA_1/OA in Figure 3, there is the measure of consumer's surplus AA_1. This is Hicks' "equivalent variation." Again, corresponding to the index OA/OA_2, there is the measure AA_2. This is Hicks' "compensating variation." In a similar way we could define a "variation" to correspond to any one of the infinite number of true quantity indexes that can be constructed to measure the shift from indifference curve I_1 to I_2.

However, as Henderson (1941) emphasized in his classic article, for any specific question only one of these measures of consumer's surplus will usually be relevant. Thus, if in Figure 3 we want to know the maximum amount of money ("tax") our individual with income OA and price p_1 will pay for the privilege of being able to buy at the lower price p_2, then it is only the compensating variation AA_2 that is relevant. On the other hand, if in Figure 1 we want to know the minimum amount of money we must pay our individual with income OA and price ratio AQ for withdrawing entirely the privilege of buying X (that is, raising its price to infinity), then it is only the equivalent variation AA'' that is relevant. Note that though the compensating variation cannot exceed the individual's income, there is no such limit on the equivalent variation, for though the individual's income necessarily sets an upper limit on what he can *pay*, it obviously cannot limit what he can *receive* (Hicks, 1956, pp. 105–6).

Thus far we have restricted the two trade situations being compared to competitive ones (from the viewpoint of the buyer) that differ only in their given prices. There is, however, no reason why we should not broaden our scope to make comparisons involving other types of situations. As we shall now see, once this is done, there will no longer be a one-to-one correspondence between measures of consumer's surplus and true quantity indexes. This is what should be expected, for as already indicated— and as the straight budget lines used in their computation show—these indexes themselves are based on the assumption of perfect competition. Indeed, we might reverse the direction of our argument and contend that index-number theory should be generalized so as to provide measures relevant for noncompetitive situations too.

In any event, let us now assume, for example, that our individual with income OA in Figure 1 is initially subject to a perfectly discriminating monopolist who has exacted from him the maximum price he is willing to pay for each successive unit, and has brought him to point D on indifference curve I. (Alternatively, we can assume that the individual has been brought to this point by an all-or-none monopolist who has forced him to take OC units of X.) Then the line segment AH measures the maximum amount of money our individual would pay to convert this situation into a competitive one with a price equal to the *average* one now being paid to the discriminating monopolist. On the other hand, our individual would be willing to pay AF to obtain a competitive price equal to the *marginal* one now being paid. Since the marginal is less than the average, AF must clearly exceed AH. Note too that the individual buying competitively at the erstwhile marginal price FG will —after paying AF— continue to consume OC units of X. Obviously, AF and AH also represent the compensating variation for a movement from the no-trade situation represented by point A to competitive trade at the prices represented, respectively, by the slopes of AD and FG. This simply reflects the fact that, from the viewpoint of welfare, no-trade and trade under a perfectly discriminating monopolist are equivalent.

Let us now consider the opposite case, in which our individual is initially buying OC units of X in a competitive market and is at K. The minimum amount that we must pay him to convert this into a situation in which he must buy this same quantity from a perfectly discriminating monopolist (or on an all-or-none basis) is *KD*. This would seem to be closest to Marshall's own notion of consumer's surplus as "the excess of the price [i.e., total expenditure] which he would be willing to pay rather than go without the thing, over that which he actually does pay." [9] Note that this surplus, too, cannot exceed income; for even though, as interpreted here, it is an amount *received* by the individual, its magnitude is determined by a hypothetical experiment in which he would be *paying* it.

All of these are relevant measures of consumer's surplus under the circumstances defined. Indeed, in principle it would seem possible to define a set of circumstances that would enable us to interpret as consumer's surplus any of the infinite ways there are of measuring the "distance" between two indifference curves. The common element of all these surpluses would be that they measure the welfare difference between two trade situations in terms of the amount of money an individual would pay—or insist on receiving—in order to move from one to another. The differing element would be a reflection of the fact that this amount of money obviously varies in accordance with the situations being compared. In brief, the "distance" between two indifference curves depends on the nature of the path followed. [10]

2.2. It is recognized, of course, that the foregoing surpluses can be presented alternatively in terms of the demand curves of Figure 2. For simplicity, we shall—in the case of compensating and equilibrating variations—restrict our attention to the total surplus, i.e., to that measuring the welfare difference between no-trade and competitive trade at a given price. In the case of the Marshallian surplus, however, no such restriction is actually needed; for according to the foregoing interpretation, this necessarily refers to the surplus on the total amount of X purchased by the individual.

Let us start with the compensating variation AA' in Figure 1. Let the price represented by the slope of AQ (or $A'Q'$) in Figure 1 equal OL' in Figure 2. Then it is clear from Section 1.1 (p. 185) that AA' can be represented by the triangular area

9. See Marshall (1920), p. 124. The first to identify *KD* with Marshall's surplus was, of course, Hicks (1946), pp. 38–41.

See, however, Appendix Note A for evidence that Marshall also thought in terms of the surplus as measured by the equivalent variation, AA''.

Actually, the interpretation of Marshall's surplus just presented differs from the usual one in ways that cannot be fully discussed here. Suffice it to say that the usual interpretation does not clearly represent the Marshallian surplus as the outcome of a comparison of perfect monopoly and competition. Instead, it essentially compares two competitive price situations (from the consumer's viewpoint), in one of which the consumer is prevented from attaining his optimum position (Mishan, 1960, pp. 240–41). In this way it defines the Marshallian surplus as *CD* in Figure 3, and describes *BE* as its counterpart. Correspondingly, it does not present the surpluses *AH* and *AF* in a Marshallian context.

We might also note that in his original article Henderson does initially describe the Marshallian surplus as "the maximum increase in returns which the seller could obtain through negotiating all-or-none bargains with each consumer" (1941, pp. 119–20). But he unfortunately concludes his article with the diagram reproduced here as Figure 3—and with the statement that the Marshallian surplus is measured by *CD* and *EB*. It is this last version that became accepted in the literature.

10. This multiplicity of measures is emphasized here because of Mishan's contention that "in all plausible circumstances" only the compensating and equilibrating variations are "tenable" (1960, p. 241; 1947–48, pp. 27, 30–32).

Mishan's contention is correct if we restrict our attention to perfectly competitive equilibrium situations; but (as is evident from the foregoing discussion) it ceases to be correct as soon as we broaden the scope of our analysis to other types of situations.

$L'VM$ defined by the price OL' and the compensated demand curve MQ. For, to repeat the argument, the maximum the individual would be willing to pay for the quantity OC' in the all-or-none experiment is given by the area $OC'VM$ under this curve. The amount he actually does pay in the compensated experiment (i.e., ''after tax'') is $OC'VL'$. Hence, since he remains on the same indifference curve, he must have been taxed a compensating payment of $OC'VM - OC'VL' = L'VM$ units of Y.

In a similar way it can be shown that the equivalent variation AA'' equals the triangular area defined by the price OL' and a compensated demand curve constructed so as to keep the individual at the utility level represented by indifference curve II in Figure 1. Clearly, if X is a normal good, this demand curve must be rightward of MQ in Fig. 2. (See Mishan, 1947–48, and the references to Hicks cited therein.)

In general, however, no such simple representation exists for the Marshallian surplus, KD, in Figure 1, for this equals the difference between the areas defined by *two* different demand curves: the first, to tell us the maximum he would pay for the given quantity of X under all-or-none conditions; the second, what he actually does pay under competitive ones. In particular, the surplus equals (Figure 2) area $OCJT$ defined by curve MP *less* the necessary smaller area $OCH'L'$ defined by curve MR. Alternatively, it equals $OCHM - OCH'L'$. Thus it can be represented either by $L'H'JT$ or by $L'VM - VH'H$.[11] From this it is clear that both the triangular area under MQ (namely, $LHM = OCHM - OCHL$) and the triangular area under MR (namely, $L'H'M = OCH'M - OCH'L'$) are overestimates of Marshall's measure, the former because its subtrahend $OCHL$ is too small, the latter because its minuend $OCH'M$ is too large. Only in the special case where the demand for X is of zero income elasticity—so that MR and MQ coincide—will the triangular area under the ordinary demand curve provide a correct measure of Marshall's consumer's surplus. For only under this assumption will the total area under this demand curve tell us the maximum the individual is willing to pay. As Hicks has shown (1946, pp. 38–40), this is indeed the assumption Marshall made.

Finally, let us consider the other Marshallian surpluses defined above: AF and AH. Since these can be interpreted alternatively as compensating variations (see p. 189) their relationship to the compensated demand curve is obvious. Note that in the zero-income-elasticity case, $AA' = AA'' = KD = AF$, so that all these measures of consumer's surplus are represented by the same triangular area.

2.3 Other aspects of these interrelationships have been sufficiently discussed elsewhere,[12] so that we can go on to some more general points.

First, consider the criticism levied against Marshall that since in the light of his budget restraint an individual cannot plan to spend more than he actually does on all

11. Thus, in the case of a normal good, the Marshallian surplus is less than the compensating one. This could also be deduced directly from Figure 1 by noting that if both X and Y are normal goods, AA' must be greater than KD.

Note, however, that this inequality is reversed in the case of an inferior good. From this it is clear that there is no basis for the contention—frequently found in the literature—that the foregoing inequality necessarily results from the inherent nature of the Marshallian and compensating surpluses.

12. See the references cited in footnote 8. See also Boulding (1945); Henderson (1941); and Hicks (1956), chs. X and XVIII.

his commodities simultaneously, consumer's surplus in the aggregate must be identically zero.[13] It is clear from the preceding discussion that this contention is based on a misunderstanding of the nature of consumer's surplus. True, Marshall's definition of this surplus (as the difference between the maximum the individual is willing to pay for a commodity and what he actually pays) does lend itself to such misunderstanding. But it is clear from other passages of the *Principles* that Marshall did conceive of consumer's surplus as measuring the welfare difference between two trade situations, and hence as remaining meaningful even when the totality of the consumer's purchases is considered.[14]

Second, let us see how the magnitude of consumer's surplus is affected by changes in price or quantity. Continuing to restrict our attention to total consumer's surplus, we note that the necessarily negative slope of the compensated demand curve (or, equivalently, the convexity of the indifference curves) implies that the lower the price at which competitive trade is initiated, the greater both the compensating and equivalent variations. This is self-evident, for the lower the price at which the individual can convert his initial endowment of Y into X, the greater the advantages of trade as compared with no-trade.

From this we can also see that (as long as the ordinary demand curve is negatively sloped) the greater the volume of the competitive trade that is opened up, the greater the compensating and equivalent variations. On the other hand, if X is an inferior good, this relationship obviously need not hold. For if the inferiority is sufficiently marked, a greater quantity will be associated with a higher demand price.

In contrast, the Marshallian surpluses AH and AF will be increasing functions of quantity even in the case of a highly inferior good. For—as the negatively sloped all-or-none curve and compensated curve of Figure 1 show—the greater the quantity of X purchased in the initial monopolistic situation, the lower its average and marginal price, respectively, hence the greater the advantage of converting these prices into uniform competitive ones.

On the other hand, the Marshallian surplus KD will not always increase with quantity consumed, even in the case of a normal good. This is the simple counterpart of the fact that KD also measures the potential profit of a perfectly discriminating monopolist, and monopoly profits are generally not a monotonically increasing function of quantity sold. That is, there is generally some finite quantity at which these profits are at a maximum.

In technical terms, the Marshallian surplus equals $OCJT - OCH'L'$ in Figure 2. Now, the all-or-none curve in this diagram is necessarily of greater-than-unitary elasticity (p. 184); hence, as the quantity of X increases, the area of the rectangle corresponding to $OCJT$ must also increase. If, now, the ordinary demand curve is of less-than-unitary elasticity, then the area of the rectangle corresponding to $OCH'L'$ will at the same time decrease, so that the surplus will increase. If, however, the ordinary demand curve is elastic, this rectangle will increase. Hence, over ranges

13. See Viner (1937), p. 575, and the reference to Allyn Young cited therein. See also Bishop (1942–43), pp. 432–33, and the description there of the debate between Marshall and J. S. Nicholson.
14. See Appendix A, below.

in which the elasticity is sufficiently pronounced, the Marshallian surplus will decrease with increases in X.

This indeterminacy can also be seen in terms of Figure 1, where the Marshallian surplus is measured as $ED - EK$. As quantity of X increases, ED must also increase; but the direction of the change in EK depends on the elasticity of demand. In graphical terms, the vertical distance between indifference curve I and the relevant initial indifference curve can either increase or decrease with X. Note that this remains true even if X is always a normal good, for normality expresses itself as a narrowing vertical distance between any two *given* indifference curves as X increases. In the Marshallian case, however, the initial indifference curve to be compared with curve I will change as X itself changes.[15]

The third point that emerges from the preceding analysis is the fundamental one that consumer's surplus is a function also of the individual's initial position. (For simplicity, the following discussion is restricted to the compensating and equivalent variations; the extension to the Marshallian surplus is immediate.) Thus, for example, if the individual were initially at K in Figure 1, both the compensating and equivalent variations would be zero at the price AQ. This absence of surplus would also manifest itself in demand-curve diagrams, for these would show a zero demand at the price AQ; hence all of the relevant triangular and rectangular areas would also be zero. Note that we are here making use of "demand" in the sense of amount purchased, and not in Wicksteed's sense of including also "reservation demand." This is as it should be, for what is measured by the compensating and equivalent variations is the increased welfare generated by the possibility of carrying out transactions in a competitive market.

Clearly, if the individual does start from the initial position K (or any other point representing a greater-than-zero quantity of X) he will—for sufficiently high prices— be a supplier of X instead of a demander. Once again, we can construct a triplet of curves corresponding *mutatis mutandis* to the all-or-none, compensated, and ordinary experiments described in the preceding section (Boulding, 1945). The relationship between these curves is depicted in Figure 4, where the negative quantities of X represent amounts supplied and OQ represents the individual's initial endowment of X. Thus the curves in this figure are of the excess-demand variety. The all-or-none curve in the negative region represents the *minimum* per unit price at which the individual will supply X rather than make no sale at all; alternatively, it represents the maximum amount of X he can supply at a given price without worsening his initial position. Just as on the demand side of Figure 4, the compensated curve on the supply side is marginal to the all-or-none curve and (in the case of a normal good) lies below the ordinary one. This latter relationship reflects the fact that whether the individual uses the market to buy or sell X, he achieves thereby a higher level of real income

---

15. Even though this is also true of the equivalent variation, no such indeterminacy characterizes that case. The reason for this difference is that no matter what the value of X in the initial situation, the equivalent variation is measured on the Y-axis—i.e., for the same (zero) value of X. Hence a higher level of utility must correspond to a higher level of Y. This is obviously not the case for the Marshallian measure just discussed.

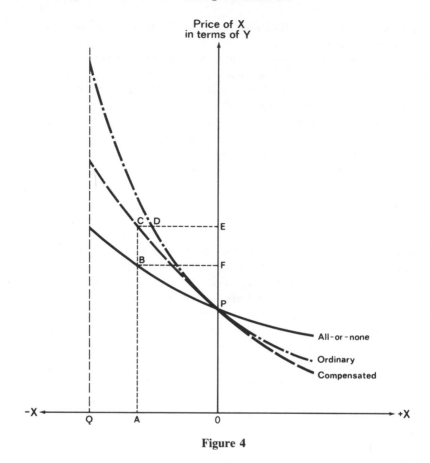

Figure 4

(i.e., higher indifference curve) and hence consumes a larger amount of X. Hence only at the point-of-no-trade P can the compensated and ordinary curves coincide.

As before, the various areas subtended by the supply curves can be used to provide different measures of consumer's surplus (Boulding, 1945). Thus area $BFEC = PCE$ is the compensating variation: the maximum amount the individual is willing to pay in his initial position for the privilege of selling X at the uniform price OE. On the other hand, the Marshallian seller's surplus has no simple representation, and the area subtended by the ordinary curve no welfare connotation, except for the case in which a zero-income elasticity for X causes the ordinary and compensated curves to coincide throughout. Note, however, that in this case the corresponding curves for Y cannot coincide, for the income effect then expresses itself exclusively in an increased demand for this commodity.

Since the initial position plays such a crucial role in the analysis of consumer's surplus, it is worth dwelling a little longer on its nature. In a modern economy individuals generally come to the market with initial quantities of factor endowments, and not commodities. Hence it is more realistic to consider Y in Figure 1 as representing the individual's own-use of these endowments: leisure, in the case of labor; enjoyment of nature, in the case of land; and so on. Accordingly, Figure 1 would then show the increased welfare the individual obtains by selling his factor services in the market and using the proceeds to buy goods. Thus we might say that the diagram shows producer's surplus, and not consumer's—though these are obviously two sides of the same coin.[16]

In the special case in which the individual's factor services have no own-use—that is, no alternative to being sold on the market—the indifference map would consist of a family of vertical lines (Figure 5). If the initial quantity of the factor is OA and the price the slope of AB, the individual's optimum is obviously at corner B, where none of the factor is retained for his own use. Because of the verticality of the indifference curves, it is meaningless to talk of exacting a compensating payment in terms of Y. But we can talk of such a payment in terms of X. This obviously equals OB. In more familiar terms, everything the individual receives in exchange for his factor services under our present assumptions is "economic rent." Note that under the present assumptions OB measures the equivalent and Marshallian surpluses as well. For it is the amount of X we must pay the individual if we now (i.e., at point B) prohibit him from selling his labor, or if we make him sell it to a monopsonist (who will take advantage of the individual's completely inelastic supply of labor to drive its price down to zero). This equality of the different surpluses is, of course, a reflection of the absence of an income effect on the demand for Y, for this demand is zero no matter what the level of X.

Returning to the case of ordinary indifference curves, we now note that the foregoing discussion exaggerates the extent of the surplus generated by permitting the individual to sell his labor on a competitive market. For if we let Y in Figure 6 once again represent the individual's leisure, and let AF represent his own production curve (that is, the amounts of X he himself can produce by foregoing leisure and working instead), then a Crusoe with no access to a market would not stay at point A, but would move instead to point E. Thus the increased welfare generated by the opening up of market facilities is represented by the movement from indifference curve II to III, and not by the movement from I to III. In other words, the advantages of trading on a market should be compared not with a no-trade situation, but with one in which the individual "trades with nature" by means of his isolated productive activity. In a modern economy, however, the greater efficiency of specialization and exchange is so overwhelming that the distance between A and E can be assumed to be negligible relative to that between A and R. For the same reason the individual in Figure 6 is represented as moving to corner A of his production curve after the market is opened up.

We note finally the complete parallelism between Figure 6 and the familiar diagram demonstrating the gains from international trade (Leontief, 1933). Indeed, the only

---

16. A fact duly emphasized by Marshall: ". . . when we have reckoned the producer's surplus at the value of the general purchasing power which he derives from his labour . . . , we have reckoned implicitly his consumer's surplus too . . ." (1920, p. 831). On this and the following paragraph, see Mishan (1959).

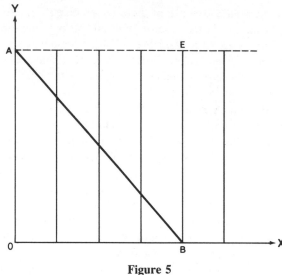

Figure 5

difference is that the "after-trade" position in Figure 6 is assumed to be one of "complete specialization." In this way we see once again that the essence of consumer's and seller's surplus (as measured by the compensating variation) are the gains from trade enjoyed by both parties to any free-market transaction.

2.4. Until now the analysis has been restricted to the case of an individual who buys only one commodity. Let us now briefly indicate some of the problems involved

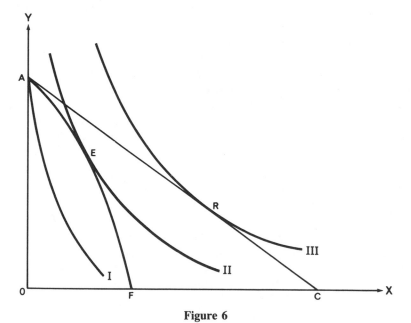

Figure 6

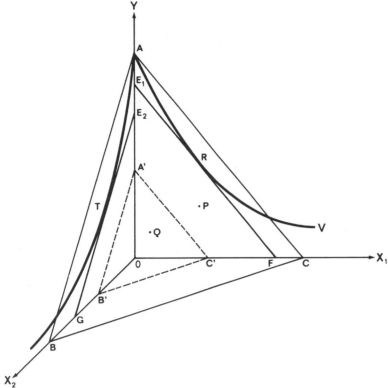

Figure 7

in extending it to the case of several commodities. For simplicity, we shall restrict our attention to the compensating variation.

In order to fix our ideas, let us consider the three-dimensional construct represented by Figure 7. Once again, Y is the (composite) commodity with which the individual is initially endowed. Let OA represent this initial endowment, and let X_1 and X_2 represent the commodities which the individual is permitted to buy at prices (in terms of Y) p_1 and p_2, respectively. Let the corresponding budget plane be represented by ABC, and let P be the point at which this plane is tangent to an indifference surface. Similarly, let $A'B'C'$ be a budget plane parallel to ABC and tangent (at Q) to that (lower) indifference surface which passes through A. Then AA' is the total consumer's surplus as measured by the compensating variation.

What must now be emphasized is that in the general case of interdependent marginal utilities it is meaningless to attempt to partition this surplus into "that part due to X_1" and "that part due to X_2," for the total increase in welfare the individual enjoys by virtue of being able to trade in X_1 and X_2 reflects the interactions between these two commodities. The welfare implications of X_1 alone—or X_2 alone—cannot logically be disentangled.[17]

17. The argument here is analogous to the one that demonstrates the meaninglessness of a cost-of-living index when both prices and money are changing. For details, see the next chapter, pp. 233–39.

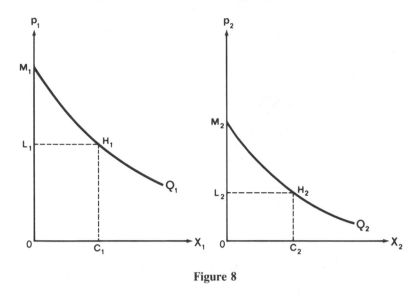

Figure 8

But what must also be emphasized is that it is difficult to conceive of policy questions for which such a disentanglement would be of interest. For what concerns us in practice is the total surplus generated by any particular action. The abstract accounting imputation of this total to particular commodities is of no operational significance.

Thus for example, we might want to determine the compensating tax that could be levied if the individual at A were permitted to buy only (say) X_1, while the market for X_2 remained closed to him. The relevant compensating variation in this case can readily be measured in Figure 7 as the distance AE_1. It is determined by the intersection with the Y-axis of that budget line in the OX_1Y plane which is parallel to AC and tangent to the indifference curve ARV (in the same plane) going through A. (The quantity AE_1 can also be represented by the relevant triangular area under the compensated demand curve corresponding to the indifference curve ARV; in other words, the demand curve drawn for the individual at A on the assumption that X_2 does not exist or is priced infinitely high.) Clearly, we would obtain a different compensating variation if instead of assuming the market for X_2 closed, we were to assume that the individual is buying a certain fixed quantity of it; or, more appropriately, if we were to assume that he is initially able to acquire X_2 at a certain price. But this is as it should be, for the nature of the policy question confronting us would then also be different.

In a similar way we can define the consumer's surplus AE_2, measuring the compensating variation for opening up only the market for X_2. The quantities AE_1 and AE_2 can be used to define the "relative importance" of X_1 and X_2 to the individual. On the other hand, it is obvious that they will not generally sum up to AA'. That is, because of the interactions noted above, the compensating variation for permitting trade in both X_1 and X_2 is not the sum of the variations for permitting trade in each one separately. In more familiar terms, consumer's surplus is not additive. For policy questions, however, this nonadditivity should not bother us.

Figure 7 can also be adapted to provide us with the relevant measures of consumer's surplus for other cases [for example, the equivalent variations for abolishing one or both of the markets for the individual at P, or the compensating (or equivalent) variations for moving from the price system p_1^0, p_2^0 to p_1', p_2']. But if consumer's surplus is to be a practical tool of policymaking, it is necessary that we be able to measure these variations not by means of indifference-map analysis, but by computing the relevant areas under observable demand curves—or, more generally, by carrying out the relevant integrations of demand functions dependent on the whole array of relative prices. The problems involved here are very complicated and still await a full and rigorous treatment.[18]

On the other hand, it is important to note that the total compensating variation in any multi-commodity case (that is, the surplus generated by introducing trade in all the commodities) can conceptually be readily computed from demand curves by making use of Hicks' well-known theorem that a group of commodities whose prices move proportionately can be treated as a single composite one.[19] Let us accordingly define the composite commodity $X = p_1 X_1 + p_2 X_2$ (where p_1 and p_2 are the prices in terms of Y), and let MQ in Figure 2 represent its compensated demand curve. Similarly, let $M_1 Q_1$ in Figure 8(a) represent the compensated demand curve for X_1 *drawn on the assumption that changes in p_1 are accompanied by proportionate changes in p_2.* A corresponding statement holds *mutatis mutandis* for $M_2 Q_2$ in Figure 8(b). Finally, let OL_1 and OL_2 be the respective prices of X_1 and X_2 corresponding to the price OL of their composite X. Since by definition the individual's expenditure on this composite good equals the sum of his expenditures on X_1 and X_2, the rectangle $OCHL$ in Figure 2 is the sum of $OC_1 H_1 L_1$ and $OC_2 H_2 L_2$ in Figure 8. By similar reasoning, $OCHM = OC_1 H_1 M_1 + OC_2 H_2 M_2$. Hence total consumer's surplus LHM can be measured as the sum of the triangles $L_1 H_1 M$ and $L_2 H_2 M_2$.[20] Needless to say, these last two triangles have no welfare connotation in themselves. We can, if we wish, *define* triangle $L_1 H_1 M_1$ as that part of the total surplus "due to" X_1, but this would be quite arbitrary. It should in particular be emphasized that this triangle is *not* a measure of the compensating variation AE_1 defined above.

We note finally that the foregoing procedure (whose simplicity stems from the fact

18. For an indication of some of the problems involved, see Little (1957), pp. 173–82 and the references to Henderson and Hicks given therein.

Little actually devotes most of his attention to analyzing the welfare implications of introducing a new good into the economy. The nature of this problem can be defined formally as follows: assume that an economy with n goods is at a certain point on its n-dimensional production surface. Introducing a new good adds a dimension to this surface. The question is then whether it is possible to move on the resulting $(n + 1)$-dimensional production surface to an $(n + 1)$-dimensional (community) indifference surface that is "higher" than the original one.

Little's discussion of the various consumer's and producer's surpluses is essentially an attempt to answer the foregoing question. At the same time Little points out certain methodological objections (similar to those which arise whenever a "change in tastes" occurs) that might make this whole question meaningless (1957, p. 173, fn.).

19. See Hicks (1946), pp. 33–34, 312–13; for a graphical representation, see Wold (1953), pp. 108–10.

20. For a different approach to the multi-commodity case, see Hicks (1956), ch. XVIII.

that it effectively reduces a multi-commodity case to a two-commodity one) indicates how total consumer's surplus can be measured in a perfectly competitive economy in which all income is from labor. The initially endowed good (Y) of this economy is, of course, potential labor service (see Figure 6). Total surplus would then be the sum of the relevant triangles under the individual demand curves for the various commodities, where each of these curves is drawn as a function of price in terms of the wage unit, on the assumption that the prices of all other commodities change in the same proportion.

3. The Marshallian Demand Curve

At several points in the preceding argument, Marshall's treatment of consumer's surplus has been mentioned in passing. It is thus desirable to present a more systematic discussion of the nature of the Marshallian demand curve, though I shall for the most part refrain from adding to the detailed exegetical disputations that have already taken place on this question (Alford, 1956; Friedman, 1949). The basic feature of the following interpretation (which is essentially a rigorization of the "traditional" one) is that despite the fact that real income increases as we move downward along the Marshallian demand curve, the curve is nevertheless identical with the one that corresponds to a constant real income. The resolution of this seeming paradox lies in drawing out the full implications of one of the key assumptions on which Marshall bases his analysis: namely, the constancy of the "marginal utility of money" (Alford, 1956; Samuelson, 1942, pp. 75–91; Stigler, 1950, pp. 388–90).

This term, of course, has nothing to do with the marginal utility of cash balances, but denotes instead what might better be called the marginal utility of expenditure. I also accept the view (though it is not essential for the following) that Marshall considers this constancy to be an approximation resulting from the assumption that the good whose demand is being analyzed (say, X) forms only a small part of the individual's total expenditure.[21,22] Marshall's two further assumptions are that the marginal utilities of the various goods are independent and diminishing.[23]

The individual's utility-maximizing position is then described by the marginal conditions

(1)
$$\frac{u_X(X)}{p} = u_Y(Y) = m,$$

together with the budget restraint

(2)
$$pX + Y = I,$$

---

21. This is the view of Samuelson (1942), p. 80, fn., and Stigler (1950), p. 370. On the other hand, it is an essential element of Friedman's interpretation that Marshall did not make this assumption (1949, p. 81). For further discussion see Appendix B, below.

22. For a rigorous analysis of the implications of this approximate constancy, see Georgescu-Roegen (1936).

23. See Marshall, *Principles*, pp. 93, 845. By "independent marginal utilities" is meant that the marginal utility of any good is dependent only on the quantity consumed of that good.

where X is the good whose demand is being analyzed, Y represents all other goods, p is the price of X in terms of Y, $u_X(\ )$ and $u_Y(\ )$ are the marginal utilities of X and Y, respectively, m is the marginal utility of money, and I is the individual's given income in units of Y.[24] Clearly, m is measured in "utils" per unit of "money" (i.e., per unit of I, which means per unit of Y) and so is dependent on the cardinal utility function chosen for the analysis. It is not invariant under a positive monotonic transformation of this function (Samuelson, 1942, pp. 76–78).

The meaning of Marshall's approximation can now be seen. If X is an unimportant good, a change in its price will cause a small variation in the individual's expenditures on it relative to his total income. Hence the total quantity of Y purchased will not be much affected, and hence $u_Y(Y)$—and therefore m—will remain approximately the same. It should be emphasized that in actuality the law of diminishing utility is assumed to hold for both X and Y; it is only the relatively small variation in the consumption of the latter that enables us to ignore it in this case.

If, for simplicity, we now assume m to remain exactly constant at m_0, we can immediately (in Marshall's words) "translate [the] law of diminishing utility into terms of price" (*Principles*, p. 94). We then have from (1),

$$(3) \qquad\qquad p = \frac{u_X(X)}{m_0},$$

or, alternatively,

$$(4) \qquad\qquad X = f(p),$$

where (to use inverse-function notation) $f(p) \equiv u^{-1}_x(m_0 p)$. Correspondingly, the demand function for Y can be deduced from (2) as

$$(5) \qquad\qquad Y = I - pf(p).$$

Now, since by assumption the marginal utility curve $u_X(X)$ is negatively sloped, its inverse—and hence the demand curve for X—must also be negatively sloped. This is the crux of Marshall's famous argument.

This argument can be reinterpreted in modern Hicksian terms by noting from (4) that Marshall's assumptions imply a demand function for X that is independent of income.[25] Hence, for example, a decrease in price will cause the amount of X demanded to increase only because of the substitution effect. It must be emphasized

24. Note that the foregoing assumptions actually imply the impossibility of any good's being an inferior one. For by budget restraint (2), an increase in I necessarily increases the demand for at least one good. This then decreases the marginal utility of that good. Hence in order to restore equality in (1), the amounts demanded of all goods must increase. (This is actually a special instance of the Paretian assumptions discussed by Hicks [1946], p. 28, fn. 21). From Marshall's discussion of the Giffen paradox, however, it would seem that he was not aware of this implication (*Principles*, p. 133).

25. Provided that the total expenditure on X is less than the individual's income. In other words, an additional (if tacit) restriction under which the individual is behaving is that Y in equation (5) cannot be negative. In graphical terms, the demand curve for X cannot lie rightward of the rectangular hyperbola representing a total expenditure on X equal to the individual's income.

Clearly, this limitation need not concern us within the framework of Marshall's assumption that X is an unimportant good.

that such a price decrease *will* generate an income effect, but as equations (4) and (5) show, this will express itself entirely in an increased demand for Y.

This zero-income elasticity of demand for X can also be deduced directly from equation (1). This is so because, if we assume an increase in I to take place, p constant, then if the marginal utility of X is declining while that of Y is constant, utility maximization will clearly lead the individual to spend all of his increased income on Y (Friedman 1935–36, pp. 153–56). By assumption, this leaves m unaffected. Thus Marshall's assumptions imply constancy of m with respect to both p and I.

There are several additional points that should be emphasized. First, the zero-income elasticity of demand for X depends no less on the two additional assumptions of declining marginal utility of X and independence of marginal utilities than on the constancy of the marginal utility of Y. Thus if we assumed, for example, that $u_X(\ )$ were also constant, then an increase in income would be used in indeterminate proportions to increase the demand for both X and Y. Alternatively, if we assumed that $u_X(\ )$ depended on Y as well as on X, then we would no longer be able to infer from equation (3)—modified accordingly—that the demand for X depended only on p, to the exclusion of I.[26]

Second, it would be a serious misinterpretation of Marshall to attribute to him the belief that the marginal utility of money (and hence the demand for a commodity) actually remains constant under a change in income, no matter how large. On the contrary, he devoted Section 3 of Book III, Chapter III of his *Principles* to an analysis of how an increase in income causes a decrease in m and hence an increase in the demand for X. In modern terminology, Section 2 of Marshall's argument analyzes the substitution effect, while Section 3 analyzes the income effect. The proper relation between these two sections is, however, somewhat obscured by a hitherto unnoticed typographical error in all editions of the *Principles* subsequent to the third.[27]

Third, there is no relationship whatsoever between constancy of the marginal utility of money and constancy of real income in the sense of staying on the same indifference curve. In general, a compensated change in price that will leave the individual on the same indifference curve will not leave m unchanged, although in the Marshallian case it will.[28] Conversely, under Marshallian assumptions a decrease in the price of X moves the individual to a higher indifference curve, on which he is consuming more of both X and Y, and yet his marginal utility of income is constant. This is no more surprising than the fact that, say, constant marginal costs do not imply constant total costs. Yet I feel that the failure to recognize this lack of relationship has been a stumbling block in the path toward an understanding of Marshallian demand theory.

Finally, nothing essential in the foregoing interpretation would be changed if instead of assuming that Marshall intended to keep m *approximately* constant, we

---

26. From this it is clear that Hicks' well-known demonstration that constancy of $u_Y(\ )$ implies zero-income elasticity of demand for X is actually invalid for it overlooks these two additional assumptions (1946, p. 26). For further details see Appendix C, below.

27. See Appendix D, below.

28. See Appendix E, below.

were to assume that he intended to keep it *absolutely* constant by means of compensating variations in the prices of other goods.[29] The main point is that the constancy achieved by these compensating variations is that of the marginal utility of money, and not (as Friedman would have it)[30] of the level of utility. In modern terms, the compensating variations are intended to eliminate the income effect not in its entirety, but only from the market for X.

We can now summarize our interpretation in the following words: the Marshallian demand curve is identical with the compensated demand curve of Section 1 above, not because it is conceptually generated by an experiment in which compensating variations eliminate the income effect created by the price change and thus leave the individual at the same level of utility, but because the income effect is assumed to expend itself entirely in other markets, leaving only a substitution effect in the market for X. For this reason the Marshallian demand curve tells us at one and the same time the maximum amount the individual would be willing to spend for X under perfectly discriminating monopoly conditions that keep his level of utility constant, and the amount he actually does spend under conditions in which a falling price raises this level. Hence it can be used as Marshall does use it to provide an accurate measure of consumer's surplus.

Appendix

(Superior figures in parentheses following key letter refer to respective text footnote.)

$A^{(9)}$ The passages from the *Principles* (with italics added) are as follows. Note that they create the impression that Marshall was thinking more along the lines of the equivalent surplus AA'' than of the surplus KD (Figure 1).

29. Note that under these assumptions we must divide all other goods into two classes, those whose prices are kept constant and thus serve as the unit of measure (denoted, say, by W) and those whose prices are varied compensatingly (say, Z). The optimum conditions then become

(a)
$$\frac{u_x(X)}{p_x} = u_w(W) = \frac{u_z(Z)}{p_z} = m,$$

(b)
$$p_xX + W + p_zZ = I,$$

where p_x and p_z are the prices of X and Z, respectively, in terms of W. All goods are now assumed to be subject to diminishing marginal utility, hence the assumption that $u_w(W)$ is constant implies that W is also constant. Thus (a) and (b) are effectively three equations in the four variables Z, X, p_z, and p_x. The first three of these variables can then be solved out as functions of the fourth. Clearly, the resulting demand function for X depends only on p_x and is independent of income.

30. Friedman relies primarily for his interpretation on Note II of Marshall's Mathematical Appendix (1949, p. 84). But it seems to me that the conceptual experiment referred to in this Note is not the compensated one described by Friedman, but rather the one described in footnote 2 above. This interpretation of the footnote also resolves the other difficulties of textual interpretation which Friedman raises earlier (1949, pp. 82–83). Furthermore, it enables the straightforward acceptance of Marshall's Appendix as a description of the same conceptual experiment described in his text, and not (as Friedman contends) of a different one. Similarly, our approach avoids the very strained interpretation of Marshall's discussion of consumer's surplus into which Friedman (by virtue of his constant-real-income approach) is forced (1949, pp. 51–52, 68–72). See the next paragraph of the text.

Note too how the correct text of Marshall's argument cited in Appendix D below makes it even clearer than in later editions of the *Principles* that whatever compensating variations Marshall is making in order to keep "other things . . . equal," their purpose is to achieve constancy of the marginal utility of money.

In other words, he derives this 45s. worth of surplus enjoyment from his conjuncture, from the adaptation of the environment to his wants in the particular matter of tea. *If that adaptation ceased, and tea could not be had at any price*, he would have incurred a loss of satisfaction at least equal to that which he could have got by spending 45s. more on extra supplies of things that were worth to him only just what he paid for them (p. 127).

. . . there might be use, when comparing life in Central Africa with life in England, in saying that, though the things which money will buy in Central Africa may on the average be as cheap there as here, *yet there are so many things which cannot be bought there at all*, that a person with a thousand a year there is not so well off as a person with three or four hundred a year here. If a man pays 1d. toll on a bridge, which saves him an additional drive that would cost a shilling, we do not say that the penny is worth a shilling, but that the penny together with the advantage offered him by the bridge (the part it plays in his conjuncture) is worth a shilling for that day. *Were the bridge swept away on a day on which he needed it*, he would be in at least as bad a position as if he had been deprived of eleven pence (p. 127, footnote).

It is a common saying in ordinary life that the real worth of things to a man is not gauged by the price he pays for them: that, though he spends for instance much more on tea than on salt, yet salt is of greater real worth to him; *and that this would be clearly seen if he were entirely deprived of it*. This line of argument is but thrown into precise technical form when it is said that we cannot trustthe marginal utility of a commodity to indicate its total utility (p. 129).

It yields to him, as consumer, a surplus consisting of the excess of the total utility to him of the commodity over the real value to him of what he paid for it. For his marginal purchases, those which he is only just induced to buy, the two are equal: but those parts of his purchases for which he would gladly have paid a higher price rather than go without them, yield him a surplus of satisfaction: a true net benefit which he, as consumer, derives from the facilities offered to him by his surroundings or conjuncture. *He would lose this surplus, if his surroundings were so altered as to prevent him from obtaining any supplies of that commodity*, and to compel him to divert the means which he spends on that to other commodities (one of which might be increased leisure) of which at present he does not care to have further supplies at their respective prices (p. 830).

B[21]   The contention that Marshall restricts his discussion of the demand curve to an unimportant commodity is supported by Stigler (1950), p. 390 by reference to the following passage from the first edition of the *Principles*:

When a person buys anything for his own consumption, he generally spends on it a small part of his total resources; while when he buys it for the purpose of trade, he looks to re-selling it, and therefore his total resources are not diminished. In

either case, the marginal utility of money to him is not appreciably changed
(p. 393).

The corresponding passage in the eighth edition appears on p. 335, with the last
sentence changed to: "In either case, there is no appreciable change in his willingness
to part with money."

Though mentioning this passage, Friedman apparently feels that it is offset by the
fact that "nowhere in Book III, Chapter III does Marshall explicitly restrict his
discussion to unimportant commodities" (1949, p. 81, fn. 45). Friedman also finds
much significance in the fact that the first time Marshall does make such an explicit
restriction is in connection with his discussion of consumer's surplus (*Principles*,
1920, p. 842), where according to Friedman's interpretation too it is necessary (1949,
p. 72). The significance of this contrast is, however, much attenuated, if not
eliminated, by Guillebaud's recent explanation that the critical passage on p. 842 was
inserted by Marshall "partly in response to a letter from John Neville Keynes who
was reading the proofs of Marshall's 1st edition of the *Principles* and asked him to
consider the possible effects on consumer's surplus of a transfer of expenditure to
other commodities" (*Principles*, variorum edition, Vol. 2, p. 832). Thus, if the vital
restriction to unimportant commodities was originally left only implicit in Marshall's
discussion of consumer's surplus, there is certainly nothing unreasonable in assuming
that it was (and is) also implicit in his discussion of the demand curve.

Another point that should be emphasized is that Marshall's discussion of the
demand curve in Book III, Chapter III (and in the attached Mathematical Notes) is
supported by repeated references to Jevons—who, in order to treat the "utility of
money as a constant" explicitly restricted his analogous discussion to the case of
goods that are not "the main elements of expenditure" (Jevons, 1879, pp. 159–60.
This was the edition used by Marshall. The corresponding passages in the fourth
edition occur on pp. 147–48).

C[26]   Hicks' argument is as follows:

> What is meant by the marginal utility of money being constant? Making our
> translation, it would appear to mean that changes in the consumer's supply of
> money (that is, with respect to the problem in hand, his income) will not affect
> the marginal rate of substitution between money and any particular commodity
> X. (For the marginal rate of substitution equals the ratio of the marginal utilities
> of X and money.) Therefore, if this income increases, and the price of X remains
> constant, the price of X will still equal the marginal rate of substitution, without
> any change in the amount of X bought. The demand for X is therefore indepen-
> dent of income (1946, p. 26).

Now, unless there is independence of the marginal utilities, an increase in money
may affect the marginal utility of X, and hence the marginal rate of substitution of
money for X, even though the marginal utility of money is constant. On the other
hand, if the marginal utility of X were also constant under a change in money, the

marginal rate of substitution could remain constant even if the demand for X were to increase.

These same results can be obtained analytically by making use of the fact that

$$\frac{\partial X}{\partial I} = \frac{\begin{vmatrix} 0 & 1 & u_Y \\ u_X & 0 & u_{XY} \\ u_Y & 0 & u_{YY} \end{vmatrix}}{\begin{vmatrix} 0 & u_X & u_Y \\ u_X & u_{XX} & u_{XY} \\ u_Y & u_{XY} & u_{YY} \end{vmatrix}}$$

(see Hicks, 1946, pp. 307–8). Hicks assumes only that $u_{YY} = 0$; but this clearly does not assure the vanishing of the numerator. It will, however, vanish if $u_{XY} = u_{YY} = 0$.

On the other hand, if $u_{XX} = u_{YY} = u_{XY} = 0$, both numerator and denominator are zero, so that the income effect with respect to X is indeterminate.

D[27]   The relevant text of Marshall's third edition (p. 170) is as follows:

An increase in the amount of a thing that a person has will, other things being equal (i.e. the purchasing power of money, and the amount of money at his command being equal) diminish his marginal demand price for it.

§3. This last sentence reminds us that we have as yet taken no account of changes in the marginal utility of money, or general purchasing power. At one and the same time, a person's material resources being unchanged, the marginal utility of money to him is a fixed quantity, so that the prices he is just willing to pay for two commodities are to one another in the same ratio as the utility of those two commodities.

Of course, a greater utility will be required to induce him to buy a thing if he is poor than if he is rich. . . .

In all subsequent editions, Section 3 is erroneously designated as starting a paragraph later than in the third edition. Furthermore, an additional paragraph has been inserted before the one beginning "This last sentence . . ." As a result, the words "last sentence" in all these editions actually refer to the sentence before the last.[1]

E[28]   In the two-commodity case it can be shown (Mosak 1942, pp. 70–71, fn. 3) that for a compensated change which keeps the individual on the same indifference curve,

$$\frac{\partial m}{\partial p} = \frac{\begin{vmatrix} 0 & u_X & u_Y \\ m & u_{XX} & u_{XY} \\ 0 & u_{XY} & u_{YY} \end{vmatrix}}{\begin{vmatrix} 0 & u_X & u_Y \\ u_X & u_{XX} & u_{XY} \\ u_Y & u_{XY} & u_{YY} \end{vmatrix}} = \frac{-m \begin{vmatrix} u_X & u_Y \\ u_{XY} & u_{YY} \end{vmatrix}}{U},$$

which is generally not zero.

1. Unfortunately, these errors have not been noted in C. W. Guillebaud's variorum edition (1961) of Marshall's *Principles*; see *ibid.*, vol. II, p. 241.

Under the Marshallian assumption that $u_{XY} = u_{YY} = 0$, this will, however, vanish. The reason this invariance characterizes both the compensated and uncompensated Marshallian cases is intuitively obvious. For these two cases differ only in the amount of Y demanded, the demand for X being the same in both. But since the marginal utility of Y is assumed constant, m must also be constant.

Bibliography

R. F. G. Alford. "Marshall's Demand Curve." *Economica*, Feb. 1956, *23*, 23–48.

M. J. Bailey. "The Marshallian Demand Curve." *Journal of Political Economy*, June 1954, *62*, 255–61.

R. Bishop. "Consumers' Surplus and Cardinal Utility." *Quarterly Journal of Economics*, May 1943, *57*, 421–49.

K. Boulding. "The Concept of Economic Surplus." *American Economic Review*, Dec. 1945, *35*, 851–69. Reprinted in *Readings in the Theory of Income Distribution*, ed. W. Fellner and B. F. Haley. Philadelphia, 1946. Pp. 638–59.

J. M. Buchanan. "*Ceteris Paribus*: Some Notes on Methodology." *Southern Economic Journal*, Jan. 1958, *24*, 259–70.

M. Friedman. "Professor Pigou's Method for Measuring Elasticities of Demand from Budgetary Data." *Quarterly Journal of Economics*, Nov. 1935, *50*, 151–63.

_____. "The Marshallian Demand Curve." *Journal of Political Economy*, Dec. 1949, *57*, 463–95. Reprinted in *Essays in Positive Economics*, Chicago 1953. Pp. 47–99.

_____. "The 'Welfare' Effects of an Income Tax and an Excise Tax." *Journal of Political Economy*, Feb. 1952, *60*, 25–33. Reprinted in *Essays in Positive Economics*. Chicago, 1953. Pp. 100–13.

N. Georgescu-Roegen. "Marginal Utility of Money and Elasticity of Demand." *Quarterly Journal of Economics*, May 1936, *50*, 533–39.

A. M. Henderson. "Consumer's Surplus and the Compensating Variation." *Review of Economic Studies*, Feb. 1941, *8*, 117–21.

J. R. Hicks. *Value and Capital: An Inquiry into some Fundamental Principles of Economic Theory*, 2nd ed. London, 1946.

_____. *A Revision of Demand Theory*. London, 1956.

W. S. Jevons. *Theory of Political Economy*, 2nd ed. London, 1879; 4th ed., London, 1911.

W. Leontief. "The Use of Indifference Curves in the Analysis of Foreign Trade." *Quarterly Journal of Economics*, May 1933, *47*, 493–503. Reprinted in *Readings in the Theory of International Trade*, ed. H. S. Ellis and L. A. Metzler. Philadelphia, 1949. Pp. 229–38.

I. M. D. Little. *A Critique of Welfare Economics*, 2nd ed. London, 1957.

N. Liviatan and D. Patinkin. "On the Economic Theory of Price Indexes." *Economic Development and Cultural Change*, Apr. 1961, *9*, 502–36. [Reproduced as chap. 9 below.]

A. Marshall. *Principles of Economics*, 8th ed. London, 1920.

_____. *Principles of Economics*, 9th (variorum) edition, with annotations by C. W. Guillebaud. London, 1961.

E. J. Mishan. "Realism and Relevance in Consumer's Surplus." *Review of Economic Studies*, 1947, *15*, 27–33.

————. "Rent as a Measure of Welfare Change." *American Economic Review*, June 1959, *49*, 386–95.

————. "A Survey of Welfare Economics, 1939–59." *Economic Journal*, June 1960, *70*, 197–265.

J. Mosak. "On the Interpretation of the Fundamental Equation of Value Theory." In *Studies in Mathematical Economics and Econometrics*, ed. O. Lange, F. McIntyre, and T. O. Yntema. Chicago, 1942. Pp. 69–74.

P. A. Samuelson. "Constancy of the Marginal Utility of Income." In *Studies in Mathematical Economics and Econometrics*, ed. O. Lange, F. McIntyre, and T. O. Yntema. Chicago, 1942. Pp. 75–91.

————. *Foundations of Economic Analysis*. Cambridge, Mass., 1947.

G. J. Stigler. "The Development of Utility Theory: II." *Journal of Political Economy*, Oct. 1950, *58*, 373–96.

J. Viner. *Studies in the Theory of International Trade*. New York, 1937.

H. Wold. *Demand Analysis*. New York, 1953.

L. B. Yeager. "*Methodenstreit* Over Demand Curves." *Journal of Political Economy*, Feb. 1960, *68*, 53–64.

9. On the Economic Theory of Price Indexes*

(with Nissan Liviatan)

One of the most fruitful interconnections between theoretical and empirical work in economics has been the use of the theory of consumers' behavior to attribute meaning to the Laspeyres and Paasche price indexes. On the meaning of these indexes as deflators of national-income magnitudes, a fairly clear consensus has been reached as a result of the discussions of Hicks,[1] Kuznets,[2] Samuelson,[3] Little,[4] and others. From these discussions one basic point should have become clear: the validity of a price index cannot be judged apart from the purpose for which it is to be used. Unfortunately, however, this lesson has not carried over sufficiently to analysis of the second use of price indexes—namely, in the computation of cost-of-living allowances. Hence, despite the protracted discussion of this question in the literature—by, for example, Staehle,[5] Lerner,[6] Allen,[7] and Samuelson[8]—there continue to persist several points of confusion and misunderstanding.

It is these points which will concern us in this paper. Section 1 reviews—with some elaboration—the accepted theory of "true" price and quantity indexes. In Section 2 the operational significance of these indexes in computing cost-of-living allowances is then examined in detail. The section concludes with a demonstration that only Laspeyres price indexes provide a valid limit for cost-of-living allowances. Section 3

Reprinted by permission from *Economic Development and Cultural Change*, Apr. 1961, *9*, 502–36, Copyright 1961 by the University of Chicago. This was a *festschrift* issue for Simon Kuznets. Advantage has been taken of this reprinting to correct various typographical errors and notational inconsistencies in the original article, as well as to make numerous minor changes for the purpose of improving clarity or style. Unfortunately, however, there are inconsistencies of labelling between Figures 6–7, on the one hand, and Figures 1–5, on the other, which were not noted until it was too late to correct; this, however, does not affect the analysis based on Figures 6–7. There is also one duly noted substantive addition at the end of section 1.

* We are indebted for most valuable comments and criticisms to Yosef Attiyeh, Giora Hanoch, David Levhari, Zvi Ophir, Eytan Sheshinski, Joseph Steinman, and Avigdor Meroz (Zirulnikov).

1. J. R. Hicks, "The Valuation of the Social Income" (1940), pp. 105–24.
2. Simon Kuznets, "On the Valuation of Social Income—Reflections on Professor Hicks' Article" (1948), pp. 1–16, pp. 116–31. See also Hicks' reply (1948), pp. 163–72.
3. Paul A. Samuelson, "Evaluation of Real National Income" (1950), pp. 1–29.
4. I. M. D. Little, *A Critique of Welfare Economics*, second edition (1957), Chapter XII.
5. H. Staehle, "A Development of the Economic Theory of Index Numbers" (1934–35), pp. 163–88.
6. A. P. Lerner, "A Note on the Theory of Price Index Numbers" (1935–36), pp. 50–56. See also the comment on this article by M. F. W. Joseph (1935–36), pp. 155–57.
7. R. G. D. Allen, "Some Observations on the Theory and Practice of Price Index Numbers" (1935–36), pp. 57–66.
8. Paul A. Samuelson, *Foundations of Economic Analysis* (1947), pp. 146–63.

then shows in detail the error of the still frequently expressed notion that the Paasche index provides a lower limit for such allowances. Indeed, this section shows that the use of the Paasche index can sometimes lead to a greater overcompensation than the Laspeyres! Section 4 concludes with a discussion of the consequences of dropping the assumption of a constant money (base) income—the assumption on which the analysis of Section 2 is based. It is pointed out that once income is variable, the cost-of-living allowance cannot be meaningfully defined—even when we use the ideal price index.

We must emphasize that this paper is concerned exclusively with the theory of index numbers as regards a given individual of fixed tastes. It does not deal with the fundamental problems of aggregation, changes in taste, introduction of new commodities, and the like which have been discussed at length in the literature.

1. True Price and Quantity Index[9]

In this section we shall define rigorously the concept of "the true index of prices." For the moment we shall not inquire as to the uses to be made of this index. Instead we shall merely set out the way in which it can conceptually be computed. The discussion of the operational significance of this index number is deferred to the next section. We shall also deal in passing with "the true index of quantities."

Our subject is a complicated one—and for that reason it is necessary to make use of fairly complicated symbols in order to avoid ambiguities. In particular, let us adopt the following notation:

A, B	indifference curves
x, y	commodities
$_xp_i, {}_yp_i$ $(i=1, 2, \ldots)$	a specific set of prices for x and y
p_i $(i=1, 2, \ldots)$	a shorthand notation for $_xp_i, {}_yp_i$
$_xq_i^A, {}_yq_i^A$ $(i=1, 2, \ldots)$	a specific combination of quantities of x and y having the following two properties: (i) it lies on indifference curve A (ii) it has a marginal rate of substitution equal to the price ratio $_xp_i/{}_yp_i$—or, in brief, the marginal rate of substitution specified by p_i
q_i^A $(i=1, 2, \ldots)$	a shorthand notation for $_xq_i^A, {}_yq_i^A$
Q_i^A $(i=1, 2, \ldots)$	a point on indifference curve A whose coordinates are q_i^A

Corresponding definitions hold, of course, for $_xq_i^B, {}_yq_i^B; q_i^B;$ and Q_i^B.

The meaning of a "true" index number is that it is derived from an assumed full knowledge of the individual's indifference map. Consider, then, indifference curve A

---

9. Cf. on this section Staehle (1935), and Samuelson (1947), pp. 146–63.

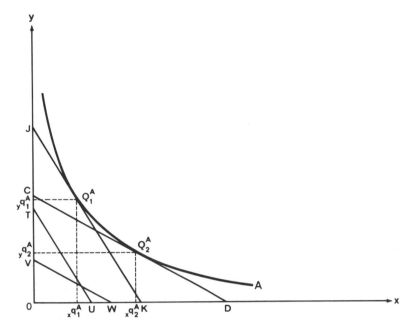

Figure 1

in Figure 1. It is convenient for our purposes to conceive of the level of utility represented by this indifference curve as being a "good" which is purchased by the individual. Denote this good by $U(A)$. The minimum cost of this good is obviously a function of the prices which prevail. Thus consider the prices p_1 whose ratio is assumed to equal the (negative of) the slope of the budget line TU in Figure 1. The minimum cost of acquiring the utility level of indifference curve A at these prices is clearly

(1) $\Sigma\, p_1 q_1^A = {}_x p_1\, {}_x q_1^A + {}_y p_1\, {}_y q_1^A,$

where the q_i^A are the coordinates of that point on the indifference curve, Q_1^A, whose marginal rate of substitution is specified by p_1.

Thus $\Sigma\, p_1 \hat{q}_1$ is defined as that level of money income necessary to bring a budget line whose slope equals $-\dfrac{{}_x p_1}{{}_y p_1}$ into tangency with the given indifference curve A. If money income were below $\Sigma\, p_1 q_1^A$, the individual would not be able to acquire the utility level of A; that is, he would not have enough money to purchase $U(A)$. On the other hand, if it were above $\Sigma\, p_1 q_1^A$, he would have more than necessary for this purpose. Thus $\Sigma\, p_1 q_1^A$ is the money income corresponding to the budget line JK (parallel to TU) whose equation is

(2) ${}_x p_1\, x + {}_y p_1\, y = \Sigma\, p_1 q_1^A.$

If, instead, prices were ${}_x p_2$, ${}_y p_2$ (or in brief, p_2), with a ratio assumed equal to the (negative of the) slope of the budget line VW, then in a similar way the minimum cost of acquiring the utility level of indifference curve A—or $U(A)$—would be

(3) $\Sigma \; p_2 q_2^A = {}_x p_2 \; {}_x q_2^A + {}_y p_2 \; {}_y q_2^A,$

where the q_2^A are the coordinates of that point, Q_2^A, on the indifference curve A whose marginal rate of substitution equals $\frac{{}_x p_2}{{}_y p_2}$. This, of course, is the point of tangency with a budget line parallel to VW—namely, budget line CD, whose equation is

(4) ${}_x p_2 \, x + {}_y p_2 \, y = \Sigma \, p_2 q_2^A.$

The true index of the change in prices from p_1 to p_2 is then defined as

(5) $I_{1,2}^A = \dfrac{\Sigma \; p_2 q_2^A}{\Sigma \; p_1 q_1^A}.$

The subscripts of this index, "1, 2," represent the initial and final prices, respectively. The superscript, "A," represents the level of utility which is being acquired. By definition, q_1^A and q_2^A in the denominator and numerator, respectively, of the foregoing index represent points Q_1^A and Q_2^A, with the following properties: (1) their marginal rates of substitution are specified by p_1 and p_2, respectively; (2) they are both on the indifference curve A—that is, they both represent the same good $U(A)$. Thus the superscript A is of critical importance; it shows that the true price index can be defined only as of a given level of utility.

In a similar way we could define

(6) $I_{2,1}^A = \dfrac{\Sigma \; p_1 q_1^A}{\Sigma \; p_2 q_2^A} \, .$

This represents the percentage change in the cost of $U(A)$ as prices are changed from p_2 to p_1. Obviously,

(7) $I_{1,2}^A \cdot I_{2,1}^A = 1.$

Thus the true price index meets the "time reversal test." [10]

Before going on we might note that our usual conception of a price index is that of a ratio of two weighted averages of prices—in which the same weights appear in the numerator and the denominator. At first sight, then, it might appear unreasonable to refer to $I_{1,2}^A$ as a "price index:" for the quantity which serves as a weight in the numerator, q_2^A, is clearly different from that which serves as a weight in the denominator, q_1^A. But as is already implicit in the preceding discussion, in a deeper sense $I_{1,2}^A$ does partake of the characteristics of a price index: for the prices of the numerator and denominator are both "weighted" by the same "quantity"—namely, the good $U(A)$, representing a given level of utility.

10. On the nature of this test, see F. E. Croxton and D. J. Cowden, *Applied General Statistics* (1941), pp. 612–14.

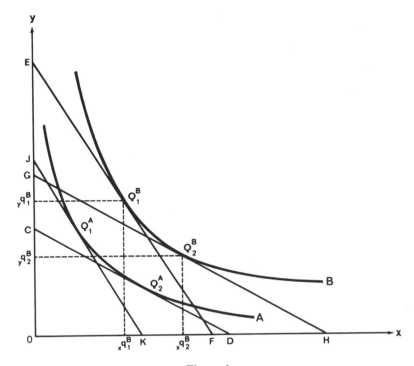

Figure 2

Let us now proceed to indifference curve B in Figure 2—whose constant level of utility represents the good $U(B)$. The true index of the price change from p_1 to p_2 in this case is

$$(8) \qquad I^B_{1,2} = \frac{\Sigma\ p_2 q^B_2}{\Sigma\ p_1 q^B_1},$$

and from p_2 to p_1

$$(9) \qquad I^B_{2,1} = \frac{\Sigma\ p_1 q^B_1}{\Sigma\ p_2 q^B_2},$$

where the q^B_1 are the coordinates of Q^B_1, and the q^B_2 are the coordinates of Q^B_2. Once again it is clear that

$$(10) \qquad I^B_{1,2} \cdot I^B_{2,1} = 1.$$

From this discussion we see that in general there are as many true indexes of the change in prices from p_1 to p_2 as there are indifference curves. We can also see that the "time reversal test" will in general not be met unless the reverse movement is traced on the same indifference curve. Thus, in general

$$(11) \qquad I^A_{1,2} \cdot I^B_{2,1} = \frac{\Sigma\ p_2 q^A_2}{\Sigma\ p_1 q^A_1} \cdot \frac{\Sigma\ p_1 q^B_1}{\Sigma\ p_2 q^B_2} \neq 1.$$

This follows from the fact that there is no necessary relationship between indifference curves A and B. Thus, for example, if indifference curve B leftward of the point of tangency Q_2^B were to have a different shape than in Figure 2, this would affect only q_1^B, while leaving q_1^A, q_2^A, and q_2^B unchanged—so that the value of the product in (11) would necessarily be affected. On the other hand, if indifference curves A and B were in some way related, there could be a relationship between $I_{1,2}^A$ and $I_{2,1}^B$. Thus, for example, if the indifference map were of a homogeneous utility function,[11] then the product of the two indexes would necessarily be unity.[12]

Let us now turn briefly to "true quantity index numbers." These are an indication of the magnitude of the shift from one level of utility [say, $U(A)$] to another [say, $U(B)$] as measured by the ratio of the money cost of acquiring $U(B)$ to the money cost of acquiring $U(A)$. Clearly, this ratio depends on the prices used to evaluate these costs. In our present case, there are two such prices—and hence two such indexes: namely,

$$(12) \qquad V_{A,B}^1 = \frac{\Sigma\ p_1 q_1^B}{\Sigma\ p_1 q_1^A} \text{ and } V_{A,B}^2 = \frac{\Sigma\ p_2 q_2^B}{\Sigma\ p_2 q_2^A},$$

where the subscripts "A, B" represent the initial and final levels of utility, respectively; and the superscript represents the price system used for weighting. These indexes have a simple graphical representation in Figure 2: namely,

$$V_{A,B}^1 = \frac{OE}{OJ} \text{ and } V_{A,B}^2 = \frac{OG}{OC}.$$

Clearly, these two are not necessarily equal. Thus there are as many true quantity indexes as there are systems of prices. On the other hand, $V_{A,B}^1$ will be greater than unity if and only if indifference curve B is above A—and the same is true for $V_{A,B}^2$. Thus if $V_{A,B}^1$ is greater than (less than) unity, the same must be true for $V_{A,B}^2$—and vice versa. That is, any two true quantity index numbers must always show the same direction of movement.

In the same way we can also define two quantity indexes of the reverse shift from B to A,

$$(13) \qquad V_{B,A}^1 = \frac{\Sigma\ p_1 q_1^A}{\Sigma\ p_1 q_1^B} \text{ and } V_{B,A}^2 = \frac{\Sigma\ p_2 q_2^A}{\Sigma\ p_2 q_2^B}.$$

11. Or any positive monotomic transformation thereof—that is, what is sometimes called a homothetic function.

12. In this case Q_1^A and Q_1^B in Figure 2 would lie on the same radius vector—and Q_2^A and Q_2^B on another. Furthermore, the following relationship would obtain,

$$\frac{OQ_1^A}{OQ_1^B} = \frac{OQ_2^A}{OQ_2^B},$$

which would in turn imply $I_{1,2}^A \cdot I_{2,1}^B = 1$. This reciprocal relationship really reflects a property of *quantity* indexes. This point cannot be analyzed fully within the confines of the present article, but see the discussion in the text immediately following.

Here again, one index will be greater than (less than) unity if and only if the other one is. It follows from these definitions that

(14) $V_{A,B}^1 \cdot V_{B,A}^1 = 1$ and $V_{A,B}^2 \cdot V_{B,A}^2 = 1$.

In other words, true quantity indexes—using the same price weights—meet the "time reversal test." On the other hand, it is clear that in general the test will not be met if different price systems are used. That is, in general

(15) $V_{A,B}^1 \cdot V_{B,A}^2 \neq 1$.

To speak somewhat loosely, if we go from indifference curve A to B by one path (Q_1^A to Q_1^B in Figure 2) and return by another (Q_2^B to Q_2^A) the relative "distances" traversed will generally not be the same.

The concept of quantity indexes is very useful in the analysis of the properties of price indexes. As we shall see we can define for every price index a corresponding quantity index. The meanings of the fundamental relations between these indexes can best be understood when formulated in terms of the familiar concepts of compensated and uncompensated price changes. Consider the price index

$$I_{1,2}^A = \frac{\Sigma\ p_2 q_2^A}{\Sigma\ p_1 q_1^A}$$

which is the ratio of the costs of U(A) at two price systems, p_2 and p_1. Let us now regard $\Sigma\ p_1 q_1^A$ as a "base income" which does not change automatically with the change in prices. Then the numerator $\Sigma\ p_2 q_2^A = I_{1,2}^A \Sigma\ p_1 q^A_1$ can be regarded as the base income adjusted—or "compensated"—for the change from p_1 to p_2 so as to enable the consumer to remain on U(A) in the new situation.

Suppose, however, that the consumer is *not* compensated for the change in prices, so that his money income remains constant at the level of the base income $\Sigma\ p_1 q_1^A$. Then obviously, he cannot remain at U(A) unless $I_{1,2}^A = 1$. Generally he must move to a different utility level, say U(B), which will be higher or lower than U(A) depending on whether $I_{1,2}^A$ is smaller or larger than unity. Thus to every initial point Q_1^A (with base income $\Sigma\ p_1 q_1^A$) and price index $I_{1,2}^A \neq 1$ there correspond two different points: the *compensated* point Q_2^A and the *uncompensated* point Q_2^B which is located on the indifference curve U(B). The compensated movement from Q_1^A to Q_2^A can accordingly be partitioned into two parts: the uncompensated movement from Q_1^A to Q_2^B and the reverse movement (along a different path) from U(B) to U(A) which shifts the consumer from Q_2^B to Q_2^A. The latter movement can be expressed in terms of a quantity index, since it is a movement between two indifference curves at a given system of prices (p_2). This is how we can associate with each price index a corresponding quantity index. In fact this quantity index is simply another way of expressing the price index.

This can be seen as follows. The equation of the *uncompensated* budget line [which is tangential to U(B)] is given by

(16) $_x p_2 x + {_y p_2 y} = \Sigma\ p_2 q_2^B$.

The quantity index which shifts this budget line to a tangential position with $U(A)$ at Q_2^A is defined as

$$(17) \qquad V_{BA}^2 = \frac{\Sigma\, p_2 q_2^A}{\Sigma\, p_2 q_2^B}.$$

However since the base income is constant (i.e., $\Sigma\, p_2 q_2^B = \Sigma\, p_1 q_1^A$) we have

$$(18) \qquad I_{1,2}^A = \frac{\Sigma\, p_2 q_2^A}{\Sigma\, p_1 q_1^A} = \frac{\Sigma\, p_2 q_2^A}{\Sigma\, p_2 q_2^B} = V_{BA}^2.$$

Let us now alternatively regard the point Q_2^B as the "initial" position and consider a change of prices from p_2 to p_1. This is associated with the index $I_{2,1}^B$ along $U(B)$, which is related to the compensated point Q_1^B. The *uncompensated* point of tangency corresponding to Q_1^B must of course be the alternative initial point Q_1^A. The reason for this is that the income $\Sigma\, p_2 q_2^B$ is equal to the uncompensated income $\Sigma\, p_1 q_1^A$, and this money income with prices p_1 defines precisely the budget line which is tangential to $U(A)$ at Q_1^A. Thus the uncompensated movement from Q_1^A as a result of a change in prices from p_1 to p_2 is precisely the opposite of the uncompensated movement from Q_2^B as a result of a change in prices from p_2 to p_1.

In computing the quantity index corresponding to $I_{2,1}^B$ we note that the former must reflect the "movement" from the uncompensated point Q_1^A to the compensated point Q_1^B. Making use of the assumption of constant money income we have

$$(19) \qquad I_{2,1}^B = \frac{\Sigma\, p_1 q_1^B}{\Sigma\, p_2 q_2^B} = \frac{\Sigma\, p_1 q_1^B}{\Sigma\, p_1 q_1^A} = V_{AB}^1.$$

Comparing (18) and (19) we see that the former quantity index is associated with a "movement" from $U(B)$ to $U(A)$ while the latter is associated with a "movement" in the opposite direction. Since $U(A)$ and $U(B)$ cannot intersect we must have:

$$V_{AB}^1 \overset{>}{\underset{<}{=}} 1 \text{ if and only if } V_{BA}^2 \overset{<}{\underset{>}{=}} 1$$

or in terms of the price indexes:

$$(20) \qquad I_{2,1}^B \overset{>}{\underset{<}{=}} 1 \text{ if and only if } I_{1,2}^A \overset{<}{\underset{>}{=}} 1.$$

In words, the price index corresponding to a change from p_2 to p_1 on $U(B)$ must be in the opposite direction to a price index corresponding to a change from p_1 to p_2 on $U(A)$. However, unlike the relation between price indexes on the *same* indifference curve, $I_{2,1}^B$ and $I_{1,2}^A$ do not satisfy the stronger, reciprocal relation, $I_{2,1}^B \cdot I_{1,2}^A = 1$. This follows immediately from the fact that the corresponding quantity indexes are not reciprocals, as we have seen earlier [equation (15)]. In other words, the relative costs of $U(A)$ and $U(B)$ at two different price systems are generally not equal.

Using the reciprocal relation between price indexes on the *same* indifference curve [see equations (7) and (10)] we may derive from (20) the following relations:

(21a) $I^B_{1,2} \lesseqgtr 1$ if and only if $I^A_{1,2} \lesseqgtr 1$

(21b) $I^B_{2,1} \lesseqgtr 1$ if and only if $I^A_{2,1} \lesseqgtr 1.$

That is, the price index corresponding to a change from p_1 to p_2 must be of the same direction on both indifference curves, and similarly the price indexes corresponding to a change from p_2 to p_1. Alternatively it can be shown that this property of price indexes follows from the fact that the corresponding quantity indexes must be of the same direction. Thus, for example, (21a) can be written as

$$V_{BA}^1 \lesseqgtr 1 \text{ if and only if } V_{BA}^2 \lesseqgtr 1.^{13}$$

Note, however, that these quantity indexes, and therefore the corresponding price indexes, are generally not equal, i.e. $I^B_{1,2} \neq I^A_{1,2}$ and similarly $I^B_{2,1} \neq I^A_{2,1}$.

The various relationships among true price and quantity indexes (when $\Sigma \, p_1 q_1^A = \Sigma \, p_2 q_2^B$) can now be summarized in the following table:

(22)

$$I^A_{1,2} = V^2_{BA} \quad \left(= \frac{OC}{OG}\right) \quad I^A_{2,1} = V^2_{AB} \quad \left(= \frac{OG}{OC}\right)$$

$$I^B_{1,2} = V^1_{BA} \quad \left(= \frac{OJ}{OE}\right) \quad I^B_{2,1} = V^1_{AB} \quad \left(= \frac{OE}{OJ}\right),$$

where the bracketed ratios measure the various indexes in terms of Figure 2. The pair of indexes in each row of (22) are reciprocals, since they relate to the same indifference curve. For any other pair of indexes, however, all we can determine is whether they move in the same or opposite direction. Thus the indexes in each column must be in the *same* direction, since both quantity indexes in the first column relate to a "movement" from $U(B)$ to $U(A)$ while those in the second column relate to a "movement" from $U(A)$ to $U(B)$. On the other hand, the indexes in each of the diagonal pairs must be in opposite directions.

It is important to note that except for the relation between price indexes in each row, all the above relations are based on the assumption that money income at Q_1^A equals money income at Q_2^B. In other words, $U(A)$ and $U(B)$ are not just a pair of arbitrarily selected indifference curves, but are vitally related in the manner described above (p. 215). On the other hand, if A and (say) C were two arbitrarily selected indifference

13. This follows from the fact that since $\Sigma p_1 q_1^A = \Sigma p_2 q_2^B$, then

$$I^A_{2,1} = \frac{\Sigma p_1 q_1^A}{\Sigma p_2 q_2^A} = \frac{\Sigma p_2 q_2^B}{\Sigma p_2 q_2^A} = V^2_{AB}$$

and

$$I^B_{1,2} = \frac{\Sigma p_2 q_2^B}{\Sigma p_1 q_1^B} = \frac{\Sigma p_1 q_1^A}{\Sigma p_1 q_1^B} = V^1_{BA}$$

curves, it would generally not be true that $I_{1,2}^A$ and $I_{1,2}^C$ must indicate the same direction. We may note, however, that in the application of price indexes to cost-of-living allowances it is precisely the pair of the "related" indifference curves which is of interest. This point will be further discussed in the concluding section of this paper.

Before concluding the discussion of the relation between price and quantity indexes we may note a related point concerning the graphical representation of price indexes. Specifically, there is no way to infer from Figure 1 anything about the direction or magnitude of the index $I_{1,2}^A$. The reason for this is that conventional diagrams such as Figure 1 reflect only "real" magnitudes. Hence only the change in relative prices is reflected in this diagram. Price indexes, however, are concerned with the change in absolute prices. Hence the only way to represent this change graphically is to introduce the uncompensated budget line, whose position relative to the compensated one is, as we have seen, a measure of V_{BA}^2 and hence $I_{1,2}^A$ ($\dfrac{OC}{OG}$ in Figure 2).

With this we have concluded our discussion of the theory of true index numbers. In the real world, of course, lack of knowledge of the indifference maps prevents our computing such indexes. However, as is well known, certain limits can be placed upon them—and it is to this question that we now turn.

To say that $\Sigma\ p_2 q_2^A$ is the minimum cost of acquiring $U(A)$ at the prices p_2, is to say that any other point on indifference curve A (on the assumption that it is convex) must—again at prices p_2—cost more. That is,

$$(23) \qquad \Sigma\ p_2 q_2^A < \Sigma\ p_2 q_i^A,$$

where q_i^A represents any other point on indifference curve A.[14] Similarly, on indifference curve B we have

$$(24) \qquad \Sigma\ p_1 q_1^B < \Sigma\ p_1 q_i^B,$$

where q_i^B represents any other point on this curve. Now, since these inequalities must hold for any point on A and B, respectively, they must also hold for $q_i^A = q_1^A$ and $q_i^B = q_2^B$. That is,

$$(25) \qquad \Sigma\ p_2 q_2^A < \Sigma\ p_2 q_1^A,$$

$$(26) \qquad \Sigma\ p_1 q_1^B < \Sigma\ p_1 q_2^B.$$

Substituting these into (5) and (9), we then obtain

$$(27) \qquad I_{1,2}^A = \frac{\Sigma\ p_2 q_2^A}{\Sigma\ p_1 q_1^A} < \frac{\Sigma\ p_2 q_1^A}{\Sigma\ p_1 q_1^A} = \text{Laspeyres index,}$$

$$(28) \qquad I_{2,1}^B = \frac{\Sigma\ p_1 q_1^B}{\Sigma\ p_2 q_2^B} < \frac{\Sigma\ p_1 q_2^B}{\Sigma\ p_2 q_2^B} = \text{Laspeyres index.}$$

14. Cf. Samuelson (1947), pp. 107–8.
The fact that p_2 and q_i^A do not have the same subscripts indicates that q_i^A could not be a chosen point under price system p_2, for its marginal rate of substitution is not that specified by p_2.

Finally, inverting these inequalities—and making use of (7) and (10)—we obtain

(29) $\quad$ Paasche index $= \dfrac{\Sigma\, p_1 q_1^A}{\Sigma\, p_2 q_1^A} < \dfrac{1}{I_{1,2}^A} = I_{2,1}^A,$

(30) $\quad$ Paasche index $= \dfrac{\Sigma\, p_2 q_2^B}{\Sigma\, p_1 q_2^B} < \dfrac{1}{I_{2,1}^B} = I_{1,2}^B.$

Unlike true indexes, the right-hand sides of (27)–(28)—and the left-hand sides of (29)–(30)—are price indexes in the ordinary sense of the term: they weight prices by the same quantities (q_1^A or q_2^B, as the case may be) in both numerator and denominator. Furthermore, these indexes can be computed on the basis of only two observations of the individual's behavior—namely, Q_1^A and Q_2^B. Unlike true indexes, they do not presume knowledge of the indifference map. This, of course, is why they are so important.

As already indicated, the two indexes on the right-hand sides of (27)–(28) are both Laspeyres indexes: for they both weight the prices by the quantities of the *initial* position. In the case of (27), however, this initial position is Q_1^A; and in the case of (28), it is Q_2^B. Similarly, the indexes in (29)–(30) are both Paasche for both weight prices by the quantities of the *final* position, as specified by $I_{2,1}^A$ in (29) and $I_{1,2}^B$ in (30).

We now note—and this is the crucial point—that in (27)–(30) we have succeeded in supplying only *one* limit for each of our four true price indexes. In other words, the Paasche and Laspeyres indexes will generally [15] *never* provide a lower and upper limit, respectively, for the *same* true index number. Only in one special case would such double limits be provided*: namely, the one in which we know that Q_1^A and Q_2^B are on the same indifference curve. For then $I_{1,2}^A = I_{1,2}^B$ and $I_{1,1}^A = I_{2,1}^B$, so that (27) and (30) yield

(31) $\quad \dfrac{\Sigma\, p_2 q_2^B}{\Sigma\, p_1 q_2^B} < I_{1,2}^A < \dfrac{\Sigma\, p_2 q_1^A}{\Sigma\, p_1 q_1^A}.$

Similarly, (28) and (29) yield

(32) $\quad \dfrac{\Sigma\, p_1 q_1^A}{\Sigma\, p_2 q_1^A} < I_{2,1}^A < \dfrac{\Sigma\, p_1 q_2^B}{\Sigma\, p_2 q_2^B}.$

But as has frequently been emphasized,[16] this is a vacuous conclusion: for if we knew that Q_1^A and Q_2^B were on the same indifference curve, we could compute the exact values of the true indexes directly from equations (5) and (6), and so would have no need to derive any limits for them. And if in addition it were true that the same level of money income prevails at Q_1^A and Q_2^B, then by definition we would have $I_{1,2}^A = I_{2,1}^A = I_{1,2}^B = I_{2,1}^B = 1.$ **

---

15. The qualification is due to the Konus case (below, p. 232) and to the case now to be discussed.

16. Cf. Staehle (1935), pp. 169–70.

* {Yoseph Zeira has pointed out to me that there is actually a second such special case: namely, that of a homothetic utility function (see above, p. 216, especially fns. 11–12). Furthermore, in contrast with the case now to be discussed, the limits in this second case are meaningful.}

** {This last sentence has been added.}

2. Index Numbers and Cost-of-Living Allowances

The standard problem of the theory of consumers' behavior is to analyze the changes in the amounts demanded resulting from a variation in one single price—while all other variables, including money income, remain constant. This change is then decomposed into a substitution effect and an income effect. The standard problem of cost-of-living allowances is analytically essentially the same—though differing in details. In particular, it is assumed that changes take place in many prices simultaneously, though still not in money income. On the other hand, what is analyzed is the magnitude of the compensating change in money income that must be made in order to offset the income effect of the aforementioned change in prices.

Let us continue to assume that we know the individual's indifference map and assume that he is initially in State Alpha, characterized by prices p_1 and money income $R_\alpha = \Sigma\, p_1 q_1^A$—or, in brief $(p_1, R_\alpha = \Sigma\, p_1 q_1^A)$. The optimum position of this individual is Q_1^A in Figure 2: the point of tangency between indifference curve A and budget line JK, whose equation, reproduced from (2) above, is

$$(33) \qquad {}_x p_1 x + {}_y p_1 y = \Sigma\, p_1 q_1^A.$$

Assume now that there occurs some sort of change—characteristically, a change over time (a worker begins living in 1961 instead of 1960) or a change over space (a U. N. official begins working in Jerusalem instead of New York [17])—which is accompanied by a change in prices from p_1 to p_2, while money income is held constant. Call this State Beta—to be denoted by $(p_2, R_\beta = \Sigma\, p_2 q_2^B)$. The optimum position in State Beta is represented by Q_2^B in Figure 2, on budget line GH whose equation is

$$(34) \qquad {}_x p_2 x + {}_y p_2 y = {}_x p_2\, {}_x q_2^B + {}_y p_2\, {}_y q_2^B = \Sigma\, p_2 q_2^B.$$

As already noted, by assumption

$$(35) \qquad \Sigma\, p_1 q_1^A = \Sigma\, p_2 q_2^B.$$

It is clear from Figure 2 that despite the equality in money income, the welfare situation of the foregoing two States is not the same. In particular, Q_2^B is on a higher indifference curve than Q_1^A. Our problem now is to make compensating changes that will return the individual to the welfare situation (i.e. indifference curve) of State Alpha.

Now, this objective could be quite simply accomplished by merely changing prices back to p_1. But by assumption, this is precisely what we are not free to do. In particular, in restoring the welfare situation of State Alpha we are required to accept the existing price structure, p_2, and to make all necessary compensating changes by means of variations in the level of money income. In other words, we must accept the slope of the budget line GH, and are free

---

17. This is the very real problem to which the U.N. has had to give an answer for its own personnel. See Statistical Office of the United Nations, Department of Economic Affairs, *Retail Price Comparisons for International Salary Determination* (1952).

only to make compensating variations in money income which will shift it into tangency with indifference curve A.

Let us call the variation that must be made in the income of State Beta in order to compensate for the change in prices a "cost-of-living allowance" —or, in brief, "c.o.l." Denote it by $T_{1,2}^A$, where the superscript denotes the welfare level which is being kept constant, and the subscripts denote the nature of the price change. It is clear from the discussion of the preceding section that our objective will be accomplished by providing the individual with c.o.l.

$$(36) \qquad T_{1,2}^A = \Sigma\, p_2 q_2^A - \Sigma\, p_1 q_1^A;$$

that is, a c.o.l. equal to the difference in the cost of utility level A at prices p_2 and p_1, respectively. This can be rewritten as

$$(37) \qquad T_{1,2}^A = \frac{\Sigma\, p_2 q_2^A}{\Sigma\, p_1 q_1^A} \cdot \Sigma\, p_1 q_1^A - \Sigma\, p_1 q_1^A$$

$$= \Sigma\, p_1 q_1^A\, (I_{1,2}^A - 1).$$

The compensated income of State Beta is then

$$(38) \qquad R_\beta^C = R_\beta + T_{1,2}^A$$

$$= \Sigma\, p_2 q_2^B + \Sigma\, p_1 q_1^A\, (I_{1,2}^A - 1) = (\Sigma p_1 q_1^A)\, I_{1,2}^A$$

$$= \Sigma\, p_2 q_2^A.$$

An individual with this compensated income will obviously have the budget line

$$(39) \qquad {}_x p_2 x + {}_y p_2 y = \Sigma\, p_2 q_2^A,$$

represented by CD in Figure 2, and tangent to indifference curve A at Q_2^A. We might note that in the case represented by Figure 2, $T_{1,2}^A$ is negative.

The foregoing development makes crucial use of the assumption that $\Sigma\, p_1 q_1^A = \Sigma\, p_2 q_2^B$. We should now recall [equation (18)] that under this assumption $I_{1,2}^A$ becomes the quantity index $V_{B,A}^2 = \dfrac{\Sigma\, p_2 q_2^A}{\Sigma\, p_2 q_2^B}$. (In the case of Figure 2, this equals $\dfrac{OC}{OG}$, less than unity.) Thus the compensated income of State Beta is essentially the original income of State Beta multiplied by a *quantity* index. The full significance of this fact will be discussed in the concluding section of this paper.

In a similar way we could assume that our initial position is State Beta, that price changes from p_2 to p_1 while money income remains constant (State Alpha), and that it is desired to make a compensating variation in the money income of State Alpha so as to restore the welfare level of State Beta. The c.o.l. in this case is

$$(40) \qquad T_{2,1}^B = \Sigma\, p_2 q_2^B (I_{2,1}^B - 1),$$

which when added to $R_\alpha = \Sigma\, p_1 q_1^A$ provides the individual in State Alpha with a compensated income represented by the budget equation

(41) $_x p_1 x + {_y} p_1 y = \Sigma \, p_1 q_1^B.$

This is EF in Figure 2, tangent to indifference curve B at Q_1^B. Once again, what we have actually done here is to multiply the original money income of State Alpha by a quantity index, $V_{A,B}^1$.

Clearly, just as there is in general no specific relationship between $I_{1,2}^A$ and $I_{2,1}^B$, so is there none between $T_{1,2}^A$ and $T_{2,1}^B$. Nevertheless, it is true that negative $T_{1,2}^A$ means a positive $T_{2,1}^B$—and vice versa. This follows from the fact that a negative $T_{1,2}^A$ means that indifference curve A is below B; hence a reverse movement must require a positive compensation. This can be shown rigorously by making use of the interrelationships between price and quantity indexes presented in equations (18)–(21) above—and of the fact that true quantity indexes always indicate the same direction of movement.

Let us return to the case in which the individual has moved from State Alpha (1960—or New York) to State Beta (1961—or Jerusalem). What must be emphasized—and what has been the source of much confusion—is that for the worker in 1961 and for the U.N. official in Jerusalem no operational meaning exists for the budget line EF—or any budget line parallel to it. For such a line refers to the relative prices of 1960 or of New York—whereas the reality in which the individual must live is characterized by the relative prices of 1961 or of Jerusalem. In other words, the only budget line which determines his behavior must necessarily have the slope of CD. The relative prices of yesteryear—or yesterplace—can provide only non-operational memories.

Let us now assume that our U.N. official has been moved from New York to Jerusalem and has been provided in the latter place with the cost-of-living $T_{1,2}^A$, so that he is at Q_2^A on CD with the income $\Sigma \, p_2 q_2^A$ (Figure 3, which reproduces the relevant positions of Figure 2). Assume now that he is moved back to New York to face once again the price p_1—but with his compensated Jerusalem income $\Sigma \, p_2 q_2^A$. This income is less than his original New York income—$\Sigma \, p_1 q_1^A$—a fact reflected by the fact that the individual's budget line is now $A'B'$, below JK. Correspondingly, he is on a lower indifference curve than he originally was at Q_2^A. In order to restore him to the welfare level of Q_2^A we must therefore provide him with a c.o.l. which—in analogy to (36)—is

(42) $T_{2,1}^A = \Sigma \, p_1 q_1^A - \Sigma \, p_2 q_2^A.$

Comparing (42) with (36) we immediately see that

(43) $T_{1,2}^A + T_{2,1}^A = 0.$

In other words, a c.o.l. based on the true index of prices meets the "time reversal test:" no matter what the nature of the compensated changes which the individual undergoes, he will always receive his initial income should he ever return to his initial point of departure.

Our example has been deliberately framed in terms of a change over space. At first sight it seems meaningless to frame it in terms of a change over time—for once we are

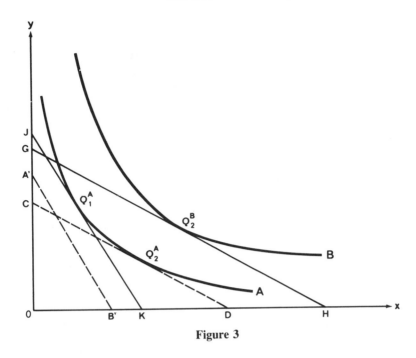

Figure 3

in 1961, the year 1960 cannot be rerun. But in some cases this can effectively be done. In particular, assume that prices in 1962 are the same as in 1960. Then the foregoing argument implies that if the individual always receives the true c.o.l, his *compensated* income in 1962 must equal that of 1960.

In a way, all this is obvious. For if the individual always receives a c.o.l. computed with a true index number, then he must always remain on the indifference curve A. Hence any two States that are characterized by the same price system (say, p_n) must also be characterized by the same point on indifference curve A (q_n^A), and hence by the same compensated money income $(\Sigma p_n q_n^A)$.

Let us now drop the assumption that we know the individual's indifference map and assume that we must compensate the individual for the change from State Alpha to Beta solely on the basis of the price and quantity information we have on these States. What can we say about the magnitude of the c.o.l. that should be paid for this purpose?

The answer is that on the basis of the theory of index numbers presented until now we can only give an upper limit to the amount that must be paid. For we saw in (37) that the amount of the true c.o.l. depends upon the true index $I_{1,2}^A$; and we saw from the discussion of the preceding section that the only limit placed on this index is the upper limit provided by the Laspeyres index of equation (27)—namely, $\dfrac{\Sigma\ p_2 q_1^A}{\Sigma\ p_1 q_1^A}$. On the other hand, the Paasche index $\frac{\Sigma \ p_2 q_2^B}{\Sigma \ p_1 q_2^B}$, is irrelevant for our present purposes. True, it does set a lower limit—but for index $I_{1,2}^B$, not $I_{1,2}^A$ [equation (30)].

In a similar way, if the initial State had been Beta and a change had taken place to State Alpha, the only relevant index would once again have been a Laspeyres and not a Paasche. For in this case equation (40) shows us that the correct c.o.l. requires an estimate of $I_{2,1}^B$, and for this we have only the upper limit of the Laspeyres index $\frac{\Sigma \ p_1 q_2^B}{\Sigma \ p_2 q_2^B}$, described by equation (28). Once again, the Paasche index $\frac{\Sigma \ p_1 q_1^A}{\Sigma \ p_2 q_1^A}$ sets a lower limit on a true index—but on an irrelevant one, namely $I_{2,1}^A$ [equation (29)].

All this is capable of a common-sense interpretation. We have seen above that a c.o.l. policy is tantamount to applying a *quantity* index to current income. Now, there are four true quantity indexes. But of these, only those two which describe the movement from indifference curve B to A can be relevant: for the purpose of our c.o.l. policy is to maintain the individual on indifference curve A. Now, of these two quantity indexes, only that one which uses *current* prices can be relevant; for, as sufficiently emphasized above, the prices that at one time prevailed cannot be determinants of the individual's *current* behavior and welfare. This narrows down the class of possibly relevant quantity indexes to one—namely, $V_{B,A}^2$; and this—as we saw in (18) above—equals the true price index $I_{1,2}^A$, the limit on which is set only by the Laspeyres price index.

Note how in this way the theory of c.o.l. differs from the theory of demand. For when in the latter we decompose the effects of a price change into the substitution and income effects (for, say, the purpose of establishing the negatively sloped demand curve for a non-inferior good) it generally makes no difference whether we measure the income effect by the movement from Q_1^B to Q_1^A (i.e., by $V_{B,A}^1$) or by the movement from Q_2^B to Q_2^A (i.e. by $V_{B,A}^2$). In the case of determining the compensating c.o.l. for a change in price from Alpha to Beta, on the other hand, only $V_{B,A}^2$ is relevant; for Q_2^A is the only point at which a utility-maximizing individual can be on indifference curve A in a world in which p_2 prices prevail. In other words, the only income effect that is operationally meaningful for purposes of the foregoing c.o.l. is the one corresponding to the p_2 prices.

We have emphasized this point because it has continued to be the source of much confusion in the literature. What has been well recognized is that the Laspeyres and Paasche indexes provide limits for two different true indexes—referring respectively to two different levels of welfare ("standards of living"). But what has not been seen is that *the Paasche index provides a limit for a true index number which can never be relevant for a c.o.l. policy.*

Thus, consider the change from State Alpha to Beta. If the purpose of the c.o.l. policy is—as usual—to assure the Alpha standard of living, then, as has been sufficiently emphasized above, only $I_{1,2}^A$—and hence only its Laspeyres (upper) limit—is relevant. But what discussions of the Paasche index in the literature seem to have in mind is a c.o.l. policy designed to assure that the Beta standard of living is maintained; for this purpose, it is contended, the Paasche (lower) limit to $I^B_{1,2}$ is relevant.[18] But this is clearly wrong. For if we have moved from State Alpha to Beta, then the obvious way to carry out the "policy" of "assuring" the Beta standard of living is simply to leave the individual alone! And surely we need compute no index number for this purpose.

This same argument holds *mutatis mutandis* for the reverse change from Beta to Alpha. Here again we need obviously compute no index number in order to maintain the Alpha standard of living—whereas only $I^B_{2,1}$ and its (upper) Laspeyres limit is relevant for maintaining the Beta standard of living. Thus once again no operational meaning can be assigned to the Paasche price index.

Before concluding this section we might note one further point of a completely different nature. Drop the assumption that the indifference map is known, and assume that the c.o.l. is given in accordance with the Laspeyres index. Assume that this c.o.l. is used to compensate our U.N. official who moves from New York (budget line I in Figure 4) to Jerusalem (budget line II). Thus his compensated budget line in Jerusalem is III. Here, however, he will not choose his original New York basket, Q^A_1, but—in accordance with the theory of revealed preferences—will find his optimum at some point southeast of Q^A_1—say, Q^C_2. Assume now that our U.N. official is moved back to New York—and that his c.o.l. is computed with his (compensated) Jerusalem basket as a base. This brings him to budget line IV on which (again, by the theory of revealed preference) he chooses Q^D_1—obviously superior to his original New York position Q^A_1. In brief, the Laspeyres c.o.l.—unlike the true c.o.l.—does not meet the "time reversal test."

It is clear that a U.N. official who enjoyed a Laspeyres c.o.l. of this type could crisscross his way to economic bliss by shuttling back and forth from New York to Jerusalem! This absurdity is avoided by the fact that when the official is shifted back to New York, we need not make an estimate of what he needs in order to be just as well off as he originally was in New York. For—on the assumption that New York prices have remained constant—we know from our past observations that we will leave him in such a position by simply returning him to his original budget line I. And this, of course, is what is done in practice: a c.o.l. is defined for each city, regardless of the path used to get there. In this way the "time reversal test" is effectively met. But note that this is accomplished by dispensing with the use of the Laspeyres c.o.l. More precisely, a U.N. official receives the Laspeyres c.o.l. only when he moves from New York to some other city. But a move from some other city to New York or

---

18. This is the only way we can interpret the discussion of such writers as R. Frisch, "Some Basic Principles of Price of Living Measurements" (1954), p. 415, and G. J. Stigler, *The Theory of Price* (1952), p. 90. The discussion in Allen (1935), p. 60, is also ambiguous on this point.

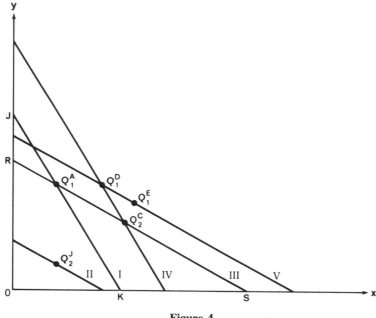

Figure 4

between any other two cities is not compensated by a Laspeyres c.o.l. weighted by the quantities of the point of departure.[19]

3. The Relationship Between Paasche and Laspeyres Price Indexes

Let us continue with our assumption that the initial money incomes of States Alpha (represented by point Q_1^A in Figure 5) and Beta (represented by Q_2^B) are the same. Let us also denote the Laspeyres index of the change in prices from State Alpha to Beta by

$$(44) \qquad _LI_{1,2} = \frac{\Sigma \; p_2 q_1^A}{\Sigma \; p_1 q_1^A}.$$

Clearly, we can also define the Laspeyres index of the price change from Beta to Alpha—$_LI_{2,1} = \dfrac{\Sigma \; p_1 q_2^B}{\Sigma \; p_2 q_2^B}$; but this will not concern us in what follows.[20]

The individual's original Beta budget line is represented by GH in Figure 5—whose equation, it will be recalled, is

$$(45) \qquad _xp_2 x + {}_yp_2 y = \Sigma \; p_2 q_2^B.$$

---

19. This, of course, is the nature of the U.N. practice; see the study cited in footnote 17. On the other hand, the U.N. does not use a Laspeyres index (see p. 11 of the aforementioned study) and so does not even assure that their officials are at least as well off as in New York! It uses instead Fisher's "ideal index number," which has no welfare meaning.

20. Cf. equations (27)–(28). The extension of all that follows to the case of the reverse movement from Beta to Alpha is left as an exercise for the reader.

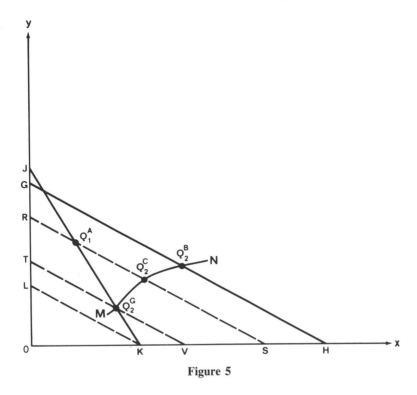

Figure 5

If we compensate him with a Laspeyres c.o.l., then his compensated Beta income—by analogy with (38)—is

$$(46) \qquad R_\beta^c = (\Sigma \, p_2 q_2^B) \, {}_L I_{1,2}$$

$$= \Sigma \, p_2 q_1^A.$$

(Here we have again made use of the assumed constancy of money incomes.) Thus his new budget equation is

$$(47) \qquad {}_x p_2 x + {}_y p_2 y = \Sigma \, p_2 q_1^A.$$

Graphically, this must parallel his original Beta budget line (the c.o.l. has not affected prices—which remain p_2) and pass through the point Q_1^A (line RS in Figure 5). As a result of the compensation the individual is obviously better off than he was in State Alpha. For his new budget enables him to acquire the Alpha basket Q_1^A (this is the essential meaning of the Laspeyres c.o.l.) and also opens up possibilities that were not available to him in State Alpha. Hence he will probably move southeast on RS to one of these possibilities (say, Q_2^C) which by his revealed preferences is superior to Q_1^A. This is the graphical representation of the fact that ${}_L I_{1,2}$ is greater than $I_{1,2}^A$. We note also that—on the assumption of the constant money income—the value of the Laspeyres index can be read directly off the graph as $\dfrac{OR}{OG}$.

Can any lower limits be placed on the necessary c.o.l.? The literature offers two main possibilities—depending on the degree of information available.[21] If we know only the data about States Alpha and Beta, then a lower limit on the individual's compensated Beta income is one which just brings his budget line entirely within the triangle of choice of the Alpha basket, Q_1^A; for then the individual would definitely be worse off than in Alpha.[22] This is represented by the line LK in Figure 5. The economic interpretation of this line is that the individual's money income is changed in such a way as to enable him to purchase the same maximum quantity of that good which has become relatively cheaper. In other words (and now the matter becomes obvious) his original Beta income is changed in the same proportion as that price which increased proportionately least.[23] Thus our limits are

$$(48) \qquad \frac{_jp_2}{_jp_1} < I_{1,2}^A < {_L}I_{1,2},$$

where the subscript j denotes that commodity whose price increased relatively least from State Alpha to Beta.[24]

This is not a very helpful limit. But we can do better only if we have additional information. Thus assume now that we know the whole income-expenditure curve generated by changing money income while holding prices constant at p_2. Represent this by MN in Figure 5. Then the intersection of MN with the Alpha budget line JK determines a point Q_2^G which (1) is inferior to Q_1^A and (2) will be chosen at the prevailing Beta prices, p_2, and with the compensated Beta income, $\Sigma\ p_2 q_2^G$. The budget line corresponding to this compensated income is TV in Figure 5.

In this way we derive the limits

$$(49) \qquad \frac{\Sigma\ p_2 q_2^G}{\Sigma\ p_2 q_2^B} < I_{1,2}^A < {_L}I_{1,2}.$$

If the individual's original Beta income is compensated in the proportion ${_L}I_{1,2}$, he will be brought to Q_2^C in Figure 5; correspondingly, let us denote the q_2^C as the "overcompensated Beta quantities." Similarly, q_2^G will be denoted as the "undercompensated Beta quantities." Thus equation (49) parallels the Slutzky under- and overcompensations for the income effect which emerge from the revealed-preference approach to the theory of demand.[25] For infinitesimal changes, then, these limits will converge on the true index $I_{1,2}^A$—which (as the discussion of Section 1 above shows) is essentially defined by

21. Cf. the succinct presentation in Samuelson (1947), pp. 156–60.

22. We are abstracting here—and elsewhere—from corner solutions.

23. Cf. Lerner (1935–36) and Joseph (1935–36) in footnote 7.

24. In an analogous way the commodity whose price increased most would give us an upper limit represented by the budget line parallel to GH—and starting from point J on the ordinate. But if the individual was not at corner J in State Alpha, this limit must always be above the Laspeyres one—and so can be ignored.

25. See P. A. Samuelson, "Consumption Theorems in Terms of Overcompensation rather than Indifference Comparisons" (1953), pp. 4–7.

(*cont.*)

use of the Hicks compensation for the income effect.[26] But in the practical application of index number theory we are, of course, never interested in infinitesimal changes.

We can reach a fuller understanding of the limits described by equation (49) by noting that, by assumption, $\Sigma\ p_1q_1^A = \Sigma\ p_1q_2^G$ and $\Sigma\ p_2q_2^C = \Sigma\ p_2q_1^A$ which means that

(50) $\dfrac{\Sigma\ p_1q_2^G}{\Sigma\ p_1q_1^A} = 1$ and $\dfrac{\Sigma\ p_2q_2^C}{\Sigma\ p_2q_1^A} = 1.$

In other words, the Laspeyres *quantity* index of the *under*compensated Beta quantities relative to the original Alpha ones is unity; correspondingly, any compensation greater than that described by the lower limit of (49) will cause this quantity index to be greater than unity—so that we will no longer be sure that the individual is worse off than he originally was in Alpha. Similarly, the Paasche *quantity* index of the *over*compensated Beta quantities relative to the original Alpha ones is also unity; correspondingly, any compensation less than $_L I_{1,2}$ will make it impossible for us to say that the individual is definitely better off than in Alpha.[27]

We note finally that by virtue of the fact that $\Sigma\ p_1q_1^A = \Sigma\ p_1q_2^G$, together with the assumption that $\Sigma\ p_1q_1^A = \Sigma\ p_2q_2^B$, equation (49) can be rewritten as

(51) $\dfrac{\Sigma\ p_2q_2^G}{\Sigma\ p_1q_2^G} < I_{1,2}^A < {_L}I_{1,2}.$

Thus our lower limit can be presented as a price index weighted by the *undercompensated* Beta quantities. This index has sometimes been referred to in the literature as a ''Paasche price index.'' [28] But this is a misleading description. For the Paasche price index in the ordinary sense of the term is one whose weights are the *actual* Beta quantities, not the *undercompensated* ones.

This distinction is fundamental not only from the theoretical viewpoint, but also from the practical. For whereas the actual Beta quantities are obviously known from mere observation of State Beta, the undercompensated Beta quantities can be determined only if we have the much more extensive information on the income-consumption curve *MN* provided by a budget study conducted at p_2 prices. And, for the same reason, whereas the actual Beta quantities can be determined fairly accurate-

---

At the same time it must be emphasized that Samuelson is at best misleading in implying that the Slutzky under- and overcompensations parallel ''the dual role that the Laspeyres and Paasche index numbers play as upper and lower bounds'' (*ibid.*, p. 7). The lower limit of (49) is clearly *not* the ordinary Paasche price index; but see the discussion of equation (51) which follows.

26. On the difference between the Slutzky and Hicks compensations—and their equality in the infinitesimal case—see J. L. Mosak, ''On the Interpretation of the Fundamental Equation of Value Theory'' (1942), pp. 69–74.

27. Cf. the discussions of the Laspeyres and Paasche quantity indexes in Hicks (1948) and Kuznets (1948).

28. Cf. Allen (1935), p. 60.

ly by direct observation, the determination of the undercompensated Beta quantities involves us in all the additional problems of the statistical estimation of economic relationships.

We also suspect that the reference to the lower limit of (51) as a "Paasche index" has contributed to the continuing misconception (despite all the contrary implications of the literature) that the Paasche index in the ordinary sense of the term provides a lower limit for $I_{1,2}^A$. For this reason it is worth dealing with this point in further detail.*

To compute the c.o.l. on the basis of the Paasche index of the change in prices from p_1 to p_2 means to multiply the Beta income by

$$PI_{1,2} = \frac{\Sigma\ p_2 q_2^B}{\Sigma\ p_1 q_2^B}.$$

This in turn means that the individual's Paasche-compensated Beta budget line becomes

$$(52) \qquad {}_x p_2 x + {}_y p_2 y = \Sigma\ p_2 q_2^B\ \left(\frac{\Sigma\ p_2 q_2^B}{\Sigma\ p_1 q_2^B}\right)$$

$$= \left(\frac{\Sigma\ p_1 q_1^A}{\Sigma\ p_1 q_2^B}\right) \Sigma\ p_2 q_2^B,$$

where we have once again made use of the assumption that $\Sigma\ p_1 q_1^A = \Sigma\ p_2 q_2^B$. The parenthetical expression is a quantity index whose magnitude (in terms of Figure 6) equals $\dfrac{OJ}{OZ}$. Thus the income described by budget equation (52) is the original Beta income multiplied by this proportion. Thus the compensated Beta budget line described by (52) is the locus of points whose cost—at the Beta prices, namely, p_2—equals $\dfrac{OJ}{OZ}$ times the cost of the original Beta basket, Q_2^B. Now, one such point must clearly be that determined by the intersection of the Alpha budget line and the radius vector going out to Q_2^B—namely, Q_2^H. For, by construction $\dfrac{OQ_2^H}{OQ_2^B} = \dfrac{OJ}{OZ}$, so that the basket represented by Q_2^H is one whose components (i.e., respective quantities of x and y) are each $\dfrac{OJ}{OZ}$ times the corresponding components of Q_2^B. Hence the money cost of Q_2^H (at p_2 prices) must be $\dfrac{OJ}{OZ}$ times the costs of Q_2^B. Hence the Paasche-compensated Beta budget line described by (52) must parallel GH and pass through Q_2^H, as represented by WW_1 in Figure 6. (Note, however, that we are *not* assuming that Q_2^H is the optimum point on WW_1.) From this construction it is also clear that the Paasche index can then be read directly off the graph as $\dfrac{OW}{OG} = \dfrac{OJ}{OZ}$, which is less than unity.

*{In order to avoid possible confusion, let me note that due to an oversight which was noticed too late to be corrected, the points labelled Q_1^A, Q_2^B and the budget lines labelled JK, GH in Figures 6–7 differ respectively from the points and budget lines so labelled in Figures 1–5. Obviously, however, this does not affect the argument which follows.}

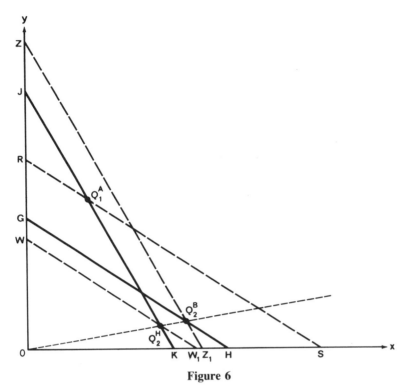

Figure 6

Note that in the case described by Figure 6—namely, one in which Q_1^A and Q_2^B are each outside the other's triangle of choice—we must necessarily have

(53) $_PI_{1,2} < 1$ and $_LI_{1,2} > 1.$

From this it of course follows that in this case

(54) $_PI_{1,2} < _LI_{1,2}.$

But this, of course, tells us nothing about the relationship of the Paasche index to the *true* index—and hence it is a *non sequitur* to infer from (54) that

(55) $_PI_{1,2} < I_{1,2}^A < _LI_{1,2}.$

Let us now drop the assumption that the Beta basket is outside Alpha's triangle of choice—and examine the implications for the relationship between the Paasche and Laspeyres indexes of different possible locations of the Beta basket. This comparison will be carried out on the assumption that the price and money income situation of State Beta remains the same—so that the Beta budget line GH is unchanged. Hence the Laspeyres index also remains the same and equal to $\dfrac{OR}{OG}.$

Assume first that the original Beta basket was not Q_2^B, but Q_2^F in Figure 7. Then the budget line determined by the intersection of JK and OQ_2^F is obviously identical with the original Beta one—namely, GH. Hence by the pre-

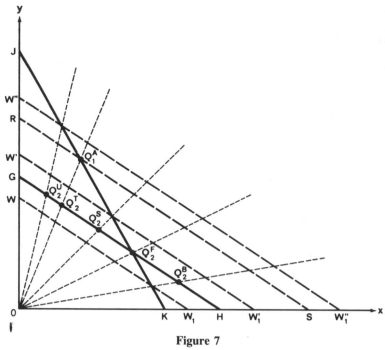

Figure 7

ceding argument $_pI_{1,2} = 1$. Note that in this case "compensating" the Beta income by the Paasche index will definitely leave the individual worse off than in State Alpha. For he will then be at point Q_2^F—which is clearly inferior to Q_1^A. Hence in this special case—in which the so-called "Konus condition" [29]

$$(56) \qquad \Sigma\, p_1 q_1^A = \Sigma\, p_1 q_2^F$$

is satisfied—the Paasche index does provide a lower limit to the true one. But this is an unnecessarily complicated way of saying that the individual in State Beta is already worse off than he was in State Alpha—and so will stay worse off if we just leave his income alone.

Assume now that the original Beta basket was Q_2^S. Then the Paasche-compensated budget line is $W'W'_1$—so that $_pI_{1,2} = \dfrac{OW'}{OG} > 1$. Clearly, however, the Paasche index is still less than the Laspeyres ($\dfrac{OR}{OG}$). If, however, the original Beta basket was Q_2^T then the Paasche-compensated and Laspeyres-compensated Beta budget lines are identical—namely, RS. Hence the two indexes are equal. This fact emerges quite simply from their respective formulas: for the proportions of x and y in the Beta basket (Q_2^T) are then the same as in the Alpha basket (Q_1^A); hence it cannot make any difference whether prices are weighted by Alpha or Beta quantities.

29. Staehle (1935), pp. 173 ff.

Consider finally the case in which the original Beta basket was Q_2^U. Then the Paasche-compensated Beta budget line ($W''W''_1$) lies above the Laspeyres compensated one (RS)—so that the Paasche index is greater than the Laspeyres! Thus paying a Paasche c.o.l. in this case will lead to a greater overcompensation than paying a Laspeyres c.o.l.

To summarize, the relevant dividing line for the relationship between the Paasche and Laspeyres indexes is the radius vector to the Alpha basket—OQ_1^A. The Paasche index is less than, equal to, or greater than the Laspeyres one according as the Beta basket is rightward, on, or leftward of this radius vector. Now, for the Beta basket to be leftward of OQ_1^A means that its quantity of y relative to x is greater than that of the Alpha basket—and this despite the fact that Figure 7 shows us that the price of y relative to x has increased from State Alpha to Beta. From this we can conclude that if there are sufficiently strong substitution effects to assure the relative decrease in demand for those commodities whose relative price increases, then the Paasche index will in actual practice be less than the Laspeyres; but this, of course, does *not* imply that it must be less than the true index.

There remains the case in which Q_1^A is within Q_2^B's triangle of choice; this is left as an exercise for the reader.

4. The Case of Changing Money Income

Up to this stage the analysis has been carried out on the assumption that money income is constant. The effect on our analysis of relaxing this crucial assumption can be illustrated by the simple example of Figure 8.

The parallel lines AA' and BB' represent the budget lines in States Alpha and Beta respectively with the corresponding observed "baskets" Q^A and Q^B. Suppose now that the consumer moves from Alpha to Beta. What is the c.o.l. allowance that has to be given in order to compensate the consumer for this change? The answer clearly depends on the causes of the shift from AA' to BB'.

Suppose first that the only change was in money income. In this case no c.o.l. allowance has to be paid since, by definition, the purpose of this allowance is to compensate for a change in *prices* and not for changes originating in other causes. It is of course possible to compensate the consumer for the change in money income by paying him $\Sigma\, p_1 q_1^A - \Sigma\, p_1 q_1^B = R_\alpha - R_\beta$, or

$$(57) \qquad \Sigma\, p_1 q_1^B \left[\frac{\Sigma\, p_1 q_1^A}{\Sigma\, p_1 q_1^B} - 1 \right] = \Sigma\, p_1 q_1^B [V_{BA}^I - 1]$$

which will bring him back to the original situation. Note however that (57) is a compensation by a quantity index for the change in money income.

Suppose alternatively that the budget line shifted to BB' as a result of a proportionate increase in prices with money income unchanged. In this case the c.o.l. allowance $T_{1,2}^A = R_\alpha(I_{1,2}^A - 1)$ will be positive and will compen-

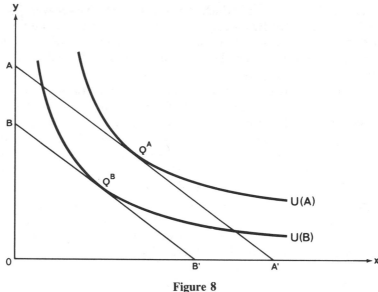

Figure 8

sate him for the change in prices by bringing him back in State Beta to the budget line of the original situation. This brings out clearly the idea that when dealing with $T_{1,2}^A$ we should not just look at the actual change in welfare but inquire whether it resulted from changes in *prices*.

We come now to the problem of determining the c.o.l. allowance when both prices and money income change simultaneously. This is the general case with which we have to deal in practice. It is therefore surprising that in the literature on price indexes it has not been realized that a *partial* compensation for price changes alone by means of a c.o.l. allowance is meaningless.

In demand theory we often deal with a compensating variation in money income for a change in the price of a given commodity. This however is always based on the assumption that there is no other change involved. In particular it is assumed that when price changes, money income remains constant. Suppose that money income changes *simultaneously* with the price. If we still want to compensate for the change in price alone we must be able to disentangle the effect of each variable (i.e., price and money income) on the change in welfare and to compensate for that amount of welfare lost (or gained) as a result of the change in price alone.

Problems of this sort are meaningless in ordinal utility functions since any partition of a change in welfare (i.e., of the distance between indifference curves) is entirely arbitrary. In our particular problem it can be shown that even if utility were *measurable* it would still be impossible to disentangle the effects of changes in money income and prices on utility.[30] The reason is that these effects are not simply *additive*, i.e., the effect of a change in price on welfare must depend on the associated change in money

30. See proof in appendix.

income, since only *"real"* changes can effect welfare. It follows that *partial* compensation for a change in prices, when money income changes simultaneously, is a meaningless concept. At the same time it is obvious that we may define a *total* compensation by paying the consumer, after the change, a sum of money which will enable him to attain his original indifference level.

It should be stressed that this is a general problem, and our difficulties arise not from the fact that we happen to be dealing with changes in money income. For suppose that money income is constant but the prices of x and y change. We can illustrate this case by using Figure 2 where we interpret *EF* as the original budget line and *CD* as the existing one. We are now asked to compensate the consumer for the change in the price of y only. We know that this price has risen, but there is obviously no variation in the existing money income which can be meaningfully said to compensate for the change in $_yp$ alone. It is also clear that there is no conceptual problem involved in defining a *total* compensation for the change in both prices. This is done by shifting the budget line *CD* to the position *GH* where the consumer is back at the original indifference level.

This leads to our general conclusion which can be stated as follows. Suppose the consumer was at a given income-price situation Alpha and an associated utility level $U(A)$, and then moved to an income-price situation Beta associated with $U(B)$. There is then only one meaningful compensating variation in R_β, namely changing R_β so that the consumer is brought back to $U(A)$.[31] This is what we mean by total compensation. No operational meaning can be attached to any attempt to partition this magnitude into components associated with changes in specific variables. It is for this reason that we can define a cost of living allowance only when *money income* is constant, since then the c.o.l. allowance is identical with total compensation. Similarly, we can meaningfully compensate the consumer for a change in money income only when *prices* are constant. Thus we can always compensate for partial *changes* (i.e., when not all our income-price variables change), but we cannot meaningfully define a partial *compensation* (i.e., a compensation for changes in a subset of the variables which changed simultaneously).

What is now left to consider is the apparent contradiction between our assertion that the c.o.l. allowance for price changes is meaningless when money income changes simultaneously and the fact that we can always meaningfully define the true price index. There is however no real contradiction involved. As we shall see, the meaning of our ability to define (conceptually) $I_{1,2}^A$ is that we can always define a *quantity* index which, when applied to R_β, will compensate the consumer for the *entire* change in welfare between the two situations. Alternatively this means that we can always define a price index for *deflating* the change in money income in a meaningful way. All this however is related to the concept of *total compensation*. On the other hand the cost of living allowance is concerned with compensation for the change in prices only and it is this concept which is meaningless when money income changes simultaneously with prices.

31. For a more precise formulation see appendix.

The above argument can be put in formal terms as follows. Consider a change from State Alpha to Beta which involves changes in both money income and prices. We can always meaningfully define the "true *standard* of living allowance" (or *total* compensation) $S_{\alpha\beta}$ which is the amount of money which must be added to R_β in order to keep the individual at the same indifference level as in State Alpha. This is defined as

$$(58) \qquad S_{\alpha\beta} = \Sigma\, p_2 q_2^A - R_\beta = \frac{\Sigma\, p_2 q_2^A}{\Sigma\, p_2 q_2^B} \cdot R_\beta - R_\beta = R_\beta \cdot (V_{B,A}^2 - 1).$$

Thus $S_{\alpha\beta}$ is always associated with a quantity index.

Define now the index of the change in money income as follows:

$$(59) \qquad M_{\alpha\beta} = \frac{R_\beta}{R_\alpha} = \frac{\Sigma\, p_2 q_2^B}{\Sigma\, p_1 q_1^A}.$$

Using the definition of the true price index $I_{1,2} = \dfrac{\Sigma\, p_2 q_2^A}{\Sigma\, p_1 q_1^A}$, we may deflate the nominal change $M_{\alpha\beta}$ and obtain the index of the "real" change,

$$(60) \qquad V_{A,B}^2 = \frac{M_{\alpha\beta}}{I_{1,2}^A} = \frac{\Sigma\, p_2 q_2^B}{\Sigma\, p_2 q_2^A}.$$

Comparing with (58) we see that $V_{A,B}^2$ is simply the reciprocal of $V_{B,A}^2$, the quantity index which we used for the standard of living allowance. We may accordingly write (58) as

$$(61) \qquad S_{\alpha\beta} = R_\beta \left[\frac{I_{1,2}^A}{M_{\alpha\beta}} - 1 \right] = R_\beta \left[\frac{1}{\dfrac{M_{\alpha\beta}}{I_{1,2}^A}} - 1 \right].$$

Formulation (61) clearly shows that in order to leave the consumer at $U(A)$, a positive compensation has to be paid in Beta if prices rose more than income ($I_{1,2}^A > M_{\alpha\beta}$), while a negative compensation has to be paid (i.e. R_β has to be reduced) if $M_{\alpha\beta} > I_{1,2}^A$. It is important to note that $S_{\alpha\beta}$ is not affected by $I_{1,2}^A$ as such but only by the ratio $\dfrac{M_{\alpha\beta}}{I_{1,2}^A}$, i.e. by the "quantitative" or "real" aspect of the change in nominal income. It is in this application as a deflator of $M_{\alpha\beta}$ that $I_{1,2}^A$ is always meaningful. But it should not be overlooked that "deflation" is related to the concept of total compensation and not to that of c.o.l. allowances.

Consider now the true c.o.l. allowance

$$(62) \qquad T_{1,2}^A = R_\alpha\, (I_{1,2}^A - 1).$$

T was defined for constant income so that we have $R_\alpha = R_\beta$ and $M_{\alpha\beta} = 1$. Substituting in (61) we obtain

$$(63) \qquad S_{\alpha\beta} = R_\beta \left[\frac{I_{1,2}^A}{M_{\alpha\beta}} - 1 \right] = R_\alpha\, (I_{1,2}^A - 1) = T_{1,2}^A,$$

i.e. the cost-of-living allowance is identical with the standard of living allowance, and it is for this reason that T is meaningful when income is constant.

When money income is variable we may of course still pay the consumer the amount $T_{1,2}^A$; but this has nothing to do with compensation for price changes. The reason is that after the payment, the consumer will *not* be on the original indifference level (since this can be accomplished only by $S_{\alpha\beta}$). Now, since a compensating variation in money income can be defined only on a *given* indifference level, $T_{1,2}^A$ can have no operational significance when money income is changing.[32]

In conclusion we may state that when both prices and money income change simultaneously the use of price indexes for determining c.o.l. allowances has no economic meaning. That is, there cannot be any logical relation between the c.o.l. allowance and the compensation for the change in prices. This applies to the true price index and therefore to the Laspeyres price index as well. The only meaningful application of the price index is as a deflator of the change in money income. This however is redundant, since "deflation" results in a quantity index which can be computed directly.

All this does not mean that we cannot analyze the welfare implications of paying c.o.l. allowances when money income is changing. Thus, in a world where money income never falls below the "base period income" the Laspeyres c.o.l. allowance ensures that the individual will always be able to attain at least the standard of living which he enjoyed in the base period. If this is the purpose of the c.o.l. allowance then the c.o.l. policy involves a serious "overcompensation" when money income is rising. The above purpose could be achieved much more efficiently by computing the Paasche quantity index and paying a "standard of living allowance" whenever this index is less than unity.

What all this amounts to is that we can meaningfully devise policies protecting the consumer against losses of welfare compared with some "base." Economists should realize however that, when money income is changing, it is impossible to formulate policies which have to do with "that part of the change in welfare which is due to the change in *prices*." The latter concept is meaningless—and so is any "compensating" cost-of-living allowance associated with it.

Appendix

Our argument concerning total and "partial" compensating variations in money income for changes in welfare between two situations can be stated more precisely as follows.

Consider two given situations which are characterized by the following income-price vectors

$$\alpha = (R^\alpha, p_1^\alpha \ldots p_n^\alpha) \qquad\qquad \beta = (R^\beta, p_1^\beta \ldots p_n^\beta).$$

32. The reader may note that it is identically true that $S_{\alpha\beta} = T_{1,2}^A + \Delta R$ where $\Delta R = R_\alpha - R_\beta$. It is important to realize that this partitionng is nothing more than an accounting identity when $\Delta R \neq 0$. All it says is that we can pay $S_{\alpha\beta}$ in two parts $T_{1,2}^A$ and ΔR. In the same way $S_{\alpha\beta}$ can be paid in three parts or in two arbitrary parts which are different from $T_{1,2}^A$ and ΔR. Only the *total* is significant.

Where R is money income and $p_1 \ldots p_n$ are the prices of the n commodities. With these vectors we associate the utility levels $U(\alpha)$ and $U(\beta)$. Suppose the consumer moves from α to β. This results in a change in utility $U(\beta)-U(\alpha)$. Now there is only one meaningful way to compensate the consumer for the change from α to β and this is by changing β in such a way as to bring him back to $U(\alpha)$, that is, to "keep utility constant." This can be done in many different ways but we confine ourselves to manipulation of R_β only. We define accordingly the compensating vector

$$C_{\alpha\beta} = (S_{\alpha\beta}, 0, 0 \ldots 0),$$

where the zeros indicate that compensation is not associated with manipulating prices but only money income. Our problem of compensating for the change from α to β is then defined as follows. Find $C\alpha\beta$ which satisfies

(A-1) $U(\beta + C_{\alpha\beta}) = U(\alpha) = U[\alpha + (\beta - \alpha) + C_{\alpha\beta}]$,

that is, $C_{\alpha\beta}$ is to compensate for $\beta - \alpha$. The reader may note that this is exactly analogous to finding rates of substitution along a given indifference curve. This is the meaning of the fact that our procedure is independent of the utility index.

In a similar way we may consider the rate of substitution along the indifference level $U(\beta)$ for a change from β to α. Define a compensating vector

$$C_{\beta\alpha} = (S_{\beta\alpha}, 0, 0 \ldots 0)$$

such that

(A-2) $U(\alpha + C_{\beta\alpha}) = U(\beta) = U[\beta + (\alpha - \beta) + C_{\beta\alpha}]$;

that is, $C_{\beta\alpha}$ compensates for the change $\alpha - \beta$. The C's are the only meaningful compensations that we are allowed to make for changes from α to β and conversely.

We call the component S the "*standard* of living allowance" since it is a *total* compensation for the change in welfare between two situations. Thus $S_{\alpha\beta}$ compensates for all components of $\beta - \alpha$ *simultaneously*. It is also legitimate to say that $S_{\alpha\beta}$ compensates for the group of all non-zero components of $\beta - \alpha$. Thus when $R_\alpha = R_\beta$ we may interpret $S_{\alpha\beta}$ as compensating for change in prices, so that S equals the cost of living allowance T. Similarly if prices in α and β are the same, $S_{\alpha\beta}$ can be said to compensate for any subset of $\beta - \alpha$ if all other components are equal to zero.

The problem of partial compensation can be formulated as follows. Suppose the consumer moves from State Alpha to Beta as a result of a change in both income and prices. The corresponding change in utility is $U(\beta)-U(\alpha)$. Find a compensating vector $C_{\alpha\beta} = (S_{\alpha\beta}, 0,0 \ldots 0)$ which compensates for that part of $U(\beta)-U(\alpha)$ which is associated with the change in prices only. In ordinal utility theory the partitioning of the distance $U(\beta)-U(\alpha)$ is obviously meaningless, since we can always apply any arbitrary positive monotonic transformation to U.

This partitioning is however impossible even if we are willing to assume that utility is *measurable*, since in order to solve the problem it is necessary that there should be no interaction between the effects of R and p_i on U. In other words U must be of the following additive form:

(A-3) $\qquad U(R, p_1 \ldots . p_n) = U^R(R) + U^p(p_1 \ldots . p_n).$

This possibility is, however, ruled out since U must be homogeneous of degree zero in R and the p's. That is, we may always write (A-3) as

(A-4) $\qquad U\left\{\dfrac{R}{p}, \dfrac{p_1}{p}, \ldots . \dfrac{p_n}{p}\right\}$

where p is some price index (with fixed weights). In other words, for any *finite* changes the effect of R on utility cannot be independent of the level of prices.[33] The "partial" compensation is not defined even for measurable utility.

Bibliography

R. G. D. Allen. "Some Observations on the Theory and Practice of Price Index Numbers." *Review of Economic Studies*, Oct. 1935, *3*, 57–66.

F. E. Croxton and D. J. Cowden. *Applied General Statistics*. New York, 1941.

R. Frisch. "Some Basic Principles of Price of Living Measurements." *Econometrica*, Oct. 1954, *22*, 407–21.

J. R. Hicks. "The Valuation of the Social Income." *Economica*, May 1940, *7*, 105–24.

———. "The Valuation of the Social Income: A Comment on Professor Kuznets' Reflections." *Economica*, Aug. 1948, *15*, 163–72.

M. F. W. Joseph. "Further Notes on Index Numbers. II. Mr. Lerner's Supplementary Limits for Price Index Numbers." *Review of Economic Studies*, Feb. 1936, *3*, 155–57.

S. Kuznets. "On the Valuation of Social Income—Reflections on Professor Hicks, Article." *Economica*, Feb., May 1948, *15*, 1–16, 116–31.

A. P. Lerner. "A Note on the Theory of Price Index Numbers." *Review of Economic Studies*, Oct. 1935, *3*, 50–56.

I. M. D. Little. *A Critique of Welfare Economics*, 2nd ed. Oxford, 1957.

J. L. Mosak. "On the Interpretation of the Fundamental Equation of Value Theory." In *Studies in Mathematics and Econometrics*, ed. O. Lange, F. McIntyre, and T. O. Yntema. Chicago, 1942. Pp. 69–74.

P. A. Samuelson. *Foundations of Economic Analysis*. Cambridge, Mass., 1947.

———. "Evaluation of Real National Income." *Oxford Economic Papers* (new series), 1950, *2*, 1–29.

———. "Consumption Theorems in Terms of Overcompensation rather than Indifference Comparisons." *Economica*, Feb. 1953, *20*, 1–9.

H. Staehle. "A Development of the Economic Theory of Index Numbers." *Review of Economic Studies*, June 1935, *2*, 163–88.

G. J. Stigler. *The Theory of Price*, rev. ed. New York, 1952.

United Nations Publications

Statistical Office of the United Nations, Department of Economic Affairs. *Retail Price Comparisons for International Salary Determination*. Statistical Papers, Series M, No. 14. New York 1952.

33. Throughout our analysis we are not concerned with infinitesimal changes, since the technique of analyzing such changes (viz., the differential calculus) essentially assumes away the main problems with which we deal in this article.

10. The Chicago Tradition, the Quantity Theory, and Friedman[*][1]

I must begin this paper with an apology for being over a decade late; for I should have written it as an immediate reaction to Milton Friedman's by now well-known 1956 essay on "The Quantity Theory of Money—A Restatement."[2, 3] But the recent appearance of Friedman's *International Encyclopedia* article on the quantity theory[4] (though, as will be shown in Part IV below, it differs significantly in its doctrinal aspects from the earlier paper) provides an appropriate, if tardy, occasion to raise some basic questions—from the viewpoint of the history of monetary doctrine— about the validity of Friedman's interpretation of the quantity theory of money, and of its Chicago version in particular.

Reprinted by permission from *Journal of Money, Credit and Banking*, Vol. 1 (February 1969), 46–70. Copyright © 1969 by the Ohio State University Press. All rights reserved. Appears here with the minor modifications and additions with which it was reprinted in my *Studies in Monetary Economics*, New York, 1972.

*This paper was written during 1968 while I was visiting at M.I.T. under a research grant from the National Science Foundation (NSF Grant GS 1812). I am grateful to both institutions for making this work possible.

I am happy to express my deep appreciation to Mr. Stanley Fischer of M.I.T. for his invaluable assistance at all stages of the preparation of this paper—and particularly in the examination of the relevant literature. In addition, I have benefited from discussions with him and from his criticisms of earlier drafts.

I am also indebted to my Jerusalem colleagues Yosef Attiyeh, Yoram Ben-Porath, and Giora Hanoch whose thoughtful suggestions have greatly improved the general organization of this paper, as well as the discussion of specific points.

As usual, it is a pleasure to thank Miss Susanne Freund for her careful and conscientious checking of the final manuscript and its references.

Because of its concern with historical questions, this paper refers to reprinted works by the date of original publication; for convenience, however, the page references themselves follow the pagination of the reprinted form as indicated in the bibliography.

Needless to say, responsibility for the interpretations and views presented in this paper remain entirely my own.

1. I would like to dedicate this paper to the memory of Miguel Sidrauski. His untimely death in August 1968 was a great loss, not only to his family and friends, but to the economics profession in general—and particularly to the development of monetary theory. Though I do not think Miguel had a strong interest in the history of doctrine, I hope that—as a Chicago graduate—he would have been interested in reading the final product of a work whose beginnings he witnessed.

2. In *Studies in the Quantity Theory of Money*, ed. M. Friedman (1956), pp. 3–21.; referred to henceforth as "Quantity Theory I."

3. In self-defense, I might, however, note that I have on previous occasions discussed in passing some of the points presented below—and have also emphasized the Keynesian nature of Friedman's essay. Thus see my "Indirect-Utility Approach to the Theory of Money, Assets, and Savings" (1965a), p. 54, note 5 (this is the proceedings volume of an International Economic Association Conference held at Royaumont in March 1962); and *Money, Interest, and Prices*, 2nd ed. (1965b), p. 81, note 8. See also the implicit criticism contained in my *International Encyclopedia* article on "Interest" (1968), p. 480b. See also below, p. 255.

4. "Money: Quantity Theory" in (1968), pp. 432–47; referred to henceforth as "Quantity Theory II."

The argument of the present paper is as follows: In both of the foregoing articles, Friedman presents what he calls a "reformulation of the quantity theory of money." In Part IV, I shall show that this is a misleading designation and that what Friedman has actually presented is an elegant exposition of the modern portfolio approach to the demand for money which, though it has some well-known (albeit largely undeveloped) antecedents in the traditional theory, can only be seen as a continuation of the Keynesian theory of liquidity preference.

The main purpose of this paper, however, is to describe (in Parts II and III) the true nature of the Chicago monetary tradition. In this way I shall also demonstrate the invalidity of Friedman's contention (in his 1956 essay) that this tradition is represented by his "reformulation of the quantity theory." As a minimum statement let me say that though I shared with Friedman—albeit, almost a decade later—the teachers at Chicago whom he mentions (namely, Knight, Viner, Simons, and Mints), his description of the "flavor of the oral tradition" which they were supposed to have imparted strikes no responsive chord in my memory.

Friedman offers no supporting evidence for his interpretation of the Chicago tradition. This is unfortunate. For questions about the history of economic doctrine ıre empirical questions. And the universe from which the relevant empirical evidence must be drawn is that of the writings and teachings of the economists in question. No operational meaning can be attached to the existence of a "tradition" which does not manifest itself in at least one of these ways.

From this it will be clear that my examination of this evidence in what follows should not be interpreted as a criticism of the individuals involved. On the contrary, I would consider it unjustified to criticize them for not having fully understood and integrated into their thinking what we have succeeded in learning only in the course of the subsequent development of Keynesian monetary theory. My quarrel is only with those who imply that such an understanding and integration existed before, or independently of, this development.

I would like finally to emphasize that my concern in this chapter is with the analytical framework of the Chicago monetary tradition, and not with its policy proposals as such. Correspondingly, I shall not—except incidentally—discuss the relation between these proposals and those of Friedman. Let me, however, note that though there are, of course, basic similarities, there are also significant differences— particularly about the degree of discretion to be exercised by the monetary authorities.[5]

5. This will become clear from a comparison of Friedman's policy (namely, expanding the quantity of money at a constant rate) with the contracyclical monetary policy advocated by Simons and Mints (see Propositions (4) and (5) on p. 246 below; see also p. 247 and especially fn. 19). One might also note Jacob Viner's criticism of Friedman's policy proposals in his (Viner's) "The Necessary and the Desirable Range of Discretion to be Allowed to a Monetary Authority" (1962), pp. 244–74.

Friedman himself discusses some of these differences explicitly in his paper on Simons referred to in fn. 22 below—and implicitly in his *Program for Monetary Stability* (1960), pp. 86–90. See also M. Bronfenbrenner, "Observations on the 'Chicago School(s)' " (1962), pp. 72–73.

Another interesting question which lies beyond the scope of the present paper is the extent to which the policy views of the Chicago school in the 1930s represented those of other quantity theorists of the period. {See next chapter.}

I. Friedman's Chicago

Friedman begins his 1956 essay with the explanation that (1956, pp. 3–4):

Chicago was one of the few academic centers at which the quantity theory continued to be a central and vigorous part of the oral tradition throughout the 1930's and 1940's, where students continued to study monetary theory and to write theses on monetary problems. The quantity theory that retained this role differed sharply from the atrophied and rigid caricature that is so frequently described by the proponents of the new income-expenditure approach—and with some justice, to judge by much of the literature on policy that was spawned by quantity theorists. At Chicago, Henry Simons and Lloyd Mints directly, Frank Knight and Jacob Viner at one remove, taught and developed a more subtle and relevant version, one in which the quantity theory was connected and integrated with general price theory and became a flexible and sensitive tool for interpreting movements in aggregate economic activity and for developing relevant policy prescriptions.

   To the best of my knowledge, no systematic statement of this theory as developed at Chicago exists, though much can be read between the lines of Simons' and Mints' writings. . . . It was a theoretical approach that insisted that money does matter. . . .

   The purpose of this introduction is not to enshrine—or, should I say, inter—a definitive version of the Chicago tradition. . . . The purpose is rather to set down a particular "model" of a quantity theory in an attempt to convey the flavor of the oral tradition. . . .

Friedman then goes on to present this model. Since I am interested only in the doctrinal aspects of the question, it is sufficient to cite the model's basic features. In Friedman's words (1956, p. 4, italics in original):

1. The quantity theory is in the first instance a theory of the *demand* for money. It is not a theory of output, or of money income, or of the price level. Any statement about these variables requires combining the quantity theory with some specifications about the conditions of supply of money and perhaps about other variables as well.
2. To the ultimate wealth-owning units in the economy, money is one kind of asset, one way of holding wealth. . . .
3. The analysis of the demand for money on the part of the ultimate wealth-owning units in the society can be made formally identical with that of the demand for a consumption service. As in the usual theory of consumer choice, the demand for money (or any other particular asset) depends on three major sets of factors: (a) the total wealth to be held in various forms—the analogue of the budget restraint; (b) the price of and return on this form of wealth and alternative forms; and (c) the tastes and preferences of the wealth-owning units.

From these and other considerations Friedman arrives at a demand function for money of the form

$$M = g(P, r_b, r_e, \frac{1}{P}\frac{dP}{dt}, w, Y; u),$$ (1)

where M is the nominal quantity of money; P, the price level; r_b is the interest rate on bonds; r_e, the interest rate on equities; $(1/P)(dP/dt)$, the rate of change of prices—and hence the negative of the rate of return on money balances; w, the ratio of nonhuman to human wealth; Y, money income; and u, "variables that can be expected to affect tastes and preferences." [6] Friedman then makes the familiar assumption that this function is homogeneous of degree one in P and Y, and hence rewrites it as (1956, p. 11, equation 11):

$$\frac{M}{P} = f(r_b, r_e, \frac{1}{P}\frac{dP}{dt}, w; \frac{Y}{P}; u).$$ (2)

Alternatively, dividing (1) through by Y, he obtains

$$Y = v(r_b, r_e, \frac{1}{P}\frac{dP}{dt}, w, \frac{Y}{P}; u) \cdot M.$$ (3)

"In this form the equation is in the usual quantity theory form, where v is income velocity" (1956, p. 11).

As an aside, I might note that at no point in the foregoing exposition does Friedman mention the name of Keynes. Indeed, one cannot escape the impression that even the term "liquidity" is being avoided.[7]

Friedman does recognize that "almost every economist will accept the general lines of the preceding analysis on a purely formal and abstract level." But Friedman defines three distinguishing features of the quantity theorist, of which the first is that the quantity theorist

> accepts the empirical hypothesis that the demand for money is highly stable. . . . The quantity theorist need not, and generally does not, mean that the . . . velocity of circulation of money is to be regarded as numerically constant over time. . . . For the stability he expects is in the functional relation between the quantity of money demanded and the variables that determine it. . . .

The other two features are that the quantity theorist believes that "there are important factors affecting the supply of money that do not affect the demand for money" and that the demand for money does not become infinitely elastic (viz., absence of a "liquidity trap") (1956, pp. 15–16).

There is no question that these last two features are generally found (either explicitly or implicitly) in presentations of the quantity theory. But it is equally clear to me that the first—which is crucial to Friedman's interpretation—is not. Correspondingly, one of the basic points that will be examined in the following discussion

---

6. Friedman (1956), pp. 4–10; the quotation is from p. 9.

7. Cf., e.g., *ibid.*, pp. 5, 14, and 19.

of the Chicago economists is whether they did indeed think in terms of a stable velocity in Friedman's functional sense.

II. The Other Chicago

As against the foregoing, let me now describe a Chicago tradition of monetary theory whose approach, contents, and language can be represented by the following summary-propositions.[8]

1. The quantity theory is, first and foremost, not a theory of the demand for money, but a theory which relates the quantity of money (M) to the aggregate demand for goods and services (MV), and thence to the price level (P) and/or level of output (T); all this in accordance with Fisher's $MV = PT$.

2. V is not constant; on the contrary, a basic feature of economic life is the "danger of sharp changes on the velocity side"; or in other words, the danger "of extreme alternations of hoarding and dishoarding." [9] These "sharp changes" in turn are due to anticipations of changing price levels, as well as to the changing state of business confidence as determined by earnings. [10] Thus if individuals expect prices to rise and earnings to be good, they will dishoard—that is, increase the velocity of circulation. But the crucial point here is that these expectations will be self-justifying: for the very act of dishoarding will cause prices to rise even further, thus leading to further dishoarding, and so on. In this way a "cumulative process" of expansion is set into operation which "feeds upon itself" and which has no "natural" limit. [11] Conversely, an indefinite "cumulative process" of hoarding, price declines and depression, and further hoarding is set into operation by the expectation that the price level will fall and/or that earnings will be poor. Thus the economic system is essentially unstable. [12]

3. Such a cumulative process might possibly take place—albeit in a much less severe form—even if the quantity of money in the economy were to remain constant. [13] In the actual world, however, the process is highly exacerbated by the

8. The following is primarily a summary of Simons' views, which were largely accepted by Mints. Knight's analysis is the same, though—quite characteristically—he seems to have had less faith than did Simons and Mints in the policy proposals. For Viner, I have been able to find clear evidence only on the first proposition. Nevertheless, Viner (together with his colleagues) did advocate government deficit financing as a means of combating unemployment.

For references to the relevant writings of the foregoing (as well as further comments on Viner's position) see Appendix I below. Cf. also J. R. Davis, "Chicago Economists, Deficit Budgets, and the Early 1930s" (1968), pp. 476–82.

9. Simons, "Rule versus Authorities in Monetary Policy" (1936), p. 164 (this passage is cited in full in Appendix 1 below). That by "hoarding and dishoarding" Simons means changes in velocity is clear from p. 165; see also the reference cited in the next footnote.

10. See Simons, "Banking and Currency Reform" (1933), as quoted in Appendix I below.

11. Knight, "The Business Cycle, Interest, and Money: A Methodological Approach" (1941), pp. 210–11, 223–24.

12. See Appendix I for supporting quotations from Simons, *Personal Income Taxation* (1938), p. 222, and "Hansen on Fiscal Policy" (1942), p. 188, and from Knight's "The Business Cycle, Interest, and Money" (1941), pp. 211 and 224.

13. See the quotation from Simons, "Rules versus Authorities in Monetary Policy" (1936) p. 164, reproduced in Appendix I below. See also *ibid.*, p. 331, footnote 16, and Mints, *Monetary Policy for a Competitive Society* (1950), pp. 120–22.

"perverse" behavior of the banking system, which expands credit in booms and contracts it in depressions. As a result the quantity of money (M) and near-moneys (and hence V) increases in booms, and decreases in depressions.

4. In accordance with (2) and (3), the government has an obligation to undertake a contracyclical policy. The guiding principle of this policy is to change M so as to offset changes in V, and thus generate the full-employment level of aggregate demand MV. If prices are downwardly flexible, the operational rule which will assure the proper variation in M is that of increasing M when P falls, and decreasing it when P rises. In any event, it is "inconceivable" that a sufficiently vigorous policy of (say) expanding M in a period of depression would not ultimately affect aggregate spending in the required manner.

5. The necessary variations in M can be generated either by open-market operations or by budgetary deficits. The latter method is more efficient, and in some cases might even be necessary. Budgetary deficits, in turn, can be generated by varying either government expenditures or tax receipts. From the viewpoint of contracyclical policy, this makes no difference—for either method changes M; but from the viewpoint of the general philosophy of the proper role of government in economic life, the variation of tax receipts is definitely preferable. Hence, a tax system which depends heavily on the income tax is desirable not only from the viewpoint of distributive justice, but also from the viewpoint of automatically providing proper cyclical variations in tax receipts.

Before going on to bring out the flavor of these propositions as contrasted with that of Friedman's presentation, I would like briefly to indicate three reasons for the emphasis I have given in the foregoing to the writings of Simons. First, at the Chicago which concerns us, Simons was undoubtedly the dominant figure in discussions of monetary and fiscal policy. (In Friedman's presentation too there is more emphasis on the writings of Simons and Mints than on those of Knight and Viner.) Second, Simons' writings on these questions were the earliest by far of the writers here considered. And, third, they were sufficiently early to represent the Chicago tradition in its pristine—and pre-Keynesian—form.

The significance of this last point will become clear from our discussion of Mints at the end of this part. In connection with the first reason, I might note that Mints repeatedly makes clear his indebtedness to Simons.[14] Again, I would conjecture that Knight's writings referred to above also reflect Simons' influence. Similarly, in my recollections of student days at Chicago—and I think I can safely speak for my fellow students at the time—it is Simons who stands out sharply as the major source of intellectual stimulation and influence in all that regards monetary and fiscal policy. In the slang of those days, most of us were "simonized" to some degree or other.[15]

14. Cf., e.g., *Monetary Policy for a Competitive Society* (1950), p. vii. {Cf. also Mints' letter to me reproduced on p. 285 below.}

15. In a letter to me commenting on this paper, Martin Bronfenbrenner disagrees with this evaluation of Simons' influence and states that "Simons was wasted on the undergraduates; few graduate students other than tax technicians took his 'Fiscal Policy' course, 361."

My opinion is still that expressed in the text. But I must admit that—in contrast with most graduate students—I also did my undergraduate work at Chicago, and that my first impressions of Simons were accordingly formed in that context. I should also note (though again I am not sure that it is relevant) that Bronfenbrenner's recollections refer to the period 1934–36 whereas mine are for 1941–46.

Let me turn now to the propositions themselves. The contrast drawn by Proposition (1) is that between the transactions approach to the quantity theory and the cash-balance approach emphasized by Friedman. Now, it is a commonplace of monetary theory that these two approaches can be made analytically equivalent. Indeed in his general discussion of monetary influences, Fisher himself vividly shows (1913, pp. 153–54) that he was thinking in terms of a demand for money. Nevertheless, if we consistently find a treatment in terms of the transactions approach, we can take this as some indication that the economists in question did not primarily approach monetary theory from the viewpoint of the demand for money. Or at least we cannot take it as an indication that they did![16]

Indeed, it is a much closer approximation to the flavor of the Chicago tradition to say that basically it was not interested in a systematic analysis of the demand for money:[17] for it believed so strongly that "the supply of money matters" that—for the policy purposes which were its main concern—the exact form of the demand function for money did not matter at all, aside from the critical (though sometimes implicit) assumption "that additional money in unlimited amounts would [not] be hoarded in its entirety." For then no matter what the demand for money—in the language of Simons and Mints, no matter what the extent of hoarding—its adverse effects could be offset by a sufficient increase in M. "Much hoarding would simply require a larger addition to the stock of money." [18] The possibility that destabilizing lags could interfere with the efficacy of such a monetary policy—a problem which has received so much attention in recent years—was either not seen (Simons) or not given much weight (Mints [19]).

It should therefore not surprise us that Simons did not present a detailed analysis of the demand for money. Indeed, despite his frequent references to "hoarding," there does not seem to be any point in his writings in which he even uses the term "demand for money." Another, and related, manifestation of the lack of interest in such an analysis is the fact that Simons did not spell out the details of the mechanism by which an increase in the quantity of money was supposed to increase the volume of spending on goods and services. Instead, he sufficed with the simple, sometimes implicit, and frequently mechanical statement that an increase in M increased aggregate demand MV.

Again, even the influence of the rate of interest on the demand for money was not

16. Actually, Friedman draws a sharper distinction on this score between the transactions and cash-balance approaches than I would; thus compare his "Quantity Theory II" (1968), pp. 437–38 with my *Money, Interest, and Prices*, (1965b), pp. 166–67.

17. It is noteworthy that the work on the empirical nature of the demand function for money that was done at Chicago during the 1940s was carried out under the inspiration not of the "Chicago oral tradition," but of the Keynesian model builders at the Cowles Commission, which was then located at the University of Chicago. See in particular Lawrence Klein, "The Use of Econometric Models as a Guide to Economic Policy" (1947), p. 125 ff., and *Economic Fluctuation in the United States, 1921–1941* (1950), pp. 95–101.

18. The last two quotations in this paragraph are from Mints, "Monetary Policy," (1946), p. 67. See also *ibid.*, p. 61 and *Monetary Policy for a Competitive Society* (1950), pp. 48–49. Cf. in this connection the quotation (given in Appendix I below) from Viner's "Schumpeter's *History of Economic Analysis*" (1954), as reprinted in *The Long View and the Short* (1958), p. 365.

19. Mints, *Monetary Policy for a Competitive Society*, (1950), p. 138 ff. Mints ascribes the suggestion that such a destabilizing influence might occur to Milton Friedman, who by then was his colleague (*ibid.*, p. 138, fn. 8).

consistently recognized by the Chicago school of the 1930s and 1940s. Thus even though Knight discussed cyclical variations in the rate of interest, he did not take account of the possible influence of such variations on the velocity of circulation.[20] Similarly, though (as indicated in Proposition (3)) Simons and Mints did emphasize the influence of near-moneys on velocity, it was the *volume* of these money substitutes to which they referred, not to the *rate of interest* upon them.

Let me turn now to the "extreme alternations" in velocity described in Proposition (2). It is not clear from the writings of the Chicago school whether it believed that the very fact that prices were, say, increasing would cause an indeterminate flight from money—so that there could exist no stable functional relationship between velocity and the anticipated rate of change of prices; or whether velocity was unstable because of the nature of the expectations function which generated a sequence of ever-increasing anticipated rates of price changes which operated through a stable demand function to generate ever-increasing (or decreasing) changes in the quantity of money demanded; or whether there were other forces in the economy (of which those described in Proposition (3) are an example) which generated such a divergent sequence—or whether it believed that a combination of some or all of these factors was at work. But in any event one point is clear: there is no place in their writings in which the aforementioned Chicago economists even hint that they were thinking in terms of Friedman's crucial assumption of a velocity which is a stable function of (among other variables) the anticipated rate of change of prices.[21, 22]

There were other respects in which the Chicago tradition lacked some of the basic ingredients of the flavor of the "model" which Friedman has presented of it. In particular, whereas (as indicated above) this tradition was primarily concerned with the relation between the stock of money and the flow of expenditures, Friedman's primary concern is with the relation between the stock of money and the stocks of other assets. I shall return to this point in Part IV below. But let me now admit that with respect to this comment—and, even more so, with respect to much of what has

20. See the discussion of Knight in Appendix I below.

21. See in this context the statement by Frank Knight (from his *Risk, Uncertainty and Profit*, (1957), p. xlv) quoted in full Appendix I.

22. I might at this point note that in his recent paper on Simons, Friedman cites the passage referred to in footnote 13 above and then concludes that:

> There is clearly great similarity between the views expressed by Simons and by Keynes—as to the causes of the Great Depression, the impotence of monetary policy, and the need to rely extensively on fiscal policy. Both men placed great emphasis on the state of business expectations and assigned a critical role to the desire for liquidity. Indeed, in many ways, the key novelty of Keynes' *General Theory* was the role he assigned to "absolute" liquidity preference under conditions of deep depression [1967, p. 7].

But Friedman gives no indication of the fact that this interpretation of Simons is hardly consistent with that of his 1956 essay, with its emphasis on the functional stability of *V* and, even more to the point, on the absence of a "liquidity trap" (cf. pp. 244–45 above).

In this paper, Friedman also contends that "had Simons known the facts as we now know them [about the monetary history of the U.S. during the Great Depression], he would, I believe," have been less concerned with " 'the danger of sharp changes on the velocity side' " (ibid., p. 12). Without discussing the validity of this conjecture {cf., however, below, ch. 12, pp. 295–97}, I shall merely note that it is not relevant to the question which concerns me here—namely, Simons' actual approach to the quantity theory.

been said above about the lack of interest at Chicago in the demand for money—Lloyd Mints was at least a partial exception. Thus even though it is not at all comparable—in either detail or precision—with Friedman's exposition, Mints' *Monetary Policy for a Competitive Society* contains a more explicit analysis of the asset-demand for money than any earlier Chicago discussion.[23] But it is highly significant that the chapter in which this analysis is presented (Chapter 3) is followed by a special appendix on Keynes' theory of liquidity preference. Similarly, as shown in Appendix II, it was in this context (and not in that of the quantity theory of money) that Mints' lectures on the asset-demand for money were given. It is also noteworthy that the few Chicago doctoral theses of the period 1939–1950 that were concerned with the choice of money as a component of a portfolio of assets generally took Keynes as their point of departure and gave no indication that they saw this approach as stemming from the Chicago tradition (see Part III below).

Thus the picture which emerges from all this is that by the 1940s the Chicago School itself had—quite understandably—been influenced by Keynesian monetary theory. Accordingly, not only did it begin to evince an interest in a systematic analysis of the demand for money, but it frequently did so from the Keynesian viewpoint of money as one component of an optimally chosen portfolio of assets. Indeed, it had to use this viewpoint in order to explain why it rejected some aspects of the Keynesian theory: namely, the Keynesian concentration on the choice between money and bonds, and the related interpretation of interest as a monetary phenomenon; and the emphasis on the possibility of indefinite hoarding (the "liquidity trap"), and the related Keynesian conclusion that money could not matter enough, so that only a policy of increased government expenditures could deal adequately with the problem of unemployment.[24]

III. The Oral Tradition of Chicago

The preceding discussion of the Chicago School has been based on its writings. It is, however, the "oral tradition of Chicago" which Friedman primarily claims to represent—and to which, accordingly, I shall now turn.

A priori it seems unlikely that scholars who had presented a consistent—and sometimes lengthy—statement of their views in print would have provided a significantly different presentation in their classroom discussions. Fortunately, there is no need to rely solely on such a priori considerations—or even on my memories of these classroom discussions as contrasted with those of Friedman. For there is concrete evidence on their nature in the form of lecture notes which I took during my graduate studies at Chicago in the period 1943–1945.

Of course, these lecture notes are subject to all of the standard reservations about the accuracy with which students understand their teachers. Furthermore, they constitute only one observation on these teachings. But at the present moment this is

---

23. Mints (1950), ch. 3; see also ch. 9 and especially pp. 210–11. See also Mints' *History of Banking Theory* (1945), pp. 219–22, and Mints (1946), pp. 63 *et passim*.

24. See again the references to Mints in the preceding footnote. See also the discussion of Knight in Appendix I.

one more than has yet been provided on the question. It should also be noted that if we accept (as I do) the fact that there was a "tradition" at Chicago, then we can also assume that there was a high degree of continuity between what was taught in my student days and what was taught before.

Mints devoted several lectures to the quantity theory at the beginning of his course on "Money." After presenting Fisher's equation of exchange (with no discussion of the determinants of V—or of the Cambridge K, to which he also referred), Mints went on to formulate the quantity theory of money in a way which has remained sharply etched in my memory—and which has always represented for me "the flavor of the Chicago tradition":

> Some attempts [have been made statistically] to verify quantity theory by showing that $MV + M'V' = PT$ is true. But quantity theory says that P *is the dependent variable*. So [in order to verify theory] would have to show that exist consistent time lags. Have to establish *causal relationship*. Formula itself is a truism—doesn't need verification. Formula $\neq$ quantity theory.

> . . .

> Mints prefers following statement of quantity theory: P is the dependent variable (in the long run) of the equation $MV = PT$. But in the short run all the variables tend to move together. [Classnotes, Econ. 330, June 28 and July 3, 1944; italics in original.] [25]

For our purposes (see end of preceding part), it is also most significant that Mints' discussion of the demand for money from a viewpoint which is closer to the portfolio approach did not occur in his lectures on the quantity theory, but a month later in the context of his discussion of Keynes' theory of liquidity preference. Here Mints said:

> Really four factors to be kept in equilibrium: (1) price level (2) rate of interest (3) demand for cash (liquidity preferences) and (4) quantity of money.
> Methods of disposing of cash:
> (1) Hold in cash
> (2) Purchase consumer's goods
> (3) Purchase producer's goods
> (4) Lend on short term
> (5) Purchase long-term bonds
> (6) Purchase corporation shares.
> Keynes assumes that doubts about the future affect only (5).
> But uncertainties affect (2) and especially (3). Demand will fall off for these, prices there will fall, profits decrease, and [hence] beginning of unemployment, etc. [Classnotes, Econ. 330, Aug. 4, 1944.]

---

25. It is noteworthy that this distinction between the quantity theory and the identity $MV + M'V' = PT$ is also emphasized by Friedman in his encyclopedia article; see Friedman (1968), pp. 434–36.

Mints then went on to present a discussion which closely parallels that of the first part of Chapter 3 of his *Monetary Policy for a Competitive Society* (1950).

Some other notes from Mints' lectures, as well as relevant notes from the lectures of Knight and Simons, are reproduced in Appendix II. The evidence of these notes leads unmistakably to one simple and unsurprising conclusion: the oral tradition of the Chicago School of monetary theory was entirely reflected in its written tradition; whatever was not in the latter was also not in the former.

Let me turn now to the doctoral theses written at Chicago during the period in question.[26] As we all know, students' theses reflect the interests, approach, and all too frequently even the views of their teachers. It is therefore interesting to see what we can learn about the Chicago tradition from this source. This is all the more legitimate in the present context in view of Friedman's assertion (1956, p.3) that "Chicago was one of the few academic centers at which the quantity theory continued to be a central and vigorous part of the oral tradition throughout the 1930s and 1940s, whose students continued to study monetary theory and to write theses on monetary problems."

The list of relevant theses is presented in Appendix III. Even after taking account of the small number of theses which were being submitted in those days (a total of 46 for the 1930s and 52 for the 1940s), one is struck by the paucity of monetary theses written at Chicago during the 1930s. The fact that from 1931 through 1938 only one such thesis was submitted speaks for itself. The number is decidedly greater for the 1940s. Nevertheless, a casual comparison with the list of doctoral theses submitted at Harvard shows that even during the 1940s there were at least as many monetary theses being submitted at Harvard as at Chicago (though admittedly the total number of theses submitted at the former was three times as large).

Let me turn now to the far more important question as to the contents of the Chicago theses. The situation can be described quite simply: several of the theses are primarily descriptive and contain little, if any, analysis. To the extent that the theses refer to the quantity theory of money, they do so in terms of Proposition (1) on p. 245 above;[27] none of them do so in terms reminiscent of Friedman's "reformulation." Few theses even reflect a portfolio approach to the demand for money. Furthermore, those that do, draw their primary inspiration from Keynes or his supporters.[28] Similarly, the influence of the rate of interest on the demand for money is rarely mentioned, even in

26. Without disclaiming any responsibility for what follows, I would like to express my appreciation to my assistant, Mr. Stanley Fischer, who has carefully gone through the monetary theses written at Chicago during the period 1930–50—and on whose excellent notes I have relied heavily.

I would also like to thank Professor Lester Telser of the Department of Economics at the University of Chicago and his secretary Mrs. Hazel Bowdry for their help in obtaining a complete list of Chicago theses and microfilms of those discussed here, as well as information about theses committees.

27. Thus see, e.g., Benjamin F. Brooks, "A History of Banking Theory in the United States Before 1860" (1939), p. 354; Marion R. Daugherty, "The Currency School-Banking School Controversy" (1941), p. 54; Roland N. McKean, "Fluctuations in Our Private Claim-Debt Structure and Monetary Policy" (1948), pp. 51, 98, and 103. See also the references to Leland Bach's thesis in fn. 31.

28. Thus see, e.g., Martin Bronfenbrenner, "Monetary Theory and General Equilibrium" (1939), pp. iii, 43, 45, 156–57; McKean (1948), ch. 4, and especially pp. 52, fn. 5, and 57–59; and William W. Tongue, "Money, Capital and the Business Cycle" (1947), chs. 1 and 2.

appropriate contexts,[29] and when there is a mention, it is again largely inspired by Keynesian monetary theory.[30]

Of particular interest in the present context is Leland Bach's thesis on "Price Level Stabilization: Some Theoretical and Practical Considerations" (1940). In his general analysis and policy proposals, Bach presents the position of the Chicago School as summarized in the five propositions of Part II above.[31] Furthermore, in the process of so doing he refers explicitly (on pp. 35–36) to an "oral tradition" at Chicago which he describes in the following terms:

> The explanation of the cycle may, for our purposes, be ultimately reduced to the existence of two basic factors, the first redivisible into two more or less separate elements. These two sub-factors in the first are (a) psychological shifts by consumers, entrepreneurs, and investors, leading to changes in the propensities to hoard, consume, and invest, and (b) perverse fluctuations in the volume of money in the system (M plus M' in the Fisherian notation). The second basic factor is the existence of "sticky" prices throughout large sectors of the economy, of which many are cost-prices, so that costs have a tendency to move more slowly than do the more flexible selling prices.*

> *On this reduction to essentials I am indebted to Professor Mints, although it has been in the nature of an "oral tradition" at Chicago for some time and can be found in many writers, but only more or less obscured.

It might be noted that at the time Bach wrote this footnote, the tradition was indeed largely oral: for all that then existed in print was Simons' brief discussions; the writings of Knight and Mints had yet to appear (see Appendix I).

In concluding this discussion of the Chicago School, I would like to emphasize once again that its purpose has not been either to praise or to criticize—and surely not to criticize the writers of the theses—but only to convey the flavor of the Chicago tradition as it really was.

29. Cf., e.g., Arthur I. Bloomfield, "International Capital Movements and the American Balance of Payments, 1929–40" (1942), pp. 578–79; McKean (1948), p. 80.

In all but the last chapter of his thesis (see especially ch. 4), McKean follows Simons (to whom he repeatedly refers—pp. 3, 32, 52, 68, *et passim*), in being concerned with the volume of liquid assets and debts, and not the rates of return upon them (cf. above, p. 248). On the other hand, his discussion of 100 percent money in the last chapter (see especially pp. 174–77) explicitly takes account of the effect on the demand for money (and hence velocity) of changes in the rates of interest on money substitutes.

30. See again the references cited in fn. 28. See also McKean (1948), p. 100, who, however, refers to the influence of the quantity of money on the interest rate as "the very old argument, revived in the thirties" (*ibid.*, p. 99).

It might be noted that at some points McKean's thesis also reflects the influence of Milton Friedman, who had joined the Chicago staff in 1946. Thus see the reference to Friedman in McKean's discussion of the simultaneous influence of the interest rate on the demand for money and on savings (p. 101, fn. 1). Somewhat less relevant for our present purpose are McKean's many references in chs. 1–2 and on p. 191 to Friedman's discussions of the problem of lags in monetary policy and of the proper framework for monetary and fiscal policy.

31. See especially pp. 42–45 and 72–75 of Bach's thesis.

IV. The Quantity Theory, Friedman,
and Keynesian Economics

As indicated in my opening remarks, the nominal occasion for the appearance of this paper is the recent publication in the *International Encyclopedia of the Social Sciences* of Friedman's article on the "Quantity Theory." From the substantive viewpoint, the "reformulation of the quantity theory" which Friedman presents on pp. 439–42 of this article is essentially the same as the one he presented in his 1956 essay (see Part I above). But from the doctrinal viewpoint which engrossed us in Parts II and III, there is a fundamental difference: for Friedman now makes no attempt to present this reformulation as a "model of the oral tradition of Chicago." Indeed, neither the Chicago School nor its individual members are even mentioned.

On the other hand, as just indicated, Friedman does continue to denote his presentation as a "reformulation of the quantity theory." The only support he adduces for this nomenclature is that "Fisher and other earlier quantity theorists explicitly recognized that velocity would be affected by, among other factors, the rate of interest and also the rate of change of prices" (1968, p. 436b).

That such a recognition existed, there can be no doubt.[32] But—as I have indicated elsewhere (1968, p. 480b) [33]—the real question is the extent to which the "earlier quantity theorists" recognized the full and precise implications of these effects: the extent to which they consistently took account of these effects at the appropriate points in their discussions. For one of the fundamental facts of the history of ideas is that in general the full implications of a set of ideas are not immediately seen. Indeed—as has been frequently noted—if they were, then all mathematics would be a tautology; for its theorems are implicit in the assumptions made. The failure to see such implications is also familiar from many episodes in the history of economic doctrine: for example, from the tortuous and faltering manner in which the full implications of the marginal productivity theory were developed.[34]

Thus there is indeed a striking passage in Fisher's *Rate of Interest* (1907, p. 212) about the "convenience" of money holdings which makes an individual willing to forgo the interest that he could earn.[35] But the only echo of this passage in *The Purchasing Power of Money* is a passing reference (1913, p. 152) to the influence of the "waste of interest" on velocity. Furthermore, it is clear that Fisher did not integrate this influence into the general analysis of this book. Indeed, this influence is not mentioned at any other point in it: neither in the analysis of the effects of the higher interest rates which mark the "transition period" (Chapter IV), nor in the detailed

---

32. For specific references to writings of Walras, Wicksell, the much neglected Karl Schlesinger, Fisher, and the Cambridge school (Marshall, Pigou, and especially Lavington) which discuss or at the least refer to the influence of interest on the demand for money, see my *Money, Interest, and Prices* (1965) pp. 372, 545, 556, and 576–80.

33. Cf. also my *Money, Interest, and Prices*, (1965b), p. 372.

34. See G. J. Stigler, *Production and Distribution Theories* (1941).

35. This passage is slightly elaborated upon in *The Theory of Interest* (1930), p. 216, where Fisher refers to the "liquidity of our cash balances [which] takes the place of any rate of interest in the ordinary sense of the term."

description of the determinants of the velocity of circulation (Chapter V),[36] nor finally in the statistical investigation of the theory, with its description of how velocity varied during the periods examined (Chapters XI–XII).

I find this last omission particularly significant. For the empirical investigator is confronted with a concrete situation in which he is called upon to take account of the major theoretical variables which might explain the data (even if some of these variables will subsequently be rejected as statistically insignificant); hence this situation provides a proper and operationally meaningful test of whether the influence of a variable has been "fully recognized." It should therefore be emphasized that the failure even to mention the rate of interest as a possible explanation of the observed variations in the velocity of circulation also characterizes the writings of Carl Snyder (1924, 1925, 1935), to whose empirical work (as well as that of Fisher) Friedman refers (1968, p. 436b). And a similar picture obtains for the earlier studies by James W. Angell (1933, 1936) [37] and Clark Warburton[38] (1945, 1946) to which Selden refers (1956, pp. 184–85) in his survey of empirical investigations of the income velocity of circulation in the United States.[39] Furthermore, the fact that Angell and Warburton mention the influence of interest only in their later studies—and in explicit response to issues raised by Keynesian monetary theory[40]—reinforces my basic contention that the "early quantity theorists" did not of themselves fully recognize this influence.

It is true that the aforementioned empirical studies were primarily concerned with explaining the observed price level in the market, and not the demand function for money. But to press this point too far in the present context is to admit that these "early quantity theorists" did not really have a major concern with the properties of this demand function. Furthermore, even within the context of these empirical studies it is quite appropriate to investigate the possibility that observed deviations from the hypothesized V (whether assumed constant or secularly declining) can be explained in terms of changes in the interest rate—provided the observed V is assumed to equal the

36. Fisher's discussion here is in terms of the "habits of the individual," the "systems of payments in the community," and "general causes"—by which he means "density of population" and "rapidity of transportation" (*ibid.*, p. 79).

37. Angell's detailed and systematic analysis of the velocity of circulation is almost entirely in terms of the timing and mechanics of the payment process. The passing references to interest on pp. 57–58 of the article and pp. 164–65 of the book do not change this basic picture. Note too the discussion of "idle balances" on pp. 140 ff. of the book, which is devoid of any reference to the interest rate.

38. Warburton's primary concern is with the secular trend in velocity, which he explains in terms of the mechanism of the payment process and a greater-than-unity income elasticity of demand for cash balances (1946, pp. 443–44); see also pp. 86–90 of his 1949 article cited in fn. 40 below.

39. Nearly half of the studies surveyed by Selden are by Angell and Warburton.

40. Thus see James W. Angell, *Investment and Business Cycles* (1941), chs. 6 and 9. Similarly, Warburton first deals with this influence in his reply to Tobin's criticism (from the viewpoint of Keynes' liquidity-preference theory) of his (Warburton's) earlier work; see Clark Warburton, "Monetary Velocity and Monetary Policy" (1948), pp. 304–14. It is against this background that one must also read Warburton's discussion of the rate of interest in his later "Secular Trend in Monetary Velocity" (1949), pp. 89–90.

desired *V*. In fact, this is what Warburton did in his later (1949) study, though he concluded that this possibility should be rejected.

In any event, it is significant that the first empirical study (to the best of my knowledge) which explicitly deals with the influence of interest on the demand for money is the 1939 Keynesian-inspired study by A. J. Brown on "Interest, Prices, and the Demand Schedule for Idle Money." [41] I might also add that this is the first such study which discusses a *functional relationship* between the demand for money and "the rate at which the general price-level has lately been changing." [42] This discussion can well be contrasted with Fisher's imprecise statement (1913, p. 63) that when money "is depreciating, holders will get rid of it as fast as possible." Furthermore, Fisher sees this as an unstable process which will cause a further rise in prices which will again increase *V* "and so on" (1913, p. 63). In my discussion of the Chicago quantity theorists (above, p. 248), I have already stressed the difference between this view and the stable relationship between the demand for money and rate of change of prices described by Friedman—and by Brown.

I have dwelt at length on the treatment of the rate of interest in Friedman's "reformulation" as compared with the actual writings of the quantity-theorists because this difference can be well defined and hence clearly observed in the literature. But I attach no less significance to other—and more subtle—differences, which also characterize Friedman's 1956 essay. Thus Friedman's presentation (1968, p. 440a) of the demand for money is first and foremost in terms of the demand for an asset; for him the income variable in the demand function is primarily "a surrogate for wealth, rather than [as in the quantity theory] a measure of the 'work' to be done by money." Correspondingly, as I have noted elsewhere (see note 3 above), Friedman is primarily concerned with the optimal relationship between the stock of money and the stocks of other assets, whereas the quantity theorists were primarily concerned with the relationship between the stock of money and the flow of spending on goods and services. Furthermore, their discussions of this relationship either did not make the distinction between stocks and flows—or at least were imprecise about it. Similarly, quantity theorists paid little, if any, attention to the effects on the rate of interest and other variables of shifts in tastes as to the form in which individuals wished to hold their assets. [43]

And now to our main point: all of the foregoing are precisely the differentia of Keynesian monetary theory as compared with the traditional quantity theory. They are the basic components of a theory of portfolio choice of which there are undoubtedly antecedents in the Cambridge cash-balance school (particularly as represented by Lavington) and before, but whose analytical structure as it now exists stems from the publication during the 1930s of Keynes' *Treatise on Money* (vol. 1, pp. 140–46),

41. As reprinted in T. Wilson and P. W. S. Andrews (eds.), *Oxford Studies in the Price Mechanism* (1951), pp. 31–51.

42. *Ibid.*, p. 34; unfortunately, Brown goes on to represent this rate by the absolute difference $p_t - p_{t-1}$, instead of the ratio of this difference to p_t (or p_{t-1}), where p_t represents the price level p at time t.

43. These differences also prevail between Friedman and the Chicago tradition; see above, pp. 248–49.

Hicks' "Suggestion for Simplifying the Theory of Money" (1935, pp. 13–32), and Keynes' *General Theory* (1936, pp. 166–72, 222–29). Subsequent valuable contributions to this analysis were made—during the 1940s and early 1950s—by, among others, H. Makower and J. Marschak (1938), Franco Modligliani (1944, especially pp. 190–201), R. F. Kahn (1954, especially pp. 236–43), Joan Robinson (1951), Harry Markowitz (1952, pp. 77–91), and James Tobin (1955, especially pp. 104–7). And in direct continuation of this intellectual line of descent, Milton Friedman provided us in 1956 with a most elegant and sophisticated statement of modern Keynesian monetary theory—misleadingly entitled "The Quantity Theory of Money—A Restatement." [44]

Actually, a careful reading of Friedman's encyclopedia article would seem to indicate that he has taken account of criticisms of his earlier exposition and that—at least in part—he himself now recognizes this intellectual indebtedness. Thus, first of all, he now describes (1968, p. 439b) his reformulation as one "that has been strongly influenced by the Keynesian analysis of liquidity preference." [45] Similarly, the term "liquidity"—which had been avoided in the 1956 essay—is now used. [46] Second, he admits (1968, p. 438b) that the Keynesian analysis of the demand for money lays "greater emphasis on current interest rates" than did the "earlier quantity theorists." Third, Friedman now recognizes (1968, p. 441b) that the "earlier quantity theory" envisaged the process of monetary adjustment in terms of the relation between the stock of money and the flow of expenditures—"to the almost complete exclusion" of the Keynesian approach, which envisages it in terms of the relation between the stock of money and other assets, particularly bonds. Furthermore, Friedman himself accepts (1968, pp. 441b–42a) as "plausible" the Keynesian approach that "any widespread disturbance in money balances . . . will initially be met by an attempted readjustment of assets and liabilities, through purchase and sale"—though he goes on to explain how the resulting change in prices will also "establish incentives to alter flows of receipts and expenditures." [47]

In view of all this, one can only regret that Friedman has persisted—even within the confines of an international encyclopedia—in presenting his exposition of the demand function for money as a "reformulation of the quantity theory."

44. For a somewhat more detailed account of this intellectual genealogy, see again the references cited in fn. 3 above.

45. Although Friedman refers to Johnson's 1962 *American Economic Review* survey article immediately after this statement, I think that it can safely be assumed to reflect his own view as well.

46. " . . . the services rendered by money relative to those rendered by other assets—in Keynesian terminology . . . liquidity proper" (Friedman, 1968, p. 460b).
Compare this with the corresponding passage on p. 14 of the 1956 essay, cited in fn. 7 above.

47. Though he does not refer to it at this point, Friedman's discussion here essentially summarizes the analysis presented in his and Meiselman's paper on "Relative Stability of Monetary Velocity and the Investment Multiplier in the United States, 1897–1958," (1963), pp. 217–22. In this analysis, Friedman and Meiselman distinguish their approach from the Keynesian one in terms of the range of assets involved in the monetary adjustment.

Appendix: The Empirical Evidence

I. The Writings[1]

The sources for the first four[2] summary-propositions at the beginning of Part II are as follows:

Henry C. Simons

> *A Positive Program for Laissez Faire* (1934). As reprinted in *Economic Policy for a Free Society* (1948), p. 64.
> "Rules versus Authorities in Monetary Policy" (1936). As reprinted in *Economic Policy for a Free Society* (1948). Pp. 164–66, 170–72, 326 (fn. 5), 331 (fn. 16).
> *Personal Income Taxation* (1938), p. 222.
> "Hansen on Fiscal Policy" (1942). As reprinted in *Economic Policy for a Free Society* (1948), p. 188.
> "Banking and Currency Reform" (1933), p. 3 and Appendix, p. 2.[3]

The passage from the Appendix to "Banking and Currency Reform" reads:

> But any general change in business earnings will affect promptly the speculative temper of the community. Larger profits breed optimism; they stimulate investment and induce dishoarding (reduction of idle cash reserves). Producers will become more anxious to borrow for purposes of increasing inventories, expanding production, and increasing plant capacity. Lenders will have fewer misgivings about the ability of borrowers to repay. People generally will increase their lending and investment at the expense of their idle reserves of cash. In a word, the velocity of circulation will increase. But this change, in turn, means a larger volume of business and higher product-prices, and thus still larger earnings. The further increase of earnings, moreover, will induce further increase in the velocity of money. And so on and on, until the initially sticky prices which govern costs do finally move upward markedly and rapidly—or until some fortuitous disturbance (perhaps a mere speculative scare) happens to establish a sharp reversal of the trend in product prices. On the other hand, once earnings

1. See fns. 8 and 10 on p. 245 above.
2. I have not provided specific sources for Proposition (5)—which does not really bear on the issue at hand, and which has been included in the text only for the sake of completeness. {Documentation for this proposition is, however, provided in ch. 12 below (pp. 302–3).}
3. "Banking and Currency Reform" is an unpublished and unsigned memorandum dated by Aaron Director as November 1933 and ascribed by him largely to Simons; see the Bibliography in Simons (1948), p. 313. See also Friedman (1967), p. 2, fn. 1 and Reeve (1943), p. 317, fn. 45. (I am greatly indebted to Friedman and Director for providing me with a copy of this memorandum.)

Actually, the date which appears at the end of the memorandum (p. 15) is "November 17, 1953"; this is clearly an error.

Friedman (1967, p. 2, fn. 1) describes the Appendix to the memorandum as a "partial exception to the statement that Simons nowhere set forth a consistent statement of his theory." However, except for its explicit relating of velocity to business earnings (see the passage which follows immediately) the theoretical presentation of the Appendix to this memorandum seems to me to be no more detailed or systematic than Simons' other writings.

begin to decline, forces will be set in motion to continue and accelerate the trend—and perhaps with more striking results, for the crucial, sticky prices are peculiarly resistant to downward pressure.

The passages from Simons' writings referred to in fns. 9, 12, and 13 above are as follows:

Once a deflation has gotten under way, in a large modern economy, there is no significant limit which the decline of prices and employment cannot exceed, if the central government fails to use its fiscal powers generously and deliberately to stop that decline. Only great government deficits can check the hoarding of lawful money and the destruction of money substitutes once a general movement has gotten under way. [*Personal Income Taxation*, 1938, p. 222.]

The bottom of an uncontrolled deflation, for all practical purposes, is nonexistent—with adverse expectations causing price declines and with the actual declines aggravating expectations, etc. ["Hansen on Fiscal Policy," 1942, p. 188.]

With all its merits, however, this rule [of holding the quantity of money constant] cannot now be recommended as a basis for monetary reform. The obvious weakness of fixed quantity, as a sole rule of monetary policy, lies in the danger of sharp changes on the velocity side, for no monetary system can function effectively or survive politically in the face of extreme alternations of hoarding and dishoarding. It is easy to argue that something would be gained in any event if perverse changes were prevented merely as to quantity, but the argument is unconvincing. The fixing of the quantity of circulation media might merely serve to increase the perverse variability in the amounts of "near moneys" and in the degree of their general acceptability, just as the restrictions on the issue of bank notes presumably served to hasten the development of deposit (checking-account) banking. ["Rules versus Authorities in Monetary Policy," 1936, p. 164.]

Lloyd W. Mints
   A History of Banking Theory (1945), pp. 218–22.
   "Monetary Policy" (1946), especially pp. 61, 63, 67.
   Monetary Policy for a Competitive Society (1950). Ch. 3 (especially pp. 29, 32–35, 39–41, 48–49, 69–70), ch. 6 (especially pp. 120–22, 138–42), and ch. 9 (especially pp. 194, 202–3, 207, 210–11, 227).

Frank H. Knight
   "Economics" (1951). As reprinted in *On the History and Method of Economics* (1956), pp. 15, 30.
   "The Business Cycle, Interest, and Money: A Methodological Approach" (1941). As reprinted in *On The History and Method of Economics* (1956), pp. 210–11, 213, 223–24.

Preface to 1948 reprint of *Risk, Uncertainty and Profit*, pp. xlii–xlv.

The passages from Knight referred to in footnotes 12 and 21 are as follows:

. . . in the case of money, just what does set a boundary to a movement of general prices in either direction, and especially the downward movement, becomes something of a mystery. [''The Business Cycle, Interest, and Money,'' 1941, p. 211.]

Up to a point, socialist critics have been right in regarding cycles and depressions as an inherent feature of ''capitalism.'' Such a system must use money, and the circulation of money is not a phenomenon which naturally tends to establish and maintain an equilibrium level. Its equilibrium is vague and highly unstable. Its natural tendency is to oscillate over a fairly long period and wide range, between limits which are rather indeterminate. [*Ibid.*, p. 224.]

My chief ground for disagreement with the Keynesian theory of money is the belief that in view of these facts, [viz., the instability of V]—some, or most, or all of them well recognized by Keynes as well as others—supply and demand curves for ''liquidity'' have no solid foundation and are not a sound basis for action but are ''theoretical'' in the bad and misleading sense. [*Risk, Uncertainty and Profit*, 1948, p. xlv.]

It might be noted that in his discussion of Keynes' theory of liquidity preference in his 1941 article, Knight readily recognizes that the rate of interest ''must equalize the attractiveness of bonds and of money for holding'' (p. 221), and earlier in this article he also describes the holding of money as an alternative to the holding of other assets (p. 210). Knight does not, however, take this dependence of the demand for money on the rate of interest into account in his discussion of variations in the velocity of circulation during the course of the business cycle—despite his discussion of the cyclical changes in the rate of interest (pp. 219–20).[4] All that is discussed in this context is the influence of price expectations.

Jacob Viner[5]
> *Studies in the Theory of International Trade* (1937), pp. 40–45, 131, *et passim.*
> ''Schumpeter's *History of Economic Analysis*'' (1954). As reprinted in *The Long View and the Short* (1958), 365.

---

4. On p. 223, Knight does refer to high ''liquidity preference'' and low interest rates in depressions; but he does not refer to a causal relationship between these two phenomena (i.e., to a movement along a demand curve for money), and instead presents them as parallel consequences of the same cause—namely, the depression.

5. For methodological reasons, I have restricted myself to writings of the period in question (1930–50)—or at least not too long afterward; hence I have not taken account of Viner's 1962 article on monetary policy cited above in note 5 of the text.

"International Aspects of the Gold Standard" (1932). As reprinted in *International Economics* (1951), pp. 137–40.

The discussion on pp. 40–45 of the *Studies* shows that Viner thought of the quantity theory as specifying a causal relationship between the quantity of money and its value. The effect of anticipations of price increases in increasing the velocity of circulation is indicated on p. 131.

The passage from Viner's review of Schumpeter is an instance in which it would have been most appropriate for Viner to have indicated (if he had so believed) that the quantity theory specified not the constancy of the velocity of circulation, but the constancy of the functional relationship between this velocity and the variables that determine it. Instead, he merely emphasizes that exponents of the quantity theory

would not find variability of velocity disturbing for their theory, provided the variations in velocity were not inverse to those in quantity—or, perhaps, even if they were, provided the amplitude of variation of velocity was less than that of quantity.

It is also interesting to note that Viner goes on in this passage to say that

the quantity theory of money [can be] understood as holding only: (1) that an authority powerful enough to make the quantity of money what it pleases can so regulate that quantity as to make the price level approximate to what it pleases, and (2) that the possibility of existence of such power is not inconceivable *a priori*.

The foregoing writings thus reflect Viner's agreement with Proposition (1) in the text as well as his rejection of the constancy of V. At the same time, Viner did not develop the inconstancy of V into the cyclical theory presented by Proposition (2).

I might also note that in his 1932 Harris Foundation lecture on the gold standard Viner discussed the problem of price stablization in the following terms:

A country on the gold standard binds itself to all the vagaries of gold as a standard of value. . . . A standard of value fluctuating erratically in its own value must be an important factor in initiating and in accentuating the recurrent cycles of expansion and depression from which the modern world has suffered. [pp. 137–38.]

He then went on to

express [the] individual view [that] we know too little as yet of the possibilities of [price] stabilization to take immediately any major steps in that direction. [pp. 138–39.]

What Viner did, however, advocate was "continuous experimentation . . . with the possibilities of stabilization . . . in the hope that something can still be made of the gold standard" (p. 139).

II. The Lectures[6]

The only relevant passage I have been able to find in my notes from Simons' lectures are from his course on "Economics of Fiscal Policy." This passage reads:

Only thing that has stopped deflationary movement is that government begins to get insolvent too. (Fears that cheap money really would set in.) So inevitably get government deficit which works to stop deflation. No automatic recovery—nothing in system to bring this about. This Simons' theory of business cycles: deflation [continues] until government action. No stability in economy—so that's why have fluctuations to begin with.

Should we obtain deficits by (1) revenue changes or (2) spending changes? Simons in favor of (1). [Classnotes, Econ. 361, Apr. 20, 1945.]

My lecture notes from Mints' courses contain the following additional relevant passage, taken from his discussion of the Cambridge cash-balance approach:

In modern theory, demand for money said to have unitary elasticity. Assume that V and T constant. Then P changes directly proportionate with M. [Real] value of total money remains the same. [A diagram of a rectangular hyperbola appears at this point].

Some have said on basis of postwar I experience that η for money $\neq 1$. E.g., total quantity of money increased 10 times, while goods that could be purchased with this [i.e., a unit of money] decreased 1/15 (?). But in this case have been changes in V and T—contrary to our assumptions. So assume that has been shift from one demand curve to another (also with $\eta = 1$) according as V and T change. [More diagrams follow here]. [Classnotes, Econ. 330, June 30, 1944.]

Mints concluded his course on "Money" with a discussion of policy, in which (among other things) he stated:

If [government] stabilizes price level, will stabilize aggregate demand and thus prevent unemployment. Inconceivable that federal government couldn't so increase cash balances of public that it wouldn't want to purchase goods. [Classnotes, Econ. 330, Aug. 11, 1944.]

Most of Mints' discussions of policy matters were, however, contained in his course on "Banking Theory and Monetary Policy" (Economics 331). The material presented here closely paralleled the corresponding discussions in his books on *A History of Banking Theory* (1945) and *Monetary Policy for a Competitive Society* (1950).

There is nothing of relevance in my lecture notes from Viner's courses (economic theory, international trade). In my notes from Knight's lectures on economic theory there is a passage that repeats the analysis of his article on "The Business Cycle, Interest, and Money: A Methodological Approach" which had appeared a few years before (see Appendix I). Indeed, the notes refer explicitly to this article and read:

(cont. on p. 264)

6. See Part III above.

III. Doctoral Theses on Monetary Problems Submitted to The University

Author	Title of thesis
Ernest R. Shaw	The Investment and Secondary Reserve Policy of Commercial Banks
Francis A. Linville	Central Bank Cooperation
Benjamin F. Brooks	A History of Banking Theory in the United States Before 1860
Martin Bronfenbrenner	Monetary Theory and General Equilibrium
Joseph E. Reeve	Monetary Proposals for Curing the Depression in the United States, 1929–1935
George Leland Bach	Price Level Stabilization: Some Theoretical and Practical Considerations
Mrs. Marion R. Daugherty	The Currency School-Banking School Controversy
Benjamin Caplan	The Wicksellian School—A Critical Study of the Development of Swedish Monetary Theory, 1898–1932
Arthur I. Bloomfield	International Capital Movements and the American Balance of Payments, 1929–1940
R. Craig McIvor	Monetary Expansion in Canadian War Finance, 1939–1945
Don Patinkin	On the Inconsistency of Economic Models: A Theory of Involuntary Unemployment
William W. Tongue	Money, Capital and the Business Cycle
Roland N. McKean	Fluctuations in Our Private Claim-Debt Structure and Monetary Policy
Joel W. Harper	Scrip and Other Forms of Local Money
Raymond H. McEvoy	The Effects of Federal Reserve Operations, 1929–1936

of Chicago: 1930–1950

Thesis committee[7]	Date of submission
L. D. Edie,* S. P. Meech, L. W. Mints	1930
H. D. Gideonse (?), L. W. Mints, J. Viner	1937
F. H. Knight, L. W. Mints,* J. Viner	1939
F. H. Knight, L. W. Mints, H. Schultz,* J. Viner	1939
G. V. Cox, L. W. Mints,* J. Viner	1939
L. W. Mints, H. C. Simons, J. Viner	1940
G. V. Cox, L. W. Mints, J. Viner*	1941
O. Lange, H. C. Simons, J. Viner	1942
O. Lange, L. W. Mints, J. Viner*	1942
R. Blough,* J. K. Langum, L. W. Mints	1947
P. Douglas, H. G. Lewis, J. Marschak,* T. Yntema	1947
O. Lange (?), H. G. Lewis, F. H. Knight, L. W. Mints*	1947
A. Director, E. J. Hamilton, L. A. Metzler, L. W. Mints*	1948
S. E. Leland,* L. W. Mints, H. C. Simons (?)	1948
E. J. Hamilton, L. A. Metzler, L. W. Mints*	1950

7. Where known, the committee chairman is designated by an asterisk attached to his name.

Keynesian economics. The older viewpoint assumed ideal neutral money: money only an intermediary, so really have barter [economy]. Say's law—*loi des debouchés*. Under ideal competition [conditions?] wouldn't have any money used as medium of exchange—just as unit of account.

Keynes didn't do anything not adumbrated in previous writings. Instead of saying: "Every supply of goods a demand for other goods"—said: "Every supply of goods a demand for money." [Keynes] hypostatizes money under name "liquidity preference." People want money as such—for its own sake—not as immediate purchasing power.

Knight says demand for money highly speculative—especially in investors' market and even in consumers' market. If consider changes in prices relative to changes in interest rate—former much greater than latter. So if foresee rising prices will borrow money to buy goods; and when foresee lower prices will hurry to sell now. And the anticipation itself will create the price change—and this is cumulative. "Every speculation on the future value of goods is a speculation on the future value of money." Essential fact in slump is just that. In a boom everybody begins to realize that prices are really too high—overcapitalization. All changes in the value of money tend to be cumulative—an unstable equilibrium.

In wheat futures markets have same thing—anticipation creates changes. But there, there is an equilibrium dependent on well-known objective facts. So damped oscillations. But no definite known equilibrium value of money. Everyone might know that [value of] money is too high—but question is whether it will continue to rise—don't know where the breaking point is.

Knight doesn't know how to stabilize price level—and at what height to stabilize it. [Classnotes, Econ. 301, July 24, 1945.]

I cannot resist citing in addition the following typical Knightian remark, which occurred at a later point:

In medieval times [men] didn't look for remedies since thought everything from God who was good—so everything good. Now science is the God—and we think that must be remedy for every disease. Maybe there is no answer to the business cycle: [maybe] have to let it take its course. [Classnotes, Econ. 301, July 26, 1945.]

Postscript

(i) Further Comment on Friedman

Friedman's reaction to the article reprinted in this chapter has been ambivalent. Thus in his concluding comments in a subsequent symposium in which I also participated (Patinkin 1972), Friedman (1972, p. 941) refers at one point to the article and states that "Patinkin has made a real contribution to the history of thought by examining and presenting the detailed theoretical teachings of Simons and Mints, and I have little quarrel with his presentation.'' Now, the correct presentation of these "theoretical teachings" is precisely the major purpose of the foregoing article; it is accordingly puzzling that at other points in his concluding comments Friedman (1972, pp. 907 and 930–33) alleges that my article gives a "misleading," if not "highly misleading," impression of the Chicago tradition. Furthermore, and more important, the evidence with which Friedman attempts to support this allegation is irrelevant. For this evidence consists primarily of the detailed documentation (*ibid.*, pp. 939–40) of a point which was never in question, and which is indeed subsumed under my Propositions 4 and 5 above: namely, the fact that in the early 1930s Jacob Viner advocated a highly activist central-bank and fiscal policy as the means of dealing with unemployment. More generally, Friedman's implications to the contrary notwithstanding, his description of the Chicago policy position (*ibid.*, pp. 936–41) is basically the same as the one summarized on p. 246 above.

(ii) Correspondence with Jacob Viner

In November 1968 I sent a draft of the preceding paper to Frank Knight, Lloyd Mints, and Jacob Viner, respectively, with a request for comments. Mints did not reply. From Knight I received a brief though warm note (dated March 19, 1969) declining comment, and adding: ". . . to be frank, I'm very definitely 'retired' from economics—in fact from any serious 'work,' beyond fairly light reading'' (see above, p. 44, fn. 25). From Viner, I at first did not hear; but some months later, after sending him a reprint of the published article, I received a long letter which led to the following correspondence (all of which was typewritten). This correspondence is reproduced here with the kind permission of the late Mrs. Jacob Viner. Some explanatory footnotes have been added:

Princeton, November 24, 1969.

Dear Patinkin,

Many thanks for the copy of your article on "The Chicago Tradition." Perhaps I should apologize for not acknowledging receipt of your earlier draft. If so, here goes. Physical circumstances oblige me to ration strictly expenditure of energy even on correspondence. The issue you raised was one that I never was interested in, nor even knew much about, nor could contribute anything really significant to, from either my fallible memory or my disordered records.

At Chicago, from late in 1929 to early 1933 I was, for me, fairly deeply engaged in policy promotion, but that is not what your piece is about. In this area, both my memory and my records indicate that the Department was in practically perfect accord. As far as my teaching at Chicago was concerned, as the Department operated throughout my membership in it, graduate courses were as narrowly specialized as the members chose to make them. I chose to exclude from my courses consideration of monetary-fiscal doctrine, of business cycles, of what we now call "economic development," except as such consideration was unavoidable when I was dealing with the early history of international trade theorizing. I fear I even excluded them from my thinking. Such specialization as I practised I would have regarded then—as I do even more so now—as foolish or even immoral if practised on undergraduates, or in contacts with the lay world, but I neither taught undergraduates nor wrote textbooks. What went on in other courses than my own I neither knew nor sought to know.

It was not until after I left Chicago in 1946 that I began to hear rumors about a "Chicago School" which was engaged in *organized* battle for laissez faire and "quantity theory of money" and against "imperfect competition" theorizing and "Keynsianism." I remained sceptical about this until I attended a conference sponsored by University of Chicago professors in 1951. The invited participants were a varied lot of academics, bureaucrats, businessmen, etc., but the program for discussion, the selection of chairmen, and everything about the conference except the unscheduled statements and protests from individual participants were so patently rigidly structured, so loaded, that I got more amusement from the conference than from any other I ever attended. Even the source of the financing of the Conference, as I found out later, was ideologically loaded. There is a published account of the proceedings of the Conference,[a] but it does not include the program, etc. as presented to the participants to direct their discussion. From then on, I was willing to consider the existence of a "Chicago School" (but one not confined to the economics department and not embracing all of the department) and that this "School" had been in operation, and had won many able disciples, for years before I left Chicago. But at no time was I consciously a member of it, and it is my vague impression that if there was such a school it did not regard me as a member, or at least as a loyal and qualified member. In any case, I am not well-informed about the past or the present of such a "school," and therefore I have had nothing to contribute to the recent inquirers about the intellectual history of this putative "school."

Whatever may be the proper evaluation of my outside-the-battle record in this respect, it did quite probably contribute substantially to the fact, whose memory I cherish deeply, that in my thirty years at Chicago my personal relations with my economist colleagues were on my part, and as far as I know mutually, uninterruptedly marked by mutual affection and respect.

With best wishes,
Cordially yours,
[signed] Jacob Viner

Jerusalem, December 21, 1969

Dear Viner:

I greatly appreciate your taking the time and energy to write me your recollections of the "Chicago School."

Your letter is indeed most interesting. I might also add that since writing the

---

a. This is presumably a reference to *Defense, Controls, and Inflation: A Conference Sponsored by The University of Chicago Law School*, ed. Aaron Director, Chicago, 1952. This contains the proceedings of a conference that took place in 1951 and included Viner among its participants (*ibid.*, p.x).

article, I came across your paper in the volume edited by Leland Yeager, *In Search of a Monetary Institution*—which also makes your position on the "Chicago School" quite clear.

It may be that I shall be reprinting my article in a collection of essays that I am planning to put out.[b] In this connection, I would like very much to be able to add a footnote citing various passages from your letter, in order to present your view of the "school" and your relationship to it. I would greatly appreciate it if you could let me know if you agree to this.

Sincerely yours,
[signed] Don Patinkin

Princeton, January 15, 1970.

Dear Patinkin,

I dislike being difficult, but I have misgivings as to authorizing quotations from my letter which in the context which you may put them could seem to assert or suggest that as an individual or in concert with others at Chicago or elsewhere I was a participant in controversy against what I ever consciously regarded or publicly or privately labelled as existentially a "Chicago school." I am perfectly happy to have my past views on monetary theory on record. But I don't trust my unaided memory and my manuscript papers are at present not in completely chronological arrangement. Perhaps I can best comply with your wishes if you let me see in advance what references you propose to make to my letter.

Except for Knight, I don't think your bibliography touches anything pre–1933. But "money", of course, was referred to in courses at Chicago (including the business school) before 1933. In your article, I miss references to Angell as (for a year, I think) teaching assistant—for me—and perhaps also as graduate student at Chicago, with the possibility, therefore, of "Chicago" influence on him or of his influence on Chicago. Carl Snyder participated in at least one conference on monetary policy at Chicago,[c] and I still remember the inside information he gave us (in 1931?) on the issues and the facts as to "money" supply as seen at the Federal Reserve Bank of New York—facts which clash with those postulated for the period by Friedman. You should also look at '*A Memorandum Presented To A Member Of The House Committee On Military Affairs, April 26, 1932*' (mimeographed) which was wholly on monetary and fiscal policy. The signatures will, I think, interest you: Cox, Director, Douglas, Gideonse, Knight, Millis, Mints, Schultz (Henry), Simons, Viner, [Chester] Wright, Yntema.

I gather that the concept of 'liquidity' is for you a key concept in distinguishing schools of monetary theory. I don't know the history of the *term* and I

b. Ultimately published as *Studies in Monetary Economics*, New York, 1972.

c. This is presumably a reference to the Harris Foundation Lectures of 1932, in which both Snyder and Viner participated; see Harris Memorial Foundation, *Gold and Monetary Stabilization*, ed. Q. Wright (Chicago, 1932), p. 166.

have what is undoubtedly only a very sketchy notion of the history of the *idea*. I don't know whether I have ever used the term in print, but my concern with the idea goes back to my undergraduate days in Montreal. I then constituted the accounting staff of a small manufacturing concern and handled its credit relations with its bank. (Incidentally, bank rates of interest in Canada were invariable, and negotiations with banks related only to the size of the "line of credit"). From that time on I was conditioned to regard all macro-statistics of 'money' I might encounter as "promiscuous aggregates". When I came back to Chicago in 1919, I was strengthened in this by my colleague, J. O. McKinsey, who talked and wrote from a very realistic managerial point of view on the importance of "cash budgeting", and, in effect, on the importance of "liquidity", to a business firm. When I went to the Treasury in 1934 I encountered Lauchlin Currie and found we shared some views in common on the complex nature of, in effect, "liquidity". Later, when he left the Treasury for the Federal Reserve Board he followed a suggestion of mine on the accumulation of statistical data relating to the effect of the financial activities of government on the "liquidity" of the economy. I am sure that in my correspondence files there is material relevant to all this,[d] and also that he then published some of his findings.

As further bits of evidence relating to my own monetary notions, I enclose (1) a Xerox of a page from the original of my contribution to the Wieser Festschrift (*Die Wirtschaftstheorie der Gegenwart,* Vienna, 1928, vol. iv), (this page has never appeared in print in its English version); (2) a recent letter of mine to the *New York Times,* which relates to some activity of mine some fifteen years or so ago whose circumstances I still appear to be bound to keep confidential. The present relevance of these items, I take it, is to the imprecision of the concept of "money," as used in current and ancient theorizing and in all statistical series I know about, as potentially a simple statistical quantity.

I have turned over all my books to the Princeton University Library, but some day in the near future I hope to go to the Library to explore what Patinkin and Keynes mean by "money" and "liquidity" and how, *if at all,* they construct their own promiscuous aggregates to represent them quantitatively.
Sincerely yours,
[signed] Jacob Viner

The following are, respectively, (1) the page from the Wieser *festschrift* and (2) the letter to *The New York Times* which Viner enclosed with his letter:

(1) It would be regrettable if the foreign reader were to get the impression that there is on all of these questions a perfect unanimity of opinion among American economists. Some American economists have been hostile to this mode of explanation of the mechanism of adjustment of international balances, because it seems to involve acceptance of the quantity theory of the value of money. But

d. There is indeed a voluminous correspondence with Currie in The Jacob Viner Papers at Princeton University Library; I am indebted to Shlomo Maital for this information.

although the classical economists did expound the theory of international trade in terms of a rigid quantity theory of money, the modern American expositions of the theory of international trade make little or no appeal to the quantity theory of money. They merely take for granted, on *a priori* grounds, or they demonstrate inductively, that price levels do tend to reflect in some degree changes in the stock of gold. They grant freely that by deliberate banking policy, or as the result of cyclical variations in business conditions, the influence of gold movements on price levels may for a time be neutralized by counter-movements in the volume of bank deposits and bank-note circulation, or in the rapidity of circulation of money, and that the influence of gold movements on price levels can be clearly traced only if proper allowance is previously made for the influence on price levels of changes in banking policy, banking methods, or business conditions other than those which are themselves the results of the gold movements.

(2) Bank Commitments [e]

To the Editor:

Officers of the Federal Reserve System are complaining that the American banking system is making too slow and too small a contribution to the fight against inflation. Some American bankers are saying that their hands are tied by outstanding ''commitments to lend'' which their customers are currently calling upon them to meet.

If this is true, it is important, and information as to the extent of and behavior through time of such aggregate commitments could conceivably be of considerable value both to the monetary authorities and to the professional and academic interpreters in terms of the state of the national economy. But no public source exists today where statistics as to commitments to lend are obtainable.

Some years ago, the staff of the Board of Governors of the Federal Reserve System did attempt a spot survey of the commitment-to-lend situation in the New York money market, including total commitments per bank and total receipts per bank from fees charged for the commitments.

Since, however the inquiry was on a strictly voluntary basis and many banks were noncooperative, the results were inconclusive except as to the one fact that commitments to lend were not an unusual phenomenon in the New York money market. Presumably for this reason, the report containing the results of the inquiry never emerged from the printers'-proof stage.

Today an inquiry of the same sort would not need to be on so purely voluntary a basis. Even if each bank were required only to report on a periodic basis its receipts from commitment fees, and if the Federal Reserve were to make public only its summation by regions of the amounts of such receipts, this of itself would serve to provide a good statistical basis for estimating the aggregate size and behavior through time of outstanding commitments.

Banks of course have obligations to their customers extending beyond their

e. Appeared with this caption in Letters to the Editor in *The New York Times* of July 6, 1969.

commitments to lend and their deposit liabilities, such as agreed-upon "lines of credit" and tacit understandings that the "needs" of their customers for loans will be reasonably taken care of. As compared to commitments, however, lines of credit and tacit understandings, dollar for dollar and probably also over-all, have much less power to "tie the hands" of bankers who wish to cooperate with the efforts of monetary authorities to check inflation by checking the expansion of credit.

For instance, lines of credit and tacit understandings are less susceptible to legal enforcement, are more subject to elastic interpretation at the discretion of the banker, and are ordinarily applicable in the absence of renewal for shorter periods of time. Jacob Viner

Princeton, N.J., June 28, 1969

Jerusalem, February 9, 1970

Dear Viner:

Thank you very much for your letter of January 15, and the additional information which it contains.

I can well understand your interest in seeing whatever quotation I may from your earlier letter. I am, therefore, enclosing Footnote 13 of my paper with the additional paragraph, which I would now like to add.[f]

Also enclosed is a revised version of Footnote 5,[g] in which I refer to the article you wrote, edited by Yeager, and which is referred to in Footnote 13.

I would greatly appreciate hearing from you as to whether you agree to letting me quote you in this manner.

Thank you once again for your interest and help.

Sincerely yours,
[signed] Don

Princeton, Feb. 23, 1970.

Dear Patinkin,

I have no comment to make on your note 5.

In your note 13, you say: "For Viner, I have been able to find evidence only on the first proposition. It should, however, be noted that he did not take a position on the policy of price stabilization, . . ."

I am not at all sure that I know what you are attributing, or denying, to me here. I feel fairly confident, however, that what you say is not confirmed by the items of mine to which J. R. Davis [1968] refers and by the following items to which he does not refer:

---

f. As a result of subsequent changes, this paragraph did not appear in fn. 13 (which corresponds to fn. 8 on p. 245 above) of the reprinted article, but at the end of Appendix I there (*Studies in Monetary Economics* (1972), p. 113). The paragraph cited three sentences from the third paragraph of Viner's first letter to me; since this letter has been reproduced here in its entirety, this paragraph has not been included in Appendix I above.

g. This version more or less coincided with fn. 5 on p. 242 above.

Review of P. W. Martin, *The Problem of Maintaining Purchasing Power*, 1931, *J.P.E.*, June, 1932, pp. 418–419.

"International Aspects of the Gold Standard," in Harris Foundation Lectures, *Gold and Monetary Stabilization*, Chicago, 1932, reprinted in my *International Economics, Studies*, Free Press, Glencoe Ill., pp. 123–140.

I expressly indicated in one or more of these items, that I did not regard velocity as stable, and I hope I never said or implied that I did not accept price-level stabilization as in the long run *an* appropriate and major objective.

Your quotation from my letter is O.K. But could you add that the emphasis on "organized" was in the original letter, (if it was)?

I trust that my comments will not cause you any trouble.

With best wishes,
Sincerely yours,
[signed] Jacob Viner

As a result of this letter, I added the references to Viner's Harris Foundation Lectures at the end of Appendix I above. For some reason, however, I did not add any reference to Viner's review of Martin's book. The most relevant passages here are the following:

Mr. Martin criticizes at some length the doctrine expounded by many of the classical economists, and especially by J. B. Say, that since goods themselves constitute the demand for goods, general overproduction is impossible. He uses general overproduction to mean either (1) output or (2) capacity for production in excess of the amounts which the available amounts of purchasing power can absorb at remunerative prices. No one who had lived through any period of widespread business depression and unemployment could possibly have denied the existence of "general overproduction" when so defined. . . .

In the author's own account there is perhaps undue emphasis on the significance for control of manipulation of the volume of purchasing power. There is ground for maintaining that, given the prejudices and the obsessions of statesmen, bankers, and economists, the problem of unemployment is as much a problem of regulating wage rates, interest rates, rents, and the prices of monopoly commodities as one of regulating the amount of purchasing power. For a single country under the gold standard and suffering from severe unemployment, deflation of monopoly prices and of money costs may be the only way out. And for unemployment due to maladjustments in relative prices rather than to falling price levels as a whole, an artificially stimulated expansion of purchasing power may accentuate instead of remedy the evil if the elements which had superior price-bargaining power before the inflation still retain it under the inflation and employ it to intensify the non-equilibrium divergences in relative prices. In any case, both the purchasing power and the price sides of the picture call for analysis, whereas only one side receives it here. But this book embodies an important contribution, of whose timeliness and thought-provoking quality there can be no question.

Bibliography*

J. W. Angell. "Money, Prices and Production: Some Fundamental Concepts." *Quarterly Journal of Economics*, Nov. 1933, *48*, 39–76.

———. *The Behavior of Money*. New York, 1936.

———. *Investment and Business Cycles*. New York, 1941.

M. Bronfenbrenner. "Observations on the 'Chicago School(s).' " *Journal of Political Economy*, Feb. 1962, *70*, 72–75.

A. J. Brown. "Interest, Prices, and the Demand Schedule for Idle Money." *Oxford Economic Papers*, May 1939, *2*, 46–69. Reprinted in *Oxford Studies in the Price Mechanism*, ed. T. Wilson and P. W. S. Andrews. Oxford, 1951. Pp. 31–51.

J. R. Davis. "Chicago Economists, Deficit Budgets, and the Early 1930's." *American Economic Review*, June 1968, *58*, 476–82.

†A. Director, ed. *Defense, Controls, and Inflation: A Conference Sponsored by The University of Chicago Law School*. Chicago, 1952.

I. Fisher. *The Rate of Interest*. New York, 1907.

———. *The Purchasing Power of Money*, rev. ed. New York, 1913 (reprinted New York, 1963).

———. *The Theory of Interest* (1930). New York, 1954.

M. Friedman. "The Quantity Theory of Money—A Restatement." In *Studies in the Quantity Theory of Money*, ed. M. Friedman. Chicago, 1956. Pp. 3–21.

———. *A Program for Monetary Stability*. New York, 1960.

———. "The Monetary Theory and Policy of Henry Simons." *Journal of Law and Economics*, Oct. 1967, *10*, 1–13.

———. "Money: Quantity Theory." In *International Encyclopedia of the Social Sciences*. New York, 1968. Vol. 10, pp. 432–47.

†———. "Comments on the Critics." *Journal of Political Economy*, Sept./Oct. 1972, *80*, 906–50.

——— and D. Meiselman. "The Relative Stability of Monetary Velocity and the Investment Multiplier in the United States, 1897–1958." In *Stabilization Policies* (Commission on Money and Credit). Englewood Cliffs, N.J., 1963.

†Harris Memorial Foundation. *Gold and Monetary Stabilization*, ed. Q. Wright. Chicago, 1932.

J. R. Hicks. "A Suggestion for Simplifying the Theory of Money." *Economica*, Feb. 1935, *2*, 1–19. Reprinted in *Readings in Monetary Theory*, ed., F. A. Lutz and L. W. Mints. Philadelphia, 1951. Pp. 13–32.

H. G. Johnson. "Monetary Theory and Policy." *American Economic Review*, June 1962, *52*, 335–84.

R. F. Kahn. "Some Notes on Liquidity Preference." *The Manchester School*, Sept. 1954, *22*, 229–57.

J. M. Keynes. *A Treatise on Money*. London, 1930.

———. *The General Theory of Employment, Interest and Money*. New York, 1936.

L. R. Klein. "The Use of Econometric Models as a Guide to Economic Policy." *Econometrica*, Apr. 1947, *15*, 111–51.

*References in text to works listed here as reprinted are to the date of original publication; the page references, however, follow the pagination of the reprinted form.

Items marked with a dagger appear only in Postscript.

————. *Ecomonic Fluctuations in the United States*, 1921–41. New York, 1950 (Cowles Commission Monograph No. 11).

F. H. Knight. "The Business Cycle, Interest, and Money: A Methodological Approach." *Review of Economic Statistics*, May 1941, *23*, 53–67. Reprinted in *On the History and Method of Economics*. Chicago, 1956. Pp. 202–26.

————. "Economics." *Encyclopedia Britannica*, 1951. Reprinted in *On the History and Method of Economics*. Chicago, 1956. Pp. 3–33.

————. *On the History and Method of Economics*. Chicago, 1956.

————. *Risk, Uncertainty and Profit*. New York, 1948 (reprinted New York, 1957).

H. Makower and J. Marschak. "Assets, Prices and Monetary Theory." *Economica*, Aug. 1938, *5*, 261–88. Reprinted in *Readings in Price Theory*, ed. G. J. Stigler and K. E. Boulding, Chicago, 1952. Pp. 283–310.

H. Markowitz. "Portfolio Selection." *Journal of Finance*, Mar. 1952, *7*, 77–91.

L. W. Mints. *A History of Banking Theory*. Chicago, 1945.

————. "Monetary Policy." *Review of Economic Statistics*, May 1946, *28*, 60–69.

————. *Monetary Policy for a Competitive Society*. New York, 1950.

F. Modigliani. "Liquidity Preference and the Theory of Interest and Money." *Econometrica*, Jan. 1944, *12*, 45–88. Reprinted in *Readings in Monetary Theory*, ed. F. A. Lutz and L. W. Mints. Philadelphia, 1951. Pp. 186–239.

D. Patinkin. "An Indirect-Utility Approach to the Theory of Money, Assets, and Savings." In *The Theory of Interest Rates*, ed. F. H. Hahn and F. P. R. Breckling. London, 1965. Pp. 52–79. (a)

————. *Money, Interest, and Prices*, 2nd ed. New York, 1965. (b)

————. "Interest." In *International Encyclopedia of the Social Sciences*. New York, 1968. Vol. 7. Pp. 471–85.

†————. "Friedman on the Quantity Theory and Keynesian Economics." *Journal of Political Economy*, Sept./Oct. 1972, *80*, 883–905.

†————. *Studies in Monetary Economics*. New York, 1972.

J. E. Reeve. *Monetary Reform Movements*. Washington, D.C., 1943.

J. Robinson. "The Rate of Interest." *Econometrica*, Apr. 1951, *19*, 92–111.

R. T. Selden. "Monetary Velocity in the United States." In *Studies in the Quantity Theory of Money*, ed. M. Friedman. Chicago, 1956. Pp. 179–257.

H. C. Simons. *Personal Income Taxation*. Chicago, 1938.

————. *A Positive Program for Laissez Faire*. Public Policy Pamphlet No. 15, ed. Harry D. Gideonse. Chicago, 1934. Reprinted in Simons (1948), pp. 40–77.

————. "Rules versus Authorities in Monetary Policy." *Journal of Political Economy*, Feb. 1936, *44*, 1–30. Reprinted in Simons (1948), pp. 160–83.

————. "Hansen on Fiscal Policy." *Journal of Political Economy*, Apr. 1942, *50*, 161–96. Reprinted in Simons (1948), pp. 184–219.

————. *Economic Policy for a Free Society*. Chicago, 1948.

C. Snyder. "New Measures in the Equation of Exchange." *American Economic Review*, Dec. 1924, *14*, 699–713.

————. "The Influence of the Interest Rate on the Business Cycle." *American Economic Review*, Dec. 1925, *15*, 684–99.

————. "The Problem of Monetary and Economic Stability." *Quarterly Journal of Economics*, Feb. 1935, *49*, 173–205.

G. J. Stigler. *Production and Distribution Theories*. New York, 1941.

J. Tobin. "A Dynamic Aggregative Model." *Journal of Political Economy*, Apr. 1955, *63*, 103–15.

†J. Viner. "Die Theorie des auswärtigen Handels." In *Die Wirtschaftstheorie der Gegenwart* [Wieser *Festschrift*], IV, 1928. Pp. 106–25 [Part III of this article appears in the original English version in Viner (1951), pp. 40–48.]

†———. Review of *The Problem of Maintaining Purchasing Power* by P. W. Martin. *Journal of Political Economy*, June 1932, *40*, 418–19.

———. "International Aspects of the Gold Standard." In Harris Memorial Foundation, *Gold and Monetary Stabilization*, ed. Q. Wright, 1932. Reprinted in Viner (1951), pp. 123–40.

———. *Studies in the Theory of International Trade*. New York, 1937.

———. *International Economics*. Glencoe, Ill., 1951.

———. "Schumpeter's *History of Economic Analysis*." *American Economic Review*, Dec. 1954, *44*, 894–910. Reprinted in Viner (1958), pp. 343–65.

———. *The Long View and the Short*. Glencoe, Ill., 1958.

———. "The Necessary and the Desirable Range of Discretion to be Allowed to a Monetary Authority." In *In Search of a Monetary Constitution*, ed. L. B. Yeager. Cambridge, Mass., 1962. Pp. 244–74.

C. Warburton. "The Volume of Money and the Price Level Between the World Wars." *Journal of Political Economy*, June 1945, *53*, 150–63.

———. "Quantity and Frequency of Use of Money in the United States, 1919–45." *Journal of Political Economy*, Oct. 1946, *54*, 436–50.

———. "Monetary Velocity and Monetary Policy." *Review of Economics and Statistics*, Nov. 1948, *30*, 304–14.

———. "The Secular Trend in Monetary Velocity." *Quarterly Journal of Economics*, Feb. 1949, *63*, 68–91.

†Q. Wright. See Harris Memorial Foundation.

Unpublished Materials

Author's Lecture Notes of Following Courses:
    Frank H. Knight:
        Economics 301: "Price and Distribution Theory." Summer 1945.
    Lloyd W. Mints:
        Economics 330: "Money." Summer 1944.
        Economics 331: "Banking Theory and Monetary Policy." Winter 1944.
    Henry C. Simons:
        Economics 361: "Economics of Fiscal Policy." Spring 1945.
[H. C. Simons]. "Banking and Currency Reform." [Chicago, 1933] [See p. 257, fn. 3, above.]
University of Chicago Ph.D. Dissertations as listed in Appendix III.

Lloyd W. Mints (ca. 1938)

11. More on the Chicago Monetary Tradition *

In a paper a few years ago on the nature of the Chicago School {see preceding chapter} I suggested that it would be interesting—though beyond the scope of that paper—to examine "the extent to which the policy views of the Chicago School in the 1930s represented those of the other quantity-theorists of the period" (above, p. 242, fn.5). Thomas Humphrey's recent note (1971) casts some interesting light upon this question, and I shall accordingly begin with some comments on it. I conclude with some general observations on the relations between the Chicago School of the 1930s and its contemporaries. I might note that the multifarious nature of these interrelationships raises the question of the proper basis of distinction between "Chicagoans" and "non-Chicagoans"—a question that I shall not, however, deal with here.

Humphrey's main point is that the present Chicago School as represented by Milton Friedman has been influenced by the work of American quantity theorists "outside The University of Chicago" during the 1930s and 1940s. More specifically:

> the work of these non-Chicago economists has its roots in and emanates from the earlier Fisherine tradition and thus represents a clear and direct line of development from the earlier approach to the contemporary one. In fact, several of the doctrines currently espoused by Chicago monetary economists originated not with Friedman's mentors, but with these non-Chicago quantity theorists (Humphrey 1971, p. 12).

In support of this contention, Humphrey cites evidence from the writings of Carl Snyder, Lionel Edie, Lauchlin Currie, and Clark Warburton—and states (1971, p.

Reprinted by permission from *Southern Economic Journal*, Jan. 1973, *39*, 454–59. Published originally under the title "On the Monetary Economics of Chicagoans and Non-Chicagoans: Comment." This was a comment on Thomas M. Humphrey's "Role of Non-Chicago Economists in the Evolution of the Quantity Theory in America 1930–1950" (1971). Slightly revised and expanded, in part by the reinsertion of material which was for various reasons deleted at the time.

* Work on this note was carried out in part while I was a Mills B. Lane Visiting Scholar at the University of Georgia in the fall of 1971. I am grateful to Robert R. Dince and Richard H. Timberlake of the University of Georgia for helpful comments on an earlier draft. I am also grateful to Martin Bronfenbrenner and Clarence E. Philbrook for their comments during a seminar at the University of North Carolina, Chapel Hill, where the latter part of this note was discussed. I have also benefited from the criticisms of Milton Friedman and George Stigler. Needless to say, none of the foregoing are to be held responsible for the views here expressed.

Finally—and with sadness—I express my deep indebtedness to the late Samuel H. Nerlove for his invaluable comments on an earlier draft of this note—comments which throw penetrating light on the respective roles of various economists at Chicago in the period under discussion. These comments are reproduced in the Appendix.

17) that only Warburton's influence is acknowledged by Friedman and Schwartz in their *Monetary History of the United States* (1963).[1]

Let me first of all say that Lionel Edie was not—strictly speaking—a "non-Chicagoan." In particular, the Annual Register of the University of Chicago for the academic years 1926/27–1928/29 (which in each case actually refers to the following academic year) list him as a professor of finance in what was then called the "School of Commerce and Administration" (and is now the Graduate School of Business).[2] During this period Frank H. Knight and Jacob Viner were full professors in the Department of Economics, Lloyd W. Mints, an assistant professor, and Henry C. Simons, first a lecturer and then an assistant professor. Indeed, according to the *Register*, in the academic year 1927–28 both Edie and Mints taught—in different quarters—the graduate course on "Money and Banking." Furthermore, in one case Edie was the chairman of a Ph.D. thesis committee of which Mints was a member (cf. p. 263 above).

It would nevertheless seem that from the viewpoint of the actual intellectual interaction between Edie and his colleagues in the Department of Economics, Humphrey is essentially correct in listing Edie as a "non-Chicagoan." For—as the late Samuel H. Nerlove (for many years Professor at The University of Chicago School of Business) wrote me [3]—"there was practically no real intellectual contact between Edie and the Economics Faculty during the short time he was in residence at Chicago." It is also noteworthy that Edie's many writings on monetary policy (1928, 1929, 1931, 1934, 1935) do not seem to contain any references to his colleagues in the economics department.[4]

In my opinion, however, Humphrey (1971, p. 13) is overstating the case when he writes that Edie preferred a policy of expanding bank credit at a steady rate to one directed at stabilizing the price index, on the grounds that the latter policy "was handicapped by the existence of imperfectly understood links as well as variable lags and required too much discretion (choice of the index) to be left with the monetary authority." I do not think that the pages of Edie's book (1931, pp. 29–30, 42–43, 114–15) on which Humphrey bases this statement can really be interpreted as referring to "imperfectly understood links" or to "variable lags"—certainly not in

1. Actually, Friedman and Schwartz do refer in this book to Carl Snyder (1963, pp. 252, 370, 374, 692). I should also note that in their subsequent volume on *Monetary Statistics of the United States*—which describes in detail the derivation of the series used in their *Monetary History*—Friedman and Schwartz do discuss the work of Currie (1970, pp. 268–70). They restrict themselves, however, to Currie's statistical work, and mention neither his monetary analysis nor his policy recommendations. Thus Humphrey's basic contention is unaffected. This is also the way in which Friedman and Schwartz (1970, pp. 270–71) treat the work of James Angell, mentioned below.

2. Note that the title page of the book by Edie (1931) that is cited by Humphrey (1971, p. 13) lists Edie's affiliations as "Vice-President, American Capital Corporation, Formerly Professor of Finance, University of Chicago."

3. In a letter commenting on an early draft of this note; reproduced in the Appendix.

4. It is true that Edie was one of those who gave a paper at the 1932 Harris Foundation Lectures on "Gold and Monetary Stabilization" which took place at The University of Chicago. But most of the participants in this conference (who included Angell and Snyder, as well as Irving Fisher) were non-Chicagoans—as was Edie at that time.

the sense that these terms are used today by Friedman and others to support their contention that the attempt to stabilize the price level might actually be destabilizing. Instead Edie's objections to price-level stabilization are stated in the following terms:

> Important as a stable unit is, the difficulties and dangers in attempting to attain it are great. Not least among these is the failure of economists to supply the scientific knowledge necessary for performance of the task. Economists have not agreed upon an index number to be used as a measure of the purchasing power of money. Although admitting that stabilization means *prevention* of undue fluctuations, and that prevention necessitates *forecasting*, nevertheless, they have been slow to develop a forecasting technique that can command confidence (1931, p. 30, italics in original).

I might also note that Edie did not seem to have too strong a preference for the growth-rate rule as against the price-stabilization rule. Thus in his earlier book on *Money, Bank Credit, and Prices* (1928, pp. 92, 470–93) he seems to be advocating the price stabilization policy—despite his many reservations about it. (It might be noted that Edie [1928, pp. 474–75] defines the central-bank policy necessary to achieve this stabilization not in terms of changes in the quantity of money or volume of credit, but in terms of the rediscount rate.) Again, in Edie's later book on *Dollars* (1934, pp. 278–79) he seems to be advocating the policy rule of price stabilization.

With reference to the other writers whom Humphrey cites (viz., Snyder, Currie, and Warburton), he [Humphrey] has little to say on what I would consider to be an even more interesting aspect of the question: namely, why the "original" Chicago school itself apparently did not refer to them? Insofar as Warburton is concerned, it is fair to say that this omission reflects the fact that his major studies (reprinted in Warburton, 1966) began appearing only in the mid-1940s—by which time Simons and other members of the Chicago School had long since formulated their position (see preceding chapter). Thus Reeve's (1943) comprehensive study of monetary discussions in the 1930s does not even contain a reference to Warburton.

This explanation may also hold—though with considerably less justification—for the case of Currie. For though Currie wrote some ten years before Warburton, his [Currie's] work appeared after the main features of the Chicago School position had been formulated. Indeed, in connection with his advocacy of "100% money" (which idea he apparently developed independently of the Chicago School), Currie himself referred (1934c, p. 156, fn.) to the 1933 Chicago memorandum on "Banking and Currency Reform" (cf. preceding chapter, p. 257). Similarly, Currie (1934b, p. 146, fn. 2) expressed his "substantial agreement" with C. O. Hardy (who was also connected with The University of Chicago, and who was indeed a teacher of Simons and Mints) [5] on the question of proper central-bank policy. Still, I agree with Humphrey's implication that the Chicago School should subsequently have taken

---

5. See again Professor Nerlove's letter in the Appendix.

more account of Currie's work.[6] And to this I would add that it should also have taken account of the work of Angell (1933, 1936).[7]

Though it does not bear on the present subject, there is one aspect of Humphrey's discussion of Currie which I would like to correct. This is Humphrey's statement (1971, p. 13) that "Currie was the first American economist to replace the transaction velocity concept with the income velocity concept." This is not the case. Currie's first published work making use of income velocity (a concept which he attributed to Schumpeter [1933, p. 91]) appeared in the same issue (November 1933) of the *Quarterly Journal of Economics* in which Angell (1933) employed the same concept, though denoting it as "circular velocity." Indeed, Currie subsequently wrote a note (1934a) to explain their different statistical findings. Furthermore, both Currie in his 1931 Ph.D. thesis (1931, p. 5, fn. 5) and Angell in the article just cited (1933, p. 43, fn. 5) refer to the use of the similar concept "circuit velocity" some ten years before by the American economists Foster and Catchings (1923, chapters 18–20, especially pp. 311–12). Similarly, Edie's 1928 textbook (pp. 395–98) includes a discussion of income velocity. Thus neither Angell nor Currie can be credited with having introduced this concept into the American scene.

There still remains the question as to why the original Chicago School did not refer to the work of Carl Snyder. And, frankly, what I find even more puzzling is a question which Humphrey does not discuss: namely why, in its policy discussions, the Chicago School of the 1930s and 1940s did not do justice to Irving Fisher—despite the fact that long before the Chicago School, Fisher had advocated the policy of stabilizing the price level as a means of mitigating—if not eliminating—cyclical fluctuations ("booms and depressions"). More specifically, ever since his *Purchasing Power of Money* (1911, chapter 4), if not before, Fisher had contended that business cycles were caused by the "dance of the dollar": by a changing price level which was not fully reflected in the nominal rate of interest, which failure therefore caused a change in the real rate of interest as perceived by entrepreneurs, and which change therefore caused them to undertake unwarranted expansions (or contractions) in their activities. Consequently, the way to prevent this succession of expansions and contractions was to stabilize the price level by means of a "compensated dollar." [8]

In the writings of Simons, I have not found any reference to these views of Fisher. And though Mints (1950, p. 10) did recognize that Fisher was "in more recent years . . . the strongest supporter of stabilizing the price level," he wrongly implied that this was only because of considerations of distributive justice to creditors and debtors, and not because price stability was "a necessary condition for the

6. On Currie's subsequent close connections with Viner, see pp. 268 above and 286 below. I might here also note that the index to Reeve's study (1943)—which had its origin as a Ph.D. thesis completed at Chicago in 1939 under a committee consisting of Mints (chairman), Viner, and G. V. Cox (above, p. 262)—has almost as many references to Currie as to Simons.

7. Who, incidentally, also studied at Chicago in the year (1919–20) between taking his A.B. degree at Harvard and beginning his graduate studies there. During that year, Angell served as Viner's teaching assistant (see above, p. 267).

8. Cf. Fisher (1920, 1923, 1925, 1932, and 1934). For a brief survey of Fisher's views on this point, see my "Non-Neutrality of Money in the Quantity Theory" (1972).

effective operation of a competitive system.'' As has just been emphasized, how-ever—and as Mints himself had earlier recognized (1945, p. 272)—this was precisely Fisher's view of the matter. In contrast, Fisher (1935, p. ix) did refer to the Chicago School, and particularly Henry C. Simons, as being among the primary advocates of ''100 percent money''—a proposal to which Fisher gave his unequivocal support.

In order to avoid any possible misunderstanding, I wish to emphasize that what I find puzzling here is the relation of the Chicago School to Fisher's policy views, as distinct from his theoretical contributions. Insofar as the latter are concerned, the theoretical framework of the Chicago School was explicitly based on Fisher's de-velopment of the quantity theory in terms of the equation of exchange, $MV + M'V' = PT$. Correspondingly, the chapters of Fisher's classic work on the *Purchasing Power of Money* (1911) in which this equation was explicated were required reading at Chicago (cf. above, pp. 5, 245, and 250).

Humphrey rightly notes (1971, p. 17) that the present Chicago School with its emphasis on the empirical verification of hypotheses is closer in spirit to the work of Snyder and Warburton than to the original Chicago School. To this observation I would add that it is also closer to Fisher—who devoted two chapters (11 and 12) of his *Purchasing Power of Money* to the statistical verification of his equation of exchange. Fisher also continued in later years to be concerned with empirical aspects of the economic problems he discussed.

The present Chicago School is also closer to Fisher in emphasizing his basic distinction between the nominal and the real rate of interest (Humphrey, 1971).[9] To the best of my knowledge, Simons did not explicitly refer to this distinction; nor did Mints, in his book on monetary policy (1950)—though he does mention it in passing in his history of banking theory (1945, pp. 53, 211). This is to be contrasted with the important role the distinction plays in the writings of Friedman and his associates (Friedman, 1956, 1971).

In conclusion, let me observe that the picture of monetary economics in the 1930s that emerges from Humphrey's note (1973) as well as from the foregoing discus-sion—and which accords with the larger picture that has been documented in the detailed studies of the period by Reeve (1943) and, more recently, Davis (1968, 1971)—is one of widespread ferment with respect to questions of both monetary theory and policy. Thus contrary to Friedman's implication,[10] the Chicago School of that time cannot be represented as an isolated center of monetary studies and of belief in the importance of money. What seems, however, to be true is that in some important respects it behaved as if it were—as is evidenced by the failure of Simons and Mints to refer in either their writings or their lectures (as reflected in my class

---

9. Fisher's deep conviction in the importance of this distinction is best demonstrated by the fact that in 1925 he persuaded the Rand-Kardex Company—of which he was a founder and major stockholder—to issue what he called (1934, p. 112) ''the first 'Stabilized Bond' in history,'' or what we would today call an indexed bond. The index clause, however, was not to become operative unless the price level changed by more than 10% (Fisher, 1934, pp. 112, 387–89; Reeve, 1943, p. 164).

10. ''Chicago was one of the few academic centers at which the quantity theory continued to be a central and vigorous part of the oral tradition throughout the 1930s and 1940s, where students continued to study monetary theory and to write theses on monetary problems'' (Friedman, 1956, p. 3).

notes) to the work of their contemporaries, even when it bore them out on the importance of monetary factors, and even when it incorporated similar (if not identical) policy proposals. More specifically, Simons' writings in the first half of the 1930s give little, if any, indication that there was then and in earlier years a relatively high degree of agreement among economists from different backgrounds—and different countries [11]—in support of price stabilization as a contracyclical policy.

I strongly suspect, however, that the classroom teaching at Chicago during my student days (the early and mid-1940s) differed in this respect from that of a decade before. Specifically, I would not be surprised if in the early and mid-1930s these teachings contained many more references to the wider academic support for the kind of monetary policies taught at Chicago. Similarly, it may well be that the sense of isolation that I experienced during the early 1940s in part simply reflected the fact that at that time Chicago was indeed isolated in its continued advocacy of price stabilization as a contracyclical policy, by virtue of the fact that by then most of the leading academic centers (and Harvard in particular) had been converted to the advocacy of Keynesian fiscal policy for this purpose.

Obviously, none of this changes the basic fact that the Chicago School in the 1930s played a leading role in the realm of monetary-policy discussions. On the other hand, one thing is clear from the above: Chicago was not the center of empirical work on monetary economics in the 1930s; indeed, little, if any, such work was done then at Chicago. True, there was nowhere at that time a real "center" of empirical work in monetary economics. Nevertheless, the fact is that the major empirical work on monetary economics that was done during this period was carried out at Harvard (as represented by Currie 1931,[12] 1933, 1934b, 1934c) and Columbia (as represented by Angell 1933, 1936).

The failure of such empirical work to develop at Chicago in the 1930s stands in sharp contrast with the fact that Chicago was at that time the home of two outstanding empirical economists, both of whom had at least some interest in monetary matters: Henry Schultz, who participated in the 1932 Harris Foundation Lectures and was one of the signatories of its policy proposals (1932, p. 163), and Paul H. Douglas, who in 1935 wrote a book on *Controlling Depressions* whose policy proposals (pp. 277–81) were largely in accord with the "traditional" Chicago ones.

Still, the more relevant fact is that the people primarily responsible for the teaching of monetary and fiscal policy at Chicago during the 1930s, Simons and Mints, were themselves just not interested in empirical work—and the vital importance of such personal tastes in influencing the nature of the research carried out at an academic institution is something we have all experienced. Furthermore, we must remember the general intellectual atmosphere of the economics profession in the 1930s, which

---

11. Notably, Pigou and Keynes in England and Wicksell in Sweden; cf. Patinkin, 1972 and references there cited.

12. This was Currie's Ph.D. thesis on "Bank Assets and Banking Theory" carried out at Harvard under the direction of John H. Williams and S. E. Harris.

placed much less emphasis than it has come to place since the late 1940s on the obligation to subject hypotheses to empirical testing.[13]

I would, however, conjecture that the disinterest of Simons and Mints in empirical work also reflected the influence of a more specific factor: namely, the fact that they were so convinced on a priori grounds of the validity of their analysis and consequent policy proposals that they saw no need to subject these proposals to empirical study. This attitude is strikingly revealed in the following paragraph from Simons' 1935 review of Currie's *Supply and Control of Money in the United States* (1934):

> The study reflects a rare combination of penetrating theoretical insights and patient competence in the analysis of banking statistics. The highly realistic treatment will make the author's argument convincing, or at least disturbing, to many readers who would be unimpressed by "mere theory." For critical students, however, Dr. Currie's inductive verifications will be largely gratuitous—although everyone will be grateful for the excellent statistical compilation and analysis. In general, the author's fundamental insights are so sound that failure of statistical confirmation would only indicate error or inadequacy in the statistics [Simons, 1935, p. 556].

Reflecting a similar conviction, Mints in his lectures (according to my notes) said: "If [government] stabilizes price level, will stabilize aggregate demand and thus prevent unemployment. Inconceivable that federal government couldn't so increase cash balances of public that it wouldn't want to purchase goods" (cited in the preceding chapter, p. 261; cf. also Mints, 1946, p. 67). What we have since learned (in large measure, due to Friedman's own seminal contributions (1961, and references there cited)) about the fundamental problem of lags—and particularly about the implications of possibly destabilizing lags for such a policy—was either not seen (Simons) or not given much weight (Mints) (p. 247 above). So I find it highly significant that it is precisely this question of lags that has raised doubts about the efficacy of (*inter alia*) the monetary policy espoused by the original Chicago School—and has stimulated so much empirical work since the early 1960s in the effort to determine (if possible) a more optimal policy.

Appendix

At the end of October 1971 I sent a draft of this note to Professor Samuel H. Nerlove, asking him for his comments, and particularly for information on the extent of intellectual interaction between Edie and the Department of Economics, as well as on the role that Charles O. Hardy played in the development of the Chicago School. (Professor Nerlove took his M.A. degree at Chicago in 1923, and served there on the staff of the School of Business from that time and until his retirement in 1965. I regret

---

13. Cf. also Humphrey (1973).

to say that Professor Nerlove died on February 13, 1972.) To this request Professor Nerlove replied in a letter dated December 5, 1971, the main parts of which are reproduced here with his permission:

> Getting at an accurate statement of the intellectual development and im-plementation of a set of ideas is obviously exceedingly difficult, especially in relation to the development of such a complicated set of ideas as are involved in the evolution of the Quantity Theory in this country during a 20 year period, 1930–1950.
>
> Nevertheless, here are my recollections about Edie and Hardy—and as I approach three score and ten—I find that I have total recall of past events, so perhaps the following is "more accurate" rather than less accurate.
>
> Hardy was much more influential than Edie. His influence on Mints and Simons was exceedingly significant, and therefore some reference should be made to his work when he was at the Institute of Economics in Washington (now Brookings) in the so-called money and banking area. Indeed, he had an impor-tant impact on Warburton's work. Hardy was Simons' teacher (as well as Angell's and Mints' teacher) and was influential in getting him to "respect" Currie's work on the "Supply and Control of Money," as it was being de-veloped at Harvard as a Ph.D thesis.
>
> Edie had very little "real" contact with the Economics Faculty. He was brought to Chicago, over the negative reactions of the Economics group, by L. C. Marshall primarily because he had a manuscript of his forthcoming text book on "Money, Bank Credit and Prices". The Economics group did not think well of the book. . . . My distinct impression is that Edie was so uncomfortable at Chicago that at the first opportunity, and shortly after he came to Chicago, he left for a job in Detroit with an investment trust. In short, there was practically no real intellectual contact between Edie and the Economics Faculty during the short time he was in residence at Chicago. . . .

Postscript

In June 1972, I sent Lloyd Mints a draft of the foregoing article and this time (see above, p. 265) received a reply, reproduced here with his permission:

Ft. Collins, Colorado,
Sept. 21, 1972

Dear Don:

I make no claim to an infallible memory such as Sam Nerlove claimed to have had (in your quotation from him), but as I recollect the situation during the 1930's it was as follows. The primary interest of several of us at Chicago, in such public statements as were made, was in monetary policy and its relation to economic activity. We tacitly assumed that monetary behavior had an important influence on economic activity. It was the era of the great depression, and we believed that the actions of the Federal Reserve System and of the government were woefully wrong. We therefore proposed monetary actions which we believed would facilitate a return to better economic conditions. We were not concerned with the question of who should be given credit for any particular monetary theory or policy. We merely wanted to do what little we possibly could to improve economic conditions in the country.

I have always had the greatest respect for Irving Fisher. Whether I sufficiently indicated that fact in what I said or wrote I don't know. I remember distinctly (I think!) that after a talk by Warburton at the University both Simons and I were greatly pleased by what Warburton had said. I even had the impression that Warburton was grateful for our approval. I agree with Nerlove that Edie had little if any influence on the other members of the economics department at Chicago.

I was quite familiar with the writings of Angell and Currie, but whether I should have made that fact quite clear I don't know. All of us at Chicago had the greatest respect for Charles Hardy. Whether he had the extent of influence on some of us that Nerlove suggests I don't know. The one man who it is clear to me had a considerable influence on my thinking was Henry Simons. For a short time a small group of us had weekly (?) meetings at the home of Hardy. I am not sure who attended those meetings, but at least Knight, Hardy, Simons and myself must have been present. I don't remember whether Aaron Director was in Chicago at the time, but if he was he was surely present. There may have been a few others.

Sincerely,

[signed]   L. Mints

I also sent a draft of the article to Lauchlin Currie and received a reply from which the following paragraphs are reproduced with his permission (footnotes added):

Bogota, Colombia
November 29, 1972

Dear Professor Patinkin,

I've been so busy defending and implementing a plan of development I developed, and this country adopted, that I couldn't get myself in a proper frame of mind to return to the distant past. But as a local journal is publishing (in Spanish) a translation of Humphrey's article and asked me to make a few comments on my early work, I was led to think a little about it.

I was a bit unlucky in both hitting on the 100% reserve idea a few months behind Simons and of working out a statistical series for the income velocity simultaneously with Angell. However, I hardly think this justifies your remark that my "work appeared after the main features of the Chicago school position had been formulated". I think I supplied the first explanation of the main factors governing the supply of money (which Humphrey did not mention) and my work on the ownership of demand deposits was certainly new and throws light on the demand for money (in *Journal of Amer. Stat. Ass.*, Dec. 1937 [*sic*]). I took a very strong line on the distinction between what is money and what is not. If you include savings deposits in commercial banks there is no logical place to stop. As Humphrey says, I took a highly critical line on Federal Reserve Policy, though I still defended discretionary policy.

On personal relations, I knew Simons but not well. My main link with Chicago was through Viner. (He had lectured a few times at Harvard and I got to know and respect him. I was an instructor while he had then an established reputation so our relationships was more like that of professor and student).[a]

I can't account for Nerlove's remark re Hardy's getting Simons to "respect" my work, except that I did respect Hardy. Nerlove made a little slip in connection with my Ph.D. thesis, which you may have noted.[b]

· · ·

Yours sincerely,

[signed]   Lauchlin Currie

Bibliography

J. W. Angell. "Money, Prices, and Production: Some Fundamental Concepts." *Quarterly Journal of Economics*, Nov. 1933, *48*, 39–76.
———. *The Behavior of Money*. New York, 1936.
L. Currie. "Bank Assets and Banking Theory." Unpublished Ph.D. thesis, Harvard University, 1931.
———. "Money, Gold, and Income." *Quarterly Journal of Economics*, Nov. 1933, *48*, 77–95.
———. "A Note on Income Velocities." *Quarterly Journal of Economics*, Feb. 1934a, *48*, 353–54.
———. "The Failure of Monetary Policy to Prevent the Depression of 1929–1932." *Journal of Political Economy*, Apr. 1934b, *42*, 145–77.
———. *The Supply and Control of Money in the United States*. Cambridge, Mass., 1934c.
†———. "The Economic Distribution of Demand Deposits." *Journal of the American Statistical Association*, June 1938, *33*, 319–26.

a. Cf. also Viner's letter above (p. 268) on his relations with Currie.

b. The slip—which I had not noticed—was that Currie's book on the *Supply and Control of Money* was a new work, and not a revised version of his thesis; see penultimate paragraph of Nerlove's letter and fn. 12 on p. 282 above.

†Cited only in Postscript.

J. R. Davis. "Chicago Economists, Deficit Budgets and the Early 1930's." *American Economic Review*, June 1968, *58*, 476–82.

_____. *The New Economics and the Old Economists*. Ames, Iowa, 1971.

P. H. Douglas. *Controlling Depressions*. New York, 1935.

L. D. Edie. *Money, Bank Credit, and Prices*. New York, 1928.

_____. "The 1928 Hearings on the Strong Bill." *Journal of Political Economy*, June 1929, *37*, 340–54.

_____. *The Banks and Prosperity*. New York, 1931.

_____. *Dollars*. New Haven, Conn., 1934.

_____. "Monetary Stabilization from a National Point of View." *American Economic Review, Supplement*, Mar. 1935, *25*, 164–70.

I. Fisher. *The Purchasing Power of Money*. New York, 1911.

_____. *Stabilizing the Dollar*. New York, 1920.

_____. "The Business Cycle Largely a 'Dance of the Dollar.' " *Journal of the American Statistical Association*, Dec. 1923, *18*, 1024–28.

_____. "Our Unstable Dollar and the So-Called Business Cycle." *Journal of the American Statistical Association*, June 1925, *20*, 179–202.

_____. *Booms and Depressions*. New York, 1932.

_____. *Stable Money*. New York, 1934.

_____. *100% Money*. New York, 1935.

W. T. Foster and W. Catchings. *Money*. Boston, 1923.

M. Friedman, ed. *Studies in the Quantity Theory of Money*. Chicago, 1956.

_____. "The Lag in Effect of Monetary Policy." *Journal of Political Economy*, Oct. 1961, *69*, 447–66. As reprinted in *The Optimum Quantity of Money and Other Essays*. Chicago, 1969. Pp. 237–60.

_____. "A Monetary Theory of National Income." *Journal of Political Economy*, Mar./Apr. 1971, *79*, 323–37.

_____ and A. J. Schwartz. *A Monetary History of the United States 1867–1960*. Princeton, N. J., 1963.

_____. *Monetary Statistics of the United States: Estimates, Sources, Methods*. New York, 1970.

Harris Memorial Foundation. *Gold and Monetary Stabilization*, ed. Q. Wright. Chicago, 1932.

T. M. Humphrey. "Role of Non-Chicago Economists in the Evolution of the Quantity Theory in America 1930–1950." *Southern Economic Journal*, July 1971, *38*, 12–18.

_____. "On the Monetary Economics of Chicagoans and Non-Chicagoans: Reply." *Southern Economic Journal*, Jan. 1973, *39*, 460–63.

L. W. Mints. *A History of Banking Theory*. Chicago, 1945.

_____. "Monetary Policy." *Review of Economics and Statistics*, May 1946, *28*, 60–69.

_____. *Monetary Policy for a Competitive Society*. New York, 1950.

D. Patinkin. "The Chicago Tradition, the Quantity Theory, and Friedman." *Journal of Money, Credit and Banking*, Feb. 1969, *1*, 46–70. [Reproduced as chap. 10 above.]

_____. "On the Short-Run Non-Neutrality of Money in the Quantity Theory." *Banca Nazionale del Lavoro: Quarterly Review*, Mar. 1972, *100*, 3–22.

J. E. Reeve. *Monetary Reform Movements*. Washington, D.C., 1943.

H. C. Simons. "Review of *The Supply and Control of Money in the United States*, by Lauchlin Currie." *Journal of Political Economy*, Aug. 1935, *43*, 555–58.

C. Warburton. *Depression, Inflation and Monetary Policy; Selected Papers, 1945–1953*. Baltimore, 1966.

Q. Wright. See Harris Memorial Foundation.

12. Keynes and Chicago*

I am both honored and gratified to present this lecture in memory of Henry C. Simons—one of my first teachers at this University when I entered it as an undergraduate student in economics over thirty-five years ago, and a teacher who left an indelible impression upon me.[1]

I shall yet be returning to Simons this evening, but let me first emphasize that the subject of my lecture is not Keynesianism and Chicago, on which volumes could be written, but the far more restricted one of Keynes and Chicago. Specifically, there were two notable occasions on which Keynes had direct contact with Chicago: in 1931, when he came to The University of Chicago to participate in the Harris Foundation Lectures of that year; and in 1936, when his newly published *General Theory* was greeted by review articles by (among other leading economists) the two senior members of the Chicago School, Jacob Viner and Frank Knight, as well as by a brief review by that member in whose memory we have met here this evening, Henry Simons. And it is about these two occasions that I wish primarily to talk.

The subject of the 1931 Harris Lectures was the painfully current one of "Unemployment as a World Problem," and Keynes gave the keynote lecture (or rather, series of lectures) on "An Economic Analysis of Unemployment." In order to obtain a proper perspective on this lecture, we must remember that Keynes gave it less than a year after the publication of his *Treatise on Money* (1930), the work which at the time Keynes considered as his *magnum opus* and which he undoubtedly believed would be recognized for years to come as the definitive work on the pure and applied theory of money.

The Eighth Henry Simons Lecture, delivered at The Law School, The University of Chicago, May 2, 1979. Reprinted by permission from the *Journal of Law and Economics* 22 (Oct. 1979), pp. 213–32, with the addition of material on pp. 300–301 and on p. 304, fn. 30, below.

*This paper was written while serving as Ford Foundation Visiting Research Professor at the Department of Economics and Graduate School of Business of The University of Chicago. I am greatly indebted to Shlomo Maital for providing me with materials from the Jacob Viner Papers at Princeton University. I would also like to express my sincerest appreciation to Marc Levin for his invaluable research assistance and to Mrs. Marie Marchese for so efficiently typing this paper through its various drafts. The work on this paper was in part financed by NSF Grant SOC79–08281.

Because of its concern with historical questions, this paper refers to reprinted works by the date of original publication; for convenience, however, the page references themselves follow the pagination of the reprinted form as indicated in the bibliography. In particular, references to the writings of Keynes are to the new edition of his *Collected Writings*. For simplicity, I shall refer to the two volumes of his *Treatise on Money* as *Treatise* 1(2), respectively. The *General Theory* will sometimes be further abbreviated to *GT*. Specific volumes of Keynes' *Collected Writings* will be referred to as *JMK* plus the volume number (for example, *JMK* 13).

1. See "Reminiscences," pp. 4–5 above.

In retrospect, the approach of the *Treatise* was a fairly simple one. It claimed that business cycles, or (to use the term of Keynes and his contemporaries) credit cycles, are caused by the alternation of profits and losses. Now, profits are caused by the excess of the price of a product over its cost of production, and losses by a shortfall. And so Keynes' analysis of the business cycle evolved into an analysis of what determines the price per unit of output relative to the cost per unit. This is the subject and the purpose of the so-called fundamental equations—and Keynes' very choice of that term is ample indication of the significance he attached to them. I will not bother you with the obscure notation, so strange to us today, with which Keynes presented these equations. But when you finish examining these equations carefully, when you get down to their essence, what they say is the following:

$$\text{index of price} = \text{index of cost of production} + \text{index of profits}$$

—all per unit of output. And that is the fundamental equation!

Keynes recognizes that this is an identity, and indeed says so. But he also says that it is an identity which is useful for classifying causal relationships. However, if we read the *Treatise* carefully, we find that Keynes frequently shifts across the very thin and indefinite line that lies between repeating an identity and trying to endow it with more meaning than it really has. Thus by making use of a special definition of income (namely, defining it to exclude excess profits) Keynes showed that the excess of investment over saving was equal to excess profits—and then claimed that such an excess *caused* an increase in price relative to costs.

Similarly, Keynes supplemented his fundamental equations with a dynamic theory which stated that a decline in the rate of interest (more specifically, of the "market rate" relative to the "natural rate") generated an excess of investment over saving, hence raised prices relative to costs, hence generated excess profits, and hence led firms to expand their output; conversely, a rise in the interest rate would generate losses and hence a contraction of output. Correspondingly, the way to stabilize prices, hence avoid excess profits or losses, and hence cycles, is for the central bank to adopt a policy of varying the market rate of interest so as to keep it equal to the natural rate. And in particular, the cure for depressions and their unemployment is a central-bank policy designed to lower the rate of interest, hence stimulate investment, hence raise the price level relative to costs, hence generate business profits, and hence stimulate output and employment. In brief, by making use of the interest rate, the central bank could stabilize the price level, which policy was also the means of assuring the equality between saving and investment, and hence full employment.[2]

That is the policy position that we generally associate with the *Treatise*. But in recent years we have been reminded [3] that almost hidden away at the end of this book Keynes adds a crucial reservation about the applicability of this policy: namely, what he described as "the insuperable limitation on the power of skilled monetary management to avoid booms and depressions" that has its source in "international complica-

---

2. The preceding three paragraphs are reproduced in part from Patinkin (1977), pp. 4–5. For further details, see my *Keynes' Monetary Thought* (1976), chaps. 5, 6, and 12.

3. In the excellent article by Moggridge and Howson (1974).

tions.'' More specifically, in a gold-standard world (and that was the world in which Keynes was then writing), a central bank acting in isolation cannot reduce the interest rate below that of other central banks, for this will lead to the outflow of gold and hence to a dangerous loss of international reserves (*Treatise* 2, p. 335). In such a situation Keynes advocates public works as the alternative ''reserve weapon'' by which the country in question can nevertheless combat unemployment. And Keynes makes it clear that this has indeed been the situation of Britain during 1929–30, for which (he notes) he has accordingly repeatedly advocated public works as a means of dealing with its problem (*Treatise* 2, pp. 337–38)—undoubtedly an allusion (*inter alia*) to his advocacy of such works in his famous 1929 pamphlet (together with Hubert Henderson) on *Can Lloyd George Do It?: An Examination of the Liberal Pledge*. On the other hand, says Keynes, the basic interest-rate policy of the *Treatise* is more appropriate for a country like the United States, which is much less dependent than Britain on ''international trade and international lending'' (*Treatise* 2, p. 336, especially fn. 1).

That was the background of Keynes' 1931 Harris Lecture. Indeed, this lecture was essentially a song of praise to his *Treatise*. Thus Keynes began his analysis of the slump in this lecture with a verbal rendition of the fundamental equations and with the accompanying proclamation, ''That is my secret, the clue to the scientific explanation of booms and slumps (and of much else as I should claim) which I offer you'' (*JMK* 13, p. 354). Which brings me to observe that though Keynes alluded to the Bible on more than one occasion in his writings (e.g., the famous ''widow's cruse'' of chapter 10 of the *Treatise*), the verse in the Book of Proverbs (27:2), ''Let another man praise thee, and not thine own mouth'' was apparently not one of his favorites.

In any event, Keynes summarized the ''main theme'' of his Harris Lecture in the following terms:

> The cure of unemployment involves improving business profits. The improvement of business profits can come about only by an improvement in new investment relative to saving. An increase of investment relative to saving must also, as an inevitable by-product, bring about a rise of prices, thus ameliorating the burdens arising out of monetary indebtedness. The problem resolves itself, therefore, into the question as to what means we can adopt to increase the volume of investment . . . . [*JMK* 13, p. 362]

Keynes then proceeds to describe three ''lines of approach'' for achieving this objective: first, restoring confidence, about which not much can be done deliberately; second, carrying out a program of public investment, which has the practical drawback that ''it is not easy to devise at short notice schemes which are wisely and efficiently conceived and which can be put rapidly into operation on a really large scale'' (*JMK* 13, p. 364); and, finally, lowering the long-run rate of interest by a vigorous central-bank policy of open-market purchases. And it seems to me quite clear that Keynes' preference is for the third method—a preference that, in the light of what I have said above, should be interpreted as a reflection of the fact that the world was still on the gold standard (though that situation was to change radically in the fall of that year, with Britain itself taking the lead in abandoning this standard), combined with the fact that Keynes was giving this lecture in the United States and not in Britain.

Not at all surprisingly, the conceptual framework of the *Treatise* (though it is not mentioned by name) also manifested itself in much of what Keynes had to say in the Round Table discussions that accompanied the Harris Lectures.[4] This is particularly true of his contributions (cf., e.g., *Reports*, pp. 73–74, 78–84, 92–92) to the Round Table which Alvin Hansen opened with a paper on "Business Cycles, Price Levels and Unemployment," and in which he actually referred a few times to Keynes' "book" (*Reports*, p. 49; see also pp. 62 and 66).[5,6] In this discussion Keynes also reaffirmed the policy-preferences of the *Treatise*:

> I should like to try the central bank method first, uncertain how far in practice it would lead us. If that proved to be incapable of keeping things reasonably steady, then I should go in for a very great degree of state control of the rate of investment [*Reports*, p. 93].

And in a later discussion of a paper by Otto Nathan on "Public Works Construction and Unemployment," Keynes made the *Treatise*'s differential (as between Britain and the United States) advocacy of public works most explicit:[7]

> I think the argument for public works in this country is much weaker than it is in Great Britain. In Great Britain I have for a long time past agitated very strongly for a public works program, and my argument has been that we are such a center of an international system that we cannot operate on the rate of interest, because if we tried to force the rate of interest down, there is too much lending,[8] and we lose our goal [gold?]. The advantage of a government program in Great Britain is that the government can borrow at whatever the world rate of interest is, regardless of whether the investment yields that.

---

4. A two-volume record of this discussion (designated on the title-page as "Confidential—Not for Publication") exists in mimeographed form under the title Norman Wait Harris Memorial Foundation, *Reports of Round Tables: Unemployment as a World Problem* (1931), referred to henceforth as *Reports*. In a prefatory note to these *Reports* (p. ii), Quincy Wright (who was Chairman of the meetings) states that the "reports have been in nearly every instance corrected by the speakers."

The contents of these 1931 *Reports* were surveyed (with extensive quotations) some years ago by J. Ronnie Davis (1971, pp. 107–24), though without placing them in the context of Keynes' writings in the immediately preceding period.

5. Hansen (1932) was shortly afterwards to write a brief note on a technical point in the *Treatise*.

6. Keynes again made use of the theory of the *Treatise* in his contribution to the discussion of the two papers by Henry Schultz and Carter Goodrich on "Is Wage Cutting the Way Out?" In particular, Keynes analyzed a wage cut primarily in terms of its effects on the relation between savings and investment, and concluded (as did most of the other participants in the Round Table) that he would not recommend such cuts as a means of dealing with employment (*Reports*, pp. 212–17, 222).

7. This point has already been made by Moggridge and Howson (1974, p. 236), who cite the passage as reproduced by Davis (1971, p. 120).

8. By which Keynes means lending abroad, which would generate an outflow of gold; compare this passage with that in *Treatise* 2, pp. 337–38 (pp. 376–77 of the original edition). Correspondingly, I believe the last word in this sentence should have read as indicated in the brackets. This is also the way that Davis (1971, p. 120) has rendered it, though without indicating that it differs from the original text.

In this country you haven't a problem of that kind. Here you can function as though you were a closed system, and I think all your argument hitherto has been rather based on the closed system assumption. For such a system I would use as my first method operating on the long term rate of interest.

I think in this country deliberate public works should be regarded much more as a tonic to change the state of business conditions, but the means of getting back to a state of equilibrium should be concentrated on the rate of interest. That condition not being so in Great Britain, one had to lay great stress on public programs, but in this country I should operate on the rate of interest [*Reports*, p. 303].

At the same time, Keynes indicated that where a public-works policy was called for, he would recommend doing so vigorously. Again in his words:

I am sure Dr. Nathan is right, that if we just depend on traditional methods, and keep to the traditional sphere, there never will be enough government work to be more than a small factor in curing a depression of the magnitude of the present one, but I should not be so sure that it is impractical to go beyond the traditional field [*Reports*, p. 294; see also p. 300].

When pressed to explain his preference for using interest-rate policy in the United States, as against public works, Keynes did so on the grounds that the former was more in accord with the philosophy of "individualism." In Keynes' words, "I use that [namely, interest-rate policy] because I am speaking in the country which is the last home of individualism" (*Reports*, p. 84; cf. also *ibid.*, p. 92). However, on the basis of my understanding of Keynes' personality, I would like to suggest that his preference for applying interest-rate policy in the United States was motivated by an additional consideration: namely, his already-noted belief in his fundamental equations as magic formulas that could solve the world's economic ills; his willingness (as he expressed himself the year before in a letter to the Governor of the Bank of England) "to have [his] head chopped off" if these equations should be false.[9] As against this absolute conviction, however, was his recognition of the frustrating fact that the major policy implication of these equations was not applicable to his own country, Britain. But it was applicable to the United States—and so under no circumstances would Keynes give up that unique opportunity to put his magic formula to the test.

Though the Harris Lectures brought Keynes to Chicago, they apparently did not bring him into contact with the Chicago School.[10] Viner was then spending the year at the Graduate Institute of International Studies in Geneva, which in that pre-jet age meant that he did not participate in the meetings at all. And though Knight's name

9. Letter cited by Howson and Winch (1977), p. 48. For other manifestations of Keynes' "magic-formula" view of his fundamental equations, see Patinkin (1976), chap. 6.

10. I am not including under this heading Henry Schultz, who, as already indicated, played an active role in the Round Table discussions. Nor am I including Paul Douglas, who in any event did not for some reason participate in these meetings (perhaps he was away from the University then). It might be noted that Douglas and, especially, Viner participated actively in the meetings of the following year.

does appear among the members of the "Round Table Group," he participated in only one of the fourteen Round Tables which took place, and even then did not contribute more than one inconsequential remark (*Reports*, p. 481). Henry Simons (who was then an assistant professor) did participate in several of the Round Tables, but he too did so actively only once and inconsequentially (*Reports*, p. 88).[11] Only Lloyd Mints (then also an assistant professor) played a more active role. On one occasion he asked Keynes why "public works won't bring about precisely the same results" as a reduction in interest, and received the kind of answer that has already been described. Said Keynes:

> Certainly; therefore I am in favor of an admixture of public works, but my feeling is that unless you socialize the country to a degree that is unlikely, you will get to the end of the public works program, if not in one year, in two years, and therefore if you are not prepared to reduce the rate of interest and bring back private enterprise, when you get to the end of the public works program you have shot your bolt, and you are no better off. I should use the public works program to fill in the interregnum while I was getting the interest down. The public works program would in itself increase business profits, and therefore relieve people from that exceptional unwillingness to borrow.
>
> I should be afraid of that as a sole remedy. I should be afraid it would work itself out, come to an end, and then we should be back where we were unless we decided on a very definite further action [*Reports*, pp. 493–94].

On another occasion Mints asked Keynes what he thought of the possibility of reducing the rate of interest not only by "indirect means" (by which I think Mints meant open-market purchases of government securities), but also by purchasing "industrial and public utility bonds" [12]—to which Keynes replied that he would not favor such purchases "in order that the minds of those responsible for the central system should not have loaded on them the duty of judging the relative value of different classes of bonds" (*Reports*, pp. 479–80). I do not however know whether Mints was asking these questions out of conviction or out of intellectual curiosity.

Let me now jump roughly five years to the appearance of Keynes' *General Theory*. In the meantime, much has happened: Britain left the gold standard in September

11. Apparently, however, these Round Tables formed the basis for further contacts between Simons and Keynes. Thus the Simons Papers contain a handwritten note from Keynes dated 31 March 1933—though without any designation of its addressee—which reads: "Much interested by the memorandum which you kindly send [*sic*] me." This may well be a reference to the memorandum on *Balancing the Budget: Federal Fiscal Policy During Depression* which was published in January 1933 as a University of Chicago *Public Policy Pamphlet*, and whose signers included Simons, Viner, and Douglas. The main message of the memorandum was that government budget should be balanced over the business cycle, rather than annually. For details see Davis (1971), pp. 46–47.

I am indebted to Donald Moggridge for advice on the reading of Keynes' note. Moggridge has also kindly informed me that there is no further correspondence on this point in the Keynes Papers in Cambridge; nor do these Papers, or the Marshall Library collection which came from Keynes' books, contain the aforementioned pamphlet.

12. The complete passage here refers to "purchasing industrial and utility bonds by the member banks themselves"; but from Keynes' reply and the discussion which follows (which describes Mints' proposal as one which would get the government "into the bond business") I think this passage should read ". . . by the central banks themselves."

1931, which immediately led Keynes to advocate interest-rate reduction for it too. But after a short time, during which serious unemployment continued to prevail, it became clear to Keynes that such a policy was not adequate to the task. Accordingly he began to advocate public-works expenditures not as a second-best policy, but as a "first-best" one (Patinkin 1979b, pp. 162–64). And in the *General Theory* he developed the revolutionary macroeconomic theory which provided the underpinning for such a policy. According to this theory, the great degree of uncertainty which surrounds investment plans generates instability with respect to the volume of investment and also makes it unlikely that reductions in the rate of interest brought about by open-market purchases can stimulate investment (and hence employment) significantly. This effective interest-inelasticity of investment in turn implies that the additional money injected into the economy by the open-market purchase will largely be added to cash balances—that is, the demand for such balances under such uncertain circumstances is effectively highly interest-elastic. Correspondingly, government deficit-favored expenditures must be relied upon as a way of achieving full employment.

During this same period—as all good Chicagoans know, and as both Milton Friedman (on the occasion of the Henry Simons Lecture twelve years ago) and myself (on a somewhat later occasion) have spelled out in detail[13]—the Chicago School was independently developing the traditional $MV = PT$ quantity-theory approach in a way that led it to seemingly similar conclusions. In its analysis, the major cause of the cycle was the instability, not of investment, but of the velocity of circulation V, which set off cummulative movements of expansion or contraction in the economy. And the corresponding policy prescription of the Chicago School of the 1930s (more specifically, of Simons and Mints) was for the government to make appropriate changes in M that would offset these changes in V and thus maintain a constant level of what Simons called "total turnover MV" (1934, p. 64). Under the assumption of some downward flexibility in prices, it also advocated for this purpose the operational rule of varying M so as to stabilize the price level, P: increasing M when P tended to fall, and decreasing M when it tended to rise. The necessary variations in M were to be generated either by open-market operations or by budgetary deficits, which deficits in turn were to be generated by varying either government expenditures and/or tax receipts.[14]

Having mentioned Friedman's Simons lecture, let me digress briefly to dispute one of its major contentions. When in his "Rules versus Authorities in Monetary Policy" (1936) Simons chose the foregoing policy rule of keeping the price level constant, he

---

13. Though with some differences; see chap. 10 above, p. 248, fn. 22, and p. 257, fn. 3. A more significant difference—of another nature—will be discussed in the next two paragraphs.

The views of the Chicago School have also been described in J. Ronnie Davis' *New Economics and the Old Economists* (1971), chap. 3.

14. For documentation and further details, see chap. 10 above, pp. 245–52, which also refers to the views of Knight and Viner. I have not been able to find any place where Viner explicitly supported this policy prescription; on the other hand, he was already in the early 1930s advocating deficit spending, as well as the more general policy of balancing the budget only over the cycle; see Davis (1971), pp. 39–46. Cf also Viner's letter to me of February 23, 1970, reproduced on pp. 270–71 above.

did so after considering—and rejecting—an alternative rule of keeping the quantity of money constant. And he explained this choice in the following words:

> With all its merits, however, this rule [of holding the quantity of money constant] cannot now be recommended as a basis for monetary reform. The obvious weakness of fixed quantity, as a sole rule of monetary policy, lies in the danger of sharp changes on the velocity side, for no monetary system can function effectively or survive politically in the face of extreme alternations of hoarding and dishoarding. It is easy to argue that something would be gained in any event if perverse changes were prevented merely as to quantity, but the argument is unconvincing. The fixing of the quantity of circulation media might merely serve to increase the perverse variability in the amounts of "near moneys" and in the degree of their general acceptability, just as the restrictions on the issue of bank notes presumably served to hasten the development of deposit (checking-account) banking [1936, p. 164].

Now, Friedman quite reasonably says that Simon's belief in the instability of velocity was based on his interpretation of the Great Depression; but Friedman goes on to contend that had Simons then known the "facts which we now know and he did not" (1967, p. 84), he would not have interpreted the Great Depression in terms of such an instability of V, and would accordingly have chosen instead a policy rule stated in terms of the quantity of money.

I must confess that I have always found it difficult to understand the operational meaning of such statements: to understand how they can be subjected to empirical test. And what compounds my difficulty in this case is that Friedman does not specify which of the facts of the Great Depression—facts that he goes on to cite from his monumental study with Anna Jacobson Schwartz of *A Monetary History of the United States* (1962)—were not available to Simons. Surely it cannot be the facts about the decline in Federal Reserve credit outstanding to which Friedman refers (1967, p. 90); for current monthly data on the volume of this credit were being published in the *Federal Reserve Bulletin*. Nor can it be the broad facts about the changes in the money supply which Friedman cites: for monthly data on currency in circulation had long since been available, and ever since 1927 quarterly data on net deposits (including time deposits) of all banks were being published in the *Bulletin* as well as the *Annual Reports* of the Federal Reserve; and the addition of these two series yields an estimate of the money supply[15] whose changes during the Great Depression are broadly similar to those described by Friedman in his lecture.[16] Even more relevant to the question at issue (for reasons that will become clear in a moment) is the fact that in November

15. Which after subtracting deposits of mutual savings banks (for which the Federal Reserve provided separate estimates), conceptually approximates Friedman's M_2; needless to say, however, this procedure leads to double-counting of vault cash, a minor item.

16. Thus in terms of annual rates of change in M_2, Friedman (1967, pp. 89–90) describes (a) a decline at the rate of 2.3 percent from August 1929 to October 1930; (b) a decline at the rate of 13 percent from March 1931 to August 1931; and (c) a decline at the rate of 31 percent from August 1931 to January 1932. The corresponding estimates from the Federal Reserve data (for the quarters closest to these respective periods, and again in terms of annual rates of change) are (a) −5.7 percent; (b) −5 percent; and (c) −27 percent (Federal Reserve Board, *Twentieth Annual Report* (1934), pp. 141, 163).

1933 Lauchlin Currie published an article in the *Quarterly Journal of Economics* in which he provided annual estimates of the money supply for 1921–32 whose year-to-year percentage changes during the Great Depression are also similar to those described by Friedman and Schwartz.[17] And in April 1934 Currie used this series as the basis of an article which he published in the *Journal of Political Economy* on "The Failure of Monetary Policy to Prevent the Depression of 1929–32." Indeed, the major conclusion of this article was that "The [Federal Reserve] policy followed throughout 1929, so far from tending to prevent the depression, actually operated, in the view of this paper, to bring it on" (Currie 1934a, p. 176). Later in that year, Currie published a book on *The Supply and Control of Money in the United States* (1934b) in which he reproduced the monetary data of his 1933 article (pp. 31–33, 70) as well as the major conclusions of his 1934 one (pp. 144–48). And since—as the last link in this chain of events—Simons reviewed this book the following year for the *Journal of Political Economy* we can safely say that when he chose his price-stabilization rule, Simons had available to him not only monetary data that revealed roughly the same changes that Friedman has described in his lecture, but even an alternative interpretation of these data which in its broad lines agreed with the one that Friedman was later to give.[18,19]

Let me return now to our main subject. The *General Theory* appeared in February 1936 and in November of that year the *Quarterly Journal of Economics* published what was to become a celebrated symposium on the book in which Jacob Viner wrote the lead article (entitled "Mr. Keynes on the Causes of Unemployment"), followed by articles by Dennis Robertson, Wassily Leontief, and F. W. Taussig, who also acted as editor of the symposium. In a comment on this review written some twenty-five years later, Viner explained that he had been asked by Taussig to concentrate on Keynes' theory of changes in the volume of employment, which Viner interpreted as a short-run theory. As such (wrote Viner in this comment) he found the *General Theory* "a veritable landmark, in both its positive and negative or critical aspects, in the history of our discipline" (Viner, 1964, p. 255).[20] At the same time (said Viner in this comment) he remained "skeptical . . . with some propensity to be hostile" with respect to Keynes' denial "that (in a truly competitive economy) there

---

17. Thus the following are the percentage year-to-year changes in M_1 as respectively estimated by Currie and Friedman-Schwartz (the estimates of the latter appear in parentheses): 1928–29: 0.1 (1.7); 1929–30: −3.7 (−3.4); 1930–31: −6.4 (−5.6); 1931–32: −13.7 (−14.4) (Currie, 1933, p. 84; Friedman-Schwartz, 1963, pp. 710–14). A similar comparison holds with respect to the monthly estimates which James W. Angell presented in his *Behavior of Money* (1936, p. 175).

As noted above (p. 278, fn. 1), the work of Currie and Angell is not referred to in Friedman and Schwartz' *Monetary History of the U.S.* (1963); the estimates themselves are however described in their subsequent volume on *Monetary Statistics of the U.S.* (1970). For more on Currie's contribution to monetary economics, see Brunner (1968), Humphrey (1971), and Jones (1978); cf. also the preceding chapter.

18. In 1935 Currie published a second edition of his book with slightly different estimates of M_1; these differences, however, have almost no effect on the percentage changes described in the preceding footnote.

19. For another aspect of Simons' review of Currie's book, see p. 283 above.

20. On the other hand, Viner (1951, p. 13) felt that "neither in his *General Theory* or after did Keynes himself make any important application of his new doctrines and concepts to theoretical issues in the international field." (I am indebted to Jacob Frenkel for bringing this passage to my attention.)

exist powerful automatic forces which in the long run, if not counteracted by perverse governmental intervention, will restore equilibrium'' (Viner, 1964, p. 255). Viner also explained that in his review he had not discussed "Keynes' ventures in the *General Theory* into *Dogmengeschichte*,'' and added that "as a historian of thought in areas in which he was emotionally involved as a protagonist and prophet, Keynes seemed to me to be seriously lacking in the unexciting but essential qualities for the intellectual historian of objectivity and of judiciousness'' (Viner, 1964, p. 254). Amen.

As can be gathered from this, Viner's review itself was a favorable one. Unlike such review articles as those by Hicks (1937) and Meade (1937), however, it did not attempt to summarize the basic conceptual framework of the *General Theory* and instead restricted itself to presenting a balanced criticism of various individual points in it. Thus Viner identifies one of the major differences between Keynes' position and the orthodox one as lying in Keynes' denial that reduction of money wages is a remedy for unemployment. Viner contends that Keynes had failed to take account of the possibility that the decline in prices might lag behind that of wages, thus giving a temporary boost to profits, which in turn would stimulate investment and thus output (Viner 1936, pp. 247–49). On another point, and in an adumbration of discussions twenty years later, Viner also argues that consumption should be assumed to be a function not only of current income, but also of wealth and of "anticipations as to the prospective trend of income''—and that the influence of wealth acts as a stabilizing factor over the cycle (*ibid.*, p. 239, fn. 3; pp. 250–52).

Viner's major criticism, however, is of Keynes' contention that the rate of interest is determined by liquidity preference in the sense of the propensity to hoard. As against this, Viner supports Robertson's point in his contribution to the symposium that the transactions demand—and the forces of consumption and investment which lie behind it—are equally important determinants of this rate. Viner also contends that in any event such hoards are quantitatively small, since most money holdings are for transaction purposes. And in what I interpret as an allusion to the teaching prevalent at Chicago (and elsewhere), Viner also claims that "in modern monetary theory it [i.e., hoarding] is generally dealt with, with results which in kind are substantially identical with Keynes', as a factor operating to reduce the 'velocity' of money'' (Viner, 1936, p. 240).

In his reply to Viner (whose contribution Keynes described as "the most important of the four'') Keynes contended that "the monetary theorists who try to deal with it in this way are altogether on the wrong track'' (Keynes, 1936, p. 211). But at the later point at which Keynes seems to be expanding on this contention (*ibid.*, p. 216), he fails to take account of the fact that an increased propensity to hoard means a decreased velocity of circulation. Nor does he concede to Viner or to Robertson—or for that matter to anyone else at any other time—that the rate of interest is determined by savings and investment, as well as liquidity preference (Patinkin, 1976, pp. 62–63, 99).

About a year later, Frank Knight published his review article of the *General Theory* in the *Canadian Journal of Economics and Political Science* under the title "Unemployment: And Mr. Keynes' Revolution in Economic Theory'' (1937). In his opening footnote Knight states that the article will be ''primarily critical in nature,'' and he more than fulfills his promise. It is Knight at his irascible and sarcastic best—or worst. I have had the opportunity of examining Knight's copy of the *General Theory*, the one which he presumably read in preparation for writing his review, and it is filled with pencilled marginal notes of vehement dissent.[21] Thus on Keynes' statement in the Preface that ''It is astonishing what foolish things one can temporarily believe if one thinks too long alone, particularly in economics'' (*GT*, p. vii), Knight commented ''best statement in the book''—and we know of whom he was thinking. The expletive ''Nonsense!''—replaced on occasion by even stronger terms—makes a frequent appearance in these margins. There are, however, passages which Knight obviously enjoyed, such as like Keynes' scintillating description of the nature of speculative activity on the stock market, and on Wall Street in particular (*GT*, pp. 153–60—''Best thing in the Book?'').

In any event, Knight's published review is a fairly systematized—if expurgated— rendition of these marginal notes. And this is a pity: for lost in this sea of captious criticisms are some valid points. Thus Knight (1937, p. 103), alone of all reviewers, rightly criticizes Keynes' puzzling statement that profits are maximized at the intersection point of aggregate demand and supply (*GT*, p. 25).[22] Like Viner, Knight also shows that Keynes' statements about hoarding can be translated into more familiar statements about changes in velocity. In Knight's words, ''saving may be hoarded and by reducing monetary circulation lead to sales reductions or price declines with all the consequences of these in train; but familiar terms and modes of expression seem to be shunned on principle in this book'' (Knight, 1937, p. 108; see also p. 110). And like Viner and Robertson, Knight also rejects Keynes' purely monetary theory of interest. In particular, he criticizes Keynes' theory of liquidity-preference on the grounds that

> . . . it is self-evident that at any time (and at the margin) the rate of interest equates *both* the desirability of holding cash with the desirability of holding non-monetary wealth *and* the desirability of consuming with that of lending and so with both the other two desirabilities. For, to any person who has either money or wealth in any form, or to anyone who holds salable service-capacity, all three of these alternatives are continuously open (Knight, 1937, p. 113, italics in original).

Let me, however, note that this description of the desire for holding money as an alternative to holding other forms of wealth does not appear in earlier Chicago writings on money, and so can itself be regarded as reflecting the influence of Keynes' theory of liquidity preference—an influence that was to manifest itself in subsequent writings of other Chicagoans as well (see above, chapter 10, pp. 247–49, 253–56).

To the best of my knowledge, Knight's review is also the only one which points out

21. I am indebted to George Stigler for making this book available to me, and to Mrs. Frank Knight for permitting me to quote from its marginal notes.

22. Cf. Patinkin (1979a), pp. 171–73.

that though Keynes contends that he has presented a theory of unemployment equilibrium, his language at various points in the book indicates that he is really talking about a short-period situation. In Knight's words:

> The next general comment which must be made on Mr. Keynes's book as a whole is that it is inordinately difficult to tell what the author means. This is true in particular because on general issues it appears certain that he does not mean what he says. The theory is ostensibly one of equilibrium with extensive involuntary unemployment . . . and in the bulk of the exposition there is no explicit reference to cycles or oscillations and little hint that such phenomena exist. Now I for one simply cannot take this new and revolutionary equilibrium theory seriously, and doubt whether Mr. Keynes himself really does so. Scattered through the work are innumerable references to the short period, several which indicate that reactions are more or less reversible (*e.g.*, pp. 248, 251), and a few which run frankly in terms of comparative stability or stickiness rather than fixity (pp. 236, 237); in particular, there is a reference (p. 249) to the capacity of the economic system for remaining in a "chronic" condition of sub-normal activity for a "considerable period". This is a far cry from the "stable equilibrium" of page 30 and the tone of most of the book (Knight, 1937, p. 121).

And for this general tone, a typical Knightian explanation is provided: in modern times "the demand for heresy is always in excess of the supply and its production always a prosperous business" (Knight, 1937, p. 122, fn. 22). Knight also repeatedly emphasizes that there can be a long-period position of unemployment equilibrium only if there is absolute rigidity of the money wage rate.[23]

The editor of the *Canadian Journal* wrote Keynes asking if he would care "to write a counter-blast" to Knight's review. But Keynes declined, saying that "with Professor Knight's two main conclusions, namely, that my book had caused him intense irritation, and that he had had great difficulty in understanding it, I am in agreement. So perhaps you will excuse me if I leave the article alone" (*JMK* 29, p. 217).

This difference between Knight's and Viner's views of the *General Theory* gave rise a few years later to an incident which to begin with was probably never known to more than a few people, which slipped into oblivion afterwards, and of which I have only now learned. In 1940 The University of Chicago was making plans for the celebration of its fiftieth anniversary the following year. Among these plans was the customary one of marking the occasion by awarding honorary doctorates to outstanding scholars of the world. In this connection Jacob Viner—and this was before their wartime contacts which so deeply impressed him (see fn. 30 below)—apparently proposed awarding such a degree to Keynes. I say "apparently" because the only evidence I have of this is a lengthy letter in the Viner Papers from Knight to Viner,

---

23. There is one major exception to the generally negative tone of Knight's review: namely (as might be guessed from the above description of Knight's marginal notes), his description of Keynes' discussion of "the speculative element involved in any decision to invest" (Knight, 1937, p. 11). Knight, however, questions the novelty of this discussion, and cites Keynes' own reference to Irving Fisher's marginal rate of return over cost (*GT*, p. 140). I do not, however, see the relevance of Fisher to this discussion, whereas I do very much see the relevance of Knight's own *Risk, Uncertainty and Profit* (1921)—to which Knight, quite characteristically, does not refer.

dated August 6, 1940, which begins by expressing Knight's "shock" at having heard that Viner had made such a proposal—and which then goes on to denounce it vigorously. The main substantive basis of Knight's objection was expressed in the following words:

> I regard Mr. Keynes' neo-mercantilistic position in economics in general, and with respect to money and monetary theory in particular,[24] as essentially taking the side of the man-in-the-street, against the effort of the economic thinker and analyst to get beyond and to dispel the short-sighted views and prejudices of the former. . . . His work and influence seem to me supremely "anti-intellectual," in the only meaning of intellectual life which is worthy of approval or support.

Whether because of Knight's objections, or for other reasons, the honorary degree was never awarded.[25]

Let me turn now to Henry Simon's brief review of the *General Theory*. This appeared in the *Christian Century* for July 2, 1936 and was almost as critical as Knight's. In accordance with the nonprofessional nature of this magazine,[26] the review is practically devoid of technical analytical details and instead dwells largely on what Simons saw as the policy implications of Keynes' book. Thus Simons began by explaining that:

> Mr. Keynes' main point is that our economic system has been excessively exposed and subjected to deflationary pressures—that individual savings are likely to get dammed up in hoards, instead of flowing on to finance the production of investment-assets. With this judgment, the reviewer is inclined definitely to agree. Indeed, if the whole book could be interpreted simply as a critical appraisal of the traditional gold standard, implemented through central-bank operations, one's judgment of its main ideas might be extremely favorable.

24. What I think Knight primarily had in mind here was Keynes' purely monetary theory of interest; cf. pp. 33 and 299 above.

25. The foregoing excerpt from Knight's letter is reproduced here with the permission of the Princeton University Library. I have been informed by Shlomo Maital that there is no other material relating to this letter in the Viner Papers there. Nor is this letter or any related material to be found in the Frank Knight Papers at Chicago or in the files of the Department of Economics there.

Of the members of the Department at that time who are still with us, Gregg Lewis and Lloyd Mints have informed me that they never knew of this incident; and John Nef wrote me as follows (cited with permission from a letter dated July 18, 1979):

> I was a member of the committee for recommending the awarding of honorary degrees to the president at the time you mention and I was also a member of the special committee which recommended degrees in connection with the social sciences at the time of the fiftieth anniversary celebration of the founding of the University. I cannot remember Lord Keynes' name being brought before either of these committees. So I assume that Viner did not force the issue with Knight.

Among the individuals who did receive honorary degrees at the Fiftieth-Anniversary Convocation in September 1941 were R. H. Tawney and J. M. Clark. (From 1915–26, Clark had been a Professor of Political Economy at Chicago and a member of the teaching staff of both the Department of Political Economy and the School of Business. At the Convocation he was presented by the dean of the School of Business.)

26. I do not know why Simons chose it as a vehicle for his review; he had once before published a group of reviews there. See the bibliography in Simons (1948), p. 314.

He then goes on to criticize Keynes for advocating that, in order to solve these problems, "the state should use taxation to curtail private saving; it should supplement private consumption and investment with its own spending and it should force down and keep down the rate of interest to promote new enterprise," vehemently declaring that by suggesting these and similar measures, Keynes "may only succeed in becoming the academic idol of our worst cranks and charlatans—not to mention the possibilities of the book as the economic bible of a fascist movement." And in an obvious allusion to his own policy Simons writes:

> Mr. Keynes nowhere suggests the need for economy in the kinds of governmental interference; and he seems to disregard, or grossly to underestimate, the possibilities of controlling all the variables which his analysis emphasizes merely by controlling the quantity of money—i.e., by ordering fiscal practice (spending, taxing, borrowing and currency issue) in terms of deliberate monetary policy. He overlooks the need (clearly suggested by his own analysis) for the minimizing of monetary uncertainties and the achievement of a monetary system based on definite and stable rules. Thus, while expressing decided preference for an economic system of free enterprise, he does not seriously consider what monetary arrangements or what implementations of monetary policy are most and least compatible with that system.

At first sight this strong opposition to the policy implications of the *General Theory* seems puzzling: for, as emphasized above, the Chicago School of the 1930s also advocated government deficit spending as a means of dealing with unemployment. But whereas it visualized this as a short-run necessity, which in the course of the cycle would be balanced by a budget surplus, Keynes saw it as a necessary long-run feature of a full-employment capitalist economy. This difference reflected in turn their different views as to the long-run marginal productivity of capital, which Keynes saw as highly inelastic and thus possibly declining to zero within a generation or two (*GT*, pp. 220, 375–77), and which Knight and Simons saw as highly, if not infinitely, elastic.[27] In this connection we should also note Viner's statement in his later comment on his review that

> Aside from details, however, I would have accepted the policy implications of the *General Theory* in the monetary and fiscal field were they presented as relating to short-run or cyclical fluctuations in employment but were not extended without further analysis to long-sustained or chronic unemployment [Viner, 1964, p. 263].

But I think that there was an important policy difference even within the short-term context. For Keynes, the purpose of a deficit was to increase aggregate demand directly, which meant to increase government expenditures G in $C + I + G = Y$. For the Chicago School, however, the purpose of a government deficit was to increase

---

27. Thus in his review of the *General Theory*, Knight (p. 117, fn. 18) termed Keynes' idea of a zero marginal efficiency of capital as "fantastic." For a general discussion of Knight's views on this matter, see above, chap. 1, pp. 32–33. On Simons, see his "Hansen on Fiscal Policy" (1942), pp. 186, 192–93.

M in $MV = PT$, and this could be done either by increasing expenditures or decreasing tax revenues. In his "Positive Program for Laissez Faire" (1934) and "Rules versus Authorities" (1936), Simons was neutral with respect to these two alternatives. But in his later writings, as the need arose to define his views relative to Keynesian ones, Simons (1942, p. 210; 1944, p. 265)—and after him Mints (1950, pp. 196, 205–12)—began to express a definite preference for generating deficits by means of reducing taxes: both because it was a more flexible procedure which could subsequently be reversed, and because it involved less government activity than did increasing expenditures. Indeed, there is one passage in Simons' writings (1942, p. 205, second paragraph) which, though obscure, seems to imply that the ideal method of changing the money supply is through open-market operations. Be that as it may, Mints (1946, pp. 62–63; 1950, pp. 200–203) did not have confidence in the efficacy of such operations. Nor did Viner, many years before that.[28,29]

Let me conclude with two brief comments. First, I have already stressed the common view of Keynes and the Chicago School on the short-run instability of the economy. Another common feature was the fact that each chose what we would today call a discretionary policy to deal with this instability: the Chicago School, a policy which took the price level as its target variable, and Keynes, one which took the level of employment. Yet another common feature, and what distinguishes both Keynes and Chicago, on the one hand, from both the monetarists and fiscalists of today, on the other—in brief, what distinguishes the 1930s from the 1970s—was the absolute confidence of the economists of this earlier period in the efficacy of their respective policies: their failure to realize (as both theory and sad experience have forced us to realize since then) that uncertainty about the actual state of the world at any given moment of time compounded by the possibly destabilizing effects of lags could seriously interfere with the success of their policies. Simons did not mention this problem, Keynes gave it at best passing attention, and in 1950 Mints (p. 138) even rejected Milton Friedman's "early warnings" of this danger—warnings that Friedman (1948, 1953, and 1961) was in the process of developing into one of his most important contributions to the analysis of macroeconomic policy (cf. p. 283 above).

---

28. Namely, in his 1933 article on "Inflation as a Possible Remedy for Depression," in which Viner said:

> Now, the government can also try another method [to overcome the depression]. Instead of increasing its expenditures, it may buy its own bonds in the market with either new money printed by the printing presses or with funds which it has borrowed from the banking system for the purpose. This method is inferior to the preceding one in this respect: the preceding one gives more immediate stimulus to business. What this does is to increase the cash reserves of the banking system, and therefore, it is hoped, to give the banks the desire to put their idle funds to work. But the bankers have learned in recent years, not how to make money without lending, but that under certain circumstances the rate at which they lose money is less if they stop lending, so it is conceivable that the banking system would welcome the additional liquidity and would not increase its loans or investments. But it can be argued in support of this method that it does not weaken the budgetary situation of the government, but merely substitutes obligations of no definite maturity for long term obligations. If used at a time of growing business confidence, when business men were willing to borrow, it would make it easier and safer for bankers to lend [Viner 1933, p. 131; cited by Tavlas 1977, pp. 53–54].

29. Cf. above, chap. 10, p. 246, Proposition 5, for which this paragraph provides belated documentation (cf. p. 257, fn. 2 above).

My second point is that I have restricted myself in this lecture to the relations between Keynes and Chicago in connection with the macroeconomic theory and policy of what is effectively a closed economy. There is yet another subject which I hope someone will some day study: namely, their relations in connection with international economics. Let me for the moment only say that with respect to one of Keynes' major activities in this field, his role in the Bretton Woods agreement, he earned the approval of both Viner and Simons. In view of Viner's general belief in the desirability of fixed exchange rates, this is not surprising. And though Simons saw flexible exchange rates as "perhaps closer to the ideal scheme of things" (1944, p. 265), he did not advocate this for the postwar world, for which "a strong case can be made for nominal return to the gold standard" (1943, p. 245). And so it was not only Viner who, in reaction to Keynes' plan, wrote him in July 1943 that "we are not really far apart on any important issues," [30] but also Simons, who a month before that wrote saying: [31]

> Please accept my enthusiastic praise and endorsement of your paper on *International Clearing Union*.[32] . . . I have just finished reading the document itself and am pleased beyond even my high expectations. It strikes me not only as sound in its proposals, but as eminently judicious and statesmanlike in its whole argument.

These are the considered opinions of an American economist who, by slight reputation, has been bitterly anti-Hansen and, if not wholly anti-Keynesian, utterly opposed to your extreme American disciples. (I sometimes suspect that

30. Viner had sent Keynes an advance copy of his (Viner's) *Yale Review* article (1943) on the respective merits of the Keynes and White plans and this led to some correspondence between them. This correspondence is reproduced in *JMK* 25, pp. 320–35; the statement just cited appears on p. 326.

I might note here that there was an earlier wartime context in which Viner and Keynes met, apparently for the first time: namely, during Keynes' 1941 visit to the United States on behalf of the British government for the purpose of clarifying the terms of the Lend-Lease agreement. In particular, the Henry Morgenthau Diaries contain the minutes of several meetings in the United States Treasury during June and July 1941 (usually chaired by Morgenthau himself) in which both Keynes and Viner participated. From these minutes it would, however, appear that Viner's role in these meetings (in which there were always more than a dozen participants) was a minor one.

I am indebted to Donald Moggridge for informing me of these meetings and directing me to the Morgenthau Diaries. For a general description of Keynes' Lend-Lease negotiations (though without reference to Viner), see Harrod (1951), pp. 505–14.

It was apparently the impression of these wartime contacts, as well as of Keynes' posthumously published "Balance of Payments of the U.S." (1946), which brought Viner in later years to speak of Keynes in the following way:

> The [1946] article . . . survives as one among many other testimonies of the supreme level of statesmanship, of balanced vision, of dedication, and of endeavor to reconcile differences in conclusions when there was no difference as to basic objectives and values, on which he ended his brilliant career. The Keynes of that period was to me then, and continues to be, a heroic figure, and my admiration of him as he was then, of his personality and his intellect, was unalloyed by the qualifications which I felt, and still feel, about the Keynes of the *General Theory*, and even more, about the journalistic and polemical Keynes of the 1920's and early 1930's [1964, p. 266].

31. Typewritten letter of June 10, 1943, in Simons Papers, The Law School, The University of Chicago; reproduced with permission. Unfortunately, this letter is not reproduced in *JMK* 25.

32. The reference is presumably to the version which the British government issued as a Command Paper in April 1973.

you may not be much more tolerant than I am toward that weird amalgam of your doctrines and Schumpeter's preposterous *Entwicklungstheorie* [33] which constitutes the extreme "American Keynesism [*sic*]."') As a vigorous but inconspicuous participant in recent monetary-fiscal controversies, I think I can testify to the statesmanlike quality of the document and to its success, among reasonable people, in adjourning a bitter academic controversy in favor of common pursuit of international monetary cooperation. . . .

I think I may say that my colleagues in the Department, if invited to do so, would join me in congratulating you on your great and timely service to the cause of winning the peace.

Keynes replied with a brief letter of thanks for Simons' "handsome letter"; but unfortunately for us, he did not rise to the bait of Simons' remark about Hansen. And so we lost this opportunity of learning something about Keynes' views of his "American disciples."

Bibliography*

J. W. Angell. *The Behavior of Money.* New York, 1936.

K. Brunner. "On Lauchlin Currie's Contribution to Monetary Theory." Introduction to reprint of L. Currie, *The Supply and Control of Money in the United States.* New York, 1968.

L. Currie. "Money, Gold, and Income in the United States, 1921–32." *Quarterly Journal of Economics*, Nov. 1933, *48*, 77–95.

———. "The Failure of Monetary Policy to Prevent the Depression of 1929–32." *Journal of Political Economy*, Apr. 1934, *42*, 145–77 (a)

———. *The Supply and Control of Money in the United States.* Cambridge, Mass., 1934. (b)

———. *The Supply and Control of Money in the United States*, 2nd ed., rev. Cambridge, Mass., 1935.

J. R. Davis. *The New Economics and the Old Economists.* Ames, Iowa, 1971.

M. Friedman. "A Monetary and Fiscal Framework for Economic Stability." *American Economic Review*, June 1948, *38*, 245–64. As reprinted in *Essays in Positive Economics.* Chicago, 1953. Pp. 133–56.

———. "The Effects of a Full-Employment Policy on Economic Stability: A Formal Analysis. "In *Essays in Positive Economics.* Chicago, 1953. Pp. 117–32.

———. "The Lag in Effect of Monetary Policy." *Journal of Political Economy*, Oct. 1961, *69*, 447–66. As reprinted in *The Optimum Quantity of Money and Other Essays.* Chicago, 1969. Pp. 237–60.

———. "The Monetary Theory and Policy of Henry Simons." *Journal of Law and Economics*, Oct. 1967, *10*, 1–13. As reprinted in *The Optimum Quantity of Money and Other Essays.* Chicago, 1969. Pp. 81–93.

33. I do not know to what aspects of Schumpeter's theory of development Simons is referring. And what increases my puzzlement here is that in his "Hansen on Fiscal Policy" (1942)—a reprint of which Simons enclosed with his letter to Keynes—there is a fairly favorable reference (on p. 187, fn. 2) to pp. 1032–50 of Schumpeter's *Business Cycles* (1939).

*References in text to works listed here as reprinted are to the date of original publication; the page references, however, follow the pagination of the reprinted form.

———— and A. J. Schwartz. *A Monetary History of the United States 1867–1960*. Princeton, N.J., 1963.

————. *Monetary Statistics of the United States*. New York, 1970.

A. H. Hansen. "A Fundamental Error in Keynes' 'Treatise on Money.' " *American Economic Review*, Sept. 1932, *22*, 462. As reprinted in *The Collected Writings of John Maynard Keynes*. Vol. 5, pp. 329–30.

————. *Fiscal Policy and Business Cycles*. New York, 1941.

Harris Memorial Foundation. *Unemployment As a World Problem*, ed. Q. Wright. Chicago, 1931.

————. *Reports of Round Tables: Unemployment As a World Problem*, 2 vols. Chicago, 1931 (mimeographed).

R. F. Harrod. *The Life of John Maynard Keynes*. London, 1951. Reprinted New York, 1969.

J. R. Hicks. "Mr. Keynes and the 'Classics': A Suggested Interpretation." *Econometrica*, Apr. 1937, *5*, 147–59.

S. Howson and D. Winch. *The Economic Advisory Council 1930–1939*. Cambridge, 1977.

T. M. Humphrey. "Role of Non-Chicago Economists in the Evolution of the Quantity Theory in America 1930–1950." *Southern Economic Journal*, July 1971, *38*, 12–18.

B. L. Jones. "Lauchlin Currie, Pump Priming, and New Deal Fiscal Policy, 1934–1936." *History of Political Economy*. Winter 1978, *10*, 509–24.

J. M. Keynes. *A Treatise on Money, Vol. 1: The Pure Theory of Money*. London, 1930. As reprinted in Keynes' *Collected Writings*, vol. 5.

————. *A Treatise on Money, Vol. 2: The Applied Theory of Money*, London, 1930. As reprinted in Keynes' *Collected Writings*, vol. 6.

————. "An Economic Analysis of Unemployment." In Harris Memorial Foundation, *Unemployment As a World Problem*. Chicago, 1931. As reprinted in Keynes' *Collected Writings*, vol. 13, pp. 343–67.

————. *The General Theory of Employment, Interest, and Money*. London, 1936. As reprinted in Keynes' *Collected Writings*, vol. 7 (same pagination as original).

————. "The General Theory of Employment." *Quarterly Journal of Economics*, Feb. 1937, *51*, 209–23. As reprinted in Keynes' *Collected Writings*, vol. 14, pp. 109–33.

————. "Proposals for an International Clearing Union" Cmd. 6437, London: HMSO April 1943. As reprinted in *The International Monetary Fund 1945–1965*, ed. J. K. Horsefield, vol. 3. Washington, D.C., 1969. Pp. 19–36. (Various drafts of these "Proposals" appear in Keynes' *Collected Writings*, vol. 25).

————. "The Balance of Payments of the United States." *Economic Journal*, June 1946, *56*, 172–87.

————. *The General Theory and After, Part 1: Preparation*. Edited by D. E. Moggridge. Vol. 13 of Keynes' *Collected Writings*. 1973.

————. *The General Theory and After, Part II: Defense and Development*. Ed. D. E. Moggridge. Vol. 14 of Keynes' *Collected Writings*. 1973.

————. *Activities 1940–44: Shaping the Post-War World: The Clearing Union*. Ed. D. E. Moggridge. Vol. 25 of Keynes' *Collected Writings*. 1979.

————. *The General Theory and After: A Supplement*. Ed. D. E. Moggridge. Vol. 29 of Keynes' *Collected Writings*. 1979.

————. *Collected Writings*. London, 1971–79.

———— and H. D. Henderson. *Can Lloyd George Do It?: An Examination of the Liberal Pledge*. London, 1929. As reprinted in Keynes' *Collected Writings*. vol. 9, pp. 86–125.

F. H. Knight. *Risk, Uncertainty, and Profit*. Boston, 1921.

_____. "Unemployment: And Mr. Keynes' Revolution in Economic Theory." *Canadian Journal of Economics and Political Science*, Feb. 1937, *3*, 100–123.

J. E. Meade. "A Simplified Model of Mr. Keynes' System." *Review of Economic Studies*, Feb. 1937, *4*, 98–107.

L. W. Mints. "Monetary Policy." *Review of Economic Statistics*, May 1946, *28*, 60–69.

_____. *Monetary Policy for a Competitive Society*. New York, 1950.

D. E. Moggridge and S. Howson. "Keynes on Monetary Policy, 1910–1946." *Oxford Economic Papers*, July 1974, *26*, 226–47.

Norman Wait Harris Memorial Foundation. See Harris Memorial Foundation.

D. Patinkin. "The Chicago Tradition, The Quantity Theory, and Friedman." *Journal of Money, Credit and Banking*, Feb. 1969, *1*, 46–70. [Reproduced as chap. 10 above.]

_____. "On the Monetary Economics of Chicagoans and Non-Chicagoans: Comment." *Southern Economic Journal*, Jan. 1973, 39, 454–59. (a) [Reproduced as chap. 11 above.]

_____. "Frank Knight as Teacher." *American Economic Review*, Dec. 1973, *53*, 787–810. (b) [Reproduced as chap. 1 above.]

_____. *Keynes Monetary Thought*. Durham, N.C., 1976.

_____. "The Process of Writing the *General Theory*: A Critical Survey." In *Keynes, Cambridge, and the General Theory*, ed. D. Patinkin and J. C. Leith. London, 1977. Pp. 3–24.

_____. "A Study of Keynes' Theory of Effective Demand." *Economic Inquiry*, Apr. 1979, *17*, 155–176. (a)

_____. "The Development of Keynes' Policy Thinking." In *Economic Theory for Economic Efficiency: Essays in Honor of Abba Lerner*, ed. H. I. Greenfield et al. Cambridge, Mass., 1979. Pp. 151–66. (b)

D. H. Robertson. "Some Notes on Mr. Keynes' General Theory of Employment." *Quarterly Journal of Economics*, Nov. 1936, *51*, 168–91.

J. A. Schumpeter. *Business Cycles*. New York, 1939.

[H. C. Simons]. *Economics 201: The Divisional Course in Economics*. Chicago, n.d. (mimeographed).

_____. *A Positive Program for Laissez Faire*. Chicago, 1934. As reprinted in Simons (1948), pp. 40–77.

_____. Review of *The Supply and Control of Money in the United States* by L. Currie. *Journal of Political Economy*, Aug. 1935, *43*, 555–58.

_____. "Rules versus Authorities in Monetary Policy." *Journal of Political Economy*, Feb. 1936, *44*, 1–30. As reprinted in Simons (1948). Pp. 160–83.

_____. "Keynes Comments on Money" [Review of the *General Theory*]. *The Christian Century*, July 2, 1936, 1016–17.

_____. "Hansen on Fiscal Policy." *Journal of Political Economy*, Apr. 1942, *50*, 161–96. As reprinted in Simons (1948). Pp. 184–219.

_____. "The U.S. Holds the Cards." *Fortune*, Sept. 1944, 156–59, 196–200. Reprinted with substantial revisions as "Money, Tariffs, and the Peace." As reprinted in Simons (1948). Pp. 260–76.

_____. *Economic Policy for a Free Society*. Chicago, 1948.

G. S. Tavlas. "Chicago Schools Old and New on the Efficacy of Monetary Policy. *Banco Nazionale del Lavoro Quarterly Review*, Mar. 1977, *120*, 51–73.

University of Chicago Round Table. *Balancing the Budget: Federal Fiscal Policy During Depression. Public Policy Pamphlets*, no. 1, ed. Harry D. Gideonse. Chicago, Jan. 1933.

J. Viner. "Inflation as a Possible Remedy for the Depression." *Proceedings of the Institute of Public Affairs. Seventh Annual Session.* The University of Georgia, Athens, Ga. 1933, 120–35.

———. "Mr. Keynes on the Causes of Unemployment." *Quarterly Journal of Economics,* Nov. 1936, *51,* 147–67. As reprinted in *Keynes' General Theory. Reports of Three Decades,* ed. R. Lekachman. New York, 1964. Pp. 235–53.

———. "Two Plans for International Monetary Stabilization." *The Yale Review,* Autumn 1943, *33,* 77–107. As reprinted in Viner (1951). Pp. 192–215.

———. *International Economics.* Glencoe, Ill., 1951.

———. "Comment on My 1936 Review of Keynes' *General Theory.*" In *Keynes' General Theory, Reports of Three Decades,* ed. R. Lekachman. New York, 1964. Pp. 253–66.

Q. Wright. See Harris Memorial Foundation.

Government Publications

U. S. Board of Governors of the Federal Reserve System, *Federal Reserve Bulletin,* vol. 20. Washington D.C., 1934.

———. *Twentieth Annual Report of the Federal Reserve Board.* Washington, D.C., 1934.

Unpublished Materials

Frank H. Knight Papers. Joseph Regenstein Library, The University of Chicago.

Henry Morgenthau Diaries. The Franklin D. Roosevelt Library, Hyde Park, N.Y.

Henry C. Simons Papers. The Law School, The University of Chicago.

Jacob Viner Papers. Princeton University Library, Princeton, N.J.

Index of Names